AF600698

ON CIVIC REPUBLICANISM

Ancient Lessons for Global Politics

EDITED BY GEOFFREY C. KELLOW
AND NEVEN LEDDY

On Civic Republicanism

Ancient Lessons for Global Politics

UNIVERSITY OF TORONTO PRESS
Toronto Buffalo London

© University of Toronto Press 2016
Toronto Buffalo London
www.utppublishing.com

ISBN 978-1-4426-3749-8

Library and Archives Canada Cataloguing in Publication

On civic republicanism : ancient lessons for global politics / edited by Geoffrey C. Kellow and Neven Leddy.

Includes bibliographical references.
ISBN 978-1-4426-3749-8 (bound)

1. Republicanism – History. I. Leddy, Neven, editor
II. Kellow, Geoffrey C., 1970–, editor

JC421.O5 2016 321.8'6 C2015-906926-2

University of Toronto Press acknowledges the financial assistance to its publishing program of the Canada Council for the Arts and the Ontario Arts Council, an agency of the Government of Ontario.

Funded by the Government of Canada
Financé par le gouvernement du Canada
Canada

Contents

Part Two: The Enlightenment: An Accelerated Reception?

Preface: A Return to Classical Regimes Theory

DAVID EDWARD TABACHNICK
AND TOIVO KOIVUKOSKI

On the Plural Dimensions of *Politeia*

In politics, the term regime (derived from the Latin *regere*, to rule), describes a particular form of government or administration. So, we speak in terms of "democratic regimes" and "authoritarian regimes" as well as the "Obama regime" and the "Bush regime." Used this way, the word is merely a synonym. More often, the term regime is used in the pejorative to indicate the rule of an illegitimate leader or organization, as in the "Gadhafi regime" or a "terrorist regime." Here, it is a rhetorical tool used to describe a rogue or dangerous state or group, internationally irresponsible and devoid of civic obligations.

In contemporary political science, "regime" has been employed as a technical mode of analysis in international relations theory, where, instead of a state, government, or rogue element, a regime is any set of norms and values coupled with mechanisms of governance and regulation.[1] Through the lens of social science, "regimes theory" broadens the meaning of the word to pertain to a hodgepodge of international agencies, multilateral organizations, and regulatory bodies. In this treatment, there seems almost no limit to what qualifies as a regime: everything from a collective security pact such as NATO to the Convention on International Trade in Endangered Species of Wild Flora and Fauna. Unfortunately, if the goal of this theory is to help us better understand global politics, its overly broad definition of regime seems to stand in the way.

By contrast, classical political science defines "regime" in a rather specific way. The Greek *politeia* denotes a particular kind of *polis* or a constitutional classification of a political community. Aristotle, notably, identifies six different kinds of political regimes. Monarchy, aristocracy, and polity[2] are distinguished as "natural," because they facilitate and reflect the common good of the *polis*, whereas tyranny, oligarchy, and democracy are "unnatural" or deviations because they facilitate and reflect selfishness.[3] For Aristotle, a regime is characterized not only by the structure or composition of government (e.g., one monarch, a few aristocrats, or many democrats ruling), but also by the way public life is practised among the citizenry as a whole.

Of course, what Aristotle presents are classical archetypes that may seem irrelevant to contemporary political communities. Today, the primary geopolitical actors are large and diverse modern states as well as international institutions that would be quite alien to an ancient Greek political philosopher. Perhaps surprisingly, though, the classical approach to regimes can still accommodate the changing character of contemporary geopolitics. While the six regimes mentioned above are indeed archetypes, Aristotle recognizes that there may be different forms as well as a variety of mixtures of each. In turn, we can still at least see how this ancient account of regimes provides a familiar if not also exact description of present-day states. After all, the distinction between tyranny and democracy has animated much of American foreign policy for the last decade, if not the last half-century.

For contemporary political theory, this regimes approach may be useful because it provides three interrelated criteria to help distinguish various kinds of political rule and behaviour: (1) the structure of leadership within the regime (i.e., rule of the one, the few, or the many); (2) the level of civic engagement in the political life of the regime; and (3) whether the regime is directed towards the common good or particular aims of a few. What distinguish the variety of regimes in the classical approach are these quantitative and qualitative criteria. Accordingly, we cannot limit analysis to a study of institutions, but must also consider the common animating spirit of a political community or its civic culture that links the ways people think, including what they consider to be good, and the ways they organize themselves into associations towards those things "that are in the view of those involved good."[4]

So, a tyranny can be identified not only by the criterion that it is ruled by one leader but also by the tyrant's paranoid fear of enemies, the public's indifference to civic works, and every individual's interest in personal wealth and security. Similarly, an oligarchy is sustained as much by the impetuousness leadership of the rich few as it is by the willingness of the poor to trade their political participation for bare material need.

This link between the civic mindedness of the people and the political structures of a regime is perhaps most clearly on display in the classical account of republics. A republic is a type of regime where political structure and political culture are, in a sense, merged. *Politeia* can be taken both generically to mean any distribution of power, any regime, as well as specifically to refer to a republican constitution. This would suggest that a republic realizes the core dimensions of political life, marshalling the powers of people en masse by most fully developing the public deliberation on common goods. This is after all, and at basis, what any *politeia* consists of – deliberation on shared purposes and the means of political organization to achieve them.

A Polity in the People

Within the classical tradition the closeness of the values of a political community and the kind of government that it takes on point to a dual sense of what a *politeia*, or regime, is, consisting of both these elements of political culture and institutional organization, with the character of a regime inscribed into its people, their education, and what they consider the worth of public life to be.

Much as in the modern forms of civic republicanism, in ancient political theory the civic spirit of a people would be considered inseparable from discussions of governance. It would take a specific kind of person, for example, inculcated into a tight network of like-minded others to devote more than a month's service to a regular shift of council work, even sleeping and eating in the company of fellow citizens nearby to the *agora*; or to gather at the *ecclesiastica* from sunup to sundown to discuss the public life of one's city, as were the customs in Athens under its direct democracy. In all the kinds of regimes the ancients describe there is a sense of a common animus – what the contemporary social theorist might call the political culture of an age and people – that links the ways people think, how they have learned, and the ways they organize themselves into associations.

The ancient Greek political thinkers recognized the interrelationship between these levels of a regime as key to understanding politics. On the one hand, a virtuous citizenry would lend itself to a virtuous regime and, on the other hand, a virtuous regime would lend itself to a virtuous citizenry. The reverse was also true: ignobility lent itself to ignobility. In his *Politics*, Aristotle went so far as to classify constitutions or *politeia* under the broad categories of good and bad, right and wrong, or natural and unnatural. *Generally, he decides that a good constitution will create a political community that benefits the ruled, whereas a bad constitution will do the opposite, benefiting only the rulers and not the community as a whole, including its future generations.*

That is to say, because of the differences in the distribution of power, different kinds of regimes behave on the basis of very different reasons, with structural distinctions attached to the purposes of a particular regime. So, to take perhaps the most glaring counterpoint, tyrannies can be expected to behave differently than republics in their foreign relations, and obviously present a very different internal distribution of power. If the primary interest informing the affairs of a tyrannical regime is the preservation of a monopoly of power for the tyrant, then that core purpose could be reasonably expected to translate into an oppressive domestic security agenda and the aggrandizement of the one who rules.[5] Differently, what Aristotle identifies as a polity or what we might call a republic would be imbued with a spirit of civic participation that bristles at constraints on public life, both at home and abroad.

The first instantiations of the *Ancient Lessons for Global Politics* series[6] were focused on deviant forms of *politeia*, exploring the defining features of tyrannies, empires, and oligarchies. Those perennial forms of retrograde politics now find their natural complement in the study of a rightly ordered regime, constituted by public deliberation and legitimized by the consent of citizens having a share in the decisions that shape their lives, "ruling and being ruled in turn,"[7] with each enjoying the kind of freedom and equality that derives from active participation in public life. Here then is a substantive and broad sampling of the canon on civic republicanism by contemporary political theorists who would compare its ancient and modern articulations, reflecting on what a concern for the public good might look like.

NOTES

1 For a sampling of the sub-discipline, see Stephen Krasner, ed., *International Regimes* (Cambridge: Cornell University Press, 1983), and to counterpoint, Susan Strange, "Cave! *Hic Dragones*, A Critique of Regimes Analysis," *International Organization* 36 (1982), 479–96.

2 Polity and *politeia* are sometimes used interchangeably. However, in the *Politics*, polity is used to describe the rule of the middle class.

3 Aristotle, *Politics* 1279a20.

4 *Pol.* 1252a.

5 It is worth noting the debate around the distinctions and similarities between ancient and modern tyrannies, the latter of which are in the most egregious instances inflected with the excessive traits of modern ideologies and the levelling capacities of modern technology. See Toivo Koivukoski and David Tabachnick, *Confronting Tyranny: Ancient Lessons for Global Politics* (Roman and Littlefield, 2008). But this adaptation of an ancient vice into contemporary circumstances seems to present yet another distinction within the range of regime types that may present themselves, and a renewed reason for taking the differences among regimes as a starting point for analysis.

6 This was the subtitle for three collections edited by David Tabachnick and Toivo Koivukoski: *Confronting Tyranny* (Rowman and Littlefield, 2006), *Enduring Empire* (University of Toronto Press, 2009), and *On Oligarchy* (University of Toronto Press, 2011).

7 *Pol.* 1317b.

ON CIVIC REPUBLICANISM

Ancient Lessons for Global Politics

Introduction

GEOFFREY C. KELLOW

Republic is a noun in search of an adjective. Indeed, as a taxonomic term it seems to withdraw a Linnaean level with every generation. Virtually every modern government, regardless of its actual conduct, claims as its primary concern public things, the *res publica*. As a result, the particular adjective used to qualify the republican claim, liberal, democratic, people's, and Islamic, becomes necessary to indicate the sort of concern for things public. Of course, these adjectives possess curious qualities. Indeed, in the last two centuries the more emphatic the invocation of the public in name, the less likely in practice that the populace has any share in deliberations on political matters. As a result of this semantic confusion, understanding the republican form increasingly means not only looking across polities, but perhaps more essentially, across time. Here the semantic sleight of hand that characterizes so much modern political description disappears. In the ancient world in particular a government genuinely concerned with public things, a government committed to the very idea of public things stood in stark contrast to its alternatives. It is this essential comparison that illuminates this latest iteration of the *Ancient Lessons for Global Politics* volumes.

If in our own time the adjective is everything, in the ancient world the noun was all. The very idea of a government concerned with the things public forcefully affirmed the presence of a public concerned with government. To call one's polis a republic was to stand out against a horizon dominated by oligarchic, monarchic, and imperial alternatives. As Thucydides's Pericles declares in his funeral oration, "This is a peculiarity of ours: we do not say that a man who takes no interest in politics is a man who minds his own business, we say that he has no business at all."[1] It is this vision of republicanism, civic republicanism to be precise, that the essays in this volume address. This collection considers what ancient civic republics can say to modern republics and their citizens. Of course, the ancient republics have been speaking to us, providing lessons, for centuries. Our political, cultural, and even architectural landscape is populated with their lessons. Indeed, the unceasing accretion of republican lessons, from the Renaissance to the present poses challenges to accessing the original teaching distinct from those faced by the earlier "Ancient Lessons" volumes.

These challenges explain why this volume diverges somewhat from the earlier iterations in its treatment of these ancient lessons. We speak a language redolent with echoes of the ancient republics. We not only claim republican forms, but we speak the language of republics. But this language comes to us from sources both ancient and early modern. From the most basic definitions of public and private (*res privata, res publica*) to the sublime employment of republican name and theme in everything from the *Federalist Papers* to David's *Oath of the Horatii*, republican themes permeate every aspect of our political discourse. As a result, when we draw on republican sources today we necessarily draw on two traditions, the original civic republicanism of antiquity as well as the varied early modern reclamations and restatements that emerged from Florence to the American founding. This inevitable commingling has been with us for centuries. In the very heart of the Renaissance both Erasmus's *The Education of the Christian Prince* and Machiavelli's *The Prince* explicitly and implicitly drew on recollections of Republican Rome and Cicero's *De Officiis*. But just as importantly, both referred to republics more recently lost and lamented. For Erasmus and Machiavelli and ever since, when we recall republics we inevitably recall both ancient and modern republics. We cannot think only of Pericles and Cato; inevitably, we think also of George Washington and Piero Soderini.

On Civic Republicanism reflects this bifocal aspect of the modern republican gaze. It acknowledges that we have so long been taking on the ancient lessons of civic republicanism that it has become impossible to detach them fully from, most especially, the extraordinary recovery and amplification of those ideas in the Renaissance and Enlightenment. Unlike the regimes examined in earlier volumes the experience of empire, oligarchy, and tyranny did not prompt an early modern body of thought equal to the original and ancient lessons. Unlike civic republicanism, most of these other modern incarnations of ancient originals had no deep appetite for learning, no honest engagement with the past, no sincere republic of letters to sustain them over time and across cultures. So with a few exceptions these essays consider the challenges of modern republics in a manner shared with Erasmus and Machiavelli: they draw republican lessons from republics and writers both recent and remote in time.

There are few more contested paths in the history of political theory than that which leads from ancient to modern civic republicanism. For decades scholars have contested the character of this relationship and the substance of the debt owed to the ancients by early modern civic republican theorists. The question is essentially one of fidelity. There can be no doubt that early modern restatements of civic republicanism adopted terminology, metaphor, structure, and example from their ancient precursors. What remains unsettled is the use to which these were put. One school of thought, most prominently represented by Quentin Skinner and J.G.A. Pocock, has argued for a deep continuity between ancient and modern. Pocock in particular has famously argued of Harrington that he provided the intellectual means "whereby the county freeholder could equate himself with the Greco-Roman *polites* and profess of a wholly classical and Aristotelian doctrine of the relations between property, liberty and power."[2] This interpretation has been vigorously challenged by the work of scholars such as Harvey Mansfield and Leo Strauss. Strauss, Mansfield, and others have argued that close reliance on and careful reading of ancient sources is not in and of itself evidence of continuity with those sources. In essence, they argue that close engagement and fidelity are two different questions. Mansfield goes further to suggest that indeed such close engagement may serve to reveal important differences.[3] Both approaches have rallied impressive textual evidence to support their interpretations. At this juncture neither approach has landed a knockout blow. As such the question, for the purposes of this volume and in terms of broader inquiry, remains very much open. As a result, this volume participates in this debate only inasmuch as our contributors approach the question from a variety of positions on the spectrum between Pocock and Mansfield. Given the breadth of subjects covered, chronologically and culturally, such agnosticism on the question seems only reasonable. We may settle the character of influence for Machiavelli or Madison, but the precise admixture of inspiration, fidelity, and subversion across the span of early modern civic republicanism seems, at this juncture at least, beyond the capacity of human knowing.

If the modern portrait of civic republicanism appears to our eyes as an inseparable diptych this collection adds a third panel to the picture. The essays concern themselves with the lessons of republicanism both ancient and early modern. They consider the original ancient lessons, their various influential restatements, and lastly their real relevance for current questions of civic virtue, public life, and popular politics. These essays seek to apply the insights of Cicero *and* Machiavelli, Sparta *and* Geneva.

It is this approach that distinguishes this volume from valuable work done, both in political theory and in intellectual history, on the legacy of civic republicanism. There are countless scholarly works on ancient republican thinkers. In terms of their modern reception the two-volume collection *Republicanism* edited by Skinner and van Gelderen (2002) and Paul Rahe's monumental *Republics Ancient and Modern* stand out as central to our understanding of the relationship between ancient republican thought and early modern ideas and practice. But, as the series title suggests this volume seeks to go a step further, to apply the lessons of both ancient and modern republicanism to the modern condition, to the current state of the *res publica*.

The collection begins with Athens in crisis. Timothy Burns's essay considers the picture of public life Pericles presents in Thucydides's *History of the Peloponnesian War.* As Burns notes, even in the ancient world of civic republics the comparison between regimes provided a central element of self-understanding. In service of such understanding the austere and pious Sparta stood as an alternative to republics like Athens where self-concern unchecked by piety remained an ever-present risk to the public pursuit of the good of the city. This idea of the good of the city, the end or purpose of politics quickly emerges as a defining element of civic republics. With this idea of ends, purpose, and direction we turn to the Athens of Aristotle in David Roochnik's essay. Roochnik considers the role not of transcendence but of immanence in the republican sense of polis. His essay compares ancient and early modern attempts to, almost literally, *ground* civic republicanism. Roochnik explores the extent to which civic republicanism demands a sense of space and therefore direction, questioning whether Aristotle's contention that the civic republic requires a "small and bounded space" is any longer tenable.

We stay with Aristotle and Athens, but move from place to process and participants in the essays that follow those of Roochnik and Burns. Michael Weinman explores the Aristotelian understanding of work (*ergon*), of the citizen's work in pursuing a life in accord with reason. This work, Weinman argues, is most likely to succeed when conducted in concert with others, most obviously within a civic republican milieu. Weinman contends that this Aristotelian conception of civic work provides a way through the modern debates about place and community, liberalism and communitarianism, opened earlier by Roochnik and Burns. The discussion of work naturally suggests the discussion of the worker taken up by Wendell John Coats Jr. Coats, in developing the question of republican character in both its ancient and modern iterations, begins to draw out a distinction between the collective deliberation of popular democracy and the political participation civic republicanism demands. Revisiting concerns canvassed by Aristotle regarding Athens and Tocqueville regarding America, Coats explores the vital tension and consequences for character of the distinction between self-interest rightly understood and a civic commitment to a common good. Crystal Cordell Paris builds on the distinction between democratic deliberation and republican commitment. She begins her exploration of this terrain with an account of the Aristotelian conception of citizenship and its relationship to political deliberation. In her exploration she illuminates not only the qualities of civic republican deliberation, a deliberation tied to and embedded in an outcome for a particular community, but its modern and especially Rawlsian alternatives.

The concern with ends binds together all the essays concerning Aristotle and what begins to illuminate the distinctions between liberal democracy and civic republicanism. The first essays in this collection return again and again not to process but to outcome. All these essays consider the resources that republics ancient and modern draw upon to sustain themselves. These first essays recognize that a civic republic with a common end in mind must always be concerned with the civic means, its place in the cosmos and on the earth, and the faith, character, reason, and rhetoric of its citizens.

With Jarrett Carty's essay *On Civic Republicanism* moves into the early modern reclamations of ancient civic republicanism. In exploring Machiavelli's employment of ancient historians, especially Livy and Polybius, Carty provides a compelling account of both ancient and early modern attempts to deal with the instability, fear, and faction that two and a half centuries later James Madison would identify as the central weakness of republican government. Carty considers the extent to which Machiavelli contends that the ancient accounts of instability, of competing humours within the polis, suggested a republican route from tumult to triumph.

If Carty's essay considers the role of passions, especially desire and fear, within republics, Ryan Balot's essay, in exploring the fraught relationship between manliness and courage, considers tumult within the citizen himself. Balot attempts to understand the current resurgence of debate around manliness in modern liberal democracies by tying together ancient accounts of manliness and visions of courage in the first century of the American Republic. Balot's essay asks the question: What is the character of democratic courage in ancient Athens and modern America? The discussion of courage and manliness and its decline inevitably draws out the question of decline, and more specifically corruption, in civic republican regimes themselves.

Robert Sparling's paper looks at Montesquieu's attempt to explain and understand the role of corruption in the action of political principles. Sparling's essay, in exploring the question of corruption, suggests the beginnings of the modern appreciation of ancient principles. In Montesquieu Sparling finds a thinker exploring the relationship between ancient and modern republics understood as a studied balance between high republican principles and ever-pressing political reality. Sparling examines the extent to which ancient civic republicanism, by the lights of *The Spirit of the Laws* at least, had become a counsel of perfection. In the next chapter, Marc Hanvelt's account of courage in the work of David Hume attempts to find a middle way between the discussion of virtue in Balot and Sparling, and its likely corruption. Hanvelt considers the uncertainty and instability at the heart of accounts of both philosophic and political life in early modern Europe and suggests a Humean middle way. He identifies in Hume a conception of philosophic courage that could serve as an antidote to the failings of reclaimed and perhaps corrupted ancient notions of civic and martial valour. Such a conception, Hanvelt asserts, ties Hume to the practice of political courage embodied in Plato's account of the trial and execution of Socrates by the Athenian republic.

The collection then moves from Athens to its ancient republican alternative: Sparta. At the same time, it inevitably moves from the early modern voices of the likes of Hume and Montesquieu to that most forceful of early modern advocates for the Spartan vision of civic republicanism, Jean-Jacques Rousseau. Varad Mehta introduces the decidedly mixed legacy of Sparta in the early modern period. The "Spartan mirage" offered peculiar and ultimately deadly temptations to those moderns who sought not merely to learn from but actually recover something of the community Lycurgus made. For early modern republicans, Sparta represented the ultimate alternative to the self-interested citizen, the ultimate immersion of the citizen in the civic. This immersive account of the demands on citizens of civic republicanism gets its most famous treatment in the philosophy of Rousseau.

Brent Cusher examines in particular the nature of rhetoric, persuasion, and conviction in Rousseau's account of republican citizenship. Cusher ties together Rousseau's account of persuasion with the vision of prelude and persuasion that stands at the centre of politics in Plato's *Laws.* He considers the manifold ways in which Plato, and after him Rousseau, looked to cultivate in the citizen a commitment to the laws. The discussion of the role of persuasion in civic republican politics brings to the fore for both Cusher and Lee Ward the ancient and modern accounts of civil religion as a medium of civic conviction. Ward turns to civil religion and social institutions, especially the theatre, to illuminate this aspect of the civic republic. He discusses in particular Rousseau's account of ancient and modern theatre's role in cultivating or corrupting republican virtue. The classical theatre and the related rituals of political life, as Ward suggests, point a way towards solving or saving the republican reality of Rousseau's Geneva.

After Rousseau, and just as importantly after 1789, civic republicanism both ancient and modern came up yet again for a reappraisal. That reappraisal was perhaps most famously rendered in Benjamin Constant's speech on the liberty of Ancients and Moderns to the Paris Atheneum. The final three essays in *On Civic Republicanism* turn back to the individual. This turn, the third appraisal of the ancient legacy of civic republicanism, tempered now by restatements in word and deed of both Athens and Sparta, focuses once again on education, on the citizen. Moving from rhetoric and theatre to literature and history, Neven Leddy tackles Mary Wollstonecraft's response to Rousseau and Adam Smith, and her analysis of the place of civic republicanism in the education of girls. Leddy explains that for Wollstonecraft the reading of history was key to accessing the tradition of civic republicanism and that civic engagement was a core consequence of a historical education. Staying with the education of children, Jeffrey Wilson's surprising treatment of *Pinocchio* and Plato's *Laws* explores the imagery of cords and marionettes. Wilson then draws together the proposals of the Athenian Stranger for a new Cretan republic with Carlo Collodi's commitment to the new Italian republic whose children devoured his children's stories. Wilson presents Pinocchio as the story of a puppet who becomes a boy in part at least by becoming a member of a political community. As Wilson points out, Collodi began his story insisting that this children's story had no king. In Collodi's story, Wilson contends, Pinocchio becomes both a son and a citizen and can only become the one by becoming the other.

The nineteenth century, as Douglas Moggach observes, entailed a reconsideration of the hoped-for escape from immaturity that Kant had posited and that civic republicanism required. In a very real sense, Moggach sees in the work of both Schiller and Bruno Bauer an attempt to recover the aesthetic route to civic republicanism. Moggach investigates the ways in which, as with Roman republicanism and its decline, the nineteenth-century fate of civic republicanism became repositioned not in dialogue with oligarchy or monarchy but rather as an alternative to mass society. Mass society, characterized by self-interest, private property, and deep heteronomy now stood as both the alternative to and perhaps the inevitable fate of civic republics. Moggach considers in this light the potential, in both ancient and modern accounts, of an aesthetic encounter with the sublime to generate both an individual and common commitment to a shared ideal.

On Civic Republicanism ends with a new concern. Added on to the attempt to understand republics comparatively, to reveal limits and possibilities by looking across communities ancient and modern, the final chapters focus increasingly on the substance of civic republicanism within both cities and citizens. Civic republicanism, in both its ancient original and early modern restatements remains concerned with the *virtue* of citizens in both senses of the term. The essays concern themselves with not only what a republican regime must provide its citizens but with what its citizens must provide the republic. This symbiosis, captured in Aristotle's famous requirement that such citizens both rule and are in turn ruled, points towards the most fundamental contrast between civic republics ancient and modern. If ancient republics looked to oligarchies, theocracies, monarchies, and despotisms, and surely all these remain today, nonetheless republican thinkers today engage primarily with a wholly modern form: liberal democracy. Here the stark opposition between *res publica* and *res privata* blurs. The distinction between popular and participatory politics lacks the sharp contrasts of the ancient world's various regimes.

Modern civic republican thought occurs most often within liberal democracies not outside of and in opposition to them. Civic republicanism today acts most often as a counsel against the worst instincts of liberal democracies, not as an outright alternative to them. As the essays in this collection suggest, most modern attempts to recover the lessons of ancient civic republicanism accept the modern liberal democratic regime. Increasingly, proponents of republican virtue seek to alter the regime within the citizen. From the recovery of character advocated by Wendell John Coats to the restoration of a republican courage, tied either to thought or to masculinity, as with Hanvelt and Hume, to the possibilities of self-change described by Moggach, civic republicanism finds itself in a new dialectical position. These essays seek to understand better lessons both ancient and modern in the service of a new conversation among the citizen, society, and the state.

NOTES

1 Thucydides, *History of the Peloponnesian War*, trans. Rex Warner (London: Penguin Books, 1972), 148.
2 J.G.A. Pocock, *Politics, Language and Time* (New York: Atheneum, 1971), 114.
3 Harvey Mansfield, *Machiavelli's New Modes and Orders* (Chicago: University of Chicago Press, 2001), 35.

PART ONE

The Classical Heritage

1 The Problematic Character of Periclean Athens

TIMOTHY W. BURNS

In the famous funeral oration that Thucydides provides us with, his Pericles praises the city of Athens for having citizens who, among other things, need no Homer to sing their praises and who philosophize without growing soft (2.40.1, 41.4).[1] These and other claims, along with Thucydides's own explicit assessment of Pericles's leadership of Athens, have led modern commentators to conclude that Thucydides held Pericles to be the wisest leader of Athens, a model of human wisdom and leader of a republican civic life worthy of emulation[2] – even and perhaps especially in modern, secular liberal democracies. In the light of Thucydides's judgments in the rest of the work, however, and of his account of the war as a whole, there is reason to doubt this conclusion, and to proceed with caution in our emulation of Pericles's teaching. For Pericles never really disposes of the challenge that is posed to philosophy, or to the quest for ageless truth, by a poet like Homer. The manner in which Thucydides himself does so, moreover – that is, through an examination of the problem of justice – allows us to see a great deficiency in Pericles's understanding of the needs and potentialities of republican civic life. The same deficiency poses a long-term threat to enlightened, modern republics as much as it did to Pericles's Athens.

I

In order to assess Pericles's leadership, it is helpful to grasp first the nature of his project for Athens as it comes into sight in Thucydides's narrative of his speeches and deeds. Pericles's speeches are, of course, meant to move the Athenians to war against the Spartans and their allies, and to keep them at war. But to achieve this end, Pericles invites the Athenians to adopt wholeheartedly a new way of life towards which they had been already moving: to become islanders in their souls, to abandon once and for all their ancestral lands for the swift and powerful navy that gives Athens all good things. As he argues in his first speech, only recently has Athens become a nautical power, but nautical power comprehends the earlier, primitive, land-based fighting and economy. Being nautical requires a mastery of motion, a willingness to abandon the apparently secure footing of the settled city, and points to the establishment of a city-on-the-sea, a moving island of power. In fact, if he thought he could convince the Athenians, Pericles states, he would have them burn and abandon their own homes and take up residence on their ships. And his actual strategy does in fact entail the abandonment of the Athenians' farms and ancestral towns and villages, and the resettlement of their inhabitants within the walls built under Themistocles's leadership. Pericles would have the Athenians finally say farewell to their ancient city, to make it forever what it had been temporarily in the Persian War, "a city that is no more."[3]

Pericles is, in other words, the heir of Themistoclean Athens, the Athens that prides itself on intelligence over and against trust in divine care.[4] His project entails abandoning the traditional Greek reliance on the gods for guidance, or is a secularizing project. His very steadiness and reliability rest, he claims, on his trust in the power of human intelligence (*gnome*) to understand what course of action is called for in a given circumstance, and this confidence is the counterpart to the Spartan respect for divinely controlled fortune (*tuche*) (1.140).[5] In fact, while many other speakers appeal to gods, Pericles's only mention of a god in any of his speeches is his reported reference to the gold in the removable shield of the giant statue of Athena (2.13.5).

An encouragement of the Athenians in their intelligent artfulness or inventiveness born of experience is at the core of this secularizing project. As we learn early in the work, reliance on such artfulness represents an alternative to reliance on the moral virtue inculcated at pious Sparta, including and especially the Spartan type of courage.[6] In their famous characterizations of Athens and Sparta, for example, the Corinthians had dubbed Sparta's law-bred, awe-inspired virtue "old-fashioned," and had pitted against it Athenian artfulness, intelligence, and mastery of motion through attention to necessities. We may thus say without exaggeration that Pericles, attempting to complete the project begun by Themistocles, would finally jettison the old, pious, peaceful Athens, aiming at a wholly new, "enlightened" politics directed by human intelligence.[7]

This deeply secular, enlightened nature of Pericles's project helps explain the great appeal that his vision of political life holds for democratic thinkers of secular modernity, such as Hannah Arendt.[8] What we must not overlook, however, is how *unappealing* it was to many Athenians, or the dangerous rift that quickly developed between Pericles and the Athenian people, owing to the great suffering induced by his vision and his consequent war policy. The Athenian people were still very attached to their ancient way of life and the ancient towns of the Athenian countryside. As Thucydides makes clear, this attachment was due in no small part to the ancient temples and sanctuaries that they maintained (2.15–16). A less than obvious purpose of Pericles's funeral oration, in fact, is to overcome this rift, to win the people securely to his project. And the means that he chose to do so has made him yet more attractive to contemporary democratic theorists.

Pericles invites his fellow Athenians to fall in love with the power of Athens, to become her erotic lovers (*erastas*, 2.43.1), to direct their gaze upon her as he presents her, to become devoted to her, attached to her as worthy of their sacrifice and as promising to fulfil their deepest longings. He thereby acknowledges and to a certain extent even stresses that the way of life prescribed by the laws of the old Athens, as well as by the laws of present-day Sparta, do not and cannot satisfy the felt lack of happiness that erotic longing entails. Freely given, loving devotion to Athens – and not obedience to allegedly divine laws – can grant her citizens that for which all human beings long. The city as Pericles conceives of it is to be self-sufficient (2.36.3); it will need nothing and point to nothing beyond itself. Pericles speaks of human laws, for example, but never of divine laws. To him, the city needs the gods no more than it needs a Homer who sings the praises of the gods.[9] The Athenians, as he sees it, must and can be liberated from their ancestral piety and redirected to a love of their city and to noble deeds on her behalf.

The new, godless Athens that Pericles presents is – and this is the third thing that makes it appealing to citizens of modern democracy – a city that promises to satisfy the *individual* needs of its citizens. For it is, Pericles claims, a city whose regime gives public rewards to merit or virtue.[10] Athens treats her citizens equally and thereby allows them the opportunity to shine as individuals through devotion to her. Unlike the Spartans, whose republican way of life includes keeping a jealous guard over the enjoyment of individual pleasures, the Athenians do not begrudge such pleasures to each other. Indeed, they promote virtue by rewarding it, holding that the city that offers the best rewards for virtue will be the most virtuous city (1.37.1, 1.43.1, 1.46.1). The Spartans, by contrast, merely demand virtue (unsuccessfully) from their citizens as something good in itself. The Athenians, relatedly, have a freedom to do as they like, and they make the most of it, without external restraints. They tastefully employ the tremendous wealth that empire has made available to them in public and private establishments and enjoyments, and in festivals that drive away sadness (1.38). Their courage, too, stems not from a constant boot-camp existence, such as Sparta's citizens needlessly undergo – one that leaves the Spartans penniless, hidebound, and unhappy. Athenian courage instead arises spontaneously after an education that fills each individual with ambitious hopes of honour through outstanding service to the city (2.42 with 2.39). The result is the restless, constant activity and risk taking of the Athenians on behalf of their city.

Athens is, then, as Pericles presents her, a city to which her citizens will *intelligently* devote themselves, thereby giving themselves the best lives possible. The Athenians do not march in ignorant, fearful obedience to ancestral laws, but with a strength of soul that comes from being able to see all dangers and still face them. Athens even produces citizens who possess a versatility and grace that allows each of them to be self-sufficient.[11] Unlike Sparta, the home of harsh laws, Athens offers her citizens a reasonable happiness – a civic life that is freely chosen rather than compelled. One cannot be forced to appoint one's house tastefully or to acquire a love of the beautiful with thrift, nor to be liberal in sentiments, and it is just such characteristics that citizens of Athens possess, according to Pericles. Above all, one cannot be forced by the threat of punishment or by any other imposed necessity to love wisdom. And the Athenians, Pericles states, are "lovers of wisdom without softness"; they are, that is, open to deliberation in order to be able to act well for their city; they are intelligent doers of noble deeds.

As freely and reasonably chosen, the noble deeds that the Athenian citizens undertake will also be embraced warmly and with enthusiasm, according to Pericles. For Athens's power can give Athenians something altogether desirable, something that vanquishes the greatest of evils. The beloved Athens offers to her potential lovers immortal glory (2.43.2; cf. 2.44.4). Gazing at the power of the city of Athens, her citizens can turn towards what promises to provide something deathless. This love of immortal glory attainable through noble deeds is the most splendid aspect of the Athenians' love of the beautiful or noble. The city of Athens is given (and ought to be given) the "voluntary," unreserved, "noble" love of her citizens (2.42.4, 43.1, 43.4–6). Her lovers surrender themselves to Athens as parts to a larger whole to which they truly belong, freely relinquishing their self-centredness for noble union with their city. In this way the city of Athens, moving her lovers freely, un-calculatingly, and without compulsion to sacrifice themselves, will cause them to move beyond the ordinary moral life of any other city. Eros for Athens can move them to the greatest deeds *without* the command of rankling duty, and to benefit their city unstintingly. Behind the new Athenian virtue is – or so Pericles would have them all come to see and feel – an erotic, freely self-sacrificing love of Athens.

In addition to being secular, urbane, and liberal, then, the democratic Athens that Pericles describes reasonably and wholly fulfils the desires of each individual citizen while being devoutly communal. Little wonder that it remains so attractive to contemporary democratic theorists, who search for examples of an agonistic space that yields both freedom and devotional togetherness. Nor is it surprising that so many contemporary commentators find Thucydides's own judgment of Pericles to be one of approbation, going so far as to claim that the entire work can be understood as a vindication of Pericles's wise leadership and a condemnation of the Athenian democracy's incapacity to adhere to his policies and vision after his death.[12] But Thucydides's judgment of Pericles, and of the type of city that he would bring into being, is more ambiguous than our own moral preferences might lead us to think. An examination of Pericles's speeches in the light of the war as a whole will lead us to revise the initial and massive impression of wise leadership that has moved most of our contemporaries to their opinion. It will disclose – to use Pericles's own word – a softness that prevents Pericles from ruling wisely.

II

We begin to see the difficulty when we realize that, for all of the contempt that it expresses for Sparta, Pericles's funeral oration discloses an agreement with the Spartans on the fundamental superiority of deeds to speeches, or the need to subordinate intelligence to action on behalf of the city. For such subordination means that reasoning is not allowed to proceed after a certain point: any pursuit of wisdom that does not lead to pursuit of noble deeds is deemed "soft." Thinking must be for the city; the love of wisdom cannot be a private activity but must be subordinate to the city's good. As Pericles says, "We alone regard the one who takes no part in public affairs as useless" (2.40.2). And by thus subordinating speech or reason to deeds, Pericles makes his city's grand leadership, her imperialism and martial victories, the highest good for his city. As he says, his speech describes deeds, but those deeds themselves are the true test of virtue. And if actions or deeds are the test, then opportunity to do things, as Alcibiades will later claim, is crucial to the city and its citizens. Empire must be endless.[13]

But is it right to direct the Athenians to endless empire? As we noted, the Athenian people have an abiding concern for their rootedness, and for divine justice – a concern that remains a source of opposition to Periclean activity throughout the war. Given this concern, it is amazing how very little attention Pericles, who is himself manifestly just,[14] devotes to the question of the justice of empire in either of his first two speeches. In his first speech he addresses the question of justice in the manner of the Spartan king Archidamos:[15] he substitutes the narrow, legal matter of the Megarian decree for the larger question of the justice of ruling over other cities. And in the funeral oration, saying nothing of the justice of empire, he merely explains the characteristic traits by which the Athenians acquired their empire (2.36). He also presents the *power* of the city as the proof of her greatness (2.41) and her greatness itself as consisting in her capacity to leave everywhere memorials of good *and evil*. And, as we have seen, he bids the Athenians contemplate this power and fall in love with it (2.43).

Pericles's neglect of the question of justice is most surprising in his final speech. His addressees, having suffered terribly from the plague, are angry with him, and troubled by the thought that the plague has come to them as a divine punishment for the unjust imperial policy that had brought on the war (2.59 with 54, and cf. 6.12 with 7.77.2–4). Pericles would thus seem to be forced at last to address the question of justice, of divine justice. Now it goes without saying that Pericles does not believe the plague is a divine punishment. What is remarkable is that he makes no attempt to defend or explain his lack of belief. He merely requests that the Athenians view the plague as one of the "daimonic things" that must be borne "of necessity" – a request that is as ambiguous as speaking of medicinal chemicals as "miracle drugs." Moreover, Pericles now openly sidesteps the underlying issue of the justice of the Athenian empire, claiming that the empire "is so to speak a tyranny, and while it may have been unjust to take it, it is dangerous to let it go" (63.2, 64.2). That is, he almost declares the empire unjust, but at the same time almost excuses it. Holding on to empire provides safety, and all must realize the danger of abandoning it now. Pericles thereby gives *implicitly* an exculpation of the Athenian empire: he suggests that the compelling power of fear or, more broadly, of interest, exculpates the possible injustice. But unlike other Athenians, he does not refer explicitly to a compulsion, and so does not say whether the empire really is or is not unjust.[16] He attempts, instead, to turn the Athenians' minds from their misery by encouraging hopes of greater, future imperial conquests, declaring that of the two halves of the world, land and sea, the latter belongs altogether to them.

Even under the pressure of those who, after the plague, are angrily demanding an end to the war and even a withdrawal from the empire, then, Pericles does not budge from his silence on the empire's justice. And this silence or neglect is all the more remarkable for being so unique. Some of Pericles's fellow Athenians, after all, openly and frankly defend the empire by challenging justice, arguing that the compulsion to pursue interest governs the actions of all human beings. Whatever its specific content, these Athenians argue, justice assumes the freedom to choose it over injustice, or does not ask the impossible. But, they claim, all human beings do what they do out of a compulsion – a natural necessity – to pursue security, profit, and honour, or to pursue their own good, to the extent of their ability to do so. The strong therefore necessarily rule over the weak to the extent of their ability; the weak must submit to this necessity. To ask the strong to do otherwise is to ask the impossible, and the appearance of human beings who do otherwise is only an appearance, maintained and appealed to by those without the strength to acknowledge or resist the necessary rule of the strong. Moral responsibility, the ground of all justice, human and divine, is an illusion. The divine, if it even exists, is under the same rule of necessity.[17] Any justice worth speaking of obtains only among equals, and only so long as they are equals; it is no more than a temporary standoff, and has no transcendent support.

Now it could of course be that Pericles, recognizing that most of his audience cannot accept this argument against justice in defence of empire, simply chooses to maintain a prudent silence on this most grave question. But this explanation is not adequate. For the little that Pericles does say bespeaks no such prudential concerns on his part. On the contrary, its ambiguity comes at the expense of stating any firm limits to Athenian rule. He speaks of shame in his final speech, but only of the shame that would come to the Athenians from losing what they have (2.62), not of any shame from taking what is not theirs. He seeks to lift them from what he sees as their present despondency by reminding them that the world is their oyster, and so he presents justice, or obligation to others, as exhausted by what one owes to one's own city. And his emphasis on activity, power, and capacity, together with the very short shrift that he gives to the question of justice, must cause us to wonder whether the Athenians will in the end be able to reconcile the generosity for which he has praised them with being imperialists. In the absence of anything higher than the city itself, in the absence of something to which the city looks up, what moral limit can there be on imperialism? But can an imperial city of unlimited aims, any more than thieves who are honest among themselves, sustain a public-spirited citizenry? Pericles appears to be confident that Athens can and will – that her individuals' full flowering can and will come through an erotic devotion to Athens. Yet some Athenians, and perhaps not the least capable, may well conceive desires quite different from a devotional love of Athens. And the other loves that Pericles speaks of – love of the noble and love of wisdom – might be less conducive to public-spiritedness than he wishes. In general, ambitious Athenians' lack of restraint may extend beyond Pericles's vision. On the other hand, the common good among citizens, held to obtain somehow by Pericles, must necessarily appear terribly incomplete if there is no corresponding common good held to obtain among cities, since in the absence of the latter the former does indeed look an awful lot like the good of thieves acting honourably among themselves.[18] The Athens that Pericles praises appears to set a bad example for its own more ambitious citizens,[19] and seems to others to warrant divine punishment.[20] Rather than admiring his prudence, then, we are left to wonder, at the end of Pericles' final speech, about the sustainability of his whole secularizing and liberalizing endeavour.

We are not left to wonder long. Thucydides tells us immediately (i.e., a year before it takes place) of Pericles's death, and of Athens's eventual loss of the war under subsequent and more obviously private-spirited leaders, who eventually brought strife into the city (2.65). In the absence of belief in a public good that is more than collective selfishness, the Athenians were indeed unable to sustain the self-sacrifice, devotion, or sense of obligation that had been sustained, as it still was at Sparta, by education in obedience to the divine law. Victory by Pericles's strategy would at the very least have required a Pericles at the helm, especially since his military strategy, as we have seen, brought an unprecedented disruption of the regular life of the Athenians. Since Pericles recognized that the Athenian people (*demos*) was fickle or subject to passion, and that his fairly defensive war strategy would require a steady adherence to a long war under a leader of his calibre and manifest public-spiritedness, he appears to have thought that he would be around for the duration of the war. In designing his military strategy, Pericles had foreseen neither his own death nor the private-spiritedness of the leaders who would take his place.

It would seem, then, that in addition to having neglected the question of justice, and not foreseeing how this neglect might adversely affect future leaders, Pericles also neglected to face the possibility of his own imminent death. In fact, his avoidance of the whole subject of death in the funeral oration,[21] where one could reasonably expect him to address it, rivals his neglect of the question of justice. In Thucydides's account of the plague, sandwiched between Pericles's second and third speeches, we are shown the relation of these two failures, and the particular softness that caused them.

III

Thucydides alerts us early that he will be examining (as his Pericles did not) the question of the role that divine beings might play in human affairs, and that his account of the plague will be one of the key places where he does so. His original disclosure that he will be examining the war's causes, true and professed, is accompanied by a description of non-human motions that accompanied the war. He there singles out the plague as the greatest of these motions, and later informs us that the plague was taken as a punishment of the Athenians and therefore as the help from Apollo oracularly promised to the Spartans. The understanding of the plague as a divine punishment accords with the stated Spartan claim that the war was caused by Athenian injustice, by the Athenians' breach of the solemnly sworn or divinely sanctioned treaty between Sparta and Athens.[22]

The plague is, then, an event in which the question of causes, natural or divine, or the human ability to know causes, will most obviously be examined. But what is made most manifest in Thucydides's account of the plague is human understanding in its weakness. The plague was visible as a weakening of the power of understanding as much as of the body. Not only did it show obvious limitations to the healing art, and to sense perceptions (the bodies of the victims were cool to the touch while in fact hot inside), but the suffering it induced affected memory; the plague even caused some of those who suffered from it to become oblivious of everything, unable to recognize their family members and acquaintances (2.49.6–8). And beyond these obvious weaknesses, the plague manifests a general weakness of understanding.

The account of the plague divides itself, in fact, into two parts: a look at the plague's effect on the body, and then at its effect on the understanding. At the end of what proves to be the first part Thucydides tells us that the plague baffled description; description was at least as problematic to Thucydides as cure was to physicians. But describe it he does. Contrary to the claims of some contemporary scholarship, however, Thucydides does *not* investigate the plague as would a physician, in search of its physical cause.[23] What he turns to instead is a description of what he intriguingly calls, in the introduction to the second part, the idea (*eidos*) of the disease (2.50.1). And this second part – the bulk of the description of the plague – deals with the effect of the disease on the citizens' capacity to understand what it was that they were doing or suffering, and the illusions, of a fatal or boastful kind, to which the plague gave rise. This second part culminates in the report of a disputed oracle forewarning of the disease, and of the Greeks' interpretation of the disease as a divine punishment for the war. Presenting the *eidos* of the plague, and by an extension suggested by Thucydides himself,[24] of the war, with its speeches and deeds, Thucydides gives us an alternative to the Greeks' own account of the "great motions" in the human and non-human world that came with the war. He expresses his disagreement with the interpretation of the plague as a punishment sent by Apollo upon the Athenians, and gives us reason to see this common interpretation as one particular manifestation of a more general disease of the understanding.

Since a most significant part of the disease is its effect on the understanding, the problem of describing it accurately, just as it was in itself, is itself caused in part by the disease. Thucydides was nonetheless able, by seeing this, to reflect on his capacity to know, or on the obstacles to knowing and the limits to it. And since he was able to describe this problem, he has succeeded in describing the disease, not indeed fully but in a permanently useful manner. His description shows that he himself was cured of the disease and, if his description of the effect of the disease on the understanding is indeed accurate, he may help his readers cure themselves of similar sicknesses of understanding.

What, then, was the obstacle to understanding that became so clear in the plague? We begin at the conclusion of the description of the plague, where Thucydides makes his most open statement, in his own name, against prophecies or oracles. These, he suggests, depend for their intelligibility upon human interpretation, and the interpretations or the memories of the oracles not only vary but are determined, according to Thucydides, by the circumstances of the human beings who recall or receive them; the interpretations correspond to the sufferings of the interpreters. In this conclusion to the clear-headed description of the plague that he himself suffered from, then, Thucydides tells us that human beings will interpret oracles with a view to making their sufferings meaningful, and in a manner that suggests to them a way out of their sufferings. For many pious Athenians the meaning of the plague was that they were suffering a "punishment" for their allegedly unjust war. What has Thucydides seen so that he knows that this is not the case?

That the plague was interpreted as a punishment we learn not only at the end of Thucydides's account, but in his description of those who, while the plague was raging, pursued pleasures of the moment. To these Athenians it seemed that Apollo had now shot his devastating arrows; no greater punishment could be feared, and this one seemed inevitable. Hence, the Athenians lost their fear of the gods, and pursued publicly the pleasures they had formerly denied to themselves in public. Indeed, they came to see the pleasant as advantageous and noble and no longer as base or shameful (2.53.2–3).

Now it could appear that the Athenians who in this way lost their fear of the gods lost also their belief in the gods, and that this loss of belief in avenging gods allowed them to see the greater advantage for themselves in pursuing the pleasant rather than in pursuing what they had previously called "noble." Their suffering made somewhat more clear to themselves that they had pursued the noble not as such or for its own sake, but with the expectation of reward from the gods or at least of punishment for pursuing what they really wanted, that is, the pleasant – which they had in any case often pursued in private. The plague, in other words, may have suggested to the participants themselves that their self-sacrificing virtue was always practised as a *means*, not as an end in itself, and indeed as a mistaken means. And Thucydides appears at first to suggest just this. Yet in the full explanation of the thinking that led the Athenians to act as they did, he shows us the insufficiency of this initial appearance.

The plague showed its many witnesses that virtue, which entails service to others, came in the end to the same thing as the practice of vice; it was of no profit to its practitioners or proved to be disadvantageous.

Many therefore did now in public what they had formerly kept hidden (2.51–2). Hence, the pleasant came to be held to be both noble *and* advantageous. This means, however, that the Athenians did not come to see the pleasant simply as advantageous, but remaining attached somehow to nobility, they came to see the pleasant also as noble. The reason for this would seem to be given in the sequel: the fear of gods failed to restrain them, not because they ceased to believe in just gods, but because they believed that the plague itself was a punishment, sent by just gods, and its severity and certainty removed the fear of any other punishment. They believed, moreover, that they *deserved* to enjoy for themselves some hitherto sacrificed pleasure before suffering this terrible and final punishment. From the sufferings of the virtuous and their own suffering the Athenians did not come, as they well might have, to see such sufferings as arbitrary, without rhyme or reason, and hence as evidence of a lack of just gods. Instead, they came to see the plague as a punishment of all of them (a conclusion due in part to the knowledge each had of his own previously secret transgressions).

And in fact it was this abiding need to believe in a correspondence between one's fate and one's virtue that appears to have been responsible for the most terrible things about the plague, according to Thucydides: the utter despair of those who caught it, on one hand, and on the other the frequent deaths of those who nursed others, that is, the revelation of the lack of support for "virtue."[25] Witnessing the latter brought on a fatal despair; seeing the wretched deaths of those who seemed worthy of happiness, or at least of a better fate, some simply ceased resisting the disease. Those who caught the plague and survived, meanwhile, entertained the ridiculously boastful hope in their own immunity from *all* disease, or believed that they would lead charmed lives (2.51.6). The proper disposition seems to be indicated quietly by Thucydides himself. In a rare piece of autobiographical information, he tells us that he caught the plague (48.3), but he obviously neither gave up resisting it nor entertained the false hopes of permanent immunity that he witnessed in others. Occupying a kind of mean between these reactions, he caught the plague and lived. Thucydides was able, it seems, to bear with serenity the thought of no correspondence between desert and one's fate. And so he was able to observe and report the plague as it occurred, even to report the deeds of the non-virtuous without indignation. He displays a striking equanimity, even and especially in the face of the manifest lack of natural and divine support for allegedly self-sacrificing virtue, a capacity that enabled him to observe and to describe without flinching the horror that took place before him. Conversely, the need to see a correspondence between worth and happiness or suffering would seem to obstruct access to the world as it is.

Our deep, abiding need to believe ourselves worthy of happiness appears, on the basis of Thucydides's description of the plague, as a response to, or product of, our uniquely human awareness of our mortality. Unlike animals – to which Thucydides contrasts us in his account – we humans have an unspoken but ever-present hope that security from death can be earned through noble activity or virtue. What we hope for every day, it seems, is to become worthy of a world free of suffering, of pain.[26] But when the plague presented to the citizens an overwhelming disproportion between this hope and the wretched deaths of the virtuous, their hope of overcoming our painful, mortal lives was threatened. No wonder, then, that rather than accepting what the plague showed them – the utter lack of correspondence between fate and desert – many Athenians either despaired or openly committed crimes that would fit the impending "punishment." Thucydides, by contrast, looked at his own death and his own life without despair and without unfounded hope. What the plague is able to make clear is the necessity or inevitability of our mortality, and of our suffering, as something that must indeed be borne and cannot be overcome by noble activity.

Thucydides's account of the plague thus points to a deeper problem with Pericles's vision than we have so far seen. It is possible that the loving, virtuous devotion to Athens accompanied by the love of immortal glory may manifest not wisdom but a softness – a turning away from the truth about our mortal existence and a hope for a secular way around it. But before we can form an adequate judgment of Pericles's project, we need to examine briefly a few other striking examples of the debilitating hope to which Thucydides's account of the plague directs us.

IV

Among the many examples Thucydides offers us of human beings overcoming their despair, surmounting the disease of understanding, and saving themselves from dire circumstances brought on by the war, that of the escape of the Athenians and Plataeans from besieged Plataea is perhaps the most dramatic and certainly the most thoroughly described. The escape also recommends itself to us because Thucydides chooses to speak in this context of "Being" and "Truth,"[27] perhaps indicating by these unique usages that, in this rather unexpected place, we will be shown those human qualities that he views as constituting genuine human excellence.

The fact that half of those who had planned to escape from Plataea ultimately refused, and that others turned back en route, shows us that in addition to cleverness and diligence, courage or daring was required.[28] Those who would escape were required, paradoxically enough, to dare to pursue the safest course. That course entailed a risky exertion on their part: abandoning their city, and undergoing immediate pain by walking right through the enemy's lines barefoot on a stormy, bitter cold night. Those who escaped first recognized and then acted upon the hard truth that there was no hope for their safety otherwise, that the *only* alternative to the risk and the immediate pains involved was certain death. Having no manifest hope of deliverance, they did not succumb to the hope in anything immanifest (3.20.1–2) to deliver them from the evils that are bound up with our nature.[29] The Plataeans' courage seems, then, to be based on a toughness of mind, a capacity to recognize and accept the world as it is, without hiding inevitable pains, or succumbing to despair or false hope, so that one is able to take the kinds of risks that one must when one must, or dare to do what must be done.

Those who remained, by contrast, eventually faced a trial for treason under the Spartans, a trial that displays the abiding hope that they would, on account of their virtues, be able to get around their deaths. They upbraid their Spartan judges for being slaves of mere expediency (3.56.3), and argue that Plataean virtue shown in the Persian war, a war fought with Spartans as allies and in the name of just gods, *merits* safety now. Their Theban enemies, the Plateans remind the Spartans, were on the wrong side in that war, while the Plataeans themselves have been ever attending the graves of the Spartans who fell during it. And just as they call upon the gods, so they call upon these long-dead Spartans for help, appealing to them to recognize their just desert (3.59.2). They always expected their acts of pious caretaking of the dead to support such appeals for intercession; they certainly never dreamed that the Spartans themselves would be attacking them. And this same hope in their devotional justice and piety clearly played a part in their earlier decision to turn back from the escape made by their fellow citizens, or not even to attempt it. The hope hid from them that death was the only alternative to attempting an escape. In fact, they even lost sight of the finality of their deaths. Their entire speech to the Spartans was made,

Thucydides tells us, owing to their fear that, if they made no defence speech, they would suffer certain death and reproach themselves "afterward."[30]

In the course of the war we are given a number of other examples of the debilitating hopes that we have observed. Those whom Brasidas liberates from Athenian rule, for example, lacked, Thucydides suggests, not intelligence but the capacity to accept a difficult or trouble-filled world; they gave in to the hopeful promise of someone who, claiming to recognize their blamelessness and virtue, could set all aright, nobly acting for them against all odds, rather than for himself. They were seduced by Brasidas's speeches to believe it possible for Sparta to act in the way that others in the work, especially Athenians, claimed was impossible – to believe, that is, that a city could be freely dedicated to its friends as well as, and even at the expense of, its own perceived interest.[31] And – to take another significant example – through Nicias's hope in divine justice and pity, "he overthrew," as Hobbes puts it, "himself and his army, and indeed the whole dominion and liberty of his country."[32]

V

Having glanced, however briefly, at the way in which Thucydides addresses the question of divine justice, we are now in a better position to assess Pericles and his leadership. As we have seen, Pericles did not believe in the just gods in whom his fellow, more pious citizens believed. Yet the kind of hope that leads to belief in just gods remained alive in him, and he permitted it to inform his new, secularized vision of Athenian citizenship. The evidence suggests that the hope endured because he lacked the strength of soul to examine the problem of justice. For even his most famous speech, his funeral oration, embodies that problem.

As we've seen, Pericles claims that justice, and indeed all virtue, is rewarded in Athens, and is *therefore* practised there. Now the implication of this claim is that justice is binding on us to the extent that it is or can claim to be good for us; what does not appear good to us cannot be binding on us. But this awareness, to which justice itself points, obviously runs contrary to Pericles's abiding, deep, and expressed conviction that good things belongs by right only to those who deserve them on account of their manifest willingness to *sacrifice* what appears to be for their own good. It contradicts, that is, the other statements of Pericles about noble deeds – that such deeds are not reasonable but *uncalculated*, free, sacrificial. And such a contradiction demands a resolution from us. If in truth what seems good for human beings is compelling, as just men like Pericles periodically acknowledge, then what we wish very much to believe to be a self-sacrifice cannot be so. The human perception of what is good, and the compulsion to pursue it, would defy the obligatory demands of justice to act against what appears good for us.

Similarly, Pericles claims explicitly that the virtue that Athens honours is viewed not simply as an end, or something good in itself, but (at least in part) as a means for Athens to achieve another end – victory in war – and through it, the preservation of freedom and empire. Now if virtue, which requires one to risk one's own good, is not an end in itself, but a means to another end, its claim upon us becomes problematic. Should Athens's enemies, for example, prove that victory in war is attainable through other, better means – means that prove superior to the risk-taking virtue that Pericles praises – then might Athens not be compelled to adopt those other means in order to achieve those ends? Has not her innovation, her use of intelligence, which Pericles praises, done precisely this?[33] But if the good things that one desires can truly be acquired through cleverness rather than through virtue, then virtue, which requires sacrifice, and which rests on the expectation that worthiness is required for those good things, would be unable to provide the happiness that it promises. Science, as Churchill observes, "laughs at valour."[34]

Reflection on the superiority of art or inventiveness to virtue which Pericles's own words imply might thus have begun to open up a challenge to his deep-seated assumption that we can obtain the objects of our desire by becoming worthy of them and lose them on account of our lack of worthiness. Reflection on the problematic nature of the virtue that Pericles practises and to which he directs his fellow Athenians, could in this way have brought home to him the contradiction at the heart of his vision for Athens. It would then have called into question his subordination of all things – including the pursuit of wisdom – to the city's good.

But it is above all in the speech of Diodotos, which contains the only extended reflection on erotic longing that appears in Thucydides's work, that the secular Periclean vision of citizens' erotic longing for eternal glory is shown to suffer from the same difficulty or softness of understanding as besets more obviously pious characters in the work. Diodotos, whose own reflection on justice leads him to the same conclusion as other Athenians, explicitly traces the attempt to acquire empire to the passion of *eros*, and the hope it generates (3.45.5–6). As he suggests, eros leads to hope for things beyond and against the necessary things (cf. 3.5.99), and so to an aversion to calculation of the possible and impossible (cf. 2.40.4–5 with 40.3). Above all, as Diodotos's condemnation of both Athenian anger and the Athenians' existing, negligent imperial practices suggest, the erotic longing for freedom and empire breeds hopes of enjoying an end to all troubles (cf. 3.45.3–4 and 46.4–6 with 3.39.5 and 40.7). The imperial Athenians do not wish to achieve through empire simply rule over others, or what would today be called "power." Rather, they long for a trouble-free life, and for an eternal glory that will overcome, or at least compensate for, that greatest of troubles, death.[35]

In the light of Diodotos's remarks, the erotic Periclean quest for empire looks like the misbegotten product of the soul-in-rebellion-against-death, a soul in futile and desperate search of an alternative to our condition through a glorious devotion to the city. And in this light, Pericles's project appears not a reasonable response to an insight into his own and his city's mortality. It appears rather to be a grand diversion,[36] one that evinces an inability to see clearly or accept fully, both in his own case and that of his city, what is and is not possible for human beings to obtain on their own. The late, brief Periclean admission that it is the nature of all things to decline or give way (2.64.3) seems, in the light of Diodotos's speech, not to have been genuinely accepted by Pericles, but rather to have provoked a rebellion against nature, an erotic rebellion, which found expression in the quest for "eternal glory."[37] Diodotos, we may say, sees through the false character of the experience of that quest – the false hope on which it rests – a quest that Pericles had done his best to make the lodestar of Athens. The hope for life without troubles, or at least an eternal compensation for troubles, animates the Athenians, including those who long for glory, and that is a hope that is mistaken. Empire or rule is not the way to the human good.

We are led to conclude that no more than his pious listeners could Pericles allow himself to face the fundamental self-concern of human beings, a self-concern that would render impossible the specific kind of deeds upon which his worthiness of immortality rested.[38] Yet if the recognition in question, and so the need to be resigned to our mortality, would remove a demand for just gods, it should for the same reason remove our hope for an immortal glory through noble deeds, such as Pericles sought. However different they may be – and they are as different as Pericles and Nicias – love of the noble and piety have that hope in common. If piety would hide this recognition from us because we do not want a world to whose limits we must simply be resigned, then the Periclean love of the noble is a kind of piety, if a grand and godless kind.

Being devoted, on account of his love of deathless glory, to his city is then manifestation of a softness on Pericles's part, a softness that results in an unwarranted confidence in his own virtue or devotion to the city. Even his expectation to live for the duration of the war may have some relation to his own unstinting public spiritedness; he seems to have expected to live on thinking that he deserved to live on. This same hopefulness seems likewise to have moved him to take the civic virtue of his fellow citizens too much for granted. As we have seen, his own love of glory was not, at any rate, an adequate response to a fully grasped insight into his own and his city's mortality, but a diversion that evinces an inability to see clearly or accept fully, both in his own case and that of his city, what was and was not possible. Through the speech of Diodotos, Thucydides does his best to ensure that we overcome the need for such diversion.

As we have seen, the vision of civic life articulated by Pericles is problematic in such a way as to move some of its more talented citizens to an open pursuit of their own glory, and the many to a pious backlash against that pursuit. This alone would explain Thucydides's favourable presentation of the older alternative to that vision, represented by Sparta and cities like Chios, characterized by moderation and obedience to divine law, and the absence of the civil strife that eventually led to the downfall of Athens.[39] But if, as we have suggested, Thucydides's concern is above all with that health of human understanding that became most visible in the plague, then another reason for his favouring of Sparta and its inculcation of respect for divine law comes into view. For as the case of Pericles makes clear, a confused halfway house of godless nobility represents a turning away from the very problem of justice upon which the health in question depends; while presenting itself as the product of enlightenment, it in fact makes *less* visible that which in a harsher and more moderate regime might more easily come into sight for the thoughtful individual, who must confront the dichotomy between his own good and the common good and confront squarely the question of the divine and the significance that it alone might bestow on human life. Since, as the Corinthians argue, cities are compelled to move in the direction of the Athenians (1.71.2), both civic health and the health of understanding of genuinely outstanding individuals calls for praise of the moderate, pious Spartan alternative.[40]

VI

There is a weighty reason, however, to consider the lessons for contemporary politics that we have just drawn from Thucydides's account of Periclean civic republicanism either irrelevant or mistaken. For those who put the teachings of modern political philosophers into practice in the founding of liberal democracies like ours held that what Thucydides considered permanent human problems were in fact capable of being solved, with the right institutions.[41] And in this they followed the political philosophers themselves, who were confident that their new science of politics could make the problems that had ever unsettled human life a thing of the past. Informing that confidence was a new understanding of man *not* as an erotic being but instead as a being characterized by desires that can, if properly directed, be satisfied by rational cooperation induced by political institutions of the right kind. Now the political philosopher who most clearly advanced this argument for the first time is Hobbes. And in the prefaces to his translation of Thucydides Hobbes attributes to Thucydides the fundamental teaching about human desires that became the basis of his own political philosophy: the antithesis between salubrious fear and deleterious vanity. It therefore seems that Thucydides might provide us, as he did for Hobbes, not the cautionary counsel to contemporary civic republicanism that we have articulated, but instead a ground for confidence that liberal civic republicanism can indeed solve the problems that in our analysis have seemed so permanent to Thucydides. To indicate a difficulty with this claim, we will in conclusion look briefly at Hobbes's rationale for recommending the reading of Thucydides, which he presents in the prefaces to his translation of the work.

Hobbes introduces his fear/vanity antithesis when explaining why Thucydides had "no desire at all to meddle in the government" of democratic Athens, and when explaining Thucydides's ranking of regimes. Good counsel is ever obstructed in democratic public assemblies, he argues, because self-admission of fear is ever obstructed in them. The obstructer is vanity or self-love, which invites demagoguery, competition for reputation, and "glory of wit." But since oligarchy is not immune to such competition for eminence, only in monarchy, in which a single ruler can "reasoneth with himself," is fear able to guide public life.[42] Not only Thucydides's preference for monarchy, but even his general rhetorical strategy in the work is informed, Hobbes suggests, by this fear/vanity antithesis. His narrative offers private, indirect self-instruction, which quietly disclose to the reader the "secret aims and inward cogitations" of the actors and speakers, so that the reader, confronting no lessons or precepts from the author, may instead "draw out lessons to himself, and of himself be able to trace the drifts and counsels of the actors to their seat." In this effective, indirect way, according to Hobbes, Thucydides delivers the truth about our miserable situation. "For that men profit more by looking on adverse events, than on prosperity: therefore by how much men's miseries do better instruct, than their good success." Our vanity craves the fabulous, the mythical, and public acknowledgments of submission of others to justice; it thereby hides, to our detriment, the miserable truth. Thucydides's narrative, which contains terse contemplations about publicly dissembled but in truth causal passions, leads us to see and admit the truth for ourselves.[43] Thucydides "secretly" instructs us in the central importance of the fear/vanity antithesis, teaching the dissembling character of all publicly professed devotion to justice and nobility, and directing us to the pursuit of our own solid profit.

The fear/vanity antithesis became the core of Hobbes's subsequent political teaching, in its various iterations. Man, says Hobbes, "whose joy consisteth in comparing himself with other men, can relish nothing but what is eminent."[44] When we debate good and bad, just and unjust, or engage in what Aristotle had called and Thucydides depicts as the core of political life, we are according to Hobbes merely led vaingloriously to deadly contention and sedition – particularly so when our debates involve disagreement of opinion concerning religious doctrines.[45] Vainglory prevents us from pursuing private goods in the sensible way that can lead us, in the manner of cooperative animals, to a common accrual of private benefits.[46] But a new doctrine of justice can make possible a change in political life, away from vanity-driven contention for rule and towards indirect government of ourselves. The doctrine of "rights," of individual justified claims to good things, derived from the allegedly compelling and hence blameless fear of violent death, can guide a new, prosperous way of life. Prudential reason posits "natural laws" as the surest means to secure those rights and that prosperity. On the basis of this new doctrine, designed to replace the old contentious and vain doctrines of divine law, a new kind of politics comes into being, which aims to bring all men to renounce their vain dreams and find the this-worldly security and bodily satisfaction they crave. Leviathan, "king of the proud,"[47] weakens vanity by re-presenting the terrible fear of violent death that at bottom moves all men, or relegates vanity to peaceful ("bourgeois") pursuits in a vast new private realm ("society").

But does Thucydides lead his readers, in the way Hobbes suggests, to draw conjectures about the hidden passions behind all speeches, and thence to the fear/vanity antithesis that informs Hobbes's political thought? True, Thucydides famously argues that the truest pretext (*prophasis*) for the war, though least advanced in public speech, was that the growing greatness of Athens compelled the Athenians to go to war (1.23). It is remarkable, Thucydides suggests, that this pretext was even advanced in speech, and to this extent Hobbes is drawing out an important lesson from Thucydides. But Thucydides limits his famous claim to saying that fear was the *truest* pretext; he does not cause us to conclude that publicly advanced causes, which had to do with claims of injustice, were simply false or were advanced by all parties in bad faith. In fact, it is the Athenians at Melos who make that mistake, and unexpectedly find their closed-door session with the Melians a complete failure. Here as elsewhere, Thucydides's characters – even oligarchs – are genuinely moved by a sense of justice. Hobbes, by contrast, understands and presents Thucydides's work as teaching the reader the unreliability of all public speech about justice and hence the vital need to *not* take it seriously. The speeches and narratives concerning spoken pretexts for action are, to Hobbes, mere object lessons in public dissembling versus private truth, lessons to be learned and then extended to the dismissal of all public speech as mere pretence.[48]

While Thucydides indicates that a necessary distortion of the truth occurs in all political life, in other words, his position is only apparently shared by Hobbes, for whom any public statements about justice and nobility are dismissible as a product of vanity and hence altogether at odds with the privately acknowledged truth. For Hobbes the "few and better sort" of readers are human beings who will be easily led to discount professions of justice as deceptive. But while Thucydides certainly expected to appeal to sophisticated readers, and to draw them into reflection, his primary addressees were men like Nicias,[49] just as the best readers upon whom Plato counted were men like the morally serious Polemarchus.[50] Thucydides also signals a turn, by the third book, to an ennobling rhetoric closer to that of Homer,[51] about which Hobbes is as silent as he is about Sparta.

We heirs to Hobbes's understanding of human desires and of justice may thus run the risk of missing crucial lessons of Thucydides. And while the modern secularizing project has resources – like modern natural science – available to it which were absent from its Periclean forerunner, Thucydides's warnings remain worthy of our attention. Attempts like those made in all modern liberal regimes to direct political life away from any support for the transcendent meaning that religion provides cannot take place without an eventual terrible awareness of a moral and spiritual emptiness, and eruptions of discontent with a loss of a sense of sacred restraints on human actions. (Consider 6.27–9, 53, 60–2.) Such eruptions are most visible to us in fascistic movements of the twentieth century, but are also visible on the left, especially in its romantic and postmodern varieties, which counsel an openness to hidden pagan gods[52] or sympathy with radical Islam. Nor would Thucydides think it unreasonable to expect in modern regimes unforeseeable forms of longing and rebellion against the political order that appears to be causing a diminution of natural human aspirations. The human yearning for transcendent purpose may result in manifestations of pre-liberal religiosity, or various sorts of desperate nihilisms that aim to destroy modernity, in perverted and fanatic expressions of the natural and inevitable civic concern for the sacred and willingness to fight on its behalf. If we are to find our way to the truth and to a healthier political life than late modernity may be capable of offering, we could do much worse than returning with fresh eyes to Thucydides's work, unencumbered by Hobbes's doctrines.

NOTES

1 The funeral oration was delivered by Pericles at Athens in honor of those who had been killed during the Peloponnesian War, then in its second year, a war that lasted from 432 BC to 404 BC. References to Thucydides's text will be in the standard form of book, chapter, and line. All translations are my own.

2 See, e.g., G.W.F. Hegel, *The Philosophy of History*, trans. C.J. Friedrich (New York: Dover, 1956), 261.

3 See Thucydides1.74.3.

4 Compare 1.126.7–8 with 1.138 and 1.93.2–3, and contrast 1.106.2.

5 See Lowell Edmunds, *Chance and Intelligence in Thucydides* (Cambridge, MA: Harvard University Press, 1975).

6 See the Corinthians' words at 1.70–1, especially 71.2, and the reply of the Spartan king Archidamus at 1.84–5.1 with 1.121.4.
7 See Christopher Bruell, "Thucydides and Perikles," *St. John's Review* 82.3 (1981), 24–9, and Robert C. Bartlett, *The Idea of Enlightenment: A Post-mortem Study* (Toronto: University of Toronto Press, 2001).
8 Hannah Arendt, *The Human Condition* (Chicago: University of Chicago Press, 1958).
9 2.41.4. Pericles mentions unwritten laws that are sanctioned by shame, but he excludes mention of the gods in this very place where one would most expect it (2.37.3). He understands such laws to be in no need of superhuman support. The funeral oration in general disparages things holy or sacred just as it does things ancient. Pericles's only usage of "holy," in fact, is in our contemporary sense of "holiday": sacred festivals provide relaxation from toils.
10 1.37.1. This praise is, to be sure, sandwiched between two praises of democratic equality, i.e., the blindness of justice to class and the lack of need for wealth for participation.
11 2.41.1.
12 For a thoughtful version of this argument, see Donald Kagan, "The First Revisionist Historian," *Commentary* 85.5 (1988). See, however, Bruell, "Thucydides and Perikles," 24–9.
13 Cf. Aristotle, *Politics* 1324a5ff., and see in the next chapter the fine argument of David Roochnik on this passage. I do not agree, however, that Aristotle's argument here depends on the doctrine of "place" expounded in his works on natural science.
14 See Thucydides 2.65 with 1.140.1, 2.13.1, and 2.50.5–7.
15 1.140–1.1.
16 See Christopher Bruell, "Thucydides' View of Athenian Imperialism," *American Political Science Review* 68.1 (1974), 11–17.
17 The above statement relies on the following passages in Thucydides: 1.75–7; 3.44–6; 5.85–113; 6.18.2–3; 6.82–7. I have attempted to preserve some of the differences among the various Athenian claims while including what is either common or consequent to all of them.
18 Cf. 5.9.5 and Plato, *Republic* 334a–b, and see again, in the opening of the next chapter, the argument of David Roochnik on passages from book 8 of the *Republic*.
19 Cf. Plato, *Laws* 626c–30d; Aristotle, *Politics* 1324a5–5a15. See also Steven Forde, "Varieties of Realism: Thucydides and Machiavelli," *Journal of Politics* 54.2 (1992), 372–93.
20 See 6.15.2–4 with 6.27–9, 53, 60–1, 7.18.2–4, 7.50.4, 7.77.2–4.

21 That is, the ubiquitous euphemisms for "death," and the callousness of Pericles's words to the relatives of the fallen, suggest an insufficient grasp of the sorrow and permanence of death.
22 See 1.23, 1.87.6–88, 1.118, and 3.87.
23 While he suggests contagion as a cause (2.47.3–4, 51.5), he explicitly leaves an investigation of the material or efficient cause of the plague to others (2.48.3).
24 The description of the plague is prefaced by an echo of the title of the work as a whole – an eternal possession. See 2.48.3.
25 Thucydides speaks here (2.51.5) of those who made an attempt at virtue, i.e., those who were moved by shame.
26 Those who seemed to have attained that life, having survived the plague, were "blessed" or congratulated by the others (2.51.6).
27 3.22, *to on*, being; 3.24, *to alethes*, truth. I am grateful to Christopher Bruell for calling this to my attention.
28 As the name of the soothsayer who led the escape (Theaenetus, son of Tolmides) suggests, the enterprise required a peculiar kind of daring (*tolma*).
29 3.20.1–2. Cf. 5.103.
30 3.53.3; and consider again their appeals to the dead Spartans.
31 See Timothy Burns, "The Virtue of Thucydides' Brasidas," *Journal of Politics* 73.2 (2011), 508–23.
32 Thomas Hobbes, "Of the Life and History of Thucydides" (1629), in *Hobbes' Thucydides*, ed. Richard Schlatter (New Brunswick, NJ: Rutgers University Press, 1975), 12. See Thucydides 7.50.4, 7.77.2–4.
33 On this problem, see Burns, "The Virtue of Thucydides' Brasidas."
34 Winston Churchill, *The River War: An Historical Account of the Reconquest of the Soudan*, ed. James W. Muller (South Bend, IN: St Augustine's Press, 2015), vol. 2, chap. 21. Churchill notes in the same place that "time laughs at science."
35 See 6.24.2–3, 2.64.6, and cf. Aristotle, *Politics* 1267a1–b5. For similar hopes, see Leon Trotsky, *Lenin: Notes for a Biographer*, trans. Tamara Deutcher (New York: Capricorn Books, 1971), 127.
36 See 2.40.4, 2.59.3, 2.64.6–65.1.
37 See 2.38.1 with 2.43.2.
38 See David Bolotin, "Thucydides," in *History of Political Philosophy*, 3rd ed., ed. Leo Strauss and Joseph Cropsey (Chicago: University of Chicago Press, 1987), 19.
39 See 1.79.2, 1.84–5, 2.74–5, 7.18.2–3, 8.24.4 with 2.65.11–12, 3.81.3–85, and 6.15.2–4.

40 See in this regard the excellent analysis, by Susan D. Collins and Devin Stauffer, of the Socratic alternative to Pericles's funeral oration presented in Plato's *Menexenus*: "The Challenge of Plato's Menexenus," *Review of Politics* 61 (1999), 85–115.

41 So in the preface to his longest writing John Adams excerpts a portion of Thucydides's description of the Corcyrean civil strife (3.81–2), but upon reaching Thucydides's statement that "such things will ever be ... so long as human nature continues the same," Adams interrupts the quotation to say: "But if this nervous historian had known a balance of three powers, he would not have pronounced the distemper so incurable, but would have added – *so long as parties in cities remain unbalanced*." John Adams, *Defense of the Constitutions of Government of the United States*, in *The Works of John Adams*, vol. 4, ed. Charles Francis Adams (Boston: Little, Brown, and Co., 1865), 285.

42 Hobbes, "Of the Life and History of Thucydides," 12–14.

43 Hobbes, "To the Readers," 7, and "On the Life and History of Thucydides," 17–27.

44 *Leviathan*, ed. Edwin Curley (Indianapolis, IN: Hackett, 1994), chap. 17; cf. *De Cive* 2.5.5 and William Mathie, "Reason and Rhetoric in Hobbes' *Leviathan*," *Interpretation: A Journal of Political Philosophy* 14.2&3 (1986), 294.

45 *De Cive* 1.1.5, and consider parts 3 and 4 of *Leviathan*.

46 *Leviathan*, 17.

47 *Leviathan*, 27.

48 The ancient critic Dionysius of Halicarnassus had warned rhetoricians away from imitation of the Melian dialogue on the ground that the Athenians' arguments about divine justice were shockingly ignoble, fit only for a barbarian tyrant, and unacceptable to the fathers and mothers of Athens; Hobbes dismisses these concerns on the ground that the Athenians were merely following orders. See Hobbes, "On the Life and History of Thucydides," 24, with Dionysius of Halicarnassus, *On Thucydides*, 37–41, 49–51. For a fuller examination of the significance of Hobbes's dispute with Dionysius, see Timothy Burns, "Hobbes and Dionysius of Halicarnassus on Thucydides, Rhetoric, and Political Life," *Polis* 31.2 (August 2014), 387–424.

49 See Leo Strauss, *The City and Man* (Chicago: University of Chicago Press, 1964), 202n68.

50 See Christopher Bruell, *On the Socratic Education: An Introduction to the Shorter Platonic Dialogues* (Lanham, MD: Rowman and Littlefield, 1999), 23.

51 See Timothy Burns, "What War Discloses," in *Recovering Reason: Essays in Honor of Thomas L. Pangle*, ed. T. Burns (Lanham, MD: Lexington Books, 2010), 31–52.

52 Consider, e.g., Jean-François Lyotard, *Le postmoderne expliqué aux enfants* (Paris: Éditions Galilée, 1986), 27–8.

2 Aristotle's Topological Politics; Michael Sandel's Civic Republicanism

DAVID ROOCHNIK

In book 8 of Plato's *Republic*, the first sustained critique of democracy in Western philosophy, Socrates raises a fundamental question about the form of government that is now widely regarded as unambiguously the best. Simply put, in a political system whose primary values are freedom and equality, what will prevent the citizens from becoming staunch individualists who have little concern and make little sacrifice for the good of the community as a whole? As Socrates puts it, because it is "full of freedom" (557b) and "dispenses equality to equals and unequals alike" (558c), a democracy imposes no compulsion upon its citizens to rule or to participate in the working of their own government. Instead, it allows them to become accustomed to "gratifying the desires that occur to them" (561c). In other words, they will feel free to pursue their own conception of the good life in whatever way they see fit. As lovely as such a regime may seem to be, Socrates warns of what he takes to be a grave danger: citizens of a democracy will become resentful of any limitation or authority that is imposed upon them. He describes a regime in which leaders who do not pander to the citizens' whims will be voted out of office and whose children, raised in the intoxicating air of equality, will feel no shame or fear before their parents or elders. Teachers, he says, will be frightened of their students, the old will curry favour with the young, and slaves will be as free as masters. Even the horses will cease to respect the commands of their riders and so they will bump into "whomever they happen to meet on the roads" (563c).[1]

However hyperbolic Socrates's picture may be, it inaugurates an abiding concern that has trailed democratic institutions like a shadow since their inception in Athens 2500 years ago. In contemporary political theory this concern has been expressed as a critique of modern liberalism; more specifically, as a critique of John Rawls.

This chapter considers the work of one such critic: Michael Sandel. In formulating his own version of what has come to be known as "civic republicanism" as a response to Rawlsian "procedural liberalism," Sandel turns back to ancient Greece for inspiration. In this sense he is exemplary of the project animating this volume. For he, as Geoffrey Kellow puts it in his introduction, considers "the challenges of modern republics" by drawing "republican lessons from republics and writers both recent and remote in time" (p. 5). He does not, however, invoke Plato's critique of democratic freedom. Instead, he takes his bearings from Aristotle. What will be argued below is that Sandel's neo-Aristotelian political theory is insufficiently grounded. While it effectively and invitingly revives several prominent principles from the *Nicomachean Ethics* and the *Politics*, it does not adequately examine or even acknowledge the more theoretical background on which these claims rely. Consider the following example, which I take to be paradigmatic and will become the focus of this essay.

Sandel argues that civic life in the United States has become "impoverished" (p. 6).[2] Americans, he says, suffer from the justifiable "fear that, individually and collectively, we are losing control of the forces that govern our lives." Such forces are enormous, distant, impersonal, and, because they are indifferent to the particularities of the local, politically enervating. As a result, Sandel complains, "the moral fabric of community is unraveling around us" (3). In response, he advocates a restoration of community, of the local. Without it, he believes, political engagement will continue to evaporate. As he puts it, "People will not pledge allegiance to vast and distant entities, whatever their importance, unless those institutions are somehow connected to political arrangements that reflect the *identity* of the participants" (346). He also says:

> The global media and markets that shape our lives beckon us to a world beyond boundaries and belonging. But the civic resources we need to master those forces, or at least to contend with them, are still to be found in the *places* and stories, memories and meanings, incidents and identities, that *situate* us in the world and give our lives their moral *particularity*. (349; emphasis mine)

A local institution or community, the sort to which Sandel believes people will pledge genuine allegiance, is one in which citizens have a stake and which they can influence. It has a particularized identity expressed in "stories, memories and meanings" that differentiates it from other communities. Its boundaries are stable and recognizable; they are, so to speak, within reach.

In opposition to the prevailing theory of government – which, to reiterate, he identifies as the "procedural liberalism" championed by John Rawls – Sandel advocates a return to "a version of republican political theory" (5). Its central idea is "that liberty depends on sharing in self-government ... To share in self-rule ... requires that citizens possess, or come to acquire, certain qualities of character, or civic virtues" (6). In turn, this process of character formation requires the exercise of "soulcraft" on the part of government. In this context, the local is central: "Statecraft could be soulcraft without big government, provided that families, schools, and churches" – institutions that are by their nature particularized and small – "served as the primary agents of character formation" (326). To reinforce this conviction Sandel favourably cites Tocqueville's remarks on New England towns whose "town meetings are to liberty what primary schools are to science; they bring it within the people's reach, they teach men how to use and how to enjoy it" (27). More generally he says this: "From Aristotle's polis to Jefferson's agrarian ideal, the civic conception of freedom found its home in *small and bounded places*, largely self-sufficient, inhabited by people whose conditions of life afforded the leisure, learning, and commonality to deliberate well about public concerns" (317; emphasis mine).

As these remarks suggest, and his other writings confirm, Sandel's defence of civic republicanism is neo-Aristotelian. But there is a decisive difference between Sandel's argument and Aristotle's own. Simply put, Aristotle can make very good sense of the crucial phrase highlighted above: "small and bounded places." Sandel, it will be argued, cannot.

This chapter will unfold as follows. Part 1 will show that Sandel's defence of the local echoes lines of thought first developed by Aristotle. Part 2 will argue that Aristotle's defence of the political-local is philosophically supported by the fundamental role that locality or "place" (*topos*) plays in his physics and cosmology. In other words, Aristotle's political theory, like his conception of nature itself, is thoroughly "topological." Part 3 will argue that despite leaning heavily on Aristotle's practical philosophy, Sandel himself invokes no corresponding background theory, and as a result his political convictions are not sufficiently supported. Part 4 will conclude by raising the pivotal question that Michael Sandel's failed neo-Aristotelianism raises.

Part 1: Aristotle's Defence of the Local

That Aristotle is a staunch advocate of the local in politics can be quickly ascertained by considering his discussion of the size of the ideal "regime" (*politeia*) he sketches in book 7 of the *Politics*. First and foremost, it must be neither too big nor too small. It must be big enough to achieve self-sufficiency, which means "having everything and needing nothing" (1326b30), but it must also be very careful not to become too big.[3] For a too-big city cannot, Aristotle thinks, be well governed; that is, ruled by law (1332a25). Furthermore, "too many people will lead to more poverty, which in turn leads to instability" (1265b12) or factionalism, the disease that threatens all cities.[4] Finally and most important, a too-big city would at some point simply cease to be a city at all.

Aristotle offers concrete descriptions of his ideal city. For example, rather than expanding its trading economy, it imports only necessities unavailable at home and exports only its surplus goods. It thereby resists the temptation of *pleonexia* (1327a31), the desire always to have more. It has a navy, which in antiquity required a large number of sailors (*poluanthropian*: 1327b7) to man the oars, but maintains it only "up to that number" (1327a42) required for defence of its harbour. Unlike regimes such as Sparta and Crete, it does not have imperial ambitions and so its well-trained army is solely for the purpose of defence (1333b40). In other words, Aristotle is not unlike Timothy Burns's description of Thucydides, who is critical of Pericles for making Athens's "grand leadership, her imperialism and martial victories, the highest good for his city" (20). To gauge just how small Aristotle's ideal city must be, consider this: in order for a regime to qualify as excellent it must properly distribute the responsibilities for judging and ruling. And to do this well, "citizens must recognize one another and know what sort of person each other is" (1326b15). The ideal city now sounds like a small town in which gossip flows freely and keeps the citizens well informed of each other's characters and actions.

Aristotle acknowledges that the limitations he recommends are rarely appreciated because "most people suppose that it is appropriate for the happiest [*eudaimona*] city to be great (*megalên*) ... and they judge greatness on the basis of the number of inhabitants" (1226a10). Most people, in other words, think bigger is better. But this is false, since "to be a great city and a populous one are not the same thing" (1226a25).

In sum, the ideal city is a "small and bounded place" whose borders are visible, within reach, and respected. Nonetheless, the city cannot be too small either. First, as just mentioned, it must become self-sufficient. But second, like a work of art it must be beautiful and fine, qualities it cannot achieve if it is does not have sufficient magnitude. In general, a city does not become great "by number," but by its "capacity" (*dunamis*: 1326a12), by what it can do. Aristotle offers the following comparison: "as is the case with animals, plants and tools, for a city there is a certain proper measure (*metron*). For each of these will not achieve its own potentiality if it is too small or too big" (1326b35–8). A ship only a few inches wide or ten miles long cannot do what a ship is meant to do, sail the seas and transport cargo and men, and so is not really a ship. Similarly, living beings are big enough when they have matured, attained their proper form, and can actualize those capacities, perform those functions, that are intrinsic to their species. When it comes to politics, a city is big enough when it is self-sufficient and, most important, able to generate the conditions that allow its citizens, or at least some of them, to live excellent lives that fulfil their natures as human and political beings.

To encapsulate this line of thought, Aristotle says that the best city must be of such a size as to afford a "synoptic" view of itself; it must be "easily seen as a whole" (*eusunopton*: 1327a2). It has visible borders that are sufficiently limited to be traversed by an individual and therefore small enough to allow participation. By extreme contrast, Babylon was so big that it took three days for some parts of it to realize that it had been invaded (1276a27). As a result, Babylon, due to its vast size, was not really a city at all. (Instead, it was what Aristotle calls a "people" [*ethnos*: 1276a29].)

To understand the substance of these claims, recall Aristotle's definition of a city. It is, he says, a community (*koinonia*: 1252a1) composed of several smaller communities, such as the family, the household, and the village, which is a group of households (1252b10). The city is "prior to" and the most "authoritative" (1252a5) of these communities because it embraces them all as parts. It is a well-formed whole that "reaches a level of self-sufficiency" (1252b27). The notion of the "whole" (*to holon*) is crucial here. As Aristotle defines it in the *Metaphysics*, it is that "from which is absent none of the parts of which it is said by nature to be a whole" (1023b26). This definition comes close to that of the "all" or the "sum" (*to pan*). But there is an essential difference: in the case of an "all," the position, the order of the parts, is irrelevant. "All" the letters of BAT are "b, a, t." But these can be combined to form TAB as well as BAT. "If position does make a difference, then it is a whole" (*Metaphysics* 1024a1–3).

Alternatively formulated, the whole is that "which has a beginning, middle, and end (*telos*)" (*Poetics* 1450b27). It is an orderly, an in-formed, unity of parts. The city, then, is a whole community defined or characterized by "a certain order (*taxis*) of those who live in the city" (1274b36). This order or principle of organization is the *politeia*, the "regime" or "form of government."

A genuine city, then, does not come into being simply upon the establishment of geographical borders nor can it be constituted simply by maintaining the continuity of a population through successive generations. Instead, it requires a form (*eidos*). It must be unified by means of its *politeia*, which makes the otherwise disparate and ever changing number of its parts into a whole.

The *politeia* is the organization of the city. It designates who is and who is not a citizen, who is responsible for the judicial, legislative, executive, and military activities. It determines the kind of education citizens require. As a result, simply living within the borders of a city or being subject to its laws is not sufficient to qualify an individual as a citizen (*politês*). For a citizen in the full sense of the word "is defined by nothing other than participating in decision and ruling" (1275a24) and must be engaged in the working of the city.

The preceding discussion helps us better appreciate Aristotle's description of the "synoptic" character of the ideal city. It has a "form," an *eidos*, a word that is derived from the verb "to see." A city must thus be visible as a whole. This is possible only if it is of limited size, if its borders are within reach.

Finally, the ideal city is genuinely self-sufficient. It requires nothing other than itself in order to be fully itself. In political terms, it does not have to expand beyond its borders in order to succeed. Using some of his favourite metaphysical terminology, Aristotle says this: "A single city, the one which governs in manifest fineness, could be happy with respect to itself (*kath' heautên*), if it is possible for a city to live by itself (*kath' heautên*), using decent laws. Its form of government (*politeia*) would not be directed towards war or domination of its enemies (1325a1–4).

It should now be obvious that what Aristotle recommends is the ancestor of Sandel's civic republicanism and his corresponding defence of the political centrality of "small and bounded places," of the local. But, unlike Sandel, Aristotle rests his claims not only upon his definitions of the city, the citizen, and the regime, but on his conception of a natural world that is divided into places. His political theory is thoroughly "localized" (from the Latin *locus*, "place"), thoroughly "topological" (from the Greek *topos*, "place"), because so too is his conception of the world.

Part 2: Aristotle's Topological World

Aristotle's conception of place (*topos*) is a fundamental to his conception of nature. He begins his discussion of it (in *Physics* 4) by saying that "everyone assumes that beings (*ta onta*) are somewhere. For what is not is nowhere. For where is the goat-stag or the sphinx?" (208a29–31). We regularly, perhaps even naturally, ask where something is, for if something is it must be somewhere. To illustrate, Aristotle cites the poet Hesiod, whose *Theogony* is the story of how the world and all its objects came into being.

> That there is place, and that it is independent of bodies, and that every body is perceptible as being in a place is a reasonable belief. Thus it would seem that Hesiod spoke correctly when he made "the chasm" (*chaos*) the first of all things. For he wrote, at any rate, that "first of all the chasm came to be, and then next broad bosomed earth." He did so because he understood that it was necessary first of all for there to be room for things. Just like most people, he understood that every thing has to be somewhere and in a place. (*Physics* 208b27–33)

First, says Hesiod, there was *chaos*, the "chasm" or even "emptiness." But immediately afterwards there came earth. This line, Aristotle suggests, reveals that Hesiod understood that there must be a place for all the many beings – trees, mountains, people, rivers, nymphs – whose coming-into-being his poem describes. The earth must be there for beings cannot exist nowhere or in the empty chasm. The goal of Aristotle's analysis in *Physics* 4 is thus to provide an answer to the question "What is the where of things?" There are, he thinks, two possible answers: in a place or in the void. He opts for the former because for him the latter is no more than "a special case of place, i.e., a place with nothing in it."[5]

It is important to note that Aristotle's void is similar to the neutral or indeterminate space through which all bodies move by following the same laws of motion that are central to modern physics. Such space "is internally undifferentiated – two spaces are identical, if they are of equal dimensions."[6] With this contrast in mind, we can quickly discern the salient feature of Aristotelian place. Unlike modern space, it has a kind of "power" (208b11), which in turn is manifested in directionality. There are, Aristotle argues, six "divisions" or "directions" of place: up, down, left, right, front, back (*Physics* 208b12). The striking feature of his theory here is that, unlike us – that is, we who dwell in the unbounded and homogeneous space of modern physics – Aristotle thinks that these distinct directions are objective features of the world.

> Up and down, right and left [front and back] are not only relative to us. For they are not always the same in relation to us, but instead depend on our position so that when we turn they change ... In nature, however, each is distinct and exists independently of the others. For that which is up is not a matter of chance, but instead is to where fire or a light body moves. Similarly, what is down is not a matter of chance, but is to where heavy or earthy bodies move. They differ not only in position, but also in power. (*Physics* 208b14–22)

As indicated in this passage, Aristotle's notion of place is closely tied to his account of the natural motion of the four elements: earth, fire, water, and air. Each has its natural place towards which it will move unless otherwise impeded. Fire and air, which are light, naturally move upwards, towards the heavens, which are above the earth. An earthy or watery body, one that is heavy, naturally moves downward, towards the earth. To say it again: up and down are objective features of the world. So too are left and right. In *On the Heavens*, for example, Aristotle argues that "the beginning of the heaven's revolution is the side from which the stars rise, so that must be its right, and where they set must be its left" (285b20).

The objectivity of direction is, to put it mildly, a hard pill for us to swallow. We are vastly more accepting of the belief that directionality is relative. After all, our own version of physics requires an infinite or indefinite universe in which there can be no objectively up or down, left or right, but only relative position on an indeterminate grid. Aristotle sees things quite differently. As will gradually become more clear, he does so because his conception of nature, unlike our own, emerges from a specifically human, earth-based, and naked-eye perspective.

Aristotle defines *topos* as the limit "of the containing body" (211b14). As such, it is neither a material thing nor a part of one. Instead, it is more like the form or the shape of a thing. My computer has three dimensions and is sitting on my desk. It is made of stuff like plastic and silicon; in Aristotle's terminology, some bits of earth, air, water, or fire. The stuff has been moulded into a shape or form by the computer-maker. Its shape is visible. To reiterate an earlier point, the Greek word for "form," *eidos*, is derived from the verb "to see" and so could also be translated simply as "the look" of a thing. Rather than being a separate part, the form is the entirety of the way the computer, shaped by its outermost edge or limit, looks.

Even though it too is a limit – and for the purpose of this paper this will prove to be its decisive feature – a place is not a form. A form is the limit of that which is contained, whereas place is the limit of that which contains. A place is thus like a "vessel" (210a24). Like a bottle, it is that which things are in. Like an immovable vessel, a place "holds" change.

This is hard to understand. For example, place seems close to being a body because it is three-dimensional, but the phenomenon of "replacement" shows that it is not. There may now be water in a bottle. When the water is poured out it is replaced by air. Where there was water now there is air. And the air also could be replaced by another body. Because the same place can be occupied by different bodies, place is not body. (See *Physics* 208b1–7.) Nor, as argued above, is it a form. Instead, place "is the first unmoved limit of that which contains" (212a20).

To do justice to this complicated topic would go far beyond the limits of this paper. Fortunately, the key point here is only this: place has "power." It is the principle that renders the world directional. All beings are in places that are either up or down, left or right. In turn, it is precisely such directionality that renders the world orderly and is responsible for it being a "cosmos." Koyré defines a cosmos as "a conception of the world as a finite, closed, and hierarchically ordered whole."[7] Within its confines everything has its place in which it naturally belongs. Stars are above us, earth below, and animals like us are in-between. By contrast, in a universe of indefinite space nothing belongs anywhere or is objectively above or below, to the right or the left. Since there is no fixed and immobile centre, such directions are strictly relative.

Another fundamental, and to us jarring, point is expressed in Koyré's comment. Aristotle's world is "finite." The uppermost heavenly sphere, which is as far as the eyes can see, is its outer limit. This cosmological fact has, for Aristotle, far-reaching significance. Consider, for example, his embrace of the Pythagorean "table of opposites" (in *Metaphysics* 1.5). It asserts that the finite is to the infinite as the one is to the many, as rest is to motion, as right is to left, and finally as good is to bad. Such an evaluation sounds preposterous, for finite and infinite seem to be no more than quantitative designators and thus to be indifferent to questions of value. Nonetheless, this normative hierarchy – the finite is superior to the infinite – is central to Aristotle's thought for, again like the Pythagoreans, he counts the finite as responsible for intelligibility. As he puts it, "insofar as something is infinite it is unknowable" (*Physics* 207a26). If intelligibility is then taken to be a good, as Aristotle takes it to be, then so too should the finite.

In *On the Heavens* 1.5, Aristotle asks "whether there is an infinite body" and he pleads for the urgency of this question: "for whether there is or isn't does not make a small difference, but all the difference in respect to the study (*theoria*) of truth" (271b5–6). Everything, including his practical philosophy, hinges on the answer to this question, which for Aristotle is emphatically negative, for were the magnitude of the world to be infinite it would be unknowable. And no feature of the world is more apparent and impressive to Aristotle than its knowability.

Recall that the notions of place and natural direction are tightly connected. Unless forced to do otherwise, fire naturally moves upward to its place in the heavens. The sun rises in the East, to the right, and sets in the West, to the left. If there were an infinite body these notions would become meaningless. Aristotle explains:

> Every sensible body is in a place, and the forms and differences of place are the up and the down and before and the front and the back and the right and left. And these are not relative to us nor a matter of convention, but have been distinguished in the cosmos itself. And they could not possibly be in the infinite. Simply put, if an infinite place is impossible, and every body is in a place, an infinite body is impossible. Indeed, whatever is somewhere is in a place, and what is in a place is somewhere. (*Physics* 205b31–6a2)

To reiterate: directionality – up, down, left, right, front, back – is an objective feature of the world and renders it orderly and intelligible (and beautiful). The moon simply is above the earth; fire goes up towards its natural place, water down. The world makes sense and as a consequence must be finite.

Having eliminated the possibility of an infinite body or entity, Aristotle is not yet done with the infinite. For "if there simply were no infinite at all, many impossibilities would ensue" (*Physics* 206a10). For example, if there were no infinite we would be required to say that time has a beginning and an end, and that continuous magnitudes are not divisible into further magnitudes, two notions that are absurd. We would have to say that numbers are not infinite, which again is obviously false since there is no highest number.

What, then, remains of the infinite? It is, but only in potentiality (206a18). A line segment can be divided into infinitely many smaller segments. Each segment subtracted from the original line is limited but the procedure of subtraction cannot be completed. The infinite, Aristotle tells us, is "that which is always beyond" (207a1). It is the potential of there always being more. Differently stated, the being of the infinite is "in thinking" (*en noesei:* 203b24). We can always think of a higher number and in our minds subdivide a line segment to infinity. We can always imagine a point beyond. But Aristotle cautions against "trusting in thinking alone" (208a15). Clever people can cook up puzzles and argue on behalf of paradoxical positions. But the goal of theoretical thinking is not just being clever, or doing elegant mathematics, but remaining faithful to (or saving) the phenomena, including sensible, naked-eye, ordinary phenomena. Indeed, a fundamental requirement of Aristotelian theory is that it make sense of the world as human beings here on earth actually experience it.

That the finite is prior and superior to the infinite is also reflected in one of Aristotle's basic metaphysical principles: "For one man and a man are the same, and being a man and a man are the same" (*Metaph.* 1003b22). To be is to be this or that; it is to be determinate or singular. To be, in the fullest sense – that is, in actuality – is to be finite. Differently stated, the concept of the finite is intimately connected to that of the whole. As mentioned above, a "whole" is "that from which nothing is absent; for example, a whole man" (*Physics* 207a10). A whole is a complete (*teleion*) unity of parts. This description leads directly to the concept of the finite: "The whole and the complete (*teleion*) are either entirely the same or their natures are akin. For nothing is complete unless it has a *telos*. And a *telos* is a limit" (207a15).

A man is whole because he is a complete (*teleion*) set of parts; the list of his parts comes to an end, and each contributes to the functioning of the man. It's important to note that *teleion* can also be translated as "perfect." Something that has been gone through entirely is complete and thus "perfect." The infinite is that which cannot be gone through. Furthermore, the words "perfect" and *teleion* also have evaluative connotations. What is "perfect" is not only complete or "that from which nothing is absent," but it is also maximally good and "cannot be exceeded in its kind. For example, a perfect doctor or flutist are those who, according to the form of the excellence that belongs to them, lack nothing" (*Metaphysics* 1021b16–18).

Finally, as the use of *teleion* above suggests, the lines of thought just sketched are basic to Aristotle's teleological conception of nature. A being has a purpose determined by its form. The goal of an organism, to cite the crucial example, is to maintain itself and become perfect, whole, complete.

To sum up: Aristotle's political theory and his physics work in tandem and both require the concept of place. The *polis* is natural and is the *telos* of the human urge to enter into communities. The best city is limited and has an intelligible form or *politeia* that renders it whole. It is localized, what Sandel calls a "small and bounded place," and within its reachable boundaries its citizens are recognizable to one another. These political convictions are well grounded on Aristotle's conception of nature, which is essentially topological and teleological.

It is arguable that a similar correspondence obtains between modern liberalism and the background theory, the conception of nature, from which it emerges. As Koyré puts it, the scientific revolution of the seventeenth century is precisely the transition "From the Closed World to the Infinite Universe."[8] In the indeterminate or infinite space of the latter nothing has a natural place or belongs anywhere in particular and there is no possibility of perfection (at least here on earth). The fundamental consequence of this theory when applied to political life is that human beings are not bounded or determined to exist in one place or another. In other words, we are free ... free to choose our place. By contrast, in Aristotle's version of the closed world a woman's place, for example, is in the home, where she naturally belongs and where she is, and should be, subordinated to the man. (See *Politics* 1260a10–15.) Nonsense, the liberal replies. A woman should have the right to occupy any leadership position in the community to which she aspires and for which she is qualified. She should pursue the path, occupy the place, that she wishes. For Aristotle, a (natural) slave's place is under the thumb of a master, a principle that we moderns find repugnant. (See *Politics* 1.4.) In general, then, of fundamental practical importance in modernity is the freedom to move and this is made possible by an infinite universe where we ourselves are indeterminate beings who belong nowhere in particular. At the least, this political principle – that is, "liberalism" – is compatible with the background theory of modern physics.

Part 3: Sandel's Insufficient Aristotelianism

Michael Sandel might well agree with the preceding paragraph. In one of his many criticisms of John Rawls – specifically, of what he calls Rawls's "deontological liberalism" and its attendant doctrine of an unencumbered or atomic self – he says that "only in a universe empty of *telos* such as seventeenth-century science and philosophy affirmed, is it possible to conceive a subject apart from and prior to its purposes and ends."[9] If Sandel takes his "only" seriously, then he is claiming that modern physics is a necessary condition of modern liberalism. Therefore, a rejection of that sort of physics, that sort of background theory, would imply the rejection of its corresponding political theory. Unfortunately, however, Sandel fails to pursue this line of argument. In other words, he does not propose a conception of nature to compete with that forged in the seventeenth century nor does he realize that this is required in order to complete his neo-Aristotelian critique of liberalism. More specifically, despite his Aristotelian political convictions, he dismisses the theoretical world view that underlies them. As he puts it, "Today, no scientist reads Aristotle's works on biology or physics and takes them seriously." Even more pointedly he says: "The temptation to see the world as teleologically ordered, as a purposeful whole, is not wholly absent [even today]. It persists, especially in children." Nonetheless, Sandel insists that it remains possible to deploy basic Aristotelian notions such as place and *telos* in political discourse. Indeed, he pleads for the urgency of doing so. He speaks, for example, of "the purpose, or telos, of a university" and does not flinch at asking the teleological question "What is political association for?"[10] It is not clear how this question can possibly be meaningful in the purposeless universe that looms behind it.

An even sharper display of Sandel's odd and unsatisfying neo-Aristotelianism is found in his critique of genetic engineering. He opposes it because, to cite his favoured example of athletes, it corrupts "athletic competition as a human activity that honors the cultivation and display of natural talents." He continues: "Arguments about the ethics of enhancement are always, at least in part, arguments about the telos, the point, of the sport in question." In turn, that telos is determined by "the nature of the sport," which in turn is derived from our "natural talents." Sandel needs such Aristotelian terminology in order to make what for him is the crucial distinction between medicine and genetic engineering. The former is commendable because it "is guided by the norm of restoring and preserving the natural human functions that constitute health." By contrast, genetic engineering is problematic precisely because it knows no restraints. Instead, it represents "an unbridled act of hubris or bid for domination"; namely, the domination and transformation of our own bodies.[11]

Sandel's "case" again genetic engineering manifestly relies upon a specific conception of nature, one which generates norms; in other words, a teleological conception of nature. At the same time, however, he rejects such a view as childish. He cannot, therefore, support his normative distinction between engineering and proper medicine.

Without a background theory to buttress his political convictions, what sort of argumentative strategy does Sandel actually deploy? To use a phrase he himself does not, he engages in what might be called "practical phenomenology." He regularly appeals to "moral experience" in making his arguments. So, for example, in concluding his criticism of Rawls, he says that "the deontological vision is flawed ... as an account of our moral experience."[12] In a similar vein, he argues that the conception of the human self that underlies procedural liberalism is flawed, for "it cannot make sense of our moral experience, because it cannot account for certain moral and political obligations that we commonly recognize."[13] And this: "Unless we think of ourselves as encumbered selves, open to moral claims we have not willed" – in other words, unless we think of ourselves in a fashion radically at odds with the liberal conception – "it is difficult to make sense of these aspects of our moral and political experience."[14] Finally, consider the following. In asking how one could possibly decide between "MacIntyre's narrative conception of the person" and "the voluntarist conception of persons," Sandel suggests that "we might ask ourselves which better captures the experience of moral deliberation."[15] On this basis he opts for the former.

This sort of argumentative appeal to ordinary experience is itself Aristotelian in spirit. Consider, for example, this well-known passage from *Nicomachean Ethics* 7.

> It is necessary, just as in the other studies, to set down the phenomena (*tithentas ta phainomena*) and first of all to run through the puzzles. In this way, the reputable beliefs (*ta endoxa*) about these affections will be shown; ideally, all the reputable beliefs, but if not all, then most and the most authoritative. For if the difficulties are dissolved and the reputable beliefs are left intact, then the showing will have been adequate. (*Nicomachean Ethics* 1145b2–7)

What exactly these lines mean, and therefore in what sense Aristotle is a phenomenologist, is far from obvious. The first order of business is to clarify the relationship between the "phenomena" and the "reputable beliefs." On this issue Owen's paper remains pivotal. He convincingly showed that "*phainomena*" refers to more than empirical observations, and that as such the word can even embrace the *endoxa*, or what he calls "the common conceptions on the subject." More generally still, it can include the *legomena*, "the things said," which Owen described as "often ... partly matters of linguistic usage or ... of the conceptual structure revealed by language."[16] In other words, the *endoxa* or *legomena* are themselves phenomena; they are aspects of the way the world shows itself to us. A successful theory must leave the *endoxa* intact; it must "save the phenomena" – a phrase Aristotle does not use, but has long been associated with him – rather than contradict or negate them. It must account for and harmonize with not only the way human beings register the world through sense perception but also with the way human beings, especially those who are counted as *endoxos* or "reputable," have spoken about the world.

Aristotle's stated methodology is – and this claim can only be asserted dogmatically here – supported by his robust accounts of perception, imagination, and ordinary language (largely found in *De Anima*), accounts which are themselves embedded in the more general theoretical project of which they are components. But what gives philosophical support to Sandel's turn to ordinary experience? Nothing. When he speaks confidently of the primacy of the local, the *telos* of a university, or the "natural functions" of the human body, he has stripped these Aristotelian notions of their full meaning. In short, he operates with no background conception of nature. As a result, his political convictions, however admirably Aristotelian they may be, carry little philosophical weight.

Part 4: A Concluding Question

The argument of this paper might now be construed as terribly pessimistic, at least for critics of liberalism. If civic republicanism requires a topological world view and teleological conception of nature as support, and if that world view is no longer tenable, then Sandel's neo-Aristotelian political theory is untenable. In fact, however, this paper does not counsel despair. Instead, it is designed to raise a question, one which can best be explained by means of a short detour.

In 1935 Edmund Husserl wrote "Philosophy and the Crisis of European Humanity." There he claimed that "the European nations are sick. Europe itself, it is said, is in crisis." He offered a concise diagnosis: "I am certain that the European crisis has its roots in a misguided rationalism" that gave rise, beginning around 1600 in the work of Galileo, to mathematical physics and the technology it spawned. Commenting on a later scientific achievement, namely, Einstein's theory of relativity, Husserl pinpointed what is misguided about European rationalism.

> Einstein's revolutionary innovations concern the formulae through which the idealized and naively objectified *physis* [nature] is dealt with. But how formulae in general, how mathematical objectification in general, receive meaning on the foundation of life and the intuitively given surrounding world – of this we learn nothing; and thus Einstein does not reform the space and time in which our vital life runs its course.[17]

The universe studied by mathematical physics, the backbone of modern science, tells us nothing about the "meaning" of our lives, about the space and time, the world, in which we actually pass our time. It grants no privileged status to ordinary human experience, for it is a science thoroughly purged of anthropomorphism. To grasp what this means, and how radically it diverges from the modern scientific project, consider what Spinoza, writing around 1670, had to say: "Men commonly suppose that all natural things act like themselves." Thus, to take the prime example, because men "do all things with an end [or purpose] in view; that is, they seek what is useful," they (falsely) believe that there are "final causes" – purposes, goals, ends – built into nature itself. For Spinoza this teleological or Aristotelian conception of nature was no more than anthropomorphism run amuck. Human beings projected themselves onto the screen of a non-human universe, which in reality operates mechanically rather than purposively. They deluded themselves into seeing what they wanted to see, namely, a natural order that operates like themselves. But Spinoza's nature does not work this way. For him teleology was no more than a "misconception" that had hardened into "a superstition." The centuries spent looking for final causes had inhibited the search for real or efficient ones, and so had stopped the progress of science dead in its tracks. In defiance of what was then traditional wisdom, Spinoza proudly declared that "nature has no fixed aim in view, and … all final causes are merely fabrications of men."[18] Freed from its pathetic search for purposes, liberated by mathematics, scientific research was poised to penetrate the workings of nature itself.

Husserl's "crisis" is a response to this form of mathematized and thoroughly dehumanized science. He pleads with us to return to the phenomena and treat them as epistemically significant. In other words, he urges us to invest our own ordinary experience with evidentiary value. In making these claims he is revisiting Aristotelian terrain, for this sort of phenomenological science is, as the passage from *Nicomachean Ethics* 7 indicated, at the core of his philosophical work. In radical contrast to the moderns, Aristotle is indeed concerned with "the space and time in which our vital life runs its course." And so his conception of nature, expressed in his physics and cosmology, is topological at its core and serves as the foundation of his political theory as well. To reiterate the central (and Aristotelian) complaint this paper is levelling at Michael Sandel: he wants to revive a politics of place and he relies upon ordinary human experience in order to muster his arguments in its defence. But he stops short. While he is willing to grant that a university may have a *telos*, he thinks that nature itself has none at all. In other words, he is unwilling to follow Aristotle in extending the phenomenological project beyond the limited confines of ethics and politics. As a result, his advocacy of the political primacy of place floats without any stable support. The question his work raises, then, is this: is it possible, even at this late date, to follow Husserl's lead and insist that, like Aristotle, we must never lose sight of the phenomena, of the ordinary human experience of the world, even when we are studying non-human nature? Do we have the courage to fight against the tide of modern science and insist that our very humanity, determined as it always is by places, is epistemically significant? Aristotle does and so we must wonder whether we, especially those of us willing to defend a conception of "the small and bounded places" intrinsic to civic republicanism, can as well.

NOTES

1 Plato, *The Republic*, trans. A. Bloom (New York: Basic Books, 1969).

2 Michael Sandel, *Democracy's Discontent: America in Search of a Public Philosophy* (Cambridge, MA: Harvard University Press, 1998). Subsequent citations from this work are indicated in parentheses.

3 All translations from Aristotle are my own.

4 Aristotle assumes that the poor will always be many: "The rich are everywhere few and the poor many" (*Politics* 1279b37–8).
5 Helen Lang, *The Order of Nature in Aristotle's Physics: Place and the Elements* (Cambridge: Cambridge University Press, 1998), 68. To paraphrase her point: "where" is one of the questions the answer to which is a category. See, for examples, *Categories* 1b26 and 2a1, as well as *Metaphysics* 1017a26.
6 Ibid., 69.
7 Alexander Koyré, *From the Closed World to the Infinite Universe* (Baltimore: Johns Hopkins University Press, 1968), 18.
8 This is the title of Koyré's book cited above.
9 Michael Sandel, *Liberalism and the Limits of Justice* (Cambridge: Cambridge University Press, 1982), 175.
10 Michael Sandel, *Justice: What's the Right Thing to Do?* (New York: Farrar, Straus and Giroux, 2009), 189–92.
11 Michael Sandel, *The Case against Perfection: Ethics in the Age of Genetic Engineering* (Cambridge, MA: Harvard University Press, 2007), 29, 47, 37, 47, and 101.
12 Sandel, *Liberalism and the Limits of Justice*, 177.
13 Sandel, *Democracy's Discontent*, 13.
14 Ibid., 228.
15 Sandel, *Justice: What's the Right Thing to Do?* 223.
16 G.E.L. Owen, "*Tithenai ta Phainomena*," in *Articles on Aristotle*, vol. 1, ed. Jonathan Barnes (London: Duckworth, 1979), 182.
17 Edmund Husserl, *The Crisis of European Sciences and Transcendental Philosophy*, trans. David Carr (Evanston: Northwestern University Press, 1970), 270, 290, and 295.
18 These remarks come in the "Appendix" to part 1 of Spinoza's *Ethics*.

3 Living Well and the Promise of Cosmopolitan Identity: Aristotle's *ergon* and Contemporary Civic Republicanism

MICHAEL WEINMAN

The central suggestion here is that Aristotle's account of the human *ergon* ("work")[1] might better resolve arguments about how to adjudicate pressing questions for contemporary pluralist democracies. Debates about issues such as how (if at all) one might justify a liberal state imposing limits on the traditional practices of citizens who belong to religious minorities or on parents' ability to opt out of social provisions such as education or health care demonstrate the value of an alternative norm. The context for articulating the human "work" as such a norm is the recent exploration of transnational identity, and its promise and its problems. Attempts to ground such an identity on "universal human rights" have proved hollow and ineffectual, as do those premised on a confluence of interests due to globalization. Responding to the insufficiency of extant attempts to ground transnational identity, the Aristotelian resources called upon here offer a normative basis for a contemporary form of republican citizenship that is place-based but not place-bound: a citizenship constitutive of what is called here "a non-parochial politics of place." Such a politics is built on public deliberation that addresses itself to a local or national audience in a manner that is expressly grounded in norms whose provenance exceeds those contexts. This kind of "cosmopolitics" refuses to ground normative claims in a particular political community; it also refuses to adopt the style of cosmopolitan identity[2] that excludes itself from such a particular political community.

In what follows, the Aristotelian *ergon* will come to be seen as integral to such a politics: a way of life that is expressly political, emphasizing engagement with fellow citizens, and also cosmopolitan in its appeal to a context-independent standard of human self-actualization.

In this way, I hope to show how Aristotle's political thought can help us to think past the boundaries of the liberalism/communitarianism debates of recent times. At the deepest level, I address here the tension between rights – central for the *political* self-conception of contemporary republicans – and cosmopolitanism – just as central for their *ethical* self-conception. I cannot presume to resolve this tension here, but I do aim to offer two Aristotelian claims that point to one way they may be brought into better normative accord. First, the human work is the setting-to-work of one, whole human life in accordance with reason. Second, this work is most possible in that *polis* which is truly the *politeia*; that is, the human work is most possible only under the best, that is, the most complete, regime.[3] These two claims come together in the program for civic education Aristotle advances in his *Politics*: an education for the sake of virtue that is organized around the ultimate objective of cultivating one's capacity to choose, and to justify that choice in public. That these are Aristotle's claims, I shall argue in section 1; that the form of civic education they entail is relevant for devising an alternative normative basis for a non-parochial politics of place, in section 2, which ends with a brief conclusion that will try to show why this new normative basis holds promise, and why this promise is precisely political in nature.

1. Aristotle's *ergon* as Normative Basis for a Non-parochial Politics of Place

Can the Aristotelian *ergon* better justify rights claims not based on nation-state sovereignty than the norms generally appealed to within the liberal order? An affirmative answer entails that Aristotle's conception of the human work offers a persuasive justification for a certain kind of republican citizenship independent of nation-state conventions. Before we can judge the human *ergon* in this respect, though, we need first to understand what precisely it is.

We would do well to remember that Aristotle does not share our distinction between ethics and politics. Right from the beginning, it is clear that what we call ethics is, for Aristotle, political thinking.[4] Remembering, in this light, that the Aristotelian notion of "work" developed in the *Nicomachean Ethics*, 1.7, is already expressly a political norm, let us investigate how it can be deployed to articulate a radically different understanding of the normative framework for human possibilities – one not embedded in the liberal notion of "rights."[5] What emerges from this is the intimate intertwinement of the work (*ergon*) of the human being and the being-at-work (*energeia*) of the human being. As Frank[6] has argued, this link is vital to understanding why the *ergon* really is about flourishing, and not just "functioning." That is to say, notwithstanding the justified influence of Martha Nussbaum's "capability approach" to normative evaluation,[7] Aristotle's understanding of the human work is predicated not so much on "capacities" (or "capabilities") and the extent to which it is or is not possible for a particular human being in a particular political community to actuate such capacities, but rather on the fullness of the life led by such a human being, as part of such a living *polis*. After establishing this link in Aristotle's text, we will turn to investigate how his vision of the human work might ground something like a "non-parochial politics of place."

Aristotle's *ergon* argument begins with the reminder that we are searching for the "highest of the goods of action," the *teleion telos*, the most complete completion that alone can be the good at which all things aim. The sign of such a good is that it is always chosen only for itself and never the sake of something else – that is, this "highest good" must be both for its own sake and "that for the sake of which" all else is done. This, of course, brings us back to happiness; after all, happiness "seems to be of this sort most of all," insofar as "we choose this always in virtue of itself, and never in virtue of something else" (*Nicomachean Ethics*, 1097b1–2). There are a great many things (like virtue, honour, pleasure, and intelligence) we choose for themselves and because we believe they bring happiness, and others we choose only for the sake of something else (like money), yet only happiness exists for us as something we chose only for itself.[8]

But having said this much we feel very much brought back around to the same troublesome impasse that always arises when discussing an articulation of human flourishing: sure, we are talking about happiness when we speak of the "highest of all goods of action," but *which* happiness, *whose* happiness? Aristotle (*NE*, 1097b22–3) acknowledges this problem. How can we hope to succeed in thus defining happiness, this "unique way of being-at-work in the world," here? The answer is the well-worn terrain of the *ergon* argument itself: that short bit of text where Aristotle defines the peculiar work of the human being. This is the life of action, which Aristotle defines as the mobilization of "the aspect of us holding rational speech, of which one aspect is able to be persuaded by reason, while the other holds reason and thinks things through" (*NE*, 1098a3 5). It is no accident that when Aristotle asks just what is this "life of action," which has everything to do with living according to reason, he turns to the life processes of a human being.[9] Here he says, speaking roughly, as befits the presentation of these matters proper to a political inquiry,[10] that the first life process of the human being is nutrition and growth, the mere self-sustenance as a living thing, which human beings have in common with plants and other animals. The second life process is perception, which human beings share with other animals. Since these two life processes are shared by other forms of life, they cannot be paradigmatically human; they cannot be our peculiar work. No more than what a carpenter shares with other humans – say, being a member of a family, or digesting cooked food – could define the work of a carpenter.

With what, then, are we left as the work of the human being? It can only be the aforementioned life of action. What belongs most properly to us is not reason as a possession or property, but action which necessitates holding *logos*, both as being able to be persuaded and as being able to think things through. Still more precisely, it is not this twofold ability which constitutes our work; it is rather the setting-to-work of this ability, the *energeia* of this life of action: "One must set it [the work] down as that life at-work, for this seems to be the more governing sense" (*NE*, 1098a7).

Aristotle, then, does not describe the "function" (*ergon*) of the human being as "the active exercise of the rational faculty," but, rather, claims that "the work of a human being is a being-at-work of the soul in accordance with reason, or not without reason" (*NE*, 1098a8).[11] When the whole human soul is completely set-at-work in all its various processes, all with reason, or in any case, not against it, *then* we can say that we see the peculiar and defining work of a human being.

This much I can say here for the first of the two Aristotelian claims at work in this piece. My account of the second will be more schematic still. I here only gesture towards Aristotle's view that whatever the life of virtue is (and this is to be learned from the *Nicomachean Ethics*), it is in a certain sort of political constellation – and *only* in such – that such a life is possible, and the relevance of this commitment for contemporary debates about community membership and human rights.[12] This gesture will consist of a brief discussion of three principles of the *Politics*: (1) the *polis* is the most complete form of human community; (2)(a) the *politeia* is the life of the *polis* and, thus, some *politeia* is "best," by which is meant: most entirely a singular political community; (2)(b) this "being best" is bound up with education and the cultivation of character in all the citizens. Taken together, these principles constitute the second of the two major Aristotelian claims relevant here.

(1) The claim that the *Politics*, in its opening moments (1252a1–30),[13] argues that the *polis* is the most complete[14] form of human community is not a controversial one. But it is worth remembering a few facts regarding the presentation of what is the fundamental truth of political inquiry for Aristotle. First, that the *Politics* begins with the *polis* and its nature because this is how we will learn what the *Nicomachean Ethics* did not teach us: how the young might become good. Next, that what argues for the *polis* being the proper level of analysis is that it aims at the most "authoritative" of goods, and, for this reason, is the most "all-encompassing" of communities. Third, that the "political community" that "is called 'polis'" is not only greater than other communities (like a household, or a business enterprise), but different in kind because only the *polis* (among human communities) is a natural whole. Finally, and for this reason, we will carry out the investigation of the *Politics* in "the way it is usually carried out," that is, by dividing the whole into parts, and then reassembling the parts thus divided into a whole.

The *Politics*, we can thus see, begins with arguments about how best to cultivate characters of a certain kind. It is crucial, then, that Aristotle begins with education. No less remarkable is the all-encompassing purview of the *polis* as the subject of our inquiry: none of the other communities we form is in order, if this most authoritative one is not. This all-encompassing character of the *polis*, on closer inspection, is not to do with its conventional character (its being the biggest of the communities of which we are part), but with its natural wholeness, which will become apparent if we examine the city in the way we have examined other matters – specifically, nature. What I wish to draw on here is this natural character of both the matter and the manner of investigation in the *Politics*. It is precisely this character of Aristotle's thinking about the political, indeed the human as such, that Roochnik in this volume finds lacking in Sandel's unsuccessful (to his mind and mine) attempt to appropriate the "topological" element of Aristotle's thinking about the *polis*.[15] Roochnik[16] pursues this cosmological character of political discourse through a reading of passages from the *Physics* (especially book 4) – and, to a lesser extent, the *Metaphysics* – that need to be understood in order to understand Aristotle's argument regarding the proper size of the best city. I wish to show here that this character comes to light precisely in the two further claims at work here: the being-whole of that *polis* organized through the *politeia* that is best; and the being-whole of the soul that is educated properly within such a *polis*.

(2) The reading of the *Politics* here holds that the text is, on the whole, coherent and consistent, and that the chief interpretative issue that hangs on this consistency and coherence is that Aristotle has one view of the relation of citizen, city, and regime (*politēs, polis, politeia*), in which the nature of citizenship displays the nature of a city, and that of a city reveals that of a regime. On this understanding of the *Politics,* we may, having followed the analysis to the conclusion, look backward from the best regime to the true city and the true citizen.

This account is presented as part of the discussion of the proper size and scope of the best *polis,* which is to say – as Roochnik develops at length in chapter 2[17] – the need for it to remain small enough to be a genuine *locale,* a *topos* in which all the individuals share an understanding of themselves as inhabiting the same place. Here I can present only a schematic presentation of the highlights of this section of the *Politics,* which is as follows.

(2)(a) Beginning from the preliminary definition of citizen, gleaned from the experience of "true" democracy,[18] as "those who share in office" to "members of juries and assemblies," we arrive at the difficulty that, the cities differing as their regimes do, the citizens of many existing cities are not citizens by this definition. We can thus say that the citizens are those among whom "it is given to some or all to deliberate and to judge" (1275a31; 1275b1–10, b13). Next, the *polis* is defined as "the sufficiently-great-multitude of such persons for self-sufficient life" (1275b21). We must bear in mind that human being is not for life, but the good life, and only a good man[19] – one who lives the life of virtue – can attain to the good life. Thus, only under the best regime would the city be directed to the best ends, and would the good citizen be the good man as such (1277b–8a). Thus, in all the "right regimes," rule will be by the best. The best, those who must rule in that city which would be best – whether one, a few, or many – will be those who are virtuous. And a man always becomes serious in the same way; so "it will be more or less the same to educate a man to be political or a king" (1288a32–b1).

(2)(b) With this in mind we turn to what we know (from *Nicomachean Ethics*): the best life is the life of virtue. But "it is clear" that whatever is best for one human being is best for a city (1324a7). Thus, the life of virtue is the best life for the city. This raises two questions: (a) Which is better: the life of "active involvement in the political," or a life "of a foreigner," that is, "released from the political community"? (b) What is the best regime: that aiming at political or philosophic virtue? Only (b) will be addressed here, as it alone of the two is part of "the work (*ergon*)" of this study (1324a13–23). We need not directly answer this question, since both arguments have suasion. What we must insist on is that the best city is contingent on the virtue of its citizens; this is most complete when all the citizens are virtuous (1325a16–b30). Thus, the serious city – described just above – requires the right form of education. The rightness of education is determined by answering: what virtue will the regime inculcate in its citizens? We need an education that will result in all the citizens being "serious," that is, capable of choosing (1332a28–b10). Finally, we conclude that this education must follow the division of the soul: it must cultivate in both the reasoning and desiring the best possible ends (1333a16–4a10).

One cannot avoid noticing that the question raised about the nature of the life of virtue, and the relative value of the life of *theoria* and political life, remains unanswered[20] – on the grounds that such a question is not to be addressed in a political work (and remember that that designation applies to what we call ethics, too) – identifies the non-political life of contemplation with the life of the foreigner. This makes perfectly clear why Aristotle would never endorse the sort of cosmopolitanism made famous by Diogenes and those who champion his "From what city am I? None; for I am a citizen of the world" style of rejecting "the politics of place." The choice to be this sort of cosmopolitan (a *politēs* of the *kosmos*), on Aristotelian grounds, is not to be a citizen at all. It might be a better life, but it is an expressly non-political life.

But it is also a choice. I believe that the peculiar form of dialectic argumentation at work in these sections – in addition to showing the seriousness of the subject matter, and the difficulty in adjudicating between the contentious views under examination – is meant to model exactly the kind of education to be found in the best regime. The argument began by placing the discussion of the best regime in the context of that political arrangement under which the greatest number share the burden and privilege of choice, in order to determine that it is precisely choice (in the context of voting and judging) that constitutes citizenship. This definition of citizenship then developed into an account of what it is to be a city, to be a regime, and thus to be a good city and a good regime, resulting in an early indication of the crucial role of education. This hint at education's importance is then used to underscore the intertwinement of the best life for both city and citizen (and human as such) as the life of virtue. This is achieved, importantly, through an analysis of the question of *which life is the most choice-worthy* that issues in *aporia*, in an impasse or puzzle that Aristotle leaves unresolved. That he chooses both to bring us into this impasse and also not to solve it is crucial, I believe, because it is meant to point the way towards his view of a solution: the need for us to work it out in concert and in public. Aristotle is suggesting that the question of whether it is best to pursue the life of the non-citizen who thinks about timeless matters or the citizen who must address the concerns of one's own particular place is a puzzle that must be resolved politically. It is to this model of "public deliberation," grounded in his vision of the human work that inspires my appeal to Aristotle's thinking. This is not to say that some kernel of Aristotle's political thinking – whether this kernel is thought to come from his "realist" account of existing regimes, or rather his "idealist"[21] account of the best regime [*aristē politeia*], which he also calls the regime in the "city of prayer" [*kat' eukhēn*][22] – should serve as a rule to be unambiguously endorsed for civic republicanism today. This is surely not the case, not only because Aristotle's understanding of the fundamental unit of collective human experience – the *polis* – does not, and (as far as human probability allows one to say) will likely never again, exist, but also because what Aristotle expressly has to say about the matters at hand is incorrect.[23] But it does not follow from this concession that we do not still have something to learn from Aristotle in attempting to come to terms with global citizenship in today's democracies.

It is this that chiefly arises from tracing this line of argumentation: the best regime – notably not designated as one of the three correct regimes, but rather according to how its citizens are at-work – is the one which all those who share in the being-a-city of the city live just for the sake of doing things like going through the argument itself. This is possible only when one has been educated sufficiently to achieve the level of precision in the argument, but also when one cares enough to be interested in an inquiry about how to arrange the political community in the first place. And this, as Roochnik notes in chapter 2,[24] is itself only possible if political life is the self-conscious expression of one's *place* in an intrinsically value-laden cosmos. Put another way, the argument can only succeed when those to whom it has been presented have themselves been educated to value the life of virtue with their whole soul.[25]

2. Deploying the Aristotelian *ergon* to Renovate Contemporary Cosmopolitanism

I claim that we have learned from Aristotle (1) that our life's work is to live the life of virtue, which is *not* the use of reason for reason's sake, but to set the whole human soul to work in self-preservation, sense perception, desire, and thinking, all according to *logos*, and (2) that this is expressly a *political* proposition, insofar as such a life is possible only with the kind of "civic education" one receives in the most complete regime, and that such a regime is one in which the greatest number of citizens are most capable of the life of virtue. This is so, I have indicated (if not argued), because (a) the life of virtue is the culmination of an education of one's capacities to choose – and thus, live – well and (b) this education is a fundamentally political phenomenon, possible only under a regime of a certain kind. That is, the uniquely human way of being at work in the world is fulfilling our natural capacity to make choices for ourselves – by activating (a) our individual intellectual capacities (b) through the common capacity of *logos*, (c) as embodied beings. Among the choices made possible by this life of virtue would crucially be those related to our sense of ourselves as part of a series of communities, from the immediate to the global, with many stops in between; that is, the possibilities of a cosmopolitan citizenship. In this concluding section, we examine precisely what I believe the two Aristotelian claims recovered here mean for the normative conversation about cosmopolitanism, particularly in its intersection with civic republicanism.[26] The significance of appropriating this Aristotelian work, I hope to show, is that it points to a concrete path in which normative claims can be advanced that can only be met through the cultivation of a place-based but not place-bound education for a life of action. Such a program of civic education, I propose, gives some hope for a way out of the impasse that mark our contemporary debates about both the why and the how of developing some sort of rights regime that is not predicated on nation states and their sovereignty. In developing such a proposal, we will find – as Burns[27] states in advancing the thesis that Aristotle is neither communitarian nor relativist – that Aristotle's insistence on the *polis* as the unit of shared life in which the personhood of a human being arises is ultimately compatible with the kind of universal citizenship to which cosmopolitanism aspires.

Let us begin by remembering what I stated at the outset: if Aristotle has something to offer in terms of an alternative normative basis for contemporary cosmopolitanism, it is not his particular conclusions regarding the scale of the state or the relationship between states. Why, then, should we believe that there is any Aristotelian resource for this conversation? In answer, I point to the tension between liberalism and republicanism that the long-entrenched debate among liberals, communitarians, and adherents of discourse ethics has not, and will not, solve. Given this we would do well to turn to a form of ethics and politics that hinges precisely on the borderland of individual, community, and (human) nature that cosmopolitanism wishes to call upon as a basis for a novel kind of citizenship.

It is also worth remembering that this impasse is not merely a theoretical one; rather, we can find the same tension expressed in concrete political life, and not only in normative theory. Without being overly neat about the alignment, the recent experience of the United States (liberalism), France (republicanism), and Germany (communitarianism/"social democracy") seems to provide a different kind of evidence of the current impasse for contemporary attempts at "civic republicanism." As Raulet,[28] in particular, has shown, neither the framework of nation-state sovereignty nor any kind of global economic or political regime has the resources to provide the kind of basis for citizenship that erstwhile cosmopolitans might endorse, quite aside from the question of the legitimacy of such a project.

For these reasons, both practical and theoretical, I suggest that civic republicans return once more to an Aristotelian, or neo-Aristotelian,[29] conception of citizenship, grounded both in nature and in community, and more precisely in the way that citizens can be – and ought to be – educated.[30] What remains to be found on this well-worn ground is a position that falls precisely in the contested territory between liberalism and communitarianism that our empirical republics are muddling their way through, or failing to. What, specifically, we find in this Aristotelian "third space" is the understanding that human life is the entire setting-to-work of just one soul in (or with) just one body *and* that this setting-to-work is achieved only in a self-conscious association (a *politeia*) of individuals who are thus setting-to-work and set-to-work. This work is effected through the institution of education; specifically, an education that seizes upon the nature of the human soul itself.

On this view, the Aristotelian civic republican acknowledges a conviction that there is a human nature to which our discursively conditioned norms must appeal. At the same time, this person is clear that this claim is self-generating. It is, to paraphrase Weber, "a re-enchantment of the world that is not enchanted about its own act of enchanting." My larger suggestion is that such a "contingent foundation," and *only* such, can serve as the seed for a new way forward in articulating human rights writ large. In this case, I propose, it is this formulation of the human work, in its singular and communal respects, that best provides the resources needed to envisage or enact membership in a republic that understands itself both as a political community constituted of choice-making entities and an entity that constitutes another political community *of* such political communities.

NOTES

1 For a comprehensive treatment of the importance of "work" for Aristotle's understanding of the political project see Jill Frank, *A Democracy of Distinction: Aristotle and the Work of Politics* (Chicago: University of Chicago Press, 2005), 34–5, 49–52, 179–80 (hereafter: Frank, *Distinction*). On "work" as a translation of *ergon*, see Aristotle, *The Politics of Aristotle: Translated with an Introduction, Analysis and Notes*, trans. Peter L. Phillips Simpson (Chapel Hill: University of North Carolina Press, 1997), xxviii–ix (hereafter: Simpson, *Politics*).

2 Often associated with Diogenes, and those inspired by him in the classical context and ever since. See the conclusion to section 2 for more on this.

3 On "regime" as a translation of *politeia*, see Simpson, *Politics*, xxiv–xxvii.

4 This is stipulated here, but has been argued for in a number of recent works. See especially: Claudia Baracchi, *Aristotle's Ethics as First Philosophy* (Cambridge: Cambridge University Press, 2007) (hereafter: Baracchi, *First Philosophy*); Richard Kraut, *Aristotle: Politics Books VII and VIII. Translation with Commentary* (Oxford: Oxford University Press, 1997); Richard Kraut, *What Is Good and Why: The Ethics of Well-being* (Cambridge, MA: Harvard University Press, 2007) (hereafter: Kraut, *What Is Good*); Bernard Yack, *The Problems of a Political Animal: Community, Justice, and Conflict in Aristotelian Political Thought* (Berkeley: University of California Press, 1993) (hereafter: Yack, *Problems*); and Fred D. Miller, *Nature, Justice and Rights in Aristotle's* Politics (Oxford: Oxford University Press, 1995) (hereafter: Miller, *Aristotle's* Politics).

5 Corroboration of what follows, in terms of both my analysis of Aristotle's argument and its pertinence for contemporary approaches to human rights, can be found in Miller, *Aristotle's Politics*, 336–46, 373–8.

6 Frank, *Distinction*, 46–51, 107–8.

7 Presented in a number of important works, perhaps the most relevant with respect to the *ergon* argument and Aristotle's *Politics* would be "Aristotle on Human Nature and the Foundations of Ethics," in *World, Mind, and Ethics: Essays on the Ethical Philosophy of Bernard Williams*, ed. J.E.J. Altham and Ross Harrison (Cambridge: Cambridge University Press, 1995), 86–131; and "Human Functioning and Social Justice: In Defense of Aristotelian Essentialism," *Political Theory* 20 (1992), 202–46.

8 Cf. Aristotle, *Nicomachean Ethics*, 1097b2–6.

9 For more on this, and why this is *not* akin to "naturalism" in ethics in the contemporary sense, see Kraut, *What Is Good*, 88–91 and 131–48.

10 As Aristotle himself says explicitly at *NE*, 1098b1–8; see also 1102a. Note that the qualification is "political" and not "ethical."

11 See Baracchi, *First Philosophy* and Kraut, *What Is Good* for further argumentation for this view, and a critical discussion of a conflicting (often called "intellectualist") view.

12 For this reason, all manner of important textual and interpretive controversies will have to be ignored, while I present as provisionally definitive one reading of the relation between the *polis* as such and the multiple accounts of the best possible *polis* (cf. Aristotle, *Politics*, 1279b–88b, 1289b–97b, 1323a–42b).

13 Translations largely follow Simpson, *Politics*, with emendations; for the Greek I consulted Alois Dreizehnter, *Aristoteles' Politica* (Munich: Wilhelm Fink, 1970) and Hugh Rackham, *Aristotle: Politics* (1932), Loeb Classical Library (Cambridge, MA: Harvard University Press, 1977).

14 Here again I have in mind the fundamental role of the *telos*, and its cognate *teleion*, in Aristotle's thinking.

15 David Roochnik, "Aristotle's Topological Politics; Michael Sandel's Civic Republicanism," 41–58, this volume.

16 Ibid., part 2.

17 Ibid.

18 A "true" democracy is a *politeia*, also the word for regime. It is noteworthy that Aristotle uses the same crucial technical term in both these ways; see Simpson, *Politics* and Miller, *Aristotle's* Politics for more on this. Frank (*Distinction*, 127–8, 142) notes that *demokratia* describes a "perverted" regime, in which the *demos*, simply as the mass of poor, rules. The regime in "democratic Athens," for instance, is not such a *demokratia*.

19 In this context, Aristotle persistently speaks of *aner* (man) and not *anthropos* (human being).

20 For a full-throated defence of the position that, in the end, "*Politics* 7, read in its entirety, provides a sustained and decisive, even if implicit, argument on behalf of the theoretical life," see: David Roochnik, "Aristotle's Defense

of the Theoretical Life: Comments on *Politics* 7," *Review of Metaphysics* 61 (2008), 735.

21 It will be far beyond my purview to enter into the debates about the putative idealism and realism of various parts of the *Politics*. For an introduction to them, and an interpretive conclusion that seems to me compelling, see Simpson, *Politics*, whose views about the ordering of the books of the *Politics* I find as persuasive as his overall interpretation of Aristotle's project in the *Politics*, and for the same reasons.

22 For Aristotle's characterization of the regime described in *Politics* 7–8 as the *aristē politeia*, see 7.1.1323a14, 7.4.1325b37, and 7.13.1332a4; for that of a city in accord with one's prayers or highest hopes (*kat' eukhēn*), see 7.4.1325b37, 7.10.1330a26–7, and 7.11.1330a37. That these two are one and the same is clear from 1325b37. I thank Thornton Lockword for help on articulating this point.

23 For more on the first ground, see Miller, *Aristotle's* Politics, 335–78. On the second, see ibid. and Yack, *Problems*.

24 Roochnik, this volume.

25 It is thus my view that we need to understand Aristotle's account of the best citizen/city/regime as ultimately expressing the Socratic practice of self-reflexive dialogue as the nearest approximation to the human *ergon*.

26 In advancing an "Aristotelian and not Kantian conception of human dignity," I owe much to Martha Nussbaum, *Frontiers of Justice: Disability, Nationality, Species Membership* (New York: Belknap Press, 2006). That said, Nussbaum's Aristotle seems too little ensconced in the controversies and impossibilities of life in an actual political community, as has been noted by Peter Euben, "The Polis, Globalization and the Politics of Space," in *Political Visions*, ed. Aryeh Botwinick and William E. Connelly (Princeton: Princeton University Press, 2001); Frank, *Distinction*, 18; and Yack, *Problems*. I thus aim to offer a sympathetic corrective to Nussbaum's Aristotle, on the precisely political grounds of the second Aristotelian claim discussed above (pp. 62–5).

27 Tony Burns, "Legal Subjectivity and the Basis of Citizenship in Aristotle's Philosophy of Law," at http://works.bepress.com/cgi/viewcontent.cgi?article=1000&context=dr_burns, 4–10.

28 Gerard Raulet, *Critical Cosmology* (Lanham, MD: Lexington Books, 2005).

29 In the sense of Miller, *Aristotle's* Politics, 336n1.

30 A formulation of community, as argued above, that radically differs from communitarianism, *pace* those who would claim Aristotle as the source of their communitarianism, such as Alisdair MacIntyre: *After Virtue* (Notre Dame, IN: University of Notre Dame Press, 1984 [1981]) and *Whose Justice? Which Rationality?* (Notre Dame: University of Notre Dame Press, 1988); and those following in his wake.

4 Groundwork for a Theory of Republican Character in a Democratic Age

WENDELL JOHN COATS, JR

This essay takes its usage from Aristotle's distinction[1] between the highest form of democracy (agrarian, but still a class regime) and the lowest form of mixed regime (a polity or republic anchored in a middling class capable of the common defence), to argue for some important distinctions in the outlook of two arguably different characters populating contemporary liberal democracies. This is a distinction which democracies need to understand in light of the long-observed tendency of advanced or old democracies to render their political and civil vocabularies superfluous by reducing them in use to sub-political (especially economic and lower psychic) dimensions.[2] The focus here is on the issue of character (following Aristotle's practice in the *Rhetoric* and *Nicomachean Ethics*),[3] by which is meant a pattern of fairly settled perspectives, habits, and qualities in individuals, itself the outcome of some combination of upbringing, education, experience, and self-motivation. This focus derives from the belief that democracy can only resist its "sub-political" tendencies if there are some republican characters left around to exert influence; and from the observation that advanced democracy – in its fixation on personal happiness – is more inclined to listen to discussions of personality and psychology than to ones about constitutional forms.

Before proceeding with the general argument, let us take a moment to look at Aristotle's account of the mixed regime (polity or republic) as, by implication, the most political form of constitution. Crucial to our discussion here is Aristotle's distinction in the *Politics* between the highest form of democracy and the lowest form of mixed regime. Democracy, for Aristotle, was a perverted form of rule since its conception of justice aimed primarily at the good of a class – the many, or freeborn, or poor – rather than at the good of the whole body politic. But the mix of democracy and oligarchy which he called by the generic name for constitution (*politeia*) was distinguished by the existence and support of a middle class interested in the common advantage. The interesting question for our analysis becomes the essential difference between the highest form of democracy – that of farmers residing in the country and coming to town to vote – and the polity or republic or middle-class regime of standing laws directed towards mediation of the class conflicts of perverted regimes such as democracy and oligarchy.

Where does concern for the "common advantage" begin or arise in Aristotle's view? What distinguishes the citizens of the polity from the agrarian democrats who are "good" only in the sense that since they value farming over politics, and live in the country, they are inclined to live by standing laws (class-oriented, though) rather than diurnal decrees, and do not tend use political office for personal gain.[4]

Aristotle's reasoning here in several passages of the *Politics* is unambiguous. He traces the origins of the concern for the common advantage *in the majority of people* to participation in tactically coordinated military activity in defence of the *polis*. To say this differently, Aristotle traces the generic political constitution (polity or republic) to the evolution of tactically skilled, heavy-armed infantry arising from the middling classes (those with sufficient wealth to own heavy arms and armour), capable of repelling the attacks of both oligarchic cavalry and mobile, lightly armed democratic forces, that is, capable of preserving militarily the middling regime which cooperates through moderate politics.[5] ("For those who have authority over arms also have authority over whether the regime will last or not.")[6]

Aristotle also observes that the military function (along with the judicial and deliberative functions) *is of a similar order to the mind* rather than the body, and, hence, more political than functions that satisfy the realm of necessity.[7] (This is the problem with extreme democracy for Aristotle – it politicizes the realm of necessity, retaining the vocabulary of politics in name only.) Arguably, by saying that the military function is of a similar order to the mind rather than the body, Aristotle implies that it is through participation in cooperative military endeavours that middling citizens learn to care for the common advantage and live under laws dispensing rewards commensurate with contributions to the common advantage.

It is instructive here before proceeding to look more closely at what Aristotle says in this connection. He explicitly links the military element in cities to the soul rather than the body, to the political rather than the necessary: "If, then, one were to regard soul as more a part of an animal than body, things of this sort – the military element and ... adjudication ... and deliberation – must be regarded as more a part of cities than things regulating the necessary needs."[8] Aristotle also observes that these capacities can belong to classes or to persons, as "it often happens that the same persons bear arms and farm."[9]

As to the specific virtue of which politics or republics are generally capable, Aristotle says that it is the military virtue: "It is possible for one or a few to be outstanding in virtue, but where more are concerned it is difficult for them to be proficient with a view to virtue as a whole, but [some level of proficiency is possible] *regarding military virtue, as this arises in a multitude.*"[10]

A plausible interpretation of these brief passages is that while military virtue is obviously necessary for the survival of a city, it is just as important for its capacity to nurture a concern for the common advantage in the majority of persons, and hence is important for the sustainment of the polity or republic.

Aristotle also observes other characteristics of the middling character – it is open to reason, capable of liberality towards others, and possesses a stability deriving from its proximity to, and experience of, other classes – the rich, the poor, and the powerful. And he also observes in the *Nicomachean Ethics* that the equality among citizens in the middling constitution is like that among brothers (who are truly equal in status and outlook) in contrast to the relationship among citizens of a democracy, the equality of which resembles that among members of an entire household where the ruler of the house is weak, and everyone is allowed to do what he likes.[11]

Now, to return to this chapter's general argument, the aim here is not an ambitious attempt to prove the existence of some sort of continuous republican tradition across the ages. This would be both historically inaccurate and philosophically naive. Rather, the starting point is the conviction that advanced democracy is more of a psychological than a narrowly political and constitutional phenomenon, and should evince certain fundamental similarities in individuals any time that it occurs. Hence, one way of establishing some commonality among various republicanisms is to show what they are not, that is, how they resist and differ from the characteristics of advanced democracy. Also downplayed from this perspective will be the differences between what have been called ancient and modern republicanism, with the former putatively defined by emphasis on civic virtue (and even intellectual virtue in some cases) and the latter more by private industry, enlightened self-interest, and shrewd institutional arrangements limiting the realm for political deliberation.[12] The aim here is to attempt to "factor out" the common elements, as conveyed in the typical characters they produce, of various republicanisms, and their reaction to the increasing democratization of law and culture. Let us begin with a very compact statement of the argument, and then break it down to defend and illustrate it.

Over time, a democracy, through electoral arrangements to enact the popular will and spread equality, moves increasingly towards the reduction of its political abstractions and ideas to sub-political (material and bodily) dimensions. This occurs from deference to its own egalitarian sense of fairness and "due process" – increasingly, the only fair form of public discourse is focused upon material and tangible entities *since these are the only things which can be unambiguously equalized.* (In Platonic terms, this is to say that democracy is "the regime of the body.")[13] To focus political and social discourse over rewards upon intangibles such as spirit, intellect, talent, honour, duty, and so on, is by implication from the perspective of the egalitarian *ethos* unfair, in spirit and letter and outcomes, to those deficient in those realms, and also appears highly subjective to democracy. *Ceteris paribus*, the movement, as a democracy ages, will be *from* formal equality *to* substantive equality (*from* fairness in terms of procedures and opportunities, *to* fairness as guaranteed, substantive, egalitarian outcomes), because only the latter will be seen as meaningful and "real."

This is worrisome from the standpoint of political balance, or more carefully speaking from the standpoint of the continued existence of the "political" in any society, because (following Aristotle) the political vocabulary arises in a trade-off between intangibles such as justice and tangibles such as land and cows. Political association was for Aristotle a more complex form of association than that of families, tribes, and villages, and it required a more general and abstract vocabulary than that of logistics and economics and warfare (and this is still true for us today).

Concomitantly, as the democratic "mindset" becomes more prevalent with age, the meaning of political abstractions is reduced to substantive, material referents, if they are to have any meaning at all. As this occurs, abstractions such as the common good are *either* taken to mean more equitable distribution of material and bodily goods (such as health care), *or* they are taken cynically as rhetorical subterfuges for partisan projects. If nothing is done to resist this tendency, politics gradually ceases to be rational dialogue among competing conceptions of a common object of good (and the means to attain it) within an authoritative context making such a dialogue possible, and becomes simply a smokescreen for various wills to power – with the attendant loss of a realm for the relatively free and contingent play of intellect and persuasion in the choice of common courses of action.

What this chapter calls the "republican character" in a modern liberal democracy resists this reductionist tendency, and continues to take into consideration as well in pursuing her private interests, the general context making the moderate pursuit of these feasible, and whether the attainment of all her interests would be favourable to the common good, understood as the health of the political system of which she is a part. The "republican character" evinces a manageable tension between public and private interests.

In making clearer the meaning of this compactly stated argument, there are three salient issues which need to be unpacked and illustrated. First is the claim that democracy is the "regime of the body" and over time tends to reduce its vital political abstractions to material and bodily and psychological referents. The second is the claim that this occurs because the democratic "mindset" (whether of elites or masses) has great difficulty in treating ideas of the common good, and the authoritative context making politics possible, as real or meaningful. The third is the claim that what is here called the "republican character" may be defined in part by the ways in which it differs from the "democratic character." On the first point, democracy as the "regime of the body," let us begin by looking at some relevant ideas of two well-known Western observers of democracy, Plato and Alexis de Tocqueville, and then search for more contemporary illustration.

In Plato's *Republic*, written under and during the fourth-century Athenian democracy, we are presented with an indictment of democracy for eliminating the governmental and cultural restraints upon the appetites or the appetitive part of the *psyche*, in the name of freedom and of the equality of pleasures. Too much freedom eventually ends in too much slavery or tyranny, both individually and politically. The majority of human beings are likened (without a hint of irony) to copulating and fattening cattle for their inability to rise above a life dominated by the appetites,[14] and we are presented with the paradox that democracy is conditionally good only for the few philosophic souls erotically drawn to a greater good than those of power, money, status, and sex. ("It is impossible that a multitude be philosophic.")[15] This release from the senses and lower appetites also makes the philosophic or dialectic class capable of an "overview" of all the arts in a city, and hence capable of the abstraction necessary for political rule of a city.

Plato's implication here is that the appetitive life is not capable of sufficient abstraction from the intense demands of the body and the family to generate political life. Political life, by implication, arises in the "etherealization" of conflicts arising from demands of the body for sensual satisfaction and for species perpetuation. It is only political abstraction (e.g., the idea of justice for an entire *polis*) which can, under rare, favourable conditions, transcend these demands, and generate a political life and a political vocabulary which are not merely smoke-screens for the assertion of substantive wants and interests (as cynics have always claimed all politics is). Plato precedes Aristotle here, in the implication that the danger in advanced democracy is loss of the perspectival distance and abstraction requisite for the generation of constitutional structures capable of channelling and limiting the demands of the body (and the family that perpetuates it).

The second volume of the French aristocrat Alexis de Tocqueville's *Democracy in America*, written in the late 1830s after a long visit to the United States, and showing strong intellectual influences of the aristocrats Plato and Montesquieu,[16] makes an argument similar to Plato's about democracy – it is always in danger of falling below the level of the political in its fixation on material and physical well-being, and in its love of equality.[17] Tocqueville's solution, following Montesquieu, is to recommend the English model – maintenance of systemic political balance by cultivation of the countervailing passion of liberty through institutions for local control, an independent judiciary, freedom of the press, and cultivation of economic self-sufficiency for as many as possible. Tocqueville also develops the idea (which he observes practised in the United States) of self-interest, rightly understood[18] as an approximation or as an alternative to civic virtue and traditional patriotism and adds to the mix the importance in the American case of religion as counterweight to democratic materialism. (We shall return to the concept of enlightened self-interest momentarily in deciding whether it is in accord with the "republican character.")

Following Tocqueville's focus on the United States of America as the laboratory of democracy, let us try to isolate in contemporary American political and legal culture the democratic tendency to reduce its political abstractions to sub-political meanings and to conflate the authoritative context for politics and policies with the policies themselves. In this brief space it is not possible to determine the empirical question of how extensively this elusive tendency is occurring – the aim is rather to illustrate what the claim means, in more concrete and contemporary terms.

Let us begin by looking in some detail at a relatively recent United States Supreme Court case, not for its outcome or decision so much as for the reasoning behind the majority opinion and the dissenting opinion, which are illustrative of the two "characters" we are in search of. Again, this case is explored here not as typically "American," but rather as typical of advanced democracy.

In the 1989 "flag-burning" case (*Texas, Petitioner v. Gregory Lee Johnson*) the US Supreme Court took up the issue of whether public burning and denunciation of the American national flag fell within "the small class of fighting words likely to provoke the average person to retaliation and thereby cause a breach of peace."[19] Justice Brennan (writing for the majority), argued that no reasonable onlookers could have taken Johnson's generalized dissatisfaction with the *policies* of the federal government as an insult or an invitation to exchange fisticuffs. Brennan's reasoning here is revealing for our distinction between the "republican" and "democratic" characters. In his mind, apparently, no reasonable person could be driven to violence over a political abstraction or symbol because, by implication, these are not real or meaningful. It is in the reasoning of the dissenting opinion of Justice Stevens that there are evident the kinds of distinctions associated with the "republican character." Stevens argued that the national flag differs from other political symbols (such as state flags) because it is a controlling symbol representing the ideas of liberty and equality which characterize the entire society (in Aristotelian terms, its conception of political justice or who should rule). Stevens argued further that Brennan was mistaken in asserting that the respondent was prosecuted for expressing his dissatisfaction with the *policies* of the country. On Steven's view there is a fundamental difference between policies and fundamental ideas such as liberty and equality that provide the authoritative context within which specific policies are pursued.[20]

For our purposes, there are two important logically implied differences in the reasoning of the two justices. Stevens makes a qualitative distinction between the authoritative context for policies and the policies themselves, and Brennan does not, treating both as parts of a homogeneous continuum. Second, Stevens treats political abstractions such as "liberty" and "equality" as real and motivating on their own, while Brennan does not. Arguably, both differences flow from the inability of the advanced democratic personality to grasp the full meaning of higher-order political abstractions such as the "common good" or "political authority" in its fixation on equalizing short-term, individual, and collective physical, material, and lower-psychic well-being.

In another quick attempt to locate and illustrate the tendency of advanced democracy to reduce its political abstraction to sub-political dimensions, let us consider the views of John Rawls's influential late-twentieth-century work *A Theory of Justice*, sometimes characterized as a theoretical defence of the liberal welfare state. The popularity of Rawls's ideas precludes the necessity of a lengthy exposition of them here; nor is it necessary for the purposes of our analysis of the differences between the republican and democratic characters to mark the various modifications in his views in the decades following the publication of *A Theory of Justice* in 1971. Let us simply look at those of his ideas relevant to our analysis.

First, it is clear that Rawls's picture of a just society is not one of formal equals deferring to one another's particular talents and characteristics, and united in mutual understanding of their obligations to a system of political authority and to one another. There is virtually no discussion of the problems of preserving political authority and political and economic order, beyond the implied assumption that a government which provided the basic social primary "goods" (rights and liberties, opportunities and powers, income and wealth, and "a sense of one's worth")[21] as a matter of individual rights, and which tolerated various "life-plans" consistent with those rights, need not fear violent revolution, economic failure, or external invasion. In fact, there is little interest here in politics as practices and procedures for working out the meaning of justice; rather, we are given a set of antecedently formulated moral principles to be given force, apparently, through the influence they can gain in high national courts.

Second, one is struck at (what sounds like a fulfilment of Tocqueville's prophesies of dangerous democratic developments) the dependency of citizens under "justice as fairness." Their conceptions of their own self-worth depend heavily upon the esteem of others, who will, presumably, withhold their respect where the primary social goods are lacking in a person. Self-reliance, the strength to hold conflicting duties and desires in balanced tension, and individual independence and judgment do not appear prominent in Rawlsian personae.

A third democratic aspect of Rawls's theory of justice is the radically egalitarian and resentful impulse behind the idea ("the original position") that justice requires negating insofar as possible inherited talents or defects, and other characteristics such as beauty and grace. Combined with the idea that society is a great resource pool devoted to the material and psychic relief of all, but especially the least advantaged, the general picture that emerges is similar to the one criticized as extremely democratic by thinkers from Plato to Tocqueville and Nietzsche: demands for guarantees of equality and individual happiness leading to no higher purpose than group or species solidarity, and masked behind the cry for individual diversity over *marginalia* in the midst of a prevalent conformity. To say this differently, Rawls's account of a just society does not provide for sufficient separation of issues of formal legitimacy from those of substantive benefits to be considered "republican-like."

Before attempting a concise statement of the content of the "republican" and "democratic" characters and the possible reasons for the differences between them, let us look first at how contemporary attitudes towards the use of armed force, in the United States especially, are emblematic of advanced democracies (and monarchies and empires), rather than republics anchored in a middling citizenry. I allude to the advent of specialized "all-volunteer" military forces, and the concomitant drop in the military experience of most citizens (and especially political and social elites). Let us explore momentarily what is lost when the majority of citizens have no exposure to military life, or, more positively, what is gained from even brief military experience in peacetime. In what sense is the claim of theorists from Aristotle to Machiavelli to modern proponents of citizen armies that capacity for military service is an important part of the republican character[22] still valid for our time? Here is an attempt at stating what is implied in this idea.

First, the idea of common defence of a political union is an abstraction (whether grasped conceptually in a definition or in a symbol, e.g., a flag), and as such requires the ability to think generally in order to be understood. Furthermore, the willingness to act upon this idea, at risk of life or at least hardship, suggests that the abstraction of the common defence is treated as *real*, not simply as an epiphenomenon (as in Justice Brennan's reasoning in the "flag-burning" case).

Second, the idea of defence, properly understood to include initiatives to preclude and ward off attack, comprehends the ability to imagine a future undesirable state of affairs to be prevented by a lesser, immediate sacrifice, and, as such, bespeaks and nourishes a fairly complex time sense (of which, more momentarily) capable of transcending the pull of present appetite and impulse.

Third, the ability to apply armed force, even in a technological age, requires entrance into a world of practical and physical action, and pulls the personality away from words and thoughts only (whether reflective or calculative). This is perhaps the truth in the recurring insight that military service is one way of making citizens out of otherwise self-interested bourgeoisie.

Fourth, for individuals raised in an advanced democracy (where culture as well as electoral arrangements have been democratized), military life may be their only opportunity to see rules strictly enforced; to see the utility in a functioning system of authority; and to have the opportunity to issue commands themselves. Said differently, military service may be the opportunity to learn, as Aristotle says, to "rule and be ruled" by one another. (As we have observed, in the *Politics* Aristotle treats military activity, along with deliberative and judicial functions, as of a similar order to life of the mind, not the body.)

Arguably, all these aspects of taking part in the common defence of a political union resist tendencies towards extreme democracy in the human character. The abstraction of duty and sacrifice pull away from democracy's appetitive and materialist tendencies by providing first-hand experience of responsibility for the common good. The requirement to be adept in a world of physical danger pulls away from the tendency of especially commercial democracy to specialize the personality in a world of mental calculation. The habits and skills of collective and individual self-defence move the personality away from extreme dependence on specialists in armed force. Experience in "ruling and being ruled" gives insight into the problems of those in political and governmental office at any moment, and, hence, insight into whether they are abusing their authority at any moment. Finally, and arguably, the habit of sacrificing and risking for a future state of affairs all work to inculcate a fairly complex time sense, which mixes hope for a better world with realistic expectations about the recurring tensions in the past and present ones.

Let us try now to specify more carefully the attributes of the "republican" character vis-à-vis the "democratic" character by focusing on what is arguably the ground of their differences – their respective sense of time.[23] The view I presented here is that regardless of the particular language used in the historical circumstances, perhaps the most important distinction between the "republican" and "democratic" characters is a different and more expansive sense of time which makes meaningful and real the problem of the general good, and of the achievement and preservation of public authority. For whatever complex, evolutionary reasons, the personality here called "democratic" finds it extremely difficult to grasp the problem of the general good as real – it remains for this personality largely epiphenomenal or even fraudulent. Perhaps this is why Aristotle found that the distinguishing excellence of the polity or republic was the use of arms[24] – that is to say, by implication, that military service is a concrete way of grasping and acting upon the issues of the common good (or a common object of good) *for the majority of people.* In the Romanized, Stoic version of this idea, emphasis was placed upon maintenance of a tension (*intentio*) of body and soul as essential to both military and civilian life, capable of resisting the corrosive effects on character (*habitus*) of both pleasure and pain. For Cicero, in particular, this healthy tension was achieved and maintained through imitation of military discipline and through disciplines such as oratory: "The soul must strain every nerve in the performance of its duties; in this alone does duty find its safeguard."[25]

To pursue this line of reasoning, what is here designated the "republican" character has a more complex time sense than the democratic, and possibly than the aristocratic as well. It is a time sense constituted in a *tension between* the transient and appetitive aspects of experience *and* the more general and enduring aspects, both of which are grasped as important and real. The various debates over civic corruption since the Renaissance, and the various ways to combat it – military service, agrarian occupations, enlightened self-interest – are illuminated by viewing the problem in this light.

Let us restate the problem starting with the issue of civic corruption and its relation to time sense. The common element one sees in almost all historic debates over civic corruption is the idea of extreme dependency, whether upon a dictator, or upon powerful economic interests, or upon personal appetite, *or upon one another*. Power in such situations becomes increasingly "phenomenal," immediate, and unstable, as it is based more upon perceptions about what others are likely to do, rather than upon more abiding forms of influence such as constitutional authority. As more power calculations focus (through growth and ease and transparency of communication) upon the likely and contingent effect of every word and action of the circumstantially powerful – the dictator, the masses, the corporations – the predominant sense of time becomes "phenomenal" rather than seasonal, cyclical, or transcendent. (And if there is transcendent thinking, it is in an existentialist direction of future power scenarios further down the time-stream.)

To say this in more conventional language, in extremely democratic situations, where every shift in power perception is of "constitutional" significance, there is in time no constitution (or ordering) in actual fact. On the other hand, a time sense which was so disdainful of the contingent, the phenomenal, and the appetitive as to exclude them from constitutional significance, in its political form would be called "true aristocracy" (total dedication to the public good) and in its philosophical form "Platonic" (true reality as a realm of pure ideas). The "republican character" spans these two time senses by incorporating them as a tension in a single individual citizen, under a constitutional system making such an outlook viable. This was arguably the outlook of the most intelligent and influential of the founders of the United States, and is also the basis for the stability and longevity of their system. That is to say, the stability resides in the comprehensiveness of the outlook nurtured by their constitutional arrangements, incorporating for different seasons three ways of viewing time – as the never changing (e.g., maxims about human nature and ambition), the slowly changing (e.g., customs and laws). and the ever changing (e.g., policies and the market).

Such a view of the republican character, as one grounded in a manageable tension between the immediate and the recurring (or abiding) may assist us in finding a common ground in various historical ideals which we have inherited as "republican." Consider in this regard the following claims – that the republican character is not atheistic (the French case to the contrary notwithstanding);[26] that it bears some relation to the country and agriculture; that it can be constituted in "enlightened" commerce as well; that it is capable of competently bearing arms; that it is "amateurish" (i.e., resists extreme specialization in the personality); that it cares for the common or general good, or is habituated to civic virtue; that it has origins in the traditional family; and so on.

Each of these emphases has the effect of resisting extreme dependence on forms of power and influence generated exclusively by perceptions and calculations about likely shifts in power – that is, they all anchor the personality in something outside the ephemeral, while permitting it, in varying degrees, to value as well the transient, the contingent, or the appetitive event. For example, belief in dependence on a Creator, dependence on the soil, belief in the utility of the abstractions of "self-interest rightly understood," and the abstract capacity to grasp the importance of a public realm of action and meaning, all move the personality away from radical dependence on the short-term perceptions of others (as in credit markets), and towards generation of a tension within the personality between dependence and independence, characteristic, for example, of Aristotle's middling citizen. Military service (and gentlemanly "amateurishness" generally) moves the personality towards a tension between thought and action, and between authority and appetite (as in the case of the soldier prepared one minute to use lethal force to disarm an adversary and the next minute to care for him as a dependent once disarmed). In the same vein, the deference learned towards the authority of parents in traditional families may provide an initial understanding of formal authority (distinguished from mere power) for those born in otherwise democratic regimes.

May not a meaningful account of the "republican" character be given spanning both ancient and modern experience which distinguishes it from the true aristocrat's complete devotion to the common good, on the one hand, and from the democratic preoccupation with appetitive self-interest, on the other? May it be specified as a character characterized by a middle position, existing in a tension between the ephemeral and the recurring, between appetite and authority, and between dependence and independence with regard to others? If there is a significant distinction between ancient and modern forms of this republican balance, it might be in the tendency of the ancient Graeco-Roman world to locate the balance in the regime as a whole between classes, and of the modern world to locate the tension or balance self-consciously within individual citizens. But for our purposes in analysing political character, too much should not be made of this difference. Ancient writers such as Aristotle and Cicero strained towards the equivalent of the modern ideal, and modern defenders of commerce such as Adam Ferguson hearken back to ancient ideas of wholeness. For example, Aristotle's polity or republic is grounded in middling individuals who understand the claims of both the oligarch and the democrat and transcend them both in striving for the common advantage; Cicero (a favourite of George Washington) made it a major theme of his essay on duties (*De Officiis*) that the state exists to protect private property and honourable commerce; and Ferguson wrote in his essay on the history of civil society (1767) that to continue the otherwise healthy specialization of the arts and professions into the realm "of the arts which form the citizens ... the arts of policy and war, is an attempt to dismember the human character."[27]

To rehearse, it is possible to discern the *outlines* of a distinctive "republican character" here and there across two and a half millennia of Western political reflection, distinguished by the complexity of its allegiances to things both private and public. It is constituted in a complex time sense capable of maintaining a healthy tension[28] between the recurring and the ephemeral, duty and appetite, and thought and action. Its hallmark is the ability to *grasp* the significance of a public realm of authority (as the context for private pursuits), and without being single-mindedly devoted to it, still sacrifice for its preservation. And it is important for us in an age of increasing specialization of personalities and professions to distinguish the "republican character" from its less complex (or less mixed) and more highly specialized sibling, "the democrat."

This republican character can be either partisan in the Burkean sense ("when bad men combine, good men must associate") or staunchly unpartisan – it depends for our purposes on the larger intent. So long as the intent is to achieve some substantive interest for oneself or one's supporters, while still preserving a public realm of freedom under general laws, sustained by competition in government and party, there is evidence of the "republican character." By contrast, the "democratic character" sees those in government and political office as simply competitors for resources and influence or, if herself already in government service, sees her function as the aggrandizement of resources and influence for herself and her supporters, as an end in itself.

Yet anytime we find individuals raised in a commercial, democratic *ethos* of material self-interest as the basis for individual contentment, who can still grasp the idea of political authority as providing the context for this pursuit (rather than simply another form of it), we are on the trail of our catch. The "democratic character" generally finds it very difficult to recognize the difference in actual practice between the authoritative context for substantive transactions and the transactions themselves, perhaps because such a "context" has sufficient permanence and abstraction (generality) as to move outside the ephemeral democratic time sense. To say this more historically, the democratic character will generally have a very incomplete view of how much of her present circumstances is owed to her politically-minded forebears.

If it is correct that the tendency of unchecked advanced democracy is towards loss of political and individual balance through reduction of "the political" to sub-political pursuits, then residual "republican" generalists have an important and indispensable service to provide to liberal democracies in keeping alive a focus on the political or authoritative context making possible the democratic pursuit of its sub-political interests. One pedagogic strategy for nourishing expansive and imaginative minds receptive to this republican focus might be to follow in Vico's footsteps and to encourage reading of literature and texts written before the scientific and democratic generation of a culture of extreme specialization, with its view of all objects of study (including politics) as a homogeneous subject matter devoid of qualitative distinction.

NOTES

1 Aristotle, *Politics*, bk. 4, chaps. 7–9. For a sustained and cogent application of Aristotle's regime criteria to a modern regime, see Paul Eidelberg, *A Discourse on Statesmanship: The Design and Transformation of the American Polity* (Urbana: University of Illinois Press, 1974).

2 On this point (which will be developed in the chapter) one could cite Plato in the ancient world and Tocqueville in the modern. For a salient example of the psychologizing of political abstractions, see John Stuart Mill, *On Utilitarianism*, in which justice becomes a very intensely felt social utility. See also, in this connection, Rousseau's views on the cultural influence on civic virtue of women, as summarized by Lee Ward in his piece on Rousseau in this collection.

3 I take the idea of character types from Aristotle's practice in the *Rhetoric* and the *Nicomachean Ethics* of delineating types of persons such as "the young," "the old," "the mature," "the great-souled man," the "small-souled man," "the serious man," and so on.

4 Aristotle, *Politics*, bk. 6, chap. 4.

5 Ibid., bk. 3, chap. 7; bk. 4, chap. 13.

6 Aristotle, *The Politics*, trans. Carnes Lord (Chicago: University of Chicago Press, 1984), 1329a.

7 *Politics*, bk. 4, chap. 4.

8 *Politics* (trans. Lord), 1291a1.

9 Ibid., 1291a1.

10 Ibid., 1279a1–b1; emphasis added.

11 Aristotle, *Nicomachean Ethics*, bk. 8, chaps. 11 and 5.

12 See, for example, on the primacy of politics and civic virtue, Paul Rahe, *Republics Ancient and Modern* (Chapel Hill and London: University of North Carolina Press, 1992); and on intellectual virtue Thomas Pangle, *The Spirit of Modern Republicanism* (Chicago: University of Chicago Press, 1988).

Pangle is silent on all Roman criticism of Greek philosophy, as well as on the Ciceronian affinities of Locke's *Second Treatise.*

13 See, in this connection, besides book 8 of *Plato's Republic*, Leo Strauss, *The City and Man* (Chicago: University of Chicago Press, 1964), 109–15. See also J. Peter Euben, "Justice and the Oresteia," *American Political Science Review* 76.1 (1982), esp. 27: "... the triumph of the *oikos* is as dangerous as the victory of the heroic ethic. This is because exclusive preoccupation with instinctive attachments ... and biological life is too confining an ethic for living a fully just life. Its intensity precludes resolution of the dilemmas it generates. "

14 Plato, *The Republic*, 586a–b.

15 Plato, *The Republic of Plato*, trans. Allan Bloom (New York: Basic Books, 1968), 494a.

16 For an extended discussion of the influence of Montesquieu on Tocqueville (and Rousseau), see Paul Rahe, *Soft Despotism, Democracy's Drift* (New Haven: Yale University Press, 2009).

17 This is a theme of the entire second volume of *Democracy in America*, but see, esp., 2.2.10, "On the Taste for Material Well-Being in America."

18 Tocqueville, *Democracy in America*, 2, 2, 8, "How Americans Combat Individualism By the Doctrine of Self-Interest Rightly Understood."

19 *Texas, Petitioner v. Gregory Lee Johnson*, no. 88–155. Decided 21 June 1989, *Criminal Law Reporter*, 6–21–89, 45 CRL 3111.

20 Ibid., 45 CRL 3119.

21 John Rawls, *A Theory of Justice* (Cambridge, MA: Harvard University Press, 1971), 62 and 92. For an expanded account of the apolitical features of the Rawlsian project, see the essay in this collection by Crystal Cordell Paris.

22 Aristotle, *Politics*, bk. 3, chap. 9. This excursion into military character is not intended to explore what Marc Hanvelt in this collection calls "martial political courage"; rather, it is meant to show how military service augments the average capacity to grasp the idea of formal authority as the context for power, not merely another form of power. For an exploration of this distinction, see Michael J. Oakeshott, *On Human Conduct* (Oxford: Oxford University Press, 1975), 147–58, 194–6.

23 On the general importance of time conceptions for politics, see works of J.G.A. Pocock such as *Politics, Language and Time* (New York: Atheneum Publishers, 1973); and *The Machiavellian Moment* (Princeton, NJ: Princeton University Press, 1975). But whereas Pocock is engaged in the historical exercise of articulating paradigmatic ideas for different historical eras, I am engaged in the "unhistorical" exercise of trying to show that in any historical setting there are more and less complex characters afoot, with more and less complex ideas about what kinds of events in time have

meaning; and with more and less influence on political constitutions, which in turn affect the time sense of succeeding generations. For an interesting discussion of the connections between the time conceptions of modern science and modern democracy, see Wyndham Lewis, *Time and Western Man* (New York: Harcourt, Brace and Co., 1928), esp. 434–7. What Lewis calls (against the modern "time-philosophy") the "spatializing instinct of man" has similar political effects to what I am calling cyclical (vs. linear) or "recurring" time sense. See, also, the Roochnik essay in this volume on the political effects of the modern scientific focus on the concept of infinity.

24 Aristotle, *Politics*, bk. 4, chap. 4.

25 Cicero, *Tusculan Disputations*, trans. J.F. King (Cambridge, MA: Harvard University Press, 1976), 209, and throughout sections 2 and 23.

26 The case of atheistic French republicanism would appear to be an exception. For a comparison of the role of religion in the French and American revolutions, see Patrice Higonnet, *Sister Republics: The Origins of French and American Republicanism* (Cambridge, MA: Harvard University Press, 1989), esp. 90–5.

27 Quoted in Pocock, *The Machiavellian Moment* 500n95. Loosely speaking, my own essay could be said to follow in Ferguson's footsteps in its implications for commercial democracy. To see Ferguson's orientation summarized, see the essay in this collection by Varad Mehta.

28 To state the obvious, Plato (and many others) would not accept this (Stoic) idea of a healthy tension in the soul or personality. Plato, in particular, implies that it is not sustainable; rather, that psychic harmony arises in the erotic pull towards the intellectual virtues, which do not so much discipline the appetites as enlist them in pursuit of a stronger *eros*. Perhaps Tocqueville (following Montesquieu) was drawing upon Platonic psychology when he fashioned the idea of "self-interest rightly understood" as an American approximation of civic virtue and patriotism. For a discussion of Montesquieu's view that any sort of self-renunciation (pagan or Christian) contained the seeds of political fanaticism, see Rahe, *Soft Despotism, Democracy's Drift*, 10–22. For an illustration in this collection of the view that sustainable political moderation requires not maintenance of psychic tension but cultivation of the erotic pull towards the transcendent, see the chapter by Timothy Burns on Periclean Athens. Burns does not address the possibility that concessions to higher forms of *eros* have difficulty resisting the democratic and utilitarian elevation of appetite to the status of a political purpose as intellect and appetite ally against duty for frustrating their respective pursuits of pleasure.

5 Ancient, Modern, and Post-National Democracy: Deliberation and Citizenship between the Political and the Universal

CRYSTAL CORDELL PARIS

As the composite character of the term indicates, "civic republicanism" comprises two distinct and complementary elements. On one hand, the republic or *res publica*; on the other, the citizen or *civis* who, with his or her fellow citizens, constitutes the body politic. The expression "civic republicanism" thereby suggests a substantive connection between the citizen and the republic of which one is a citizen: the nature of citizenship is determined by the specific political context in which it is exercised, the duties and rights of the citizen being contingent upon the republic as both the source and guarantor of those duties and rights. Up until the contemporary period, the exercise of citizenship was understood to vary with the specific political community which at once grants citizenship and determines the conditions of its exercise. Moreover, the political community, whether it took the form of city, republic, or nation state, was conceived of as both a legal-political and a social-cultural entity. Citizens were accordingly considered to be simultaneously political actors and sharers in a common culture. The comprehensive character of the political community is expressed in the Greek term *politeia* (political regime), that is to say, a form of political organization which determines the way of life of the community as a whole.[1]

Similarly, the composite term nation state corresponds to both a legal-constitutional and a historical-cultural entity. The nation state is characterized at once by its political sovereignty and its cultural singularity. As citizens of a given nation state, individuals partake of a common political regime and identify with a specific national culture. Within the framework of the nation state, the political regime coincides with the national culture and constitutes one of its integral parts. Over against this political model, contemporary theories of constitutional patriotism and post-national citizenship envisage a division of the nation state into its component parts through the dissociation of culture and constitution, historically determined specificity and universal rational principles. Citizenship in its post-national version thus undergoes a radical transformation. The citizen is no longer considered in relation to a comprehensive whole the boundaries of which constitute the horizon of political action. Rather, the citizen becomes the moral subject of a set of democratic principles, principles which are destined to emancipate themselves from the strictures of historical-cultural particularity. Such a transformation would ultimately be made possible by a progressive transfer of political sovereignty from each particular political-cultural community to a moral community conceived of as essentially universal. As a consequence, the citizen's attachment to the particular *res publica* would lose its political character as civic republicanism gives way to moral cosmopolitanism.

1. On Ancient Citizenship: The Aristotelian Conception of Deliberation, Judging, and Ruling

In order to bring to light the political and philosophic roots of the opposition between properly political conceptions of citizenship and universalistic conceptions inspired by Kantian rationalism, an examination of the Aristotelian conception of citizenship is indispensable. For not only did Aristotle furnish one of the earliest theoretical analyses of citizenship based on the practices developed in the city (*polis*), but he also profoundly influenced subsequent conceptions of civic republicanism. It is ultimately an Aristotelian form of citizenship which defines the civic republican notion of citizenship. Two distinct but interdependent elements characterize the Aristotelian conception of citizenship. First, the citizen is distinguished by the activity characteristic of citizenship. The citizen is a political *actor*. Second, the activity of citizenship is characterized by the capacity to *deliberate*. Political deliberation requires practical reason and has as its objective decision and action. From this point of view, rhetoric is considered to play a fundamental role in the practice of citizenship. Rhetoric is the form of speech proper to the domain of political action, in which contingency and opinion reign, not predictable certitude and scientific truth. The domain of political action thus calls for an art of argument and persuasion indispensable to good decision making.

Aristotle problematizes the question of citizenship in the third book of the *Politics*. Rather than a straightforward exposition of a theory of citizenship, his discussion constitutes an examination of a series of problems (*aporiai*) related to the question of the definition of the citizen and of the citizen's specific virtue.[2] The starting point of the discussion is the affirmation that the *polis* is composed of citizens; put otherwise, the city cannot exist without a minimum number of active citizens.[3] A precise definition of the citizen as such is the subject of disagreement, not least because the criteria for citizenship vary with the political regime. Certain definitions can, at any rate, be eliminated from the outset: a citizen is not defined simply by place of residence, nor even by certain legal rights, such as the right to sue and be sued. As Aristotle, himself a metic of Athens, observes, resident aliens share a common place of residence and certain legal rights with citizens without enjoying full citizenship.[4] In the strict sense of the term, Aristotle argues, the citizen is one who shares in (*metechein*) judging (*krisis*) and ruling (*archè*). The citizen is the juryman (*dikastès*) or the member of the assembly (*ekklèsiastès*). Anticipating possible objections, the Stagirite insists that both these offices constitute *ruling* offices, despite the absence of the term for "ruling office" or "ruler" (*archè, archôn*) from their official titles, as no specific term is associated with them. Indeed, these offices are the most sovereign offices; accordingly, they are to be considered under the heading of "undetermined rule" (*aoristos archè*).[5]

As these passages suggest, Aristotle's innovation consists in adapting the analytic framework and language of political theory to the reality of political life in the *polis*. Decision making or, more generally, ruling is in fact in the hands of those who judge public and private suits as well as those who deliberate on public matters. Consequently, Aristotle proposes to call both types of offices *archè*. And it is a share in ruling that in practice distinguishes the citizen from the non-citizen, resident alien, or disenfranchised citizen. As Aristotle's analysis emphasizes, legal rights are distinct from political rights. While legal rights are, under certain conditions, granted to residents, political rights are proper to citizens. Only citizens share in determining the common destiny of the city. In this sense, a city is not to be assimilated with other forms of alliance or trade bloc, for in these cases there are no common ruling offices among the partner cities.[6] While the member cities of a military alliance or a trade bloc have certain interests in common and enjoy mutual rights and protections, they do not share in a common political association (*politikè koinônia*). It is precisely this specific form of association or community that requires of its members deliberative and ruling capacities. These capacities are to be put to the service of justice, in its punitive sense but more particularly in its positive sense; the end of political rule and the political association in general is virtuous or noble *action*: "It is for the sake of noble actions that the political association must be considered to exist, rather than for the sake of living together."[7]

Indeed, sharing a common geographic space, participating in a common social life, be it through family ties, religious customs, or cultural activities, and engaging in economic exchanges constitute necessary conditions for the existence of a city, but these necessary conditions are nonetheless insufficient to constitute a veritable association of *citizens*. The end (*telos*) of the city as such is living well (*to eu zèn*),[8] that is to say, activity in accordance with practical virtue: "Any city which is truly so called, and is not merely one in name, must be attentive to virtue."[9] Political or civic activity thus distinguishes the veritable city from a mere alliance whose members are not subject to common laws and institutions which, beyond the mere enforcement of covenants and punishment of individual injustices, promote virtue and justice.[10] The activities of deliberating, judging, and ruling with a view to justice give the citizen the opportunity to practise the political or civic virtue (*politikè aretè*) evoked by Aristotle in his conclusion of the discussion concerning the political association's specificity with respect to other types of association: "Those who contribute most to this association have a greater share in the city than those who are equal to them (or even greater) in free birth and descent, but unequal in political virtue, or than those who surpass them in wealth but are surpassed by them in virtue."[11] Illuminating the true character of the city thus leads to a clearer understanding of the citizen and civic virtue. Insofar as the end of the city is virtuous activity, the good citizen must be defined in light of the sole criterion of civic virtue rather than that of birth or wealth qualifications. In this sense, the Stagirite's argument constitutes a critique of both the democratic and the oligarchic perspective concerning justice. Justice is neither strict equality for those of free birth nor equality proportionate to wealth, but must instead be a function of virtue. It is by honouring civic virtue above all else that the city "distributes" justice according to political merit.

At the same time, the Aristotelian definition of citizenship is not strictly neutral with regard to the type of political regime. Rather, it is a definition that most closely corresponds to one regime in particular: democracy. For it is in (Athenian) democracy that the citizen shares in the ruling offices in an "indeterminate" manner: on one hand, the jury has a general function, being authorized to judge a whole range of private and public cases; on the other hand, the popular assembly is a permanent institution holding regular sessions. In regimes other than democracy, such as Sparta, the popular assembly does not exist and the jury's function is divided among different bodies convened to judge different types of cases.[12] Given the institutional specificities of the Athenian regime, the initial definition of the citizen appears too restrictive. Aristotle thus introduces a modification of the definition to render it less regime-specific, while nonetheless maintaining its substance: the citizen is defined as one who is *eligible* to share in (*koinônein*) deliberative or judicial office, even if the said offices are not for an unlimited term.[13]

This modification does not, however, resolve all the difficulties raised by the question of citizenship. As it is pointed out in the subsequent discussion, the question of the just attribution of citizenship remains. Even if one is authorized to partake of the function of citizen, does it necessarily follow that the attribution of citizenship was just? This was an objection raised against the democratic reforms instituted by Cleisthenes, which expanded citizenship to foreigners as well as slaves and resident aliens. Clearly, Aristotle does not wish to encourage the calling into question of the political rights of certain classes of citizens, as he dismisses this objection by reaffirming his functional definition: one who exercises the functions of the citizen is, by definition, a citizen.[14] This functional definition also resolves a difficulty raised by *jus sanguinis*. Insofar as the requirement that one's parents be citizens cannot apply to the founders and earliest inhabitants of a city, it is clear that, in these cases, citizenship was indeed determined by its exercise and not by ancestry.[15] Another difficulty concerns the legitimacy not of an individual's title to citizenship but rather of the decisions made by the regime's rulers. Under what circumstances and on what bases can a decision made by the city be called into question? Aristotle considers two general cases: that of the transformation of an oligarchy or tyranny into a democracy and that of a deviant democracy, that is to say, a democracy acting by force and contrary to the common interest. In the first case, a contract engaged by the previous regime would appear to be non-binding on the grounds that the rulers' authority was based on force rather than the common good. Anticipating the classification of regimes into correct and deviant regimes according to which democracy is considered to be the deviant form of "constitutional government" (*politeia*),[16] Aristotle affirms that a similar conclusion must also apply in the second case.[17] As the Federalists,[18] Tocqueville,[19] and others would later emphasize, democracy is not immune to despotic tendencies, despite its intimate connection to civic virtue.

2. On the Art and Ethics of Ancient Rhetoric

The analysis of citizenship presented in the *Politics* is completed by the treatment of deliberation and judgment in the *Rhetoric*. As we saw in the foregoing discussion, it is these aspects of ruling in particular that characterize the function of the citizen and, when exercised with a view to justice, constitute the virtue of the citizen. In the *Rhetoric* Aristotle provides an account of the central role played by speech and argument in deliberation and judgment. It comes to light in the course of this account that the art of rhetoric is the necessary corollary of the ruling activity of the citizen insofar as it gives expression to the arguments necessary for decision making while acknowledging the intrinsic limits of purely logical or rational argumentation. As an *art* rather than a science, rhetoric is adapted to the political and human reality of decision-making processes. For it must operate within the constraints imposed both by the specific structures and temporality of political institutions and by the complex nature of human reasoning. To the degree that judgment is not the product of argument or reason alone, the art of rhetoric must take into account the way in which habit, custom, character, emotion, and interest, in addition to argument, influence deliberation and sway judgment. Rhetoric is thus at the crossroads between the ethical and the analytical: "Rhetoric is composed of both analytical science and of the political science concerned with character."[20]

The art of rhetoric intervenes in precisely those contexts in which the citizen exercises specific civic functions: the assembly and the courts. These institutions occupy a space which is left partially vacant by the law, for the law is general in nature, whereas the decision and judgment apply to a specific case.[21] It is the impossibility of the law to determine in advance particular matters that gives rise to jurisprudence. However, "it is proper that laws, correctly enacted, should themselves define the issue of all cases as far as possible, and leave as little as possible to the discretion of the judges."[22] This statement should forestall any tendency to interpret Aristotelian civic virtue as an idealization of political life. Far from depicting a stylized version of citizenship, Aristotle's analysis is attentive to the limits of political virtue and to the dangers of abuses of power by citizen-rulers. It thus appears essential that the law circumscribe the decisions of the assembly and the courts: "first, because it is easier to come upon one or a small number who are of sound intelligence [*eu phronein*] and have the capacity to legislate and to judge, than a large number; next, because laws are the outcome of lengthy examination, while judgments are that of brief reflection, such that it is difficult for the judges to nobly render justice and what is fitting."[23] On one hand, this statement acknowledges the limits of human prudence; on the other, it underscores the specific temporality which characterizes political and judicial judgment. In contrast to the relatively long temporality of legislation, that of judgment is abbreviated. By consequence, political and judicial judgment is more susceptible not only to error but also to short-term or immediate considerations, including personal interest, which tend to adulterate the judging faculty.[24] Observing that the role of rhetoric in deliberation is to address a specific audience, Aristotle adds that the reasoning or calculating faculty is itself limited: "The hearers do not have the capacity to synthesize a number of elements or to calculate [*logizesthai*] beyond a certain point."[25]

Rhetoric is thus not to be confused with a pure analytical science in which logical demonstration leads to the discovery of scientific truth or indisputable necessity.[26] Rather, rhetoric is concerned with the possible, the probable, and the plausible, degrees rather than absolutes, contingency rather than certainty. In the context of political deliberation, the rhetorician must advocate not the best course of action absolutely, but the best course of action under the circumstances, the best *possible* course of action: "The one who deliberates does so not about everything but only about those things that might come to pass or not. Those things that are, or will be, the result of necessity, or that are impossible or cannot ever occur, are not subject to deliberation."[27] Moreover, insofar as rhetoric seeks to *persuade* (concerning justice and injustice in the case of forensic rhetoric, advantage and harm in the case of deliberative rhetoric, the noble and the base in the case of epideictic rhetoric), its methods and the conditions of its exercise are to be distinguished from those of science. While the discovery of truth constitutes the self-sufficient end of science, the attainment of accurate knowledge in the course of deliberation does not ensure an outcome in accordance with that knowledge. For persuasion does not in all cases follow upon knowledge: "Even if we were to possess the most exact scientific knowledge, it would nevertheless not be easy to persuade certain people using arguments arising out of that knowledge; for scientific argument belongs to instruction, which is impossible here, as it is necessary to use proofs and arguments that accord with common conceptions."[28] Persuasion presupposes not only the rhetorician's faculty to persuade, but the hearer's faculty to be persuaded. In this sense, emphasizing the sole oratorical aspect of rhetoric leads to an incomplete understanding of Aristotelian deliberation, which is equally characterized by its *dialogic* aspect. At once a practical and demonstrative art, rhetoric aims at adherence to arguments and action on the part of the hearer.[29] In the absence of an implicit dialogue between the speaker and the hearer, rhetoric would be reduced to a reflexive art of oration rather than a dialectical art of persuasion. In underscoring the distinction between the practical art and the exact science, Aristotle incites both those who study and those who practise rhetoric to be mindful of the intrinsic limits of persuasion through scientific knowledge alone.

It is important to recall, moreover, that Aristotle considers his innovation in the *Rhetoric* to be his interlinking of the "dialectical" element of persuasion, consisting in the adduction of proofs, with two other crucial elements: the emotive and the ethical. Having reproached his predecessors for placing disproportionate emphasis on the manipulation of the judges' emotions such that they are in fact *prevented* from judging (the judges in the law courts, "considering only themselves and listening for the sake of their own pleasure, give themselves over to both parties, but do not in fact make a judgment"),[30] the Stagirite treats the emotions, not as inhibitors of judgment but as contributors to the formation of judgment.[31] Emotions, which are paired by opposites – such as anger and gentleness, friendship and enmity, fear and confidence, shame and shamelessness, compassion and indignation, envy and emulation – derive not exclusively from the personal experience of pain or pleasure, but from opinions or beliefs that are capable of influencing judgment:[32] "The emotions are those affects which, in causing to undergo a change, make a difference with respect to judgments, to which are joined pain and enjoyment."[33] It is this more complete understanding of the role of emotion in deliberation that the teacher and practitioner of rhetoric must acquire. *Pathos* is then not opposed to *logos*, as Kant would affirm,[34] but rather shown to contribute to the reasoning faculty so as to produce in the hearer true conviction. It is when emotion is separated from the judging faculty that it becomes the object of inappropriate manipulation. When understood to be an integral part of judgment, however, emotion becomes a valid and indeed indispensable object of persuasion. Equipped with the knowledge of emotions, the speaker will be able to change the opinions and beliefs of the hearer relative to the matter at hand and not relative to the hearer's mere personal interest and pleasure, as is the case when the manipulation of emotion prevents judgment.[35]

As Aristotle argues in his treatises devoted to ethics, the knowledge of emotions is an *ethical* knowledge. Indeed, the province of ethical or moral virtue (*aretè èthikè*) is not only that of actions, but also that of emotions, which admit of a mean in the same way as do actions. In both emotions and actions, there exist

> excess, deficiency and the mean. For example, to be fearful or confident, to be desirous or angry or compassionate, and in general to experience pleasure and pain, either too much or not enough, is in both cases incorrect; but to experience these emotions at the right time, in the right circumstances, with respect to the right individuals, for the right reason, and in the right way, therein lies both the mean and the highest excellence, and this is the very thing which characterizes virtue.[36]

Ethical virtue presupposes the regulation of the emotions insofar as they play a role in disposing one to action. In the same way that well-regulated emotions participate in virtuous action, emotions properly influenced participate in sound judgment. The persuasion of the emotions is thus not to be considered antithetical to deliberation, but as an essential component of the art of rhetoric. However, to the extent that the rhetorician's role is to persuade rather than to provide an education in virtue, his[37] influence on the emotions cannot be expected to produce virtue in the hearer, but is limited to the more modest objective of orienting the existing emotions of the hearer, imperfectly regulated as they are, towards the best possible decision in a given case.

Consequently, the effective orator must be able to adapt his discourse to the specific audience being addressed. This means that he will be mindful of both individual characters (*èthè*) or groups of characters, such as those determined by age,[38] and *political* characters, that is to say, the specific character of the political regime in which the deliberation takes place. It is in the context of deliberative or political rhetoric in particular that knowledge of the character of the regime is paramount: "What is most important and authoritative [*kuriôtaton*] in order to be able to persuade and advise nobly is to apprehend all the regimes and to distinguish the characters, institutions, and advantage of each. For all are persuaded by considerations of advantage, and preserving the regime is advantageous. Moreover, the declaration of the sovereign authority [*kurios*] is authoritative, and the sovereign authority is determined by the regime; for there are as many sovereign authorities as there are regimes."[39] Recalling the treatment of the question of sovereignty (*to kurion*) and the classification of regimes in the *Politics*,[40] Aristotle here argues that the most effective rhetorician will possess a sufficient knowledge of the different political regimes so as to be able to grasp the cultural and institutional specificities of his own regime and, armed with that knowledge, better advocate for the interests of his regime.

Despite his sufficiently comprehensive political knowledge, however, the rhetorician is not to be assimilated with the political philosopher, whose knowledge and perspective tend to place him in the position of impartial judge of the various regimes. In contrast to the philosopher, the rhetorician must, to a certain extent, adopt the perspective of the regime of which he is a part. This implies not only knowledge of but *attachment to* the end (*telos*) of the regime.[41] Both the sovereign authority (the people, the few, the wealthy, etc.) and the end or fundamental aim is specific to each regime: liberty in the case of democracy, wealth in the case of oligarchy, etc.[42] The persuasive speaker in a democracy cannot afford to be ambivalent about his commitment to liberty. Only democratic arguments will succeed in convincing a democratic audience. In this sense, the etymology of the term "advise" or "counsel" – *symbouleuein* – is suggestive. Literally the term implies "deliberating together"; engaging in an implicit dialogue about the city, about the action and direction it must take, the rhetorician participates in a common deliberation with his fellow citizens. Therein lies the Aristotelian critique of the Sophistic conception of rhetoric as an art or technique the mastery of which is independent of ethical and political knowledge. Rejecting the notion of a technical rhetoric, Aristotle describes an intrinsically political rhetoric rooted in the practice of citizenship and in the particularity of the political regime.

3. Contemporary Theories of Deliberative Democracy: From Rhetoric to Ideal Discourse

Inasmuch as the activity of citizenship appears to be specific to democracies – an intrinsic connection underscored by Aristotle – democratic theory has an abiding concern for the way in which citizen-specific activity is transformed by the evolving institutions and practices of democratic regimes. No theorist is unaware of the significant changes brought about by the territorial and population expansion of modern democracies compared with their ancient counterparts and by the advent of representative government, which enables large democracies to continue to function in accordance with the principle of self-rule. As Madison famously argued, the distinction between a "democracy" and a "republic" lies precisely with these two criteria: in contrast to "pure" or direct (i.e., ancient) democracy, in which government by "faction" produces chronic instability, representation, in the context of a large society in which multiple parties and interests coexist, favours the general rather than particular interest and is a check on the excesses of the effective political equality of all citizens.[43] Before moving to the Enlightenment view of democratic citizenship and deliberation, however, it will be useful to contrast the Aristotelian conception with the contemporary view as it comes to light in the deliberative democratic theory of two of its most influential exponents, John Rawls and Jürgen Habermas. The aim of deliberative theory is to clarify and promote the role of public reasoning and citizen deliberation in contemporary (i.e., large and representative) democracy. In the thought of Rawls and Habermas, these questions turn largely on the conceptualization of rationality, greatly influenced by Kant's moral philosophy, that underlies their respective notions of "public reason" and "ideal discourse."

For Rawls, reasonability is a moral attitude which allows citizens of liberal democracies to tolerate the coexistence of a multiplicity of beliefs and opinions regarding the good. This notion of reasonability arises from an understanding of modern democracy according to which its fundamental challenge is the establishment and preservation of a "moral consensus" regarding democratic principles despite the pluralism of private, "comprehensive" doctrines, where democratic principles are defined in classical liberal terms: the aim of the political association is to protect individual rights and liberties on the assumption that all persons are fundamentally equal. Continuing the social contract tradition, Rawls assumes a hypothetical "original position" which creates the conditions necessary for universal agreement as to the principles of a just society. The original position is a neutral standpoint protected by a "veil of ignorance" from behind which citizens adopt an "impartial" perspective with regard to political and social arrangements, including measures of economic redistribution.[44]

Thus, in contrast to the Aristotelian conception of political deliberation, Rawls considers not ethical and political knowledge but a certain form of ignorance to be the fundamental condition of public reason. It is only when human beings are separated from the particularity of their individual characters that they can be expected to adhere to principles of justice. Similarly, in the absence of the veil of ignorance, fair deliberation is achieved only when citizens arrive at "impartiality." That is to say that, disregarding their private beliefs and opinions, citizens must deliberate with a view to *respecting* others as equal, rights-endowed individuals or, to put it in Kantian language, "ends in themselves."[45] Knowledge of and attachment to the specific political regime thus appears superfluous in Rawlsian public reason. For as Rawls insists, justice must be understood not in relation to political or civic virtue but as an attachment to a universalistic principle, that of impartiality or "fairness." Whereas Aristotelian political virtue can only be measured by the justice of one's decisions and actions as they affect the common destiny of the political community, Rawlsian justice as fairness, reflecting the Kantian universalistic perspective, is ultimately the measure of a strictly interior disposition radically disconnected from interest and inclination, "purity of heart."[46] Rationality is then not practical but reflexive, aimed not at judgment and action but tolerant respect of the rational subject. Just as the end of the political community is no longer virtuous or excellent activity but respectful tolerance, the criterion of good citizenship is no longer political virtue in the exercise of judging and ruling but rather an interior commitment to fairness.

Indeed, the notion of political rule (*archè*) itself appears to be incompatible with Rawlsian "political liberalism" insofar as the doctrine of "justice as fairness" tends to empty political deliberation of its content.[47] According to Rawls, the public use of reason must be consistent with citizens' mutual recognition of each other as equals. This requirement rejects the pertinence of political virtue to deliberation to the extent that political virtue by definition acknowledges distinctions between citizens, all of whom do not demonstrate it in identical proportions. It also precludes the role of persuasion and rhetoric in public deliberation. For persuasion presupposes a certain inequality between the one who seeks to persuade and the one who is open to being persuaded.[48] The one who hopes to contribute to sound deliberation through argumentation and influencing the emotions of the hearers must possess superior knowledge and capacity to persuade; otherwise his or her contribution will be futile at best and harmful at worst. In Aristotle's view, it is insufficient for good citizenship to be authorized to partake in ruling. It is also necessary to acquire the capacity to fulfil the functions of citizenship, whence the need for a certain education in politics, ethics, and rhetoric.

Rawls's conception of public reason, in contrast, asserts an essential incompatibility between democracy and superiority or expertise.[49] Justice as fairness sees any form of expertise as going against the egalitarian premises of liberal democratic society. It does not, however, ask whether some forms of superiority, such as political virtue, prudence, judgment, and the capacity to persuade, are necessary to healthy democracy.[50] The extent to which this important question is obfuscated by Rawls's commitment to liberal egalitarianism is shown by a remark concerning the activities of political life: "Plainly, engaging in political life can be a reasonable part of many people's conceptions of the good and for some it may indeed be a great good, as great statesmen such as George Washington and Abraham Lincoln testify. Still, justice as fairness rejects any such declaration; and to make the good of civil society subordinate to that of public life it views as mistaken."[51] In interpreting the notion of "the good" as a private question relative to mere preferences and in establishing a strict opposition between "civil society" and "public life," Rawls does not acknowledge that the fundamental question for democracy is whether the activity of those who engage in politics is good for the political community, not whether it is good for the politically active individuals themselves. A truly political theory of justice considers great political leaders not so much as examples of *self*-realization as examples of the realization of the political virtue indispensable to democratic regimes.

In their exchange concerning Rawls's theory of political liberalism, Habermas and Rawls appear to disagree about the status of political activity as it bears upon the relation between private and public "autonomy." Objecting to Habermas's giving priority to political autonomy, Rawls associates Habermas with the classical humanism tradition.[52] And yet, political virtue finds little expression in Habermasian deliberative theory. In the same way that Rawlsian egalitarianism precludes distinctions based on political virtue, judgment, and the capacity to persuade, Habermas's emphasis on the procedure of rational-critical deliberation points to a form of "ideal discourse" in which not sound judgment but equal access constitutes the standard by which political justice, or rather "legitimacy," is measured. Indeed, Habermasian ideal discourse requires the same "impartiality" as is required by Rawlsian public reason. This entails an attitude of tolerant respect towards all potential and actual participants in public deliberation. According to this view, most forcefully articulated by Rawls, no participant can bring to bear a claim to merit a greater share of participation in deliberation, no matter the basis of that claim. The Aristotelian conception of distributive justice, by which those who contribute most to deliberation and ruling have the greater share in the city, is thus implicitly rejected, insofar as the pertinence of the distinction between greater and lesser contributions to deliberation is denied by the very terms of contemporary deliberative theory. Impartiality or objectivity constitutes the sole standard of moral validity for Habermas, just as it constitutes the sole standard of reasonability for Rawls. Objectivity is guaranteed procedurally, notably by the openness of the deliberation and by the absence of coercion.[53] Pointing out the fundamental similarity between his own and Rawls's argument in this regard, Habermas concludes that in both theories, "the procedure of the public use of reason remains the final court of appeal for normative statements."[54] Justice as legitimacy, like justice as fairness, has the effect of obscuring the criterion of justice as a practical-political good.

For Habermas, the crucial aim of deliberation is the exercise of "political autonomy" by all members of society. In terms which owe a debt to the Arendtian conception of political speech and action,[55] Habermas advocates the "present exercise of political autonomy" so as to allow citizens "to experience [the act of founding the democratic constitution] as open and incomplete" and thereby "reignite the radical democratic embers of the original position in the civic life of their society."[56] Despite Habermas's expressed concern for democratic civic participation, however, he ultimately privileges the perspective of self-realization or autonomy over that of judging and ruling with a view to the common interest, those activities considered to be properly political according to the Aristotelian account of citizenship. Deliberation is not understood to be an essential component of political rule, as is the case for Aristotle; on the contrary, it is understood to be incompatible with political rule, which presupposes politically pertinent distinctions of knowledge, character, capacity, and judgment.[57] As a result, the exercise of deliberation, as a means towards "uncoerced intersubjective recognition,"[58] tends to become its own self-sufficing end. Moreover, to the extent that "ideal discourse" or "ideal role taking" requires perfect sincerity on the part of the one communicating,[59] it becomes impossible to take into account political considerations concerning the limits of purely rational persuasion and the necessity of ethical-affective knowledge in the Aristotelian sense. It thus appears that Habermas's normative approach takes its bearings not from actual political life, bound up as it is with considerations not only of reason but also of interest, but from a universalistic conception of abstract moral consciousness isolated from political particularity. This universalistic moral perspective is of a piece with a universalistic political perspective which looks towards ever wider borders as the horizon of applicability of universalistic moral principles. Consequent upon the shift away from rhetoric towards an ideal form of discourse, the political framework of rhetoric, what Aristotle called the *koinônia politikè* (the political association or community) gives way to an increasingly legalistic and transnational framework of decision making.[60]

4. A Return to Rhetoric? Enlightenment and Post-Enlightenment Views of Ancient and Modern Deliberation

If citizenship in the Aristotelian sense – in which rhetoric, deliberation, and judgment are constitutive of ruling – is implicitly rejected by contemporary deliberative theory on grounds of its incompatibility with egalitarian public reason and ideal discourse, it is important to recall that the Enlightenment period produced critical reflections on Athenian democracy which, while rejecting as unsound and impracticable the ancient form of democracy, advocated a properly political rather than a moral-universalistic conception of citizenship. That is to say, the Enlightenment critique is founded on a concern for ensuring the conditions necessary within particular, sovereign political regimes for sound political deliberation and judgment as preservatives of justice and of the common interest.

Hume, Hamilton, and Madison each articulate a critique of ancient Greek democracy from the point of view of the preservation of the democratic regime. Despite his praise of ancient eloquence,[61] Hume considers the Athenian democracy to be an unhealthy form of government in which law had little authority and decisions often lacked prudence. Putting forward the example of the *graphè paranomôn* (indictment of illegality), he denounces the injustice of a procedure by which members of the popular assembly could be put on trial for laws they had initiated on grounds that the law was unjust. Being insufficiently restricted by the law, the *graphè paranomôn* often served as a pretext for privately motivated acts themselves contrary to the public good. For example, Demosthenes had been indicted for having initiated a law, adopted by the assembly, which proportioned the taxation destined to finance warships to taxpayer income. In Hume's view, this indictment was merely the result of the wealthy citizens' resentment and demonstrates the "irregular and extraordinary" character of the *graphè paranomôn*. A procedure of this sort could only contribute to the endemic instability of the Athenian regime which was, at root, caused by the openness of the democracy and the absence of checks on the power of the popular assembly: "The whole collective body of the people voted in every law, without any limitation of property, without any distinction of rank, without controul from any magistracy or senate."[62]

An additional consequence of the significant deliberative power accorded to the assembly, which was increased by the relative paucity of laws compared with the British parliamentary regime, was the flowering of the rhetorical art. Comparing ancient Greek and Roman with British eloquence, Hume deems the former to be "sublime and passionate" and the latter to be "argumentative and rational."[63] What first appears to be the superiority of ancient to modern eloquence turns out to be the inferiority of ancient to modern politics, for the difference between the "sublime" and the "argumentative" is in fact a direct reflection of the specific character of the respective political regimes under consideration. To the inconstant and unstable Athenian democracy corresponds a sublime rhetoric, the elevation of which is proportionate to the magnitude of the dangers to which the regime is exposed. To the stable and regular British parliamentary regime corresponds a sensible eloquence free of rhetorical tropes and replete with references to legal precedents. Thus, for Hume, it is the specific character and institutional framework of the political regime that determines the character of rhetoric, deliberation, and judgment. Put another way, it is impossible to give an account of political deliberation in the absence of an analysis of its conditions, limits, and effects as determined by the particular political regime in which it takes place.

Like Hume, Hamilton and Madison reject ancient democracy as a model of sound government. While acknowledging the peaks of its greatness, they abhor its disunity and violent instability: "It is impossible to read the history of the petty republics of Greece and Italy, without feeling sensations of horror and disgust at the distractions with which they were continually agitated, at the rapid succession of revolutions, by which they were kept perpetually vibrating between the extremes of tyranny and anarchy."[64] To remedy the ills of ancient democracy while preserving the popular form of government, Madison proposes to treat the effects of faction; for its causes are permanent. Faction is consequent upon inequality – inequality of possessions, opinions, and passions, the elimination of which can be achieved only at the price of liberty itself. Pure democracy,[65] in which checks on the majority are absent, has the effect of nourishing factional passions and interests. As Madison observes, the political equality characteristic of ancient democracy does not solve the problem posed by the persistence of other kinds of inequality. It is therefore advantageous to institute a republican system of representation, whose desired effect is "to refine and enlarge the public views, by passing them through the medium of a chosen body of citizens, whose wisdom may best discern the true interest of their country, and whose patriotism and love of justice, will be least likely to sacrifice it to temporary or partial considerations."[66] Representation can create the conditions necessary for healthy deliberation by attributing deliberative power not to all citizens equally but to a select body of citizens, chosen by their compatriots, whose distinctive qualities are wisdom and an attachment to the nation and to the public good.[67] In contrast to Rawlsian and Habermasian deliberation, Madisonian deliberation adopts the criteria of political capacity and judgment ("wisdom") rather than procedural objectivity; a simultaneously affective and rational attachment to the particular political regime rather than a purely rational commitment to the universal principle of autonomy. For in Madison's view, these are the politically relevant criteria to which both political theorists and those who govern must be attentive.[68] In this way, the American founders point towards the reactivation of an Aristotelian form of citizenship and rhetoric.

Is it representation itself that accounts for the declining role of rhetoric observed by Hume in the British context? Or does the role of rhetoric depend more fundamentally on the particular character of the representative democracy? Writing two generations after the Federalists, Tocqueville gives an account of American "parliamentary eloquence" that attests to a continued role for rhetoric in democracy, a role that will necessarily be determined by the particular character of the nation.[69] Given the absence of a historical class structure in the United States, Tocqueville observes that elected representatives there tend to attribute greater importance to their office than in aristocratic parliamentary systems. For it is through elected office that they achieve a certain rank and status, whereas the rank and status of the aristocratic member of parliament are independent of his office. Moreover, the indeterminacy of social rank combined with frequent elections produces a marked uncertainty or "instability" in the American representative system; the representative must strive to "captivate" and "please" his electorate continually.[70] The electorate places great expectations in the merit and capacity of the representative, for individuals of significant political capacity are quite rare.[71] In particular, the electorate expects the representative to be an "orator," to speak often in the assembly, evoking great matters and small grievances alike. As a result, even those who do not possess noteworthy rhetorical skill are determined to take the floor and deliver a memorable oration. The quality of discourse within deliberative bodies is thus uneven and on average mediocre.

At the same time, Tocqueville highlights the paradoxical effectiveness of what he sees as becoming the new democratic rhetoric. What characterizes deliberative rhetoric in nineteenth-century America is the contiguity of considerations concerning local affairs and those touching the entire nation. While many orations make an unconvincing transition between these two levels of consideration, Tocqueville attributes the specific strength of democratic speakers to their ability to raise their discourse to the level of the nation: "That enlarges thought and elevates language."[72] Democratic rhetoric, he argues, will be distinguished by general or universal arguments: rather than addressing itself to a particular class, it will summon universal truths which appeal not only to the nation as a whole but to human beings as such. Alluding to the French revolutionary period, Tocqueville remarks that, if the French nation was able to produce discourse that echoed beyond its borders, it is precisely because the discourse was of a universal character. In contrast to the rhetoric deployed in colonial America or revolutionary France, British parliamentary eloquence was never able to incite great sympathy or interest in other nations.

Tocqueville's analysis complements Hume's observations concerning the decline of eloquence in parliamentary Britain in a thought-provoking way. On one hand, it confirms the distinction between parliamentary and democratic eloquence suggested by Hume; on the other, in acknowledging the ambiguous effects of electoral campaigns on argument and rhetoric, it raises anew the question of the stability of democratic regimes and the influence of majority opinion on political judgment and decision. More generally, it reaffirms the crucial link, first established by Aristotle, between the particular character of the political regime and that of deliberation and rhetoric. In Tocqueville's view, modern democracies like the United States – and like France in a not too distant future – require rhetoric, and even a soaring rhetoric which rises to the heights of universal truths. But crucially, democratic rhetoric is the counterpart to democratic participation, including deliberation, judging, and ruling. The various activities of citizenship occur not only in national political institutions but also, and especially, in the township, in the context of local government;[73] they also occur within juries[74] and in political and civil associations.[75] An advocate of "local liberties" as a counterweight to despotic democratic tendencies, Tocqueville suggests that the township is the object of an affective attachment at once because of citizens' effective participation in governing and the real political power, within the decentralized federal system established by the 1787 constitution, of the township: "The New England town brings together two advantages that, wherever they are found, strongly excite the interest of men – namely, independence and power … You must realize that in general the affections of men go only where strength is found. Love of native land[76] does not reign for long in a conquered country."[77] Similarly, in his analysis of the jury system, Tocqueville considers the jury as an institution which enables the citizens to exercise a share in ruling. Indeed, it is as a political, rather than a judicial, institution that the jury comes to light in Tocqueville's account. In particular, he considers it to be a "republican" institution: it "can be aristocratic or democratic, depending on the class from which you take the jurors; but it always retains a republican character, in that it places the real direction of society in the hands of the governed or a portion of them, and not in the hands of those governing."[78]

5. Conclusion

It is the link between political or civic activity, in particular on the national and local levels, affective political attachments, and effective political power or sovereignty that is called into question not only by universalistic conceptions of rationality and deliberation, but also by post-national conceptions of citizenship which advocate the development of a universal moral community independent of properly political communities.[79] According to the post-national perspective, developed notably by Habermas and those influenced by him,[80] citizens' primary attachment would be displaced from a specific culture, history, or nation, to a set of universalistic democratic principles, foremost among which are human rights, mutual recognition, non-discrimination, and tolerance. Individual adherence to universalistic principles would foster a common public culture the borders of which would correspond to practical dispositions, independent of a shared culture and national or local sovereignty. Such a common public culture would be supported by a universalistic legal framework, by which respect for human rights and claims to recognition would be ensured.

This conception of citizenship, however, largely fails to give an account of the citizen as *political actor*. Rather, the citizen is seen primarily as a *subject* of moral-legal principles, the upholding of which satisfies citizens' rights claims. How can this thin conception of citizenship foster attachment to the political community and the attendant desire to participate in the activities of citizenship, in what Aristotle called "ruling and being ruled"? Neglecting to recognize the decisive implications of this question, post-nationalists see the disposition to tolerant recognition as the essential criterion of good citizenship, thereby transforming the faculty of deliberative judgment into a means of achieving a preconceived ideal society. Ultimately, the practical disposition of respect for all claims to recognition is both the means to establishing and the end of the universalistic "political" community.

And yet, both the Aristotelian and the Enlightenment republican traditions point to the conclusion that in the absence of deliberation and judgment, directed not towards private autonomy but towards just ends, "political" action becomes a discursive exercise in intersubjective recognition rather than a practical activity oriented towards the common good of the community. It is the dissociation of citizenship from what Aristotle and modern republican thinkers considered to be the activities necessary for sound political decision making that renders the foundations for shared notions of justice uncertain. For, as Aristotle observed, the legal rights of residents are an inadequate substitute for the political rights of citizens who rule and are ruled in turn. Insofar as rhetoric constitutes a means by which opposing political opinions and persuasions are confronted with the continual necessity of common decisions and actions, renewed attention to the art of rhetoric would enable a deeper understanding of both contemporary evolutions in the republican form of government and contemporary forms of democratic political participation.

NOTES

1 Cf. Leo Strauss's discussion of the term *politeia* in *Natural Right and History* (Chicago: University of Chicago Press, 1953), 135–7.

2 More generally, *Politics* 3 contains the greater proportion of *aporiai* of the entire work. By the author's calculations, approximately two-thirds of the total number of appearances of the word "*aporia*" are to be found in book 3.

3 Cf. Aristotle, *Politica*, ed. W.D. Ross (Oxford and New York: Oxford University Press, 1957), 1274b38–41. Hereafter abbreviated to *Pol.*
4 Cf. *Pol.*, 1275a2–14.
5 Cf. *Pol.*, 1275a22–33. All translations from the Greek are my own.
6 Cf. *Pol.*, 1280a34–b5.
7 *Pol.*, 1281a2–4.
8 Cf. *Pol.*, 1280b29–40.
9 *Pol.*, 1280b6–8.
10 Cf. *Pol.*, 1280b8–12.
11 *Pol.*, 1281a4–8.
12 Cf. *Pol.*, 1275b5–12.
13 Cf. *Pol.*, 1275b13–20.
14 Cf. *Pol.*, 1275b34–6a6.
15 Cf. *Pol.*, 1275b22–34.
16 Cf., *Pol.* 3, 7.
17 Cf. *Pol.*, 1276a6–16.
18 Cf. Alexander Hamilton, John Jay, and James Madison, *The Federalist* (Indianapolis: Liberty Fund, 2001), no. 10.
19 Cf. Alexis de Tocqueville, "Of the Omnipotence of the Majority in the United States and Its Effects," in *Democracy in America*, bilingual edition, ed. Eduardo Nolla, trans. James T. Schleifer (Indianapolis: Liberty Fund, 2010), vol. 2, part 2, chap. 7.
20 Aristotle, *Ars Rhetorica*, ed. W.D. Ross (Oxford: Clarendon Press, 1959), 1359b9–11. Hereafter abbreviated to *Rh.*
21 On the general character of the law, cf. Aristotle, *Nicomachean Ethics*, 5, 10.
22 Aristotle, *Rh.*, 1354a31–4.
23 *Rh.*, 1354a34–b4.
24 Cf. *Rh.*, 1354b8–11.
25 *Rh.*, 1357a3–4.
26 On this point, cf. Carnes Lord, "The Intention of Aristotle's 'Rhetoric,'" *Hermes* 109 (1981), 326–39. Lord convincingly argues that Aristotle's "provisional assimilation of rhetoric to dialectic serves the important purpose of conferring on rhetoric a dignity capable of engaging the attention of men of intellectual and moral seriousness, and of ensuring that such men are encouraged to view rhetoric, not as an instrument of personal aggrandizement in the sophistic manner, but rather as an instrument of responsible and prudent statesmanship" (336–7).
27 *Rh.*, 1359a31–4. In *Nicomachean Ethics* 3, 3, Aristotle provides an extended discussion of this point, arguing that deliberation concerns only those matters which admit of human agency.

28 *Rh.*, 1355a24–8.

29 For a discussion of this point, cf. Chaïm Perelman, *L'empire rhétorique: Rhétorique et argumentation* (Paris: Librairie philosophique J. Vrin, 1977), 32–3 and Chaïm Perelman and Lucie Olbrechts-Tyteca, *Traité de l'argumentation: La nouvelle rhétorique* (Brussels: Éditions de l'Université de Bruxelles, 1970), 62–8.

30 *Rh.*, 1354b33–1355a1. This passage further develops Aristotle's initial statement concerning his predecessors (1354a11–18): "Now those who have composed Arts of Discourse have provided but a small part of this art, for only proofs are included in it, while the rest is an afterthought, but they say nothing concerning enthymemes, which are the body of proof, treating for the most part things extraneous to the subject. For slander, pity, anger and other such emotions of the soul do not concern the subject, but rather the judge."

31 As Bryan Garsten puts it, "The difficulty was not simply that judicial orators aroused emotions but that they aroused the wrong emotions, at the wrong times, and in the wrong way" (*Saving Persuasion: A Defense of Rhetoric and Judgment* [Cambridge, MA, and London: Harvard University Press, 2006], 123).

32 For a useful discussion of the deliberative dimension of the emotions, cf. Martha C. Nussbaum, "Aristotle on Emotions and Rational Persuasion," in *Essays on Aristotle's Rhetoric*, ed. Amélie Oksenberg Rorty (Berkeley: University of California Press, 1996), 303–23.

33 Aristotle, *Rh.*, 1378a19–21.

34 Implicitly rejecting Aristotle's practical philosophy, Kant remarks that "a mixed moral philosophy, compounded both of incentives drawn from feelings and inclinations and at the same time of rational concepts, must make the mind waver between motives that cannot be brought under any principle and that can only by accident lead to the good but often can also lead to the bad." Cf. Immanuel Kant, *Grounding for the Metaphysics of Morals*, trans. James W. Ellington (Indianapolis: Hackett Publishing Co., 1993), 22.

35 For an argument concerning the affective dimension of legislative persuasion in Rousseau and Plato, cf. Brent Edwin Cusher's contribution to this volume. While Cusher brings out the "enchanting" and "musical" character of the legislator's use of persuasion, to the exclusion of rational argument, Aristotelian rhetoric involves an artful combination of both rational and emotive persuasion.

36 Aristotle, *Ethica Nicomachea*, ed. Ingram Bywater (Oxford: Clarendon Press, 1970), 1106b17–23.

37 To avoid anachronism, the masculine pronoun will be used here and in what follows.

38 Cf. Aristotle, *Rh.*, 1388b31–90b13.

39 *Rh.*, 1365b22–9.

40 Cf. the explicit reference to the *Politics* at 1366a21–22. One should recall that the brief presentation of the classification of the regimes which appears in the *Rhetoric* does not treat the *aporiai* related to the question of sovereignty, nor does it provide an analysis of the criteria by which correct regimes are distinguished from deviant regimes, as is the case in the *Politics*. Moreover, the list of regimes includes only four out of the six regimes presented in the *Politics*: democracy, oligarchy, aristocracy, monarchy (*Rh.*, 1365b29–30). It is, however, important to note that despite its absence from the initial list of four regimes, tyranny appears a few lines later, defined as a limitless (*aoristos*) form of monarchy (1366a2). And in the immediate sequel, it is monarchy that is absent from the enumeration of each regime's end. Significantly, the distinction between the correct and deviant forms of democracy is not evoked in the *Rhetoric*, an absence which, particularly for one familiar with the *Politics*, implicitly indicates both the intrinsic and potentially dangerous connection between rhetoric, on one hand, and all forms of democracy, on the other.

41 For analyses concerning the crucial political role of emotive or affective attachments to one's political community, cf. Montesquieu, *The Spirit of the Laws*, trans. A.M. Cohler, B.C. Miller, and H.S. Stone (Cambridge: Cambridge University Press, 1989), bk. 4, chap. 5 and bk. 5, chap. 2, and Jean-Jacques Rousseau, "Considerations on the Government of Poland and on Its Planned Reformation," in *The Collected Writings of Jean-Jacques Rousseau*, vol. 11, trans. C. Kelly and J. Bush (Hanover, NH: Dartmouth College Press, 2005). For an argument concerning the crucial relevance of the passions for political life that draws on Montesquieu's political theory, cf. Rebecca Kingston, *Public Passion: Rethinking the Grounds for Political Justice* (Montreal and Kingston: McGill-Queen's University Press, 2011).

42 Cf. Aristotle, *Rh.*, 1366a2–6.

43 Cf. Hamilton, Jay, and Madison, *The Federalist*, no. 10.

44 Cf. John Rawls, *A Theory of Justice* (Cambridge, MA: Belknap Press of Harvard University Press, 1971) and Rawls, *Political Liberalism* (New York: Columbia University Press, 1993).

45 As Rawls puts it in the concluding pages of *A Theory of Justice*, "To respect persons is to recognize that they possess an inviolability founded on justice that even the welfare of society as a whole cannot override" (586).

46 Ibid., 587.

47 Wendell John Coats, Jr (chap. 4 in this volume) makes a similar argument: "There is little interest here [in Rawls's picture of a just society] in politics as practices and procedures for working out the meaning of justice." At the same time, in speaking not of political "rule" (*archè*) but rather of political "authority" or "the political or authoritative context," Coats frames his critique of Rawls somewhat differently than I do: "There is virtually no discussion of the problems of preserving political authority and political and economic order." While authority or sovereignty (*to kurion*) is certainly an essential component of Aristotelian *archè*, another – and equally essential – component is that of political participation (*metechein*). Consistent with an emphasis on the notion of authority is Coats's reading of Aristotle as "trac[ing] the origins of the concern for the common advantage *in the majority of people* to participation in tactically coordinated military activity in defence of the *polis*." Thus, it is suggested that, in "advanced democracy," military life provides a rare opportunity to learn to rule and be ruled thanks in large part to its authoritative structure. However, it is important to remember that Aristotle resists attempts to assimilate political life to military life, political virtue to military virtue. His discussion of the Spartan regime (*Pol.* 2, 9) is instructive in this respect. On one hand, he acknowledges that "military life encompasses many parts of virtue" (1270a5–6) and thus is to be recommended both for women and for men; in particular, it disposes citizens to obey the law. On the other hand, the Spartan regime is not to be taken as a model for healthy political life, insofar as it aims excessively at war and military virtue, neglecting the part of virtue that enables citizens to use leisure well (1271b2–6). This critique is developed by important arguments in *Pol.* 3, 9 (in the absence of care for the whole of virtue in the citizens, the city is a *polis* in name only, being in reality a military alliance or a trade union) and 7, 2 ("despotic" regimes, the raison d'être of which is domination, are pleonectic rather than political). Another aspect of the critique of Sparta can help to see the ways in which Aristotle envisages the cultivation of concern for the common, namely, his critique of the way in which the common meals are organized in Sparta. Aristotle points out that, unlike in Crete, they were not financed publicly, with the result of putting a burden on the poorest citizens. This result was contrary to the spirit of the law, which was to cultivate democratic participation or sharing (*metechein*) (1271a28–34). Indeed, Aristotle considers the system of common meals to be an important criterion for evaluating the civic health of a regime, and emphasizes their importance in his description of the regime *kat'euchèn* (cf. in particular *Pol.* 7, 10; 12).

48 As Bernard Yack underscores, considerations related to the (superior or inferior) character of the speaker are often decisive with respect to the persuasiveness of the argument being made. Cf. Bernard Yack, "Rhetoric and Public Reasoning:. An Aristotelian Understanding of Political Deliberation," *Political Theory* 34 (2006), 430.

49 Cf. the following statement: "In justice as fairness there are no philosophical experts. Heaven forbid!" (John Rawls, "Reply to Habermas," *Journal of Philosophy* 92 [1995], 174).

50 My critical perspective on Rawls can be usefully compared with Ryan Balot's approach in examining democratic courage (cf. chap. 7 in this volume). While Balot emphasizes the compatibility between courage and egalitarianism – in particular, gender egalitarianism – his study points at the same time to an understanding of courage that is inseparable from the notion of political virtue. Courage is accordingly analysed as political virtue, civic virtue, and military virtue. Thus, while Balot's argument demonstrates that democratic courage in no way excludes respect and equality, it also confirms that it is indispensable for democracies to cultivate healthy forms of political superiority or virtue.

51 Rawls, "Reply to Habermas," 170.

52 Ibid., 169.

53 Cf. Jürgen Habermas, *Moral Consciousness and Communicative Action*, trans. C. Lenhardt and S.W. Nicholsen (Cambridge, MA: MIT Press, 1990), 89–90.

54 Jürgen Habermas, "Reconciliation through the Public Use of Reason: Remarks on John Rawls's Political Liberalism," *Journal of Philosophy* 92 (1995), 124.

55 Cf. Hannah Arendt, *The Human Condition* (Chicago: University of Chicago Press, 1958) and Arendt, *Between Past and Future: Eight Exercises in Political Thought* (New York: Penguin Books, 1993). On the complex intellectual relationship between Habermas and Arendt, see Margaret Canovan, "A Case of Distorted Communication: A Note on Habermas and Arendt," *Political Theory* 11 (1983), 105–16. In Canovan's view, there is a fundamental disagreement between the two thinkers, despite an acknowledged debt on the part of Habermas to Arendt. That disagreement stems from Habermas's interpretation of the role of rational communication and consensus in political life: "Arendt did not share Habermas's crucial belief in the possibility of rational consensus on political questions … The fundamental flaw in Habermas's reading of Arendt is that it is excessively intellectualist. Because Habermas is himself preoccupied with *discussion*, he misses Arendt's concern with *action*. Habermas appears to believe that free politics is a matter of citizens first of all talking, and then, after they

have all formed a common conviction and will, proceeding to act as one; and he attributes this view to Arendt. But Arendt thought (as her criticisms of Rousseau's General Will show) that the whole notion of getting individuals to act as one was a dangerous illusion. What she herself stressed was the inescapable plurality of men, not just in the early stages of discussion, but in *action*" (108, 109–10).

56 Habermas, "Remarks on John Rawls's Political Liberalism," 128.

57 For an argument asserting the incompatibility between political rule and "plurality," cf. Arendt, *The Human Condition*, sect. 5, "Action."

58 Habermas, "Remarks on John Rawls's Political Liberalism," 127.

59 Cf. Habermas, *Moral Consciousness and Communicative Action*, 88 and "Remarks on John Rawls's Political Liberalism," 117.

60 To use Bernard Yack's striking terms, one might say that the "living reason" of political deliberation yields to the "dead reason" of impartial legal deliberation: "Dead reason, impartial reasoning without emotion, may be worth trying to recreate when adjudicating cases. But deliberation about what serves the common advantage requires a living reason, reasoning informed by the emotions that interest us in the consequences of our decisions. Since we need to call on our emotions to help us judge the value of competing proposals, we must be willing to accept the risks that they will mislead us as well." Cf. Bernard Yack, "Rhetoric and Public Reasoning: An Aristotelian Understanding of Political Deliberation," *Political Theory* 34 (2006), 433.

61 Cf. David Hume, "Of Eloquence," in *Essays Moral, Political and Literary* (Indianapolis: Liberty Fund, 1985), 97–110.

62 Hume, "Of Some Remarkable Customs," in *Essays Moral, Political and Literary*, 368.

63 Hume, "Of Eloquence," 108.

64 Hamilton, Jay, and Madison, *The Federalist*, no. 9, 37.

65 Madison defines pure democracy as "a society consisting of a small number of citizens, who assemble and administer the government in person" (*The Federalist*, no. 10, 46).

66 Hamilton, Jay, and Madison, *The Federalist*, no. 10, 46.

67 For an argument concerning the Madisonian theme of the distinction between democracy and republicanism, cf. Coats's chapter in this volume. Coats suggests that the republican character stands as a mean between "the true aristocrat's complete devotion to the common good, on the one hand, and … the democratic preoccupation with appetitive self-interest, on the other."

68 As Robert Sparling's analysis in chapter 8 suggests, Montesquieu shared the perspective I have attributed to the American founders with respect to

the importance of the affective dimension of citizens' attachment to their regime.

69 Cf. Alexis de Tocqueville, "Of Parliamentary Eloquence in the United States," in *Democracy in America*, vol. 3, part 1, chap. 21, 861–70.

70 Ibid., 864–5.

71 What Tocqueville refers to as the rareness of "talents" among the electorate of a given district (ibid., 865) should be understood in part to be a function of the sparsity of the American population in the mid-nineteenth century. To give an indication of the relative insignificance of the population at this time, one might compare population growth in the United States and in France from this period to the present. Whereas the US population in 1840 was approximately 5% of the current US figure, the French population around this same time was approximately 53% of its current total (excluding its overseas departments and territories).

72 Ibid., 868.

73 Cf. Tocqueville, *Democracy in America*, vol. 1, part 1, chap. 5 ("Necessity of Studying What Happens in the Individual States before Speaking about the Government of the Union") and vol. 3, part 2, chap. 4 ("How the Americans Combat Individualism with Free Institutions").

74 Cf. Tocqueville, *Democracy in America*, vol. 2, part 2, chap. 8 ("Of What Tempers Tyranny of the Majority in the United States").

75 Cf. Tocqueville, *Democracy in America*, vol. 3, part 2, chaps. 5–7, 895–917. For an argument interpreting Tocqueville's account of democratic associations as a theory of "democratic courage," cf. Ryan Balot's chapter in this volume.

76 "Native land" translates "*patrie*."

77 Tocqueville, *Democracy in America*, vol. 1, part 1, chap. 5, 111.

78 Ibid., vol. 2, part 2, chap. 8, 445.

79 Contrary to what David Roochnik's argument concerning neo-Aristotelianism would suggest (cf. chapter 2 in this volume), it is not necessary for one to adhere to Aristotle's thesis concerning the non-existence of infinite bodies or, more generally, to his cosmology, to advocate or experience a new awareness of this link, to which Aristotelian practical philosophy gives its first formulation. Indeed, a consequence of the Socratic turn from natural science to political philosophy is that, while science can certainly be invoked in support of political theory, political theory is not founded on the science of nature but on that of human beings. Along these lines, Pierre Pellegrin argues in his introduction to Aristotle's *Politics* that "for Aristotle, the inferior realities do not participate in the superior realities, *they imitate them* … What Aristotle refuses then is at once the reduction of the sphere of philosophy to simply ethical and political affairs and the absolute

dependence of the things here below, and therefore of ethical and political affairs, on the things above." Cf. Pierre Pellegrin, trans., *Les Politiques* (Paris: Flammarion, 1990), 21. My translation.

80 Cf. Jürgen Habermas, *Between Facts and Norms: Contributions to a Discourse Theory of Law and Democracy*, trans. William Rehg (Cambridge, MA: MIT Press, 1996); Jean-Marc Ferry, *Europe, la voie kantienne. Essai sur l'identité postnationale* (Paris: Les Éditions du Cerf, 2006); Jean-Marc Ferry, "Face à la question européenne, quelle intégration postnationale?" *Critique internationale* 23 (2004), 81–96; Justine Lacroix, *L'Europe en procès. Quel patriotisme au-delà des nationalismes?* (Paris: Les Éditions du Cerf, 2004).

PART TWO

The Enlightenment: An Accelerated Reception?

6 Machiavelli's Art of Politics: A Critique of Humanism and the Lessons of Rome

JARRETT A. CARTY

This book *On Civic Republicanism* broadly contemplates both ancient and modern versions and traditions of civic republican political thought; thus, it is fitting to include in these considerations Niccolò Machiavelli, whose singular contributions to this tradition became (and continue to be) immensely influential and hotly controversial. Machiavelli's place in the history of civic republican political thought is at the nexus of ancient and modern political ideas, yet this fact makes him notoriously difficult to interpret. All at once he claimed to be doing something wholly new by reviving the old republican teachings, yet also to be doing something old by dismissing the new Renaissance republicanism in favour of Rome's hitherto misunderstood example. Therefore, it behoves this volume's study of civic republicanism to consider what for Machiavelli made Rome's civic republic become one of the most storied and glorious regimes of all antiquity.

At the core of Machiavelli's teaching is an art of politics – an art of political efficacy acquired through the study of political histories. But for Machiavelli its adoption necessitated a thorough critique of the "humanism" of his day, and a re-evaluation of what the ancients, especially the ancient Romans, taught by their tumultuous histories. Machiavelli's art of politics in *The Prince* and the *Discourses on Livy* presented a forceful critique of Renaissance humanism while pointing towards a robust civic republicanism based on an ambivalent reading of republican Rome. For Machiavelli, many of Rome's political successes were to be emulated and its failures avoided, but equally important, these actions were to be truly understood and practised in a coherent art used for the maintaining of regimes. Against the ancient claims of Livy and Polybius, Machiavelli claimed that Rome's political art maintained the conflict between its two "humours" in the plebs and the nobles. Moreover, Machiavelli's *Discourses* argued that only a practice of this art would bring stability to his city and homeland, which had been hitherto plagued by humanism's errors in interpreting the causes of Rome's greatness.

Machiavelli's Critique of Humanism

The chaos of Italian Renaissance politics had invited experiments in political thought and practice. Despotisms – sometimes beneficent ones – ruled much of Italy, though several cities, like Machiavelli's Florence, had elements of a republican regime dating back to the city's founding. However, Italian political thought had a great asset: the variation in Italian regimes and politics afforded political thinkers a comparative vantage point that was unparalleled in the rest of Europe. A serious political mind had before it a myriad of Italian regimes constantly competing, conflicting, and cooperating among one another.

In his Florence, Machiavelli witnessed the rise and downfall of several regimes, including one which made him a respected civil servant, and another which imprisoned and tortured him. This Florentine regime change brought great instability. Tensions between different classes or rival families could resurface and explode; foreign allegiances and vital treaties could be upset or abandoned. Moreover, the regime change was often accompanied by revolutions in political thought. The political traditions and ideals of a city could be revived or challenged; ideas that once supported a polity could be quickly overturned. Under these internal fissures and external pressures, Italian regimes could rise and quickly fall.

To Machiavelli, the lack of a want of an art of politics was abundantly clear: the failure of so many Italian regimes and the failure to secure stability and prosperity in a land so promising, demonstrated the dire need to revive it. But for Machiavelli, "humanism" – the modern name for the Renaissance movement consisting of high scholarship and educational programs built on ancient texts of moral and ethical philosophy, history, and rhetoric[1] – had failed to teach an effectual art of maintaining the state.

To be sure, Machiavelli's relationship to Renaissance humanism was deeply ambivalent; whereas he would offer a biting critique of humanism, its influence upon him was striking, and as Renaissance scholarship has abundantly shown, he was greatly indebted to many of its achievements. For instance, scholars Hans Baron, John G.A. Pocock, or Quentin Skinner famously argued that he was part of a large "civic humanist" movement in Italian political thought, reviving classical ideas on civic republicanism – in the case of Pocock, Aristotelian ideas – and modifying them for their application to Italian politics.[2] Moreover, Machiavelli in many ways displayed the art and skill of a Renaissance humanist. Artful letter writing was a distinct mark of Renaissance humanism,[3] and Machiavelli was a talented letter writer.[4] Thus, broadly speaking Machiavelli shared with humanists the accomplishment of a man of letters: he composed histories, letters, commentaries, short stories, plays, poems, and of course political treatises.[5]

However, Machiavelli offered an unmistakable critique of humanism in *The Prince* and *The Discourses*. Therein, this critique was exemplified in his treatment of humanism's most revered thinkers: Petrarch and Cicero. Francesco Petrarcha, or Petrarch (1304–74), turned to ancient Roman authorities to bring the "dark ages" to an end through the revival of ancient virtue, rhetoric, art, and morality. Petrarch himself had looked especially to the Roman statesman and writer Marcus Tullius Cicero (106–43 BCE) to spearhead the rebirth of a cultured age: for Petrarch, Cicero was, among other things, a model teacher of ancient ethics and rhetoric. For humanism, Petrarch and Cicero were venerable father figures looked to for the rebirth of high civilization.[6]

Yet there are sparse references to Petrarch and Cicero found in the writings of Machiavelli, despite his familiarity with these heroes of the age.[7] But when he did use them, Machiavelli's forceful political critique was apparent. Consider the passage from Petrarch's *Italia mia*[8] found at the end of Machiavelli's famous concluding chapter of *The Prince*.

> Virtue will take up arms against fury,
> and make the battle short,
> because the ancient valour in Italian hearts
> is not yet dead.[9]

Petrarch's call to virtue to combat fury was also a call to ancient virtues – peacemaking, moderation, the quiet life, and magnanimity – to combat the vices of the despotic *signori*, whose wars against one another invited foreign invasions.[10] Yet Machiavelli's exhortation and call to arms, in this very same chapter, was far from extolling Petrarch's kind of ancient virtue; on the contrary, the priority of magnanimity, moderation, and the quiet life for Machiavelli only exacerbated the need for an art of politics.

Consider also Machiavelli's obvious allusion to Cicero in one of his most famous passages of *The Prince*. In his ancient classic *On Duties*, Cicero had argued that "force and fraud" were bestial, suited to the lion and fox but not human beings, and that "fraud is the more contemptible."[11] But here in chapter 18 of *The Prince*, Machiavelli stood Cicero on his head: "Since a prince is compelled of necessity to know well how to use the beast, he should pick the fox and the lion," and of the two the beasts "the one who has known best how to use the fox has come out best."[12] This lesson in *The Prince* was an inverted lesson from *On Duties*: Cicero's vice was Machiavelli's virtue.

Machiavelli's opposition to Petrarch and Cicero was not simply a small ethical dispute: it revealed his criticism of humanism and his assessment of the political crisis of the sixteenth century. Humanism did not offer a comprehensive political theory,[13] yet it insisted that high culture would make for better politics. Humanism held that a classical education of rhetoric, history and moral philosophy would make good princes. But Machiavelli's attempt at princely education – *The Prince* – rejected the political efficacy of this education. To be sure, Machiavelli's writings contained humanist rhetoric, history (both ancient and modern) and moral philosophy, but they subverted the humanist project by questioning its success and its assumptions on political virtue. By using humanism's own trademarks of rhetoric, ancient history, and moral philosophy against it, Machiavelli offered a powerful critique: humanism failed to produce good princes, failed to cultivate an art of politics, and thus failed to address the political crisis of the age.

Humanists were inspired by Rome's fine arts but neglected its political lessons. For Machiavelli, humanism exacerbated the political crisis of the age by elevating artistic and literary accomplishments of the ancient world to the detriment of political thought and practice. Through education in ancient fine arts and literature, and through a recreation of their own literature and philosophy, the humanists sought to revive ancient virtues (such as liberality) in political life. Under such an influence, Machiavelli argued, political thought became less and less about what politics was, and more about what, in view of the humanist's overarching concerns, politics ought to be.

Machiavelli's Ambivalent Rome

What then to Machiavelli was political "reality"? He looked to experience: according to the lessons of Rome, political reality was a world in which classical virtues were often neither useful nor expedient for the maintenance of state. In accordance with this reality, Machiavelli's art of politics was the art of maintaining regimes, an art devoid of overarching conceptions of the good or best regime or the kingdom of heaven, and wholly based upon what, to his thinking, politics basically was.

The essence of Machiavelli's political science was summed up in the fifteenth chapter of *The Prince*; "imagined republics" were rejected in favour of the "effectual truth." At stake in the juxtaposition, for example – though unmentioned throughout Machiavelli's works – were the merits of Plato's political philosophy, and the greatest of "imagined republics," the *Republic*.[14] His objection was not simply that Socrates's "city in speech" was impractical; such a criticism would have put Machiavelli in company with Plato's most prominent students, Aristotle and Cicero.[15] Rather, Machiavelli's primary objection was that the "city in speech" and all other "imagined republics" were creations contrived from visions of what politics ought to be, to the detriment of effective government.

Machiavelli's "effectual truth" was opposed to the imagined republics because it jettisoned the metaphysics that girded them. It was not that Machiavelli rejected Plato's metaphysics in particular and argued for his own; rather, he rejected the notion that metaphysical considerations had any meaningful bearing on his art of politics. In a negative sense they did: insofar as metaphysics inspired imagined republics and obscured political realities, it impeded the art of maintaining the state.

In rejecting the imagined republics, Machiavelli appealed to the lessons from the same Roman world to which humanism too had appealed, but with his own *new* way of understanding its political teachings. His *Discourses* was infused with this ambivalence of looking back to Rome but with a new perspective. As the full title of the work suggested, it took much of its substance from the first ten books of Titus Livy's *History of Rome*. Yet in the very first paragraph of the preface to the first book, Machiavelli likened his book to "a path as yet untrodden by anyone," a finding of "new modes and orders," and a labour no less dangerous than seeking "unknown waters and lands."[16]

An ambivalence about the ancients characterized Machiavelli's art of politics: at once he made it appear in part a revival and in part an innovation. This ambivalence mimicked Italian Renaissance architecture, in which there was something new, yet also "no break with tradition, no resurrection of principles which had been entirely abandoned."[17] Likewise, Machiavelli certainly claimed to be doing something new, yet there was also a claim that his political project had a seamless connection to ancient political practice. His art of politics was accessible to both those who considered the history of Florence, and the causes of hatreds and divisions within the city, and to those who studied ancient Rome and read its histories carefully. At once Machiavelli claimed to be sailing in uncharted waters, yet to be arguing for the imitation of the ancients against those in his day who thought such imitation impossible, "as if heaven, sun, elements, men had varied in motion, order, and power from what they were in antiquity."[18] The ambivalence was purposeful: Machiavelli praised the ancients in order that he might improve on them. By presenting his project as a revival of ancient political practice, Machiavelli appealed to his age's fascination with antiquity, thus making his teaching more palatable and seemingly less radical. But in so doing, he rejected Livy and Polybius's arguments for the greatness of Rome.

Against Livy and Polybius's Rome

For Titus Livy, tumults and internal divisions in Rome between the nobles and the plebeians were a threat to its very survival. But for Machiavelli, this same conflict between the nobles and plebs favoured Rome's common good. Early in the *Discourses*, Machiavelli wrote, "I do not wish to fail to discourse of the tumults in Rome from the death of the Tarquins to the creation of the tribunes."[19] In contrast to Livy, for whom this period was a reign of confusion, Machiavelli argued that the tumults between the nobles and plebs were the "first cause of keeping Rome free."[20] Machiavelli's argument was unmistakably novel; he was alone in endorsing internal partisan conflict – often identified in his works as the "two humours" – as useful and good.[21]

In some of the more particular departures from Livy's *History of Rome*, Machiavelli also showed himself far from being a mere reviver of ancient teaching. A poignant example was his take on how Romulus had secured sole power in the founding of Rome. In his account of Romulus's murder of his brother Remus, Livy attributed it to the "same source which had divided their grandfather and Amulius: jealousy and ambition."[22] Yet Machiavelli explicitly disagreed: what Romulus "did was for the common good and not for his own ambition."[23] His disagreement with Livy came from consideration of the maxim from the same chapter, "that it never or rarely happens that any republic or kingdom is ordered well from the beginning or reformed altogether anew outside its old orders unless it is ordered by one individual."[24] Machiavelli looked at Livy's history through his new art of politics. Livy was a source and basis for the political histories of Rome, but this fact did not preclude Machiavelli from using much of Livy's substance and improving and remoulding it where the Roman historian failed to discern the effective teaching on maintaining regimes.

At the beginning of the sixth book of his *Histories*, Polybius endeavoured to explain how "in less than fifty-three years nearly the whole world was overcome and fell under the single dominion of Rome."[25] For Polybius, Rome's greatness was due to its ability to cultivate and preserve the virtues. This judgment of a regime's character, Polybius wrote, was no different from the judgment of character in a man: "The sole test of a perfect man is the power of bearing high-mindedly and bravely the most complete reverses of fortune, so it should be in our judgment of states."[26] The chief cause for Rome's success was its constitution; yet Polybius conceded that it was a complex constitution, evading classification in the three typologies of monarchy, aristocracy, and democracy. Polybius understood that the typologies were not exclusive, and that, furthermore, they were not very stable: as his regime cycles had shown, each type of regime had a vicious counterpart into which it would inevitably degenerate.

Polybius argued that the best regime was a mixed one: a state that combined the best virtues of the three types. Thus, the Roman constitution combined the good character of kingship in the office of the consuls, aristocracy in the senate, and democracy in the powers given to the plebs.[27] Therefore, Rome remained stable in the face of the natural decay of political constitutions and in the face of turmoil, its example was a "remedy for the evil which [each regime] suffered."[28]

But against Polybius, Machiavelli argued that Rome's greatness was not due to its cultivation of virtue. Instead of looking to the mixed regime, his first treatment of Rome in the *Discourses* turned to its founding. "Those who read what the beginning was of the city of Rome and by what legislators and how it was ordered," Machiavelli wrote, "will not marvel that so much virtue was maintained for many centuries."[29] Contrary to the Polybian claim that kingship and aristocracy was very different (though similar in form) from tyranny and oligarchy, Machiavelli concluded that all the regime types were pernicious because of the "likeness that virtue and vice have in [each] case."[30] Machiavelli dismissed Polybius's judgment that Rome's greatness was in its promotion of virtue through the mixed regime. Doubtless the mixed regime for Machiavelli had merit; however, the chief cause for Rome's success was not its preservation of the best of the three good types of regimes and the classical virtues they promoted. Rather, its free constitution had instituted good laws built upon good arms and knowing the effectual truths necessary for maintaining itself.

Polybius, in his comparison of Rome and other regimes, claimed that there were two essential things in its well-being: custom and laws. These customs and laws had a twofold purpose: to render the lives of citizens righteous and the character of the regime good and just.

> So just as when we observe the laws and customs of a people to be good, we have no hesitation in pronouncing that the citizens and the state will consequently be good also, thus when we notice that men are covetous in their private lives and that their public actions are unjust, we are plainly justified in saying that their laws, their particular customs, and the state as a whole are bad.[31]

Furthermore, Polybius connected the character of the regime to the well-being of the soul, as in the example of the constitution of Lycurgus. Spartan laws and customs, instituted by its constitution, promoted the invaluable virtues of "fortitude and temperance," and when these virtues were "combined in one soul or city," Polybius wrote, "evil will not readily originate within such men or peoples, nor will they be overmastered by their neighbors."[32] Even though Sparta's virtues and stability were different, Polybius argued that Rome nevertheless succeeded in maintaining good laws and customs like Sparta, and preserving itself and the goodness of its people even in times of great turmoil.

At first glance, Machiavelli's assessment of Rome in the first six chapters of the *Discourses* appeared similar to the Polybian treatment. There seemed to be a philosophical convergence: Polybius's reticence to introduce Plato's ideal regime "unless it first [gave] an exhibition of its actual working"[33] was superficially similar to Machiavelli's rejection of "imagined republics." Yet there was a major difference. Polybius dismissed Plato's city in speech, because although it was praiseworthy, it must first be shown to have actually existed. But Machiavelli objected to imaginary republics more than their impracticability; in the *Discourses* we see that Machiavelli took issue with this very vision of goodness and virtue, which in his thinking neglected the effectual truths necessary for founding and maintaining regimes.

Machiavelli began his third chapter of the *Discourses* with a glaring avowal of one of the effectual truths practised by ancient Rome, but ignored by the philosophers: "As all those demonstrate who reason on a civil way of life, and as every history is full of examples, it is necessary to whoever disposes a republic and orders laws in it to presuppose that all men are bad, and that they always have to use the malignity of spirit whenever they have a free opportunity for it."[34] Machiavelli claimed that Livy's *History of Rome* and his own study of the ancient republic demonstrated this effectual truth, and that a successful regime would be built upon it. For Machiavelli, it became a major factor in determining the strength of the Roman regime. For soon after Machiavelli opened the third chapter with the "malignity of spirit" inherent in humankind, he provided a poignant example of the Roman regime's strength. He described how "it appeared that in Rome there was a very great union between the plebs and the Senate after the Tarquins were expelled" and the nobles had taken on a "popular spirit."[35] But the nobles did not act humanely to the plebs out of goodness or some virtuous disposition; Machiavelli argued that the nobles acted this way out of fear that the plebs would not take their side in a possible conflict with the Tarquins, arguing that "men never work any good unless through necessity."[36] The Tarquinian conflict demonstrated to Machiavelli that Rome was constituted in such a way that fear and tumult were the very engine of Roman success and political virtue.[37] For Rome, the tumult between the plebs and the nobles, from its very foundation, made it great: "All the laws that [were] made in favor of freedom [arose] from their disunion."[38]

The Two Humours

For Machiavelli, the word *umore* (humour) had several meanings. It could designate the desires natural to a certain group; it could mean a certain social group within a regime; it might designate the activities produced by the interaction between certain groups; sometimes it referred to conflicts between regimes; it could even be used with an evaluative term, like healthy or malignant, to describe the forces of good and evil in a regime.[39] Most importantly for his political thought, and consistent with its use in *The Prince* and the *Discourses*, Machiavelli used *umore* to evaluate the strength of regimes. In *The Prince* he wrote that out of the conflict of the two humours, "one of three effects occurs in cities: principality or liberty or license."[40] A principality or republic was a regime built so that the conflicting humours had positive effects; licence designated the regime in which the humours were out of balance and thus produced ill effects.

Machiavelli's notion of humours was derived from a long pedigree of medical science, beginning with ancient Greek and Hellenistic physicians such as the Hippocratic school and Galen. From the ancient world to his day, medical science generally considered the constitution of the human body to be made from various humours; in Galen's view, for example, there were the four humours of blood, phlegm, yellow bile, and black bile, the balance of which would affect pain, health, sickness, and wellness. Deficiency or excess of one humour in quantity, quality, potency, or proportionality would affect one's constitution.[41] In ancient political thought, Plato, Aristotle, or Polybius looked upon a diseased regime as something analogous to a diseased body. Similarly, as disease of the body in the sixteenth century was understood through the disorder of the humours, Machiavelli understood political disease through analogous humours. In a living body, humours were active and in constant motion; a healthy body was one in which the humours were balanced in their interactions. Likewise in the *Discourses*, a healthy regime was not one in which the humours were quieted or eradicated, but one in which their moving desires and ambitions were brought together to energize the regime they constituted. Hence, Machiavelli insisted that tumult between the humours in Rome had made it great; an artful constitution of the regime had allowed it to flourish. Tumult, effectively used, maintained and aggrandized the regime.

In a disordered regime the humours wreaked destruction. The *Discourses* provided ample evidence of such excess and imbalance. For Machiavelli, so often accompanying these examples was a neglect of the effectual truths necessary to maintain regimes, a fault he thought all too apparent in the early sixteenth century. In the fifteenth chapter of the second part of the *Discourses*, Machiavelli offered examples of regimes that, through indecision, allowed ill humours to weaken them. One example Machiavelli got directly from Livy. In their war against the Romans, the Latins asked the Lavinians for aid, but the Lavinians deferred and delayed, coming "right outside the gate with their troops to give them help" only when the Latins had been defeated.[42] Another example was one in recent Florentine history, when King Louis XII of France was at war with Milan; Florence delayed ratification of a treaty with the king, on account of a humour in favour of the Duke of Milan, thereby compromising the city at the very moment when Louis was victorious over the forces of Duke Ludovico.

These delays in decision making were for Machiavelli sure signs of the want of an art of politics; it was an effectual truth that strategic decisions needed hard and fast resolve, particularly in times of war, lest malignant humours hurt and destroy the regimes they affected. Machiavelli demonstrated the effects of the resolve in strategic decision making. At the onset of the war between the Latins and the Romans, he cited the example of the Latin praetor Annius, who urged clarity and decisiveness in the Latin council's deliberations; likewise, in midst of the Punic Wars, Apollonides warned his fellow Syracusans "to detest ambiguity and tardiness in taking up a policy."[43] These examples demonstrated that resolve quelled malignant humours.

Malignant humours could be so destructive that it was often necessary to crush their leaders. Just as the lesson on resolve had been forgotten, this effectual truth was neglected time and again to the detriment of many regimes, including his own Florence. Machiavelli warned his readers with the example of Piero Soderini, gonfalonier of Florence until the Medicis returned to power in the spring of 1512.

> For besides believing that he could extinguish ill humors with patience and goodness and wear away some of the enmity to himself with rewards to someone, he judged (and often vouched for it with his friends) that if he wished to strike his opponents vigorously and to beat down his adversaries, he would have needed to take up extraordinary authority and break up civil equality together with the laws.[44]

Soderini ignored the effectual truth that it was necessary, if his regime was to survive, to "kill the sons of Brutus"; for "whoever makes a free state and does not kill the sons of Brutus," Machiavelli wrote, "maintains himself for little time."[45] Out of respect for goodness and order, Soderini allowed an ill humour to grow far out of proportion, threatening the very existence of the regime itself. For Machiavelli this was a massive mistake that ignored a necessary lesson in maintaining a regime through internal conflict.

Machiavelli's accounts of the two humours were at times unclear, but for him this confusion could be highly instructive. In the fifth chapter of the first book, they became scarcely distinguishable. Which humour was more ambitious or even which one was plebeian or noble could be confused. Was the desire to maintain more ambitious than the desire to acquire? Machiavelli collapsed the distinction between the desires: the desire to maintain produced the same desire to acquire as in the other humour, for the fear of losing possessions would not seem secure until new possessions were acquired.[46] What was clear was that "either one appetite or the other [could] be the cause of very great tumults," and this was essentially because the ambitions of each humour were similarly dynamic and malleable.[47] Machiavelli saw that fear and desire were universal passions among men, and thus ambitions would be manifested differently according to their different conditions. These conditions would dictate whether they feared for their possessions or were free to acquire without such concern. Machiavelli, as one scholar has noted, seemed to "view fear and desire as points on a continuum – one followed by and causally connected to the other."[48] Ambition for Machiavelli was ubiquitous and tempered only by conditions; these differing conditions among men created different humours. Hence, Machiavelli could remark that "whoever considers present and ancient things easily knows that in all cities and in all peoples there are the same desires and the same humors, and there have always been."[49]

Machiavelli argued that through its balance of humours Rome had not only been made stable, but that it had become *great*. He well knew that there were ancient and latter-day examples of strong states which had managed to severely restrict tumultuous faction; but Sparta and Venice were small, insular states that had suppressed conflicting humours at the cost of expansion and glory.[50] Rome's greatness and power in the world would have been sacrificed if it had similarly determined to purge its tumult. Machiavelli argued that "one inconvenience can never be suppressed without another's cropping up"; therefore, "if Rome wished to remove the causes of tumults, it removed too the causes of expansion."[51] Allowing the tumultuous humours to exist, Rome, through its constitution, was able to "vent" excessive energy so as not to bring itself to ruin. In Rome, political turmoil vented malignant humours.[52]

For Machiavelli, even the fall of the Roman republic did not contradict his argument that the enmities between the plebs and the nobles kept Rome free, though admittedly "the end of the Agrarian law [appeared] not to conform to this conclusion."[53] But for Machiavelli, this remained only an appearance, as the contention over the law took three hundred years to destroy the republic, and in would have been sooner had the Rome not vented the ambitions of the humours. The tumult was necessary to vent this ambition, otherwise the republic would have succumbed to the desires and fears of the plebs and nobles long before any rise to glory.

Machiavelli combined the two humours into a dynamic of fear and desire, the maintenance of which became the measure of Rome's strength and success. For Machiavelli, the Roman regime was in fact the model regime in understanding and dealing with this dynamic desire and fear. "Men are in motion and cannot stay steady," Machiavelli wrote; Rome was the regime which best understood and applied the effectual truths that derived from this maxim.[54] Machiavelli agreed with Livy and Polybius that indeed the Roman regime was stable. Yet for Machiavelli its stability was due not to maintaining and developing a good state through customs and laws based in a natural inclination to virtue, but to understanding the dynamic humours and knowing ultimately that men were bad and always use their "malignity of spirit." Rather than inculcating virtues such as courage or wisdom, at least as the first order of political business, Machiavelli's Rome inculcated the channelling of vice and called *that* virtue, all the while allowing desires to *expand* rather than remain static or decline. Machiavelli's political art was thus contrary to ancient wisdom – particularly Plato and Aristotle's – on the importance of reigning in *eros*, promoting the cardinal virtues, and holding to small, rooted regimes.[55] Rome, Machiavelli believed, was the proof of his art's success.

Machiavelli discouraged the emulation of imagined republics, yet the Roman regime was as deft in the art of politics as regimes could be. Yet there was also a persistent counter-example: Florence. Machiavelli's home city was an unhealthy one. Its humours waxed to excess or waned to inadequacy without balancing excesses and bringing the regime to health. Only an art of maintaining regimes could bring it to health and glory.

Conclusion

For Machiavelli, the Roman lessons of the *Discourses* would best serve Florence in her perennial political woes. Whereas Rome succeeded on using its internal conflict for the sake of glory, Florence succumbed to partisan conflict and external intrigue. A general ignorance of the art of politics in general was to blame. In his *History of Florence*, for example, Machiavelli justified his new history of his beloved city by arguing that the other histories were silent with respect to the "civil discords and internal enmities, and the effects rising from them."[56] Florence's internal divisions were quite remarkable, but their causes and effects are poorly understood. Thus he summed up the purpose of his history: "If no other lesson is useful to the citizens who govern republics, it is that which shows the causes of the hatreds and divisions within the city, so that when they have become wise through the dangers of others, they may be able to maintain themselves united."[57] The lessons on maintaining a regime through its divisions and tumult – the essential teaching of his *Discourses* through the example of Rome – was thus also the key lesson for his *History of Florence* as well as his art of politics in general. Machiavelli hoped that the study of his work would in some way recover this art, for with it Florence could not only be stable, but also great and glorious. For a civil servant who was barred from political affairs by a restored Medici regime, teaching this political art was a way to continue to serve a city he had claimed to love more than his soul.

NOTES

1 J.R. Hale, *Renaissance Europe: 1480–1520* (London: Collins, 1971), 275.

2 Hans Baron, *The Crisis of the Early Italian Renaissance* (Princeton, NJ: Princeton University Press, 1966) and "Machiavelli: The Republican Citizen and the Author of *The Prince*," *English Historical Review* 76 (1961); J.G.A. Pocock, *The Machiavellian Moment: Florentine Political Thought and the Atlantic Republican Tradition* (Princeton, NJ: Princeton University Press, 1975); Quentin Skinner, *The Foundations of Modern Political Thought*, vol. 1: *The Renaissance* (New York: Cambridge University Press, 1978).

3 See chap. 1, "Renaissance Epistolarity," in John M. Najemy, *Between Friends: Discourses of Power and Desire in the Machiavelli–Vettori Letters of 1513–1515* (Princeton: Princeton University Press, 1993); Paul Oskar Kristeller, *Renaissance Thought II* (New York: Harper & Row, 1965), 8ff. The importance of letter writing to Renaissance humanism is demonstrated by not only the production and collection of letters by literary persons of the period, but also the production of letter-writing manuals. For a famous example, see Erasmus of Rotterdam's *De conscribendis epistolis* [*On the Writing of Letters*], in *Collected Works of Erasmus*, vol. 25, ed. Charles Fantazzi (Toronto: University of Toronto Press, 1985).

4 There are two helpful compilations of Machiavelli's letters introducing the reader to his talents: Niccolò Machiavelli, *The Letters of Machiavelli: A Selection*, ed. Allan Gilbert (Chicago: University of Chicago Press, 1988) and Niccolò Machiavelli, *Machiavelli and His Friends: Their Personal*

Correspondence, ed. James B. Atkinson and David Sices (DeKalb: Northern Illinois University Press, 1996).

5 For an excellent collection of essays on the former genres, see Vickie Sullivan, ed., *The Comedy and Tragedy of Machiavelli: Essays on the Literary Works* (New Haven, CT: Yale University Press, 2000). See also Niccolò Machiavelli, *The Comedies of Machiavelli*, ed. David Sices and James B. Atkinson (Hanover, NH: University Press of New England, 1985) and Joseph Tusiani, *Lust and Liberty: The Poems of Machiavelli* (New York: I. Obolensky, 1963). In the introductory essay, Tusiani argues that Machiavelli's poetry was untypical Renaissance poetry for its realism.

6 See chap. 1, "The Birth of Humanist Culture," in Charles G. Nauert, Jr, *Humanism and the Culture of Renaissance Europe* (Cambridge: Cambridge University Press, 1995), 8–51.

7 Though he only quoted Petrarch two times in his major prose writings – once in *The Prince* (26) and once in the *Florentine Histories* (6.29) – he claimed to have read Petrarch regularly in his leisure time on the farm during his exile from active Florentine politics. This claim is found in Machiavelli's famous letter to Vettori of 10 December 1513, a letter which begins with a quotation from Petrarch's *Triumph of Eternity*: "Never late were favours divine"; *CW* 927–8, *Op.* 1158–9 (see n. 9 for these abbreviations). Cicero was quoted three times in the *Discourses* (1.4, 1.33, 1.52), though there were many allusions to him and his works in other passages in the *Prince* and *Discourses*.

8 Canzone 16.13–16.

9 Niccolò Machiavelli, *The Prince*, trans. Harvey C. Mansfield (Chicago: University of Chicago Press, 1985), chap. 26, p. 105; *CW* 96, *Op.* 298. Henceforth, direct quotations from *The Prince* will be taken from Mansfield's translation with chapter number followed by page number (*Prince* 26, 105). Quotations from the *Discourses* are from Niccolò Machiavelli, *The Discourses*, trans. Harvey C. Mansfield (Chicago: University of Chicago Press, 1996) and are also followed with chapter and page number. *CW* and *Op.* refer (respectively) to Niccolò Machiavelli, *Machiavelli: The Chief Works and Others*, 3 vols., trans. Allan Gilbert (Durham, NC: Duke University Press, 1965) and the Italian version, Niccolò Machiavelli, *Machiavelli: Tutte le Opere*, ed. Mario Martelli (Florence: Sansoni, 1971).

10 Harvey C. Mansfield, *Machiavelli's Virtue* (Chicago: University of Chicago Press, 1996), 34.

11 *De Officiis* 1.8; Marcus Tullius Cicero, *On Duties*. trans. Walter Miller (Cambridge, MA: Harvard University Press, 1997), 45.

12 *The Prince*, 18, 69–70; *CW* 64–5; *Op.* 283–4.

13 An argument soundly demonstrated by Paul Oskar Kristeller, *Renaissance Thought I* (New York: Harper & Row, 1961); cf. Nauert, *Humanism and the Culture of Renaissance Europe*, 8–51.
14 For example, Plato and Aristotle are each mentioned once in the *Discourses*: 3.6, 16 and 3.26, 2.
15 Aristotle, *The Politics*, 2, 1ff.; Cicero, *The Republic*, 2, 1ff.
16 *Discourses*, 1, preface, 5; *CW* 190; *Op.* 76.
17 J. Quentin Hughes and Norbert Lynton, *Renaissance Architecture* (London: Longmans, Green and Co., 1964), 3.
18 *Discourses*, 1, preface, 6; *CW* 191; *Op.* 76.
19 Ibid., 1.4, 16; *CW* 202; *Op.* 82.
20 Ibid. Cf. Titus Livy, *History of Rome*, 2, 23–33.
21 Mansfield, *Machiavelli's Virtue*, 92–7; "Introduction," *Discourses on Livy*, xxviii.
22 Titus Livy, *The Early History of Rome: Books I–V of The History of Rome from Its Foundation*, trans. Aubrey de Selincourt (London: Penguin Books, 1971), 1.6, 40. The grandfather (Numitor) and Amulius were sons of the Silvian kingship of the Latins; Amulius drove his older brother from the throne and unsuccessfully attempted to kill his brother's line, from which came Romulus and Remus (1.3).
23 *Discourses*, 1.9, 29; *CW* 218; *Op.* 91.
24 Ibid.
25 Polybius, *Histories*, trans. W.R. Paton (Cambridge, MA: Harvard University Press, 1979), book 6, para. 2.
26 Ibid., 6, 2.
27 Ibid., 6, 12–14.
28 Ibid., 6, 18.
29 *Discourses*, 1.1, 7; *CW* 192; *Op.* 77.
30 Ibid., 1.2, 11; *CW* 197; *Op.* 79.
31 *Histories*, 6, 47.
32 Ibid., 6, 48.
33 Ibid., 6, 47.
34 *Discourses*, 1.3, 15; *CW* 201; *Op.* 81.
35 Ibid., 1.3, 15; *CW* 201; *Op.* 82.
36 Ibid. Cf. *The Prince*, 15.
37 Cf. Montesquieu's treatment of fear and desire to promote the public good in Robert Sparling's chapter "Montesquieu on Corruption" below; I would argue that Machiavelli's treatment of Rome's greatness figures highly in Montesquieu's thinking on regime stability.
38 *Discourses*, 1.4.

39 Anthony Parel, *The Machiavellian Cosmos* (New Haven: Yale University Press, 1992), 105–7.

40 *The Prince*, 9, 39; *CW* 39; *Op.* 271. Parel, *The Machiavellian Cosmos*, 107.

41 See Mark Grant, ed., *Galen on Food and Diet* (London: Routledge, 2000), "Introduction," 1–13, and translation of Galen's "On the Humors" and "On Black Bile," 14–36; Parel, *The Machiavellian Cosmos*, 101.

42 *Discourses*, 2.15, 159; *CW* 362; *Op.* 165.

43 Ibid., 2.15, 159; *CW* 361; *Op.* 165.

44 Ibid., 3.3, 214–15; *CW* 425; *Op.* 198.

45 Ibid., 3.3, 214; *CW* 425; *Op.* 198. Cf. *Discourses* 1, 16; 3, 27.

46 Ibid., 1.5. See Mansfield, *Machiavelli's New Modes and Orders*, 47–8.

47 Ibid., 1.5, 19; *CW* 206; *Op.* 84.

48 Patrick Coby, *Machiavelli's Romans* (Lanham, MD: Lexington Books, 1999), 94.

49 *Discourses* 1.39, 83; *CW* 278; *Op.* 122.

50 Hence, for Machiavelli, Sparta was not the ancient regime fit for contemporary emulation. Sparta's fitness for modern imitation was a focus of contending Enlightenment political philosophies, as Varad Mehta aptly explains in his essay "Sparta, Modernity, Enlightenment" (chap. 10). See also Timothy Burns's treatment of Sparta (chap. 1).

51 *Discourses*, 1.6, 21; *CW* 209; *Op.* 85.

52 Ibid., 1.7.

53 Ibid., 1.37, 80; *CW* 274; *Op.* 120.

54 Ibid. 1.6, 22; *CW* 210; *Op.* 86.

55 This volume contains a wealth of scholarship on several classical Greek perspectives that contrast to Machiavelli's art of politics. Compare and contrast Thucydides's teaching on Athens, Sparta, and Pericles in Timothy Burns's chapter, or Roochnik and Weinman on Aristotle's political philosophy (chaps. 2 and 3). Though influential upon much of Enlightenment political thought, Machiavelli's argument for conflicting factions also contrasts with the attempts to curtail and limit faction in, for example, the political thought of David Hume (see Marc Hanvelt's essay below).

56 From Machiavelli's preface to the *History of Florence*, in *Florentine Histories*, trans. Laura F. Banfield and Harvey C. Mansfield (Princeton: Princeton University Press, 1988), 6.

57 Ibid.

7 Transforming "Manliness" into Courage: Two Democratic Perspectives

RYAN K. BALOT

Manliness is very fashionable today, not only among dictators, but also in the world's leading democracies. Only the naive will be surprised. US president George W. Bush often seized opportunities to show off his manly credentials, as did former president Ronald Reagan.[1] Prominent American authors such as Harvey C. Mansfield, Jr, have recently called for the revival of "manliness" in our supposedly gender-neutral society. Middle Eastern dictators still carry on the brutally manly traditions of the ancient kingdoms of the Near and Middle East. Has manliness ever been out of fashion?

No, it hasn't: manliness has been a cherished marker of status and social esteem from classical antiquity to the present. The classical republics prized manliness as their cardinal virtue. In fact, ancient writers often suggested that manliness was the best or even the whole of "virtue" – as in the Roman term *virtus*, "virtue," derived from the Latin word *vir*, "man" as opposed to "woman." The ancients typically argued that their republican forms of manliness were superior to those found in other regimes, particularly monarchies or tyrannies. As far back as the fifth century BCE, for example, Herodotus held that Greek "manliness" or "courage" (it's the same word in Greek: *andreia*) proved to be superior to that desperate, reckless "manliness" of the Persians under King Xerxes. The hyper-masculinity of the king meant the corrosion of masculinity among his servants. By contrast, Greek *andreia* was motivated by law and served the cause of political freedom; it was not driven by fear of a tyrant's punishments.

To understand manliness in a democratic perspective, I propose to examine its manifestations in the political discourse of two popularly self-governing republics: ancient Athens (from 508 to 322 BCE) and the United States of America (from roughly 1776 to 1840). Athens differed from the United States, of course, in being a comparatively small, self-contained, and direct democracy, as opposed to a representative democracy located in an extended or large-scale republic. One might point to other oppositions, too, such as polytheism versus monotheism, the premodern economy versus capitalism, and ancient "virtue" versus modern "right." Despite these differences, though, and despite the American founders' suspicion of direct democracy, I have chosen to explore Athens and early America alongside one another. As well-documented and carefully theorized embodiments of popular self-government, they both offer us significant empirical, speculative, and imaginative resources for understanding the relationship between democracy and manliness. In order to emphasize their similarity in this respect, I will consider each from the perspective of its popular sovereignty or "people-power," without, however, neglecting differences in their central practices, institutions, ideals, and intellectual foundations.

My chief point is that democracies give manliness a special character, by encouraging it to become, or at least to approximate, what it should have been in the first place, that is, courage. This idea poses an important challenge to recent exponents of "manliness." Because of their openness and self-questioning, democratic regimes specially advance the project of disentangling courage from manliness; and this is one of the key strengths of democracy. More than other regimes, democracies help their citizens to recognize that courage does not belong exclusively to men as opposed to women. Rather, democratic discourses and practices characteristically reveal that courage is the praiseworthy, firmly embedded disposition through which men and women confront dangerous or frightening circumstances in order to achieve admirable ends.[2] Discussion of this point will lead us to search for the distinctive shapes that courage might take in democracy. My approach is to evaluate the diverse perspectives on courage found in democratic Athens and in early America. Examining their special ideals of courage will both bring out important differences between these regimes and uncover the distinctive human goods that tend to be nurtured by popular republics altogether.

Contemporary Debates

Contemporary exponents of manliness usually find that men are in "crisis." Either manliness is not being used effectively, or men are now inadequate to their traditional roles, or they are too irresponsible to live up to their own commitments. Men have become soft, weak, effeminized – in short, not manly enough. The "new man" is no man at all. He is an androgynous mixture whose impurity constitutes a danger to all mankind.[3] Or have men, to the contrary, become hyper-manly, able to vindicate their manliness only in desperate acts of rage and aggression? According to many neoconservatives, notorious episodes such as the Columbine and Jonesboro shootings resulted directly from the undomesticated aggression of furious and neglected young men, who are themselves the victims of broken families and absent fathers.[4]

Undoubtedly, this ambiguity – the apparent effeminizing and hypermasculinizing of men, all at once – is unsettling to many men and women. This ambiguity, in fact, helps to explain why current perspectives on manliness vary so widely; think of the diverse views found among evangelical Christian "Promise Keepers," the "Men's Rights" movement, neoconservatives, and followers of the Jungian Robert Bly.[5] As disparate as they may be both in intention and in effect, however, these movements share two central tenets. First, they agree that men are now suffering through a profound crisis of meaning and identity – that manliness needs to be rescued or restored to a prelapsarian condition. Second, and more important for us, they strive not only to speculate about manliness or courage, but also definitively to answer the question of manliness, to define its shape, to fix its form, so as to limit the presumptive dangers of further confusion. But is it right to be unsettled by these confusions? Should we be quick to settle the questions? Or is it healthier and more democratic to "live the questions" (to quote Rilke), to embrace the provisionality of our practical responses?

According to recent exponents of manliness, the underlying cause of our social ills is clear: it's the feminists. For W.R. Newell, "Thirty years of stereotyping taught us to equate manliness with macho, piggish, violent behaviour. But according to the entire preceding tradition of the West (and, for that matter, the non-Western world), macho behaviour was considered unmanly, the very opposite of manliness. And that error, I will argue, is the source of the current crisis of manliness."[6] Newell argues that by criticizing patriarchy on the grounds of oppression, feminists destroyed all positive images of manliness. The feminist presentation of manliness led to a crisis in which young men could imagine no way to express their "rambunctious, competitive" male urges other than through acting out in reality the violence they learned from rap stars such as Eminem.[7]

Harvey Mansfield, by contrast, is less directly concerned about men's social destructiveness. Instead, he worries about the corrosion of traditional moral order, as well as the forms of fulfilment that, in his view, usually accompanied it. Despite the feminists' creation of a "gender-neutral" society, Mansfield says, "women still rather like housework, changing diapers, and manly men."[8] Nonetheless, many women have abandoned conventional domesticity. By contrast, Mansfield argues, men have sought to regain their traditional standing, and, to the extent that they have succeeded, they have done so only as a result of traumatic, world-changing events: "With the disaster of September 11, 2001, Americans were sharply reminded that it is sometimes necessary to fight, and that in the business of government, fighting comes before caring. Women were reminded that men can come in handy."[9] Traditional gender roles provided pathways to security and happiness that are now being frittered away, with no corresponding gains.

This worry leads to Mansfield's accusation that feminism is "nihilism," in so far as it "says that being a woman is nothing definite and that the duty of women is to advance that nothingness as a cause" (147). This paradoxically nihilistic duty is dangerous because women, according to Mansfield, do have a substantial nature; ignorance or neglect of the intrinsic ends of that nature leads to injustice, unhappiness, and ethical and political disintegration. By nature, women should take pride in "good housekeeping," which, along with "decorating and adornment," can be "a delight to the eye and the soul" (142). They should recognize that "women's bodies are made to attract and to please men" (155). Mansfield's attack on feminism as narrow, dishonest, and dangerous resonates with a long tradition – and a republican one at that: think of such strange bedfellows as Aristotle, Machiavelli, Rousseau, Kant, and Hegel – of supposing that men have natural and indefeasible privileges and that women's destinies lie in fulfilling men's purposes.

As Martha Nussbaum has argued, however, Mansfield's characterization of feminism corresponds badly to the work of such figures as de Beauvoir, Friedan, Gilligan, and others.[10] Moreover, and more importantly, I would say, Mansfield's antipathy to openness or provisionality in assuming gender roles, or in expressing traditionally gender-specific virtues, is both unhealthy and undemocratic. The drive to fix masculinity and femininity within essentializing stereotypes is unhealthy because it limits the possibility that men and women will cultivate the virtues traditionally associated with the other gender. Mansfield's insistence is undemocratic because it runs contrary to the openness and self-questioning characteristic of democracy at its best. Instead of being unsettled by prevailing cultural ambiguities, in fact, we might embrace provisional answers as the expression of our ongoing collective pursuit of more adequate understandings of our own questions about men and women. We might recognize in our confusions a persistent feature of popular, self-governing republics, such as Athens and America – namely, that these republics have always accommodated confusion or disorder, within limits, as the corollary to their practices of political and intellectual freedom, their rejection of traditional ideas, and their consequent openness to innovation and non-conformity. Democracy invites its citizens to "live the questions" in a deep and admirable way.

Disentangling Courage from Manliness

Instead of defending "manliness" from feminists, in fact, a more honest and constructive approach would disentangle courage from any fossilized associations with femininity and masculinity. For courage manifests itself in diverse spheres of worthy human accomplishment, not only those, such as warfare or acts of daring and aggression, which have historically characterized the display-oriented activities of a certain kind of man. Thus, when Socrates examined courage in the Platonic *Laches*, he wanted to establish an account of "courage" that encompassed "not only those who are courageous in warfare but also those who are brave in dangers at sea, and the ones who show courage in illness and poverty and affairs of state; and then again ... not only those who are brave in the face of pain and fear but also those who are clever at fighting desire and pleasure, whether by standing their ground or running away" (*Laches* 191d–e).[11]

More than this: Plato's Socrates was an intransigent critic of traditional Greek manliness and yet also a novel embodiment of authentic courage. As he pointed out to Callicles, a young man inflamed by conventional machismo, truly courageous human beings worry less about preserving their own lives through self-aggrandizing political schemes than about living nobly and well, and leaving the mere duration of their lives in the hands of the gods (Plato, *Gorgias*, 512c–e). Socrates developed new models of courage that thoughtfully transcended traditional gender roles.

We would do well to follow Socrates's example. For liberating courage from manliness enables us to grant respect more proportionately, more precisely, and more justly, to what is genuinely worthy of respect – namely, activities that are honest, generous towards others, truth-seeking, just, self-respecting, and dedicated to the common good. Granting respect in this way will free us from an all-too-familiar admiration for thoughtless audacity or recklessness, even when recklessness appears to be more noble or beautiful because of its association with "manliness."[12]

Yet courage is one of the few classical virtues (if not the only one) specifically and emphatically associated with one gender as opposed to the other. Men have long tried to preserve exclusive rights to courage, just as specifically militaristic men have often tried to use their defence of their homelands as a "protection racket" that provides them with disproportionate status and political privileges.[13] This is why we require special vigilance when well-placed authors begin to reassert these atavistic connections. Courage does not belong exclusively to men, nor is it more admirable when expressed by men. In Euripides's *Medea*, the title character (of all people) observes that women – virtually all women – show exceptional physical courage in the act of giving birth. It is no secret that women have often been in the front lines of change towards equal civil rights, distributive justice, and the emergence of democracy. Consider not only the American suffragist movement, but also the female protestors, writers, and activists who have agitated for equal pay, non-discrimination, and democracy in the Middle East.[14]

Most of these examples come from democratic contexts or movements, but perhaps critics will reply that Plato's Socrates was anti-democratic, and therefore that it takes a philosopher, not a democrat, to move beyond the equation of courage with manliness. My response to this thought is as follows: the efforts of Plato's Socrates to disentangle courage from manliness grew out of the democratic culture in which his thought arose. In Plato's dialogues, (the character) Socrates advanced in a more self-consistent way the possibilities for openness, self-questioning, and revision characteristic of the Athenian democratic experience.[15] Let me offer a single example to explain what I mean, one to which I return in a different way at the end of the chapter.

In 338 BCE, Demosthenes delivered his well-known funeral oration over the Athenians who had died at the Battle of Chaeronea. The Athenians had lost this battle to Philip II of Macedon, and at the time the Athenians, above all Demosthenes, envisioned their struggle against Philip II as a fight for their democratic freedoms altogether. Amidst many conventional *topoi*, Demosthenes concluded his speech with a single, but highly significant, twist. He says that, now that he has given an account of the ethical character and democratic principles that motivated the fallen soldiers, he will explain how their courage was stimulated in this case by referring, tribe by tribe, to the nobility and self-sacrifice of their tribal heroes. The Aegeidae, for example, recalled that Theseus, son of Aegeus, had established equality at Athens; consequently, soldiers from that tribe, Demosthenes says, could never have accepted inequality as the price of cowardly survival. Whatever we might think of Demosthenes's discussion of the emotional inspiration provided by such tribal heroes, it is crucial that he both characterizes the soldiers' own heroism as dedicated to democratic ideals such as equality and that he emphasizes the psychological forcefulness of these heroes within the Athenians' collective social imaginary.

The surprise is that many of these heroes were women. First, Demosthenes mentions the daughters of King Pandion, who took revenge on the Thracian king Tereus for raping Philomela, the sister of his wife Procne. Passing over the more grisly details of this story, Demosthenes concludes, "Therefore they decided that life was not worth living unless they, akin by race, should have proved themselves to possess equal spirit with those women, when confronted by the outrage they saw being committed against Greece" (Dem. 60.28).[16] In the same spirit, Demosthenes offers as an example of heroic courage the daughters of Leo, who "offered themselves to the citizens as a sacrifice for their country's sake" (60.29), thereby challenging the Athenians to show courage equal to their own. He then proceeds to describe the courageous activities of more traditional heroes such as Ajax and Antiochus, Heracles's son. Even in ancient Athens, and in a specifically martial context, Demosthenes held up both men and women as exemplars of the courage that he challenged his contemporaries to exhibit in their great wars of freedom.

Democratic courage, in Demosthenes's presentation, embodied openness to new ideas and willingness to reject or to improve upon tradition where possible. In the Athenian case, this openness extended not only to the inclusion of poor citizens in the military and a corresponding readiness to glorify their contributions, at state expense, in a public funeral and alongside the contributions of their aristocratic social superiors. Rather, and more important for our purposes, the Athenians' openness raised the possibility of a gender-free account of courage, in which men – even traditional fighting men – could internalize as heroes or role models not only Theseus and the "manly" sons of Heracles, but also the women whose audacious commitment to Athens's common good elicited the admiration of orators and soldiers alike. It is true that ordinary accounts of courage, even in Athens, did not always bespeak an effort to rid the city of the traditionally gendered associations of the virtues, and particularly courage. Yet Demosthenes's speech could have been delivered only in a non-traditional, inclusive, open, and free democracy ready to say and do what made sense at the time – not one inclined to repeat just any misguided platitudes that had been inherited from an outmoded past.

It is genuinely exceptional to find this degree of openness realized within actual political life in an ancient Mediterranean city. By way of comparison, consider Herodotus's story of the Egyptian King (Pharaoh) Sesostris, who subjugated many foreign nations from the Indian Ocean to Egypt. Herodotus says:

> Whenever he encountered a courageous enemy who fought valiantly for freedom, he erected pillars on the spot inscribed with his own name and country, and a sentence to indicate that by the might of his armed forces he had won the victory; if, however, a town fell easily into his hands without a struggle, he made an addition to the inscription on the pillar – for not only did he record upon it the same facts as before, but added a picture of a woman's genitals, meaning to show that the people of that town were no braver than women. (*The Histories*, 2.102)[17]

This is a far more common pattern among ancient Mediterranean peoples. What made the difference was the Athenians' democratic regime.

Manliness and Courage in Early America

When we turn to early America, we discover that "Publius" and Tocqueville, the authors with whom I primarily concern myself, often conflated courage with virility in a limiting way. (So too, as I mentioned, did the Athenian orators: their liberation of courage from its associations with manliness was only partial, occasional, and incomplete.) Yet it is crucial that, despite cultural contexts favouring traditional gender hierarchies, democracies of the past at least occasionally made space for newer, more progressive accounts of courage. By arguing that women's courage was exemplary and worthy of admiration by men, they implicitly asserted that courage did not belong exclusively to men. This view was progressive, even advanced, by comparison with the ideologies of non-democratic regimes, in which the conventionally gendered associations of courage could not even be publicly questioned.

Like Demosthenes, Tocqueville was aware that the democracy he observed exemplified openness to the possibility of women's courage. In fact, Tocqueville was convinced that the success of the Americans' democratic experiment depended on the unusual courage and vigour of the country's women.[18] In Tocqueville's view, American women were brought up to be rational, autonomous, and courageous – to the same degree, in their own spheres, as men were in their spheres. Hence, even though Tocqueville opposed gender neutrality,[19] he was adamant in praising the tough-mindedness and moral clarity that he saw as characteristic of American women:

> Thus the Americans do not think that man and woman have the duty or the right to do the same things, but they show the same esteem for the role of each of them; and they consider them as beings whose value is equal although their destiny differs. They do not give the same form or the same employment to the courage of woman as to that of man, but they never doubt her courage; and if they deem that man and his mate should not always employ their intelligence and reason in the same manner, they at least judge that the reason of one is as sure as that of the other, and her intelligence as clear. Americans, who have allowed the inferiority of woman to subsist in society, have therefore elevated her with all their power to the level of man in the intellectual and moral world; and in this they appear to me to have admirably understood the true notion of democratic progress.[20]

What Is "Democratic" Courage? American Reflections

Instead of talking about manliness, I maintain, we should be talking about courage; and, instead of thinking of either manliness or courage in universal terms, we should strive to understand their regime-specific expressions. If this view is correct, then what should courage be in popular, self-governing democracies? How might courage either consistently manifest or fruitfully counteract or newly improve the essential principles of the regime? It is striking how infrequently the combatants in our contemporary struggle, whether pro-feminist or pro-manliness, refer to the democratic regime assumed as the backdrop of their conversations.[21]

By contrast, traditional American discourse offers a more adequately democratic understanding of courage. *The Federalist* and *Democracy in America* offer three perspectives on democratic courage that are worthy of careful consideration for our purposes.[22] These central ideas are (1) courage as the political virtue by which we establish novel political institutions, free of past ideologies; (2) courage as the civic virtue by which we take initiative and take responsibility for our own lives, in concert with others; (3) courage as the military virtue by which we defend freedom in full awareness of freedom's importance for living a good human life.

First, Publius explains courage as the collective capacity of the American people to create something new and important in the world. Specifically, the courage of the American republic consisted in rational, independent self-government and thus in the rejection of traditional political ideas or hierarchies. Hence, for Publius, American courage enabled the new nation to vindicate the cause of freedom as opposed to chance and necessity, by expanding the opportunities for self-government and liberty throughout the world.[23]

At the end of his first thematic section (essays 1–14), which discusses the necessity of Union, Publius triumphantly concludes with praise of the Americans' "manly spirit":

> And if novelties are to be shunned, believe me the most alarming of all novelties, the most wild of all projects, the most rash of all attempts, is that of rending us in pieces, in order to preserve our liberties and promote our happiness. But why is the experiment of an extended republic to be rejected merely because it may comprise what is new? Is it not the glory of the people of America, that whilst they have paid a decent regard to the opinions of former times and other nations, they have not suffered a blind veneration for antiquity, for custom, or for names, to overrule the suggestions of their own good sense, the knowledge of their own situation, and the lessons of their own experience? To this manly spirit, posterity will be indebted for the possession, and the world for the example of the numerous innovations displayed on the American theatre, in favour of private rights and public happiness.[24]

Publius is arguing that the extended popular republic, united by an energetic central government, is the best political solution to America's need for security and its desire for free, republican institutions. He is duly aware that virtually all previous political philosophers had cast doubt on the possibility of extended republics. He has conscientiously explored the manifold ways in which modern federations had tended to collapse under the weight of local interests. And he would go on to show, in subsequent essays, that the free republics of classical antiquity had been too turbulent and insecure to provide model institutions for this newly independent nation. In light of these obstacles, he argues, Americans must show themselves to be non-conformists with respect to the entire European political tradition, ancient or modern. They had to think for themselves and to account for the goodness of their novel institutional designs before the entire world. The Americans' willingness to "dare to be wise," as Kant had once written, to institutionalize their freedom in ways that made sense for their existing local alliances and political cultures, required the courage of all Americans to act collectively for the welfare of the nation. The courage of republican American citizens lay not only in thinking differently, but also in pragmatically shaking off the burdens of historical legacies, contingencies, and ideals that no longer fit their new situation.

Second, Tocqueville found in America's more developed political institutions and practices certain democratic expressions of courage and self-assertion that counterbalanced America's burgeoning commitment to heroic avarice.[25] In his account of democratic jury service, for example, Tocqueville argued that the jury is a pragmatic "school" educating citizens in their civic rights and responsibilities: "The jury teaches each man not to recoil before responsibility for his own acts – a virile disposition without which there is no political virtue."[26] Both here and in the previously cited passage of *The Federalist*, we can accept the essential idea and dispense with the "manly" overtones, for what both authors aim to uncover is the disposition of courage in the sense of taking "ownership" of one's own behaviour. And it is this focus on taking initiative and accepting responsibility that underlies Tocqueville's conception of courageous democratic citizenship. From our perspective, there need be nothing especially masculine about democratic courage, but there is something essentially democratic about it, in that the quintessentially democratic civic service, jury duty, teaches citizens, in Tocqueville's view, to take responsibility for their own actions and to take initiative in asserting rights and realizing political opportunities.

This conception of civic courage is democratic both in origin and in practice.[27] In further developments of the same theme, Tocqueville observes that "in democratic countries the science of association is the mother science; the progress of all the others depends on the progress of that one."[28] In associations, whether civil or political, ordinary individuals can realize their power to think through and accomplish their own aims through uniting with their fellow citizens. Through such exemplary practices of republican citizenship, all individuals learn to take the initiative, to think and act creatively, and to take responsibility for their own lives in the context of civic friendship. They do so in such a way as to preserve their independence or autonomy, but they also come to recognize the ways in which they are naturally sociable, the ways in which they can enlarge and renew their souls, to adapt Tocqueville's language, through activities of reciprocity, recognition, and mutual assistance.

Through his analysis of democratic associations, Tocqueville offers a novel conception of distinctively democratic courage. Democratic courage is that excellence of character enabling citizens to take the initiative in constituting groups of like-minded individuals in order peaceably to create socially worthwhile goods. This is a specifically democratic mode of taking responsibility for one's own life, which Tocqueville carefully distinguishes from the modes of both despotism and aristocracy. Despots, on the one hand, make "a sort of public virtue of indifference," whereas aristocrats favour individual initiative only among the few.[29] Aristocrats also tend to reject innovation and creativity altogether, outside certain highly circumscribed spheres such as the literary or plastic arts. Although Tocqueville spoke in the gendered language that he knew, often describing courage with reference to virility, it is plausible to see in the women's movement as such, both in organizations such as NOW and in the suffragist movement and elsewhere, precisely the same embodiment of initiative and courageous willingness to take responsibility for or "ownership" of one's own life that Tocqueville praised in the democratic mother science. It should come as no surprise that Tocqueville praised the American "legislators" for entrusting citizens with the administration of local politics, so that they would come to cherish the common good and come to recognize the social power created by associational activity.[30]

Third, in the final chapters of volume 2, part 3 of *Democracy in America*, Tocqueville presents what is perhaps the culmination of the entire work: his own analysis of honour in democratic societies.[31] This may be the work's culmination, I say, because democracies face particular difficulties, according to Tocqueville, in cultivating appropriate pride in their own accomplishments. Democratic societies are, in Tocqueville's view, all too frequently driven towards quotidian, bourgeois mediocrity.

Hence, it is an urgent question whether democracy can nurture a proportionate and moderate ethos of ambition, whether it can seek honour or even greatness in a suitable way.

In more specifically military terms, in fact, democratic republics face a variety of distinctive problems. On the one hand, they must curb the turbulence of democratic military culture, which is pervaded by a novel competitiveness and bellicosity among the officers. Yet they must also keep alive civil freedoms by resisting the inevitable trends towards centralized power brought on by warfare. And finally, they must ensure that, despite the regime's egalitarian principles, the citizen-soldiers will show respect to their officers, if they happen to be recruited.

According to Tocqueville, it is impossible, for better or worse, to transform democracy into a glory-seeking, hierarchical, and militaristic aristocracy, which ordinarily encounters none of the foregoing hazards. The only real solution, he says, is the enlightenment of the citizenry: "Have enlightened, regulated, steadfast, and free citizens, and you will have disciplined and obedient soldiers."[32] Democratic maturity in freedom and self-government will carry a properly moderated and reasoned courage (not a revolutionary spirit) into the army. "Democratic peoples naturally fear trouble and despotism. It is only a question of making reflective, intelligent, and stable tastes out of these instincts."[33] Thus, democracy can, if properly educated in the practices of freedom, raise the citizenry out of instinctual behaviour and produce reflective and intelligent modes of both self-government and, as we now see, warfare. This will protect the regime against excessive governmental centralization and will produce an army "pervaded by the love of freedom and the respect for rights" characteristic of the people as a whole.[34]

Admittedly, readers might worry over Tocqueville's disturbingly admiring hints of democratic imperialism, as well as his belief that warfare as such enlarges the soul and usefully shakes citizens from the complacency of their self-satisfied materialism. For us, on the other hand, Tocqueville's idea that the democratic regime creates habits of mind for democratic soldiers is crucial. He makes the point explicit at the end of chapter 25 in this section.[35] His argument is that military courage is expressed differently in democracies and aristocracies, respectively. Democratic courage is "intelligent," its "root" lying in "the very will of the one who obeys; it is supported not solely by his instinct, but by his reason."[36] By contrast, the soldier in the aristocratic armies, that is, the serf, "acts without thinking" and is "a very formidable animal trained for war" who shows the "blind, minute, resigned, and always equable obedience that aristocratic peoples impose on" their soldiers without trouble. According to Tocqueville, democracy transforms the foundations of military courage, which is now based less on an instinctive drive than on the rational and articulate will of each individual.

What Is "Democratic" Courage? Athenian Reflections

When we ask Publius and Tocqueville to explain the ends of democracy as a regime, we discover a variety of responses, commensurate perhaps with the variety of their descriptions of manliness or courage. Both Publius and Tocqueville saw the Americans' courageous political experiment as dedicated to protecting private rights and expanding public happiness. It is logically possible, no doubt, to square these ideals with Publius's notion that the American experiment would enlarge political freedom throughout the world, and even with his idea that "justice is the end of government."[37] But alongside these stirring words, what emerges most powerfully from our examination of American courage is that neither Publius nor Tocqueville offers a clear or systematic account of the goods, whether common or individual, that courage makes available – or indeed of how courage itself is intrinsically a component of a good human life, if indeed it is so. In order to define the ends of the regime, the American tradition pointed to justice, freedom, private rights, equality, active citizenship, security, and peace. But its most prominent writers offer no coherent explanation of how these ideals might cooperate, if they do cooperate, in the living of a good democratic, or human, life.

Moreover, and more importantly, neither Publius nor Tocqueville is at all inclined to believe that the American citizens *themselves* will be able to offer an account of how their courageous activities, undertaken individually or as a collectivity, might contribute to or partially constitute a good human life. While the American republican tradition, as we have interpreted it, does offer many attractive ideas about courage and its instrumental functions, neither Publius nor Tocqueville develops the analytical vocabulary that would enable them to explain why democratic citizens, in particular, were well positioned by their regime to live excellent human lives, and how their distinctively democratic courage contributed to, made possible, and partially constituted the excellence of those lives. In order to explain that point, we would do well to return to the democratic practices and discourses of classical Athens.

Despite the ethical and political shortcomings of democratic Athens, it is possible to look to the ancient democratic past in order to recover its most meritorious possibilities. I agree with Timothy Burns (see chapter 1) that the Periclean vision of democratic Athens is unstable to the extent that it fails to consider the injustice of imperialism alongside its self-professed domestic practices of justice. From democratic ideology in general, however, it is possible to recover ideas of democracy, virtue, and human flourishing that we ourselves might find attractive.[38] For our own purposes, we can render these possibilities clear, within a more systematic framework than the Athenians themselves did, in order to see whether their intellectual resources can still bear fruit in our own day. And when we do so, I submit, we can supplement our modern traditions, specifically by uncovering a non-utilitarian paradigm in which courage is understood as both a product of the Athenians' specifically democratic regime and as an essential human excellence that at least partially constitutes a life well lived.

Let us return to Demosthenes's funeral oration, delivered after the Battle of Chaeronea in 338 BCE. After praising the fallen soldiers for scorning life and acquisitiveness, and dying in a noble cause, Demosthenes pointedly emphasized that his own role as funeral orator would be easy to fulfil if courage were these men's only admirable attribute. But in fact, he argues, their goodness consists in their development of nobility and excellence in a wide range of spheres, courage being only one element of their universal goodness. From within democratic politics, strikingly, Demosthenes voices criticisms of acquisitiveness and imperialism in ways that Tocqueville himself would have found persuasive. But, unlike his modern counterparts, Demosthenes is chiefly concerned with the excellences of character that constitute a flourishing life, and he persistently locates his treatment of courage within that rich context. Thus, in addition to their battlefield courage, the Athenians also characteristically exhibited justice, self-restraint, and self-respect based on their appropriate consciousness of their own nobility. Their courage was meaningful and praiseworthy only because it served the purposes of these even higher and more excellent qualities of soul. As the "Athenian Stranger" said in Plato's *Laws* (630c–d, 631c–d), and as Demosthenes said from within Athenian democratic politics, courage ranked at most fourth among the human excellences.

Through a long history of democratic discourse, the Athenians had arrived at a proportionate recognition of the significance of their courage: courage was important, yes, but it should not overshadow or control the other virtues. (Within the ancient Mediterranean context, one might contrast their view with the outlook of Achilles or the "Spartan mother" or the Macedonian king Alexander III, known as the "Great.") The Athenians reached this level of self-knowledge because of their cognitively rich, rationally articulate understanding of the essence and purposes of courage. Like other Athenians, the soldiers themselves had a self-conscious understanding of their courage and their military goals that was adequate to their brilliant actions. Their courage was informed by a rational account of the goods that they courageously sought. Demosthenes put this point as follows:

> Arrived at manhood they rendered their innate nobility known, not only to their fellow-citizens, but to all men. For of all virtue, I say, and I repeat it, the beginning is understanding and the fulfillment is courage; by the one it is judged what ought to be done and by the other this is carried to success. In both these qualities these men were distinctly superior.[39]

The Athenians' rational and self-conscious adherence to ideals of justice, honesty, and courage gave special point to Demosthenes's striking contrast between their physical deaths and their psychological triumph. Whereas these soldiers' deaths in battle were the product of chance or circumstance, their spirits proved to be unvanquished by any opponents.[40] "The freedom of the whole Greek world," according to Demosthenes, "was being preserved in the souls of these men,"[41] because, even in death, they stood fast in their dedication to ideals of freedom, justice, and self-government – ideals that they had raised to consciousness through their democratic discourses, rituals, and political practices.

In Demosthenes's view, the Athenians' courage was directly attributable to Athens's democratic regime, as opposed to the oligarchies and dynasties of their foes.[42] In regimes ruled by the few, he argues, soldiers are motivated at most by fear of their masters. They tend to flee danger, because they lack regime-based ideals that motivate, guide, and explain their actions. If they flee, he says, they can always ingratiate themselves with the rulers after the fact and thus be restored to favour, for purely arbitrary reasons. Democracies, by contrast, cultivate a sense of shame, which is embodied in the citizens' awareness of the regime's most praiseworthy ideals. This awareness is expressed in the reproaches made by free-speaking citizens against those who fail fully to exhibit those ideals in practice. By contrast with non-democratic political cultures, the Athenian democracy made praise and blame impartial, public, and just. As a result, democratic free speech, nobility, and courage were linked in a coherent, reflective, and publicly articulated system that gave meaning to the Athenian democrats' willingness to sacrifice their lives at Chaeronea.

Conclusion: Courage and Democracy, Ancient and Modern

The foregoing investigation has uncovered two cardinal points of difference between the Athenian and the American democracies. First, although contemporary observers in both periods identified connections between courage and the regime, the Athenians offered a more robustly democratic account. They presented their rational account of democratic courage as a self-conscious feature of public discourse, which all citizens were meant to comprehend, internalize, and make available to themselves as a guide to practical, context-specific deliberation. By contrast, Publius envisioned the Americans' manliness as passionate and instinctual, and thus as less dependent on a public, articulate discourse. Tocqueville, meanwhile, agreed with the ancient Athenians that democratic courage was rational and articulate, but he provided little explanation of the democratic discourses that fostered the development of the cognitively rich democratic courage that he found so admirable. It is fair to say that the Athenians more fully "leveraged" the specifically democratic qualities of free speech and equality in developing a regime-specific account of courage.

Second, and more important, Demosthenes (like other Athenian orators) used his funeral oration to develop a distinctive account of nobility or excellence that was meant to be intrinsically good, worthwhile, and dignified. In his vision of the Athenians' flourishing lives, courage was one of the constituents of the good life, albeit not the most important one. Courage was intrinsically worthy of choice both for this reason and for its orientation towards even higher, and also intrinsically good, ideals such as justice, loyalty, freedom, and equality. This account of human excellence and human flourishing, found incipiently in Athenian democratic ideology, was expanded and developed by Plato and Aristotle and the later ancient and medieval philosophical traditions. It is important that the ancient tradition of "eudaimonism" got its start in the culture of free speech and egalitarian social relations characteristic of the Athenian democracy.[43]

Yet, despite these differences, we have discovered in both Athens and the United States ideals of democratic courage that are specifically related to the regime – ideals that manifest democracy's central organizing principles. Whether ancient or modern, democracies encourage their citizens to make judgments for themselves about what their specific, contingent circumstances demand. The contemporary debates over manliness and courage are precisely the product of such a non-negotiable commitment to free speech and to thinking for oneself. Whichever arguments are stronger, the debate itself is the sign of a healthy, courageous democracy – one that invites its citizens to live the questions, not to shut them down in favour of traditional, essentializing stereotypes. Exploring courage openly and with an eye towards our most fundamental ideals, such as freedom, justice, and equality, is the best way to pursue the good life in common. This conception of democratic possibilities, integrally tied to democratic courage, should make us hopeful even about conversations that must work, all over again, to show that manliness is far from adequate to the human excellence encapsulated by democratic courage.

NOTES

1 On Bush's manipulation of images of "manliness," see my essay "The Dark Side of Democratic Courage," *Social Research* 71.1 (Spring, 2004), 73–106; on Reagan, see Susan Jeffords, *Hard Bodies: Hollywood Masculinity in the Reagan Era* (New Brunswick, NJ: Rutgers University Press, 1994).

2 Among the many helpful analyses of courage, see Douglas N. Walton, *Courage: A Philosophical Investigation* (Berkeley: University of California Press, 1986) and William Ian Miller, *The Mystery of Courage* (Cambridge, MA: Harvard University Press, 2000).

3 I am alluding to Mary Douglas, *Purity and Danger: An Analysis of Concepts of Pollution and Taboo* (London: Routledge and Kegan Paul, 1966).

4 See, for example, W.R. Newell, *The Code of Man: Love, Courage, Pride, Family, Country* (New York: HarperCollins, 2003).

5 A useful analysis of contemporary perspectives on masculinity can be found in Kenneth Clatterbaugh, *Contemporary Perspectives on Masculinity: Men, Women, and Politics in Modern Society*, 2nd ed. (Boulder, CO: Westview Press, 1997).

6 Newell, *The Code of Man*, xvii.

7 Ibid., xx, xxiii.

8 Harvey C. Mansfield, Jr, *Manliness* (New Haven: Yale University Press, 2006), 6, 12.
9 Ibid., 11.
10 Martha Nussbaum's review of Mansfield makes the point clearly and well: Martha C. Nussbaum, "Man Overboard," *The New Republic*, June 2006.
11 Plato, *Laches and Charmides*, trans. Rosamund Kent Sprague (Indianapolis, IN: Hackett Publishing Co., 1973).
12 For a helpful account of the ways in which activities might gain in stature through association with courage or manliness, see George Kateb, "Courage as a Virtue," *Social Research* 71.1 (Spring 2004), 39–72.
13 For an exploration of this hypothesis, see Barbara Ehrenreich, *Blood Rites: Origins and History of the Passions of War* (New York: Henry Holt and Co., 1998).
14 On Middle Eastern democracy, see, for example, Nicholas Kristoff's article on the pro-democratic uprisings in Cairo: http://www.nytimes.com/2011/02/03/opinion/03kristof.html?_r=1&hp.
15 I explore these ideas more fully in "Democracy and Political Philosophy: Influences, Tensions, Rapprochement," in *The Greek Polis and the Invention of Democracy: A Politico-Cultural Transformation and Its Interpretations*, ed. Johann P. Arnason, Kurt A. Raaflaub, and Peter Wagner (Oxford: Blackwell, 2013), 181–204. In doing so, I build on J. Peter Euben, *Corrupting Youth: Political Education, Democratic Culture, and Political Theory* (Princeton: Princeton University Press, 1997).
16 Throughout the paper, translations of Demosthenes are taken from Demosthenes, *Funeral Speech; Erotic Essay; Exordia; Letters*, trans. Norman W. DeWitt and Norman J. DeWitt, Loeb Classical Library 374 (Cambridge, MA: Harvard University Press, 1949).
17 Herodotus, *The Histories*, trans. Aubrey de Sélincourt, rev. John Marincola (New York: Penguin Books, 1954/1972).
18 Alexis de Tocqueville, *Democracy in America*, trans. Harvey C. Mansfield and Delba Winthrop (Chicago: University of Chicago Press, 2000), 2, 3.12. I have cited passages from Tocqueville in accordance with Mansfield and Winthrop's table of contents, that is, by volume, part, and chapter.
19 Ibid.
20 Ibid. On Tocqueville's discussion of the courage of American women, one might also compare the more extended treatment of Richard Avramenko, *Courage: The Politics of Life and Limb* (Notre Dame, IN: University of Notre Dame Press, 2011), 225–32.
21 While Mansfield and Newell agree that traditional liberalism strove to quash manliness (think of Hobbes's diatribes against honour), and thus

promoted feminism *avant la lettre*, only Newell pursues Tocqueville's question of whether democracy can produce great men (e.g., *The Code of Man*, 213–15). Yet, beyond these gestures, few recent writers have explored in any sustained way whether there is a distinctively democratic or republican form of courage, manliness, or femininity.

22 These texts also offer other, diverse and interesting reflections on courage to which I will not draw attention in the present context. Most important, Tocqueville found that democratic America had, indeed, constructed a novel, anti-aristocratic conception of courage – one devoted not to traditional glory or bellicosity, but rather to risk taking in the service of satisfying the acquisitive passions. Here Tocqueville uncovered an ideal of courage and manliness that was perhaps excessively consistent with the avaricious ends of the democratic regime – and hence an ideal that, through helping selfishness to accomplish its narrow ends, threatened to compromise the civil freedoms for which he so admired America. On these subjects, one should contrast the treatment of Avramenko (note 20, above). Or, differently, Publius found that individual leaders, particularly the executive, needed "courage and magnanimity" in order to resist the temporary passions and ill-considered judgments of the people, and thus to "serve them at the peril of their displeasure" (*The Federalist*, no. 71), while all branches of government required fortitude to resist the potential encroachments of other branches. These requirements of courage were peculiar to American federalism, on the one hand, and distinctive of democracies and republics, on the other, in so far as they called upon individual leaders, in a context of popular accountability, to risk their political futures for the sake of the common good.

23 On this theme, see especially David F. Epstein, *The Political Theory of* The Federalist (Chicago: University of Chicago Press, 1984).

24 *The Federalist*, no. 14.

25 *Democracy in America*, 1, 2.10.

26 Ibid., 1, 2.8.

27 For further reflections on democracy's broadening of the "field" of courage to include civic (as opposed to exclusively military) courage, see my essay "Free Speech, Courage, and Democratic Deliberation," in *Free Speech in Classical Antiquity*, ed. I. Sluiter and R.M. Rosen (Leiden: Brill, 2004), 233–59.

28 *Democracy in America*, 2, 2.5.

29 Ibid., 2, 2.4.

30 Ibid.

31 For a compatible treatment that differs somewhat in emphasis from mine, see Kateb, "Courage as a Virtue," 65–7.

32 *Democracy in America*, 2, 3.22.
33 Ibid.
34 Ibid., 2, 3.23.
35 Ibid., 2, 3.25.
36 Ibid.
37 *The Federalist*, no. 51.
38 I explore these connections in more detail in my book *Courage in the Democratic Polis: Ideology and Critique in Classical Athens* (New York: Oxford University Press, 2014).
39 Demosthenes, *Funeral Speech*, 60.17.
40 Ibid., 60.19.
41 Ibid., 60.23.
42 Ibid., 60.25–6.
43 For elaboration of this point, see my article "Democracy and Political Philosophy" (note 15, above).

8 Montesquieu on Corruption: Civic Purity in a Post-Republican World

ROBERT SPARLING

The term "corruption" has a curious place in modern political thought. It hearkens back to a philosophical tradition that conceives of civic life in teleological terms, capable of integrity, purity, or health, but ever in danger of dissolution, impurity, and disease. Corruption discourse is political morality.[1] If one eliminates the teleological dimension, one is left with no basis for the distinction between corruption and other types of crime. The ubiquity of the term is thus surprising given widespread liberal disavowal of moral "perfectionism," or indeed of political morality of any sort. Thus, the term is regularly deployed in a technocratic manner by people largely inattentive to its theoretical underpinnings.[2] The difficulty is that there are radically different deployments of the term "corruption" indicating radically divergent conceptions of the good, and the standard definition employed by the World Bank and the IMF – "abuse of public office for private gain" – raises more questions than it answers, leaving to its users the duty of determining, among other things, what constitutes abuse and what is the right relationship between public and private. As with so many polysemous political terms, the concept of corruption is a locus of political contestation.

The clash between competing conceptions of corruption is often attributed to cultural factors, with global anti-corruption campaigners being accused of cultural insensitivity, or even imperial mindsets (and with the return charge of cultural relativism).[3] And if cross-cultural deployments of the term appear to run roughshod over difference, so do trans-historic examples. The most cursory study of history reveals a wide array of activities considered acceptable in one period and corrupt in the next.[4] But before we attribute divergent uses of the concept to divergent historical or cultural perspectives, it is equally worth remembering that the clashes between competing conceptions of corruption also follow a logic of regime forms – competing conceptions of civic health depend on competing civic structures and their attendant social psychologies. If the liberal discourse of corruption has tended to eschew notions of collective purity or collective civic decay, there is an equally strong strand of civic republicanism in modern political thought that thinks of corruption in societal terms, with images of civic health borrowed from ancient Rome or the Greek *polis*.[5] But reviving republican civic virtue in the modern, commercial world is a project that has been replete with tensions and contradictions since the eighteenth century – tensions that are particularly manifest in contemporary liberal political thinkers who don (metaphorically) Roman togas.[6]

We have seen in this volume many examples of modernity's fraught relationship to classical republican virtue. It emerges with particular clarity in the chapters on eighteenth-century thought. Marc Hanvelt indicates the manner in which Hume carefully reinterpreted and subverted the classical virtue of courage; for contrast, Varad Mehta reminds us of the heady Laconophilia of Rousseau, Ferguson, and Mably. Among Enlightenment thinkers, however, none had such a subtle take on the legacy of the classical republic as Charles-Louis de Secondat, Baron de Montesquieu. And there is arguably no modern thinker who has better understood the manner in which corruption is thoroughly tied to the type of regime being discussed. Montesquieu's treatment of corruption is entirely in conversation with the classical question of the best regime. But there is something paradoxical about his adoption of this classical theme. Montesquieu employed the term corruption in a manner that was neutral, and relative to different regime forms, yet he also employed it as a normative anchor. Equally puzzling to many interpreters is Montesquieu's thoughtful ambivalence towards classical republicanism. For those seeking a substantive normative basis for corruption theory, the clearest source to turn to is the modern neo-Roman republicanism associated with Machiavelli and his subsequent "moments." But modernity's relationship to fierce Roman republicanism is – and ought to be – ambivalent at best. Montesquieu offers us a reflection on the varieties of modern corruption that simultaneously appeals to this source and rejects it in the name of a liberalism with which we are most familiar. In Montesquieu's thought we will see a particularly modern, liberal view of corruption that explains its structural, constitutional dimensions. It is a position that embraces the moral dimension of corruption discourse, but does so with highly moderated ethical ambitions that make it appealing to a liberal world wary of "perfectionism."

This chapter is structured as follows: the first section looks at both relative and absolute corruption in Montesquieu's thought. It indicates that the type of relative corruption – that which causes a regime to change form – is linked to the absolute corruption that Montesquieu sees in the "principle" of despotism. All these forms of corruption entail a shift in the affective basis of the regime away from that which turns citizens' and subjects' energies towards the public good. We will see that the two passions that most detract from human sociability are fear and desire for wealth and luxury – those passions that are most in evidence under despotism. The second section will demonstrate that Montesquieu's view of natural sociability has its anchor in his brief foray into natural law. Montesquieu's imaginary construction of the state of nature offers a thin but normatively important conception of purity, but it equally points to the essential corruptibility of human beings in political society. The third section looks at his portrayal of England, exploring the manner in which Montesquieu thought corruptibility could best be contained and moderated. Here we will note the degree to which England is awash in the corrupting passions; its moderation is a result of an extremely precarious balance of corruption. For Montesquieu, the price of heroic Roman purity was too high, bloody without and stifling within; the solution of commercial modernity is a pact with corruption – not a pact with Mephistopheles, but a pact with a grubbier, duller, more English demon, perhaps one resembling Robert Walpole.[7]

Montesquieu's Varieties of Corruption

In *De l'esprit des lois,* Montesquieu deploys the term corruption in the same manner that he employs other moral terms, straddling the descriptive and the normative. Corruption is at once something purely *relative* to a given regime (a loss of that regime's dominant passion) and *universal,* a degradation of human nature. Both these forms – the relative and the absolute – speak equally to individual character and political structures. With a classical unwillingness to separate city and soul, Montesquieu offers a series of socio-psychological analyses of different regime forms and the requisite character of their respective citizens or subjects. In this section, we will attempt to flesh out the link between the relative and the absolute.

In his threefold classification of constitutions, Montesquieu offered three types of corruption. Each type entails an alteration of the affective source of the regime – not its constitutional structure, but the dominant passion that "makes the regime move," its "principle" (*EL* 3.1). That is, every political arrangement has some sort of social-psychological force that makes individuals behave in such a way as to preserve the regime – the principles are the affective basis on which people's energies turn towards obedience. The principles are what make the public possible; without some sort of affective motivation, there would be no public at all. As we will see, if the types of corruption differ with regard to regime, they all share the quality of rendering people less public-spirited. We recall that the three regimes, republics (split into democracies and aristocracies), monarchies, and despotisms have, as principles or animating passions, virtue (love of the *patrie* and of equality), honour (love of distinctions and prerogatives), and fear, respectively. Let us look at the manner in which these principles are corrupted.

Republics are of two sorts, democracies and aristocracies. In both cases, corruption entails a diminution of virtue. "Le principe de la démocracie se corrompt, non seulement lorsqu'on perd l'esprit d'égalité, mais encore quand on prend l'esprit d'égalité extrême, et que chacun veut être égal à ceux qu'il choisit pour lui commander" (8.2). Citizens are all equal, but citizenship entails strict duties to obey the legitimately constituted powers. In this classical republican conception, the individual's liberty is not individual licence, but rather is a product of a juridical condition of being a citizen: one can speak of a free city. A Machiavellian form of citizen virtù ties people to their city. Aristocracy, another form of the republican regime, is corrupted when princes and nobles cease to have that moderating virtue that causes them to rule according to law – and hence it becomes arbitrary government, or despotism (8.5).

This Roman "political virtue" makes people place all of their energies in the service of their city. Political virtue is "l'amour de la patrie," (*EL*, Avertissement de l'auteur), the "désir de la vraie gloire, du renoncement à soi-même, du sacrifice de ses plus chers intérets" (3.5). Montesquieu expresses clearly the relationship between public and private in a classical republic:

> Quoique tous les crimes soient publics par leur nature, on distingue pourtant les crimes véritablement publics d'avec les crimes privés; ainsi appelés, parce qu'ils offensent plus un particulier, que la société entière.

> Or, dans les républiques, les crimes privés sont plus publics; c'est-à-dire, choquent plus la constitution de l'État, que les particuliers: et, dans les monarchies, les crimes publics sont plus privés; c'est-à-dire, choquent plus les fortunes particulières, que la constitution de l'État même. (3.5)

The very conception of crime differs according to constitutional form. When people have virtue, they consider all their actions to be for the republic. Hence, lax behaviour in their "private" lives is a sign of corruption. If the dominant definition of corruption today is the abuse of public office for private gain, we can see that all crimes in Montesquieu's ancient republics are corrupt, for the very desire for private gain is a corruption of virtue. There is no crime that is not equally an instance of political corruption. The converse is true of a monarchy. In a monarchy, these private ambitions are not rejected. They are moderated by a sense of honour that regulates ranks and makes people act with a degree of public-spiritedness (3.7), but their motivation is individualistic and, from a republican perspective, corrupt. Possessions are private things, and many public crimes are therefore more particularly crimes against particular nobles. Today's most prevalent definition of corruption – the abuse of public office for private gain – fits poorly in a monarchy, since in that regime public office exists for private gain (within the confines of an honour system), and any "abuse" of public office tends to be more of an abuse of other nobles or the monarch himself.

"Political virtue" entails that one's love and ambition is thoroughly linked with the good of one's city. It is, from a liberal perspective, stifling, and Montesquieu points out just how difficult it is to understand from the outside:

> Lorsque cette vertu cesse, l'ambition entre dans les coeurs qui peuvent la recevoir, et l'avarice entre dans tous. Les désirs changent d'objets: ce qu'on aimait, on le l'aime plus. On était libre avec les lois, on veut être libre contre elles. Chaque citoyen est comme un esclave échappé de la maison de son maître. Ce qui était *maxime*, on l'appelle *rigueur*; ce qui était règle, on l'appelle *gêne*; ce qui était *attention*, on l'appelle *crainte*. (3.3)

When this virtue is corrupted, one is no longer motivated by a love of the laws, but rather by *fear* of the laws. One's relationship is altered towards public things – they begin to be seen as extrinsic to oneself, and thus as oppressive, alien. We can imagine a degree of utilitarian calculus on the part of people such that they accept some laws out of self-interest, but this entire way of thinking entails a profound shift in attitudes. From the perspective of the cities without republican virtue such ancient respect (*attention*) for the laws is perverse and can only be a product of fear. For how else can we explain (the liberal might exclaim) such monstrous stifling of the individual?

Montesquieu admired this austere, republican "political virtue," but there is some debate as to the degree to which he thought it capable of being resurrected in the modern world. Certainly he argued that the English experiment with republicanism proved an abject failure because the principle of virtue was not firmly established in the people (3.3). If Montesquieu followed Machiavelli's description of popular corruption, he had too much historical sense to issue a Machiavellian call for the return of Roman *virtù*. Montesquieu appears to lament the fact that modern political thinkers no longer speak of virtue, but rather of "manufactures, de commerce, de finances, de richesses, et de luxe même" (3.3). Yet he himself suggests that this shift is permanent, particularly given the size of modern states (virtue is appropriate to smaller republics). He also hints that this shift away from virtue is somewhat desirable. Montesquieu treated the martial spirit of the ancient republics as noble, but also inhumanly cruel, and he equally thought that virtue required excessive self-abnegation. In an oft-cited passage, he compares republican virtue – the passionate love of their city and laws – to the love of monks for the rule of their order: being deprived of all normal objects for their passions, monks direct all their love towards the very rules that restrict them (5.2). This virtue is a kind of self-flagellation (presumably these monkish citizens would rather will their own subjection than not will). Nor is such virtue terribly amenable to liberty – on the contrary, it is stifling. A free regime must temper such virtue: "Qui le dirait! La vertu même a besoin de limites" (11.4).

Montesquieu's second regime, monarchy, is corrupted when princes centralize at the expense of other loci of power. In a monarchy, we recall, the principle of honour provides a limitation on the abuse of power. When this principle is corrupted, the laws of honour are no longer obeyed – the various ranks cease to play their role. Rather, the monarch devolves into a despot – one man who governs according to his own whim rather than according to established law and custom. A monarchy relies on honour because it relies on the principle that makes the nobility act in the interests of the state. In other words, a monarchy is not truly one-man rule, but is rather the rule of one supported by a vast array of nobility who are dutiful because they have prerogatives and honours that separate them essentially from the people, but that equally make them an independent, if subordinate, source of power.[8] This moderates the regime, preserving its law-abiding qualities, since nobles will insist on preserving their prerogatives and will refuse to do anything beneath their dignity. Montesquieu tells the heart-warming story of a viscount who refused to take part in the St Barthélemy massacre because it was beneath his dignity to act in such a way (4.2).[9]

Honour is a brake on the power of the monarch because it cultivates individual ambition among nobles. At the same time, honour turns the nobles' interests towards the state, and even makes them do heroic acts that verge on selflessness. Entirely bound up in their own *amour propre*, these nobles seek glory. Since honour can make people sufficiently courageous to have contempt for death itself, it is a principle that is most dangerous to despots, whose entire method of control depends on threatening people with death (3.8).

Montesquieu conceived of "selfless," virtuous political action as something constituted through a very rigorous education and set of laws that proscribe all avenues for personal interest at the expense of the city. That is to say, the "renoncement à soi-même" (4.5) that republican virtue entails is actually a cultivation of only one passion, love of the city, at the expense of the others. The self and its passions are still the source of a person's actions, but the passions are so constricted by laws that one directs one's energies towards the public good and, in this sense, against what one would have more readily desired had one not been so denatured by political education. Montesquieu portrays this republican cultivation of people's love as highly unnatural and even "pénible" (4.5). A sense of honour is much less painful and difficult to cultivate, since it appeals to passions that are easier to deploy because they are more directly self-regarding.

It is for the same reason that Montesquieu thought despotism the regime requiring the least amount of educational effort, since the principle of despotism – the passion of fear – is extremely easy to manipulate. If virtue is as difficult to cultivate as fear is easy, we get a sense that there is something highly artificial in courageous public spiritedness, and something natural in fear. But should not despotism, then, be considered the most natural of regimes? On the contrary, if Montesquieu considers timidity a natural human trait, so too are affection and sociability. Despotism actually undermines our friendships and all of our natural relationships, all the while elevating our fears to unnatural levels. "Il ne sert rien d'opposer les sentiments naturels, le respect pour un père, la tendresse pour ses enfants et ses femmes, les lois de l'honneur, l'état de sa santé; on a reçu l'ordre, et cela suffit" (3.10). Despotism, on Montesquieu's account, does violence to our very nature by placing unhealthy psychological burdens upon us, taking away our natural familial affections and our wider sense of community.

If the "principle" of despotism is fear, we might think that its corruption will entail confidence, but Montesquieu here leaves the realm of relativity – despotism, Montesquieu insists, is *essentially* corrupt, for fear is its "principle," and fear is an essentially corrupting principle: "Les autres gouvernements périssent, parce que des accidents particuliers en violent le principe: celui-ci périt par son vice intérieur, lorsque quelques causes accidentelles n'empêche point son principe de se corrompre" (8.10). This is a difficult passage – fear itself must be "corrupted" for corruption not to be total. Montesquieu is arguing that despotism only works when it is actually moderated by some accident of religion or climate. Voltaire wrote that there was no such thing as "despotism" as Montesquieu defined it, there being no regimes on earth that existed without some law.[10] But this is precisely Montesquieu's point – despotism is an ideal type. It cannot subsist without some moderating element. In the "oriental" despotism, Montesquieu acknowledges the degree to which religion moderates the regime (5.14, 12.29, 26.2). No society can exist on fear alone, and fear itself is fundamentally corrupting.

Moderate, lawful government is a fundamental good for Montesquieu because of its effects on the souls of its citizens. Montesquieu insists that there is no problem if one sociable principle is exchanged for another – a corruption of virtue into honour (or vice versa) does not alarm him, as the regime will retain some principle tying people to the public good (8.8). Arbitrary government is so harmful not because self-rule is a fundamental good, or yet because arbitrary rule entails a usurpation of natural rights, but because the despotic regime's principle, *fear*, does fundamental harm to the human psyche.[11] Human beings are corrupted by fear because they are rendered less capable of fellow feeling, or of any solidarity.[12] In Montesquieu's imaginary natural state, fear is precisely that which drives people away from one another; it is that which leads them to think primarily of their individual good. A society based on such a principle will be entirely fragmented. When one perceives oneself subject to overwhelming force of arbitrary rule, one retreats into oneself. Montesquieu is pointing out what Orwell would indicate so vividly: terror conquers love. The degradation of the women in the harem of Montesquieu's Persian despot, Usbek, vividly depicts how human relationships suffer under conditions of absolutism. In the harem, there is no solidarity: there is quite a lot of scheming and temporary alliances as people seek to establish their place in the pecking order, and there is one thrilling act of suicidal defiance as nature rears its noble head, but there are no independent sources of power, no room for independent action, and thus no room for true affection, whether in the form of romantic love or public-spiritedness.

Fear, then, is the ultimate corruptor, just as despotism is the unambiguous *summum malum* in Montesquieu's politics. But it is not the only thing that corrupts universally: let us now consider a *somewhat* corrupting influence, the desire for wealth and its attendant inequalities. If despotic regimes are based on fear, the only motivation that inspires striving in people is the desire for wealth and luxury (5.18).[13] Montesquieu articulates the standard civic-humanist view that excessive wealth leads to decadence and undermines civic freedom. This is one of the charges in his *Considérations sur les causes de la grandeur des Romains et de leur décadence*, and it is repeated in *EL* (8.2, 4). It is not merely that wealth leads to indolence and weakness – a standard trope – but that inequality undermines republican civic spirit. Montesquieu insists in particular that a democratic republic requires strict attention to equality of wealth. But immediately after making this point he qualifies it: there are such things as commercial republics. "Il est vrai que, lorsque la démocratie est fondée sur le commerce, il peut fort bien arriver que des particuliers y aient de grandes richesses, et que les moeurs n'y soient pas corrompues. C'est que l'esprit de commerce entraîne avec soi celui de frugalité, d'économie, de modération, de travail, de sagesse, de tranquilité, d'ordre et de règle" (5.6). This is quite an encomium. However, there is a danger: "Le mal arrive, lorsque l'excès des richesses détruit cet esprit de commerce" (5.6).

In aristocracies, a type of republic, Montesquieu indicates that moderation of inequality is essential for civic duty to be retained. When the aristocrats begin to enjoy privileges that are humiliating for the people, inequality begins to sting. Montesquieu continues:

> Cette inégalité se trouvera encore, si la condition des citoyens est différente par rapport aux subsides; ce qui arrive de quatre manières: lorsque les nobles se donnent le privilège de n'en point payer; lorsqu'ils font des fraudes pour s'en exempter; lorsqu'ils les appellent à eux, sous prétexte de rétributions ou d'appointements pour les emplois qu'ils exercent; enfin,

> quand ils rendent le peuple tributaire, et se partagent les impôts qu'ils lèvent sur eux. (5.8)

Montesquieu admits that the last instance is rare, but he suggests in a footnote that the aristocratic use of fraud to exempt aristocrats from paying taxes is common in "quelques aristocraties de nos jours." He does not mention which, but he does indicate that "rien n'affaiblit tant l'État."

Nothing weakens a state more than the absurdly low tax rates on capital gains and the ease with which the wealthy can evade and avoid taxation with foreign tax shelters (if the reader will excuse the anachronism); this is not merely because such practices deprive the state of revenue, but more because they make the state a mere avenue for the exploitation of one group by another. Such exploitation may be an objective fact of politics, but it is certainly harmful for social cohesion for exploitation to become completely transparent.[14] Such obvious subjugation is humiliating. And excessive wealth is not a problem only for republics. Monarchies' entire economies depend upon luxury (7.4), and this regime clearly requires vast inequalities of wealth to maintain the artificial divisions that honour demands. Nonetheless, it is important that such wealth be of secondary concern to the nobles. If nobles in a monarchy are given large monetary rewards for their services to the king, Montesquieu suggests, this is a sign that the principle, honour, has been corrupted (5.18). Indeed, the nobles ought to pay for their positions – Montesquieu defends the sale of public offices in monarchies, since venality, while corrupt from a republican point of view, has several advantages in monarchies: it fixes the estates, which Montesquieu thinks serves the interests of administration and hierarchy, it prevents the *secret* sale of offices (by corrupt and venal courtiers), and it inspires industry since wealth is required in order to get station.[15] Ultimately Montesquieu thinks that those who have attained noble stations ought not to engage in commerce at all (22.21, 22), as this desire for wealth is incompatible with the desire for honour and glory. The fact that English nobles engage in commerce has mixed the classes up and been responsible for the dissolution of a mediating institution (nobility) that makes monarchy function. The desire for wealth corrupts monarchical states.

Corruption, then, entails an alteration of people's primary desires such that they no longer serve to unite disparate individuals. In the great eighteenth-century debate about the relationship between self-interest and virtue, Montesquieu does not offer a paean to selflessness:

even the most public-spirited republican virtue is a product of an individual passion, and of the overwhelmingly powerful legal and educational structure that channels our self-love into love of the city. In monarchies, the nobility make a virtue out of what is traditionally considered a vice: *amour propre* (and, in a Mandevillean manner, Montesquieu argues for the beneficial economic effects of a monarchical luxury economy). A regime's principle is that which allows it to continue to exist as a society; the things that corrupt the regime are those that undermine its principle – save in the case of despotism, where the principle itself is anti-social and would cause the regime's destruction but for some extraneous moderating elements. In all instances of corruption, the sentiments unifying people are undermined by the two powerful passions of fear and greed. Social relationships are broken apart or transformed into perversions of their natural state. But if corruption is that which weakens the sentiments at the heart of social unity, we will want to know something about Montesquieu's conception of purity. Which sentiments are natural and salutary? In the following section we will inquire into Montesquieu's conception of nature and its laws.

Nature in Its Purity: Natural Law as a (Weak) Normative Anchor

While Montesquieu's extremely brief treatment of natural law in *EL* might appear to imply a subtle dismissal of the tradition, it is important to underline that nature remains a fundamental normative anchor in his thought. The difficulty with natural law (which, in Montesquieu's treatment, entails the basic social passions animating all human beings) is that it speaks so softly compared to history, climate, and positive laws. But this should not blind us to its centrality, and the elimination of nature as a normative basis would render Montesquieu's account of despotism and corruption void of normative force.[16] Following C.P. Courtney, I would like to insist on the importance of natural law in Montesquieu's thought, but I wish to highlight, somewhat contra Courtney, the way in which Montesquieu's natural law differs from that of most modern natural-law theorists. Courtney claims that, for Montesquieu as for other modern natural-law theorists, "When man's physical nature (the 'passions' and other amoral tendencies, or even instinct unguided by reason) takes over … the result is 'unnatural.'"[17] But Montesquieu does not treat the "laws of nature" as something to be equated with the a priori "rapports de justice" that he outlines in 1.1. The laws of nature, for Montesquieu, are derived from an attempt to imagine, in a proto-Rousseauan manner, a perfectly pre-social human being. The laws of nature are not a priori rational laws of moral relationships between intelligent beings (as discussed in 1.1), but are akin to scientific laws governing physical substances: they "dérivent uniquement de la constitution de notre être" (1.2). What is important to note here is that these laws are the results of natural *sentiments*. In the book's first chapter, when comparing human beings to animals, Montesquieu points out that animals "ont des lois naturelles parce qu'elles sont unies par le sentiment; elles n'ont point de lois positive, parce qu'elles ne sont point unies par la connaissance" (1.1). In our pre-social condition, we are bestial – and we share the beasts' virtues. It is our reason that makes us err, for our reason is imperfect: "Comme être intelligent, [l'homme] viole sans cesse les lois que Dieu a établies, et change celle qu'il établi lui-même." Passions can lead us astray ("comme créature sensible; il devient sujet à mille passions"), but this is largely because these passions are rendered dangerous by our *finite* intelligence, which is a source both of our freedom (or our perceived freedom) and our error. Human intelligence, because it is finite, is the source of error; passions are a surer guide.[18]

It is the complexity of society – and the tendency for people to try to turn that social union to individual advantage at the expense of social cohesion – that transforms early society into a Hobbesian state of war that can only be overcome with strong positive laws (1.3). Thomas Pangle is correct to note that "since Montesquieu holds that aggressiveness is less deeply rooted in human nature, and that affection is more deeply rooted, than Hobbes had thought, the political order which Montesquieu eventually indicated to be the solution to the human problem is much less strict or tough and much more soft and gentle than Hobbes's solution."[19] I would take this observation further than Pangle would wish and suggest that *EL*'s constant refrain that despotic institutions do violence to nature is an appeal to this natural sociability that Montesquieu locates in an imagined pre-social condition. It is not that this condition represents an ideal – Montesquieu intimates that it never existed and never could. It is merely that this thought experiment allows us to see our basic, uncorrupted natural inclinations.

This is not to say that Montesquieu was offering starry-eyed optimism about human nature; on the contrary, he treated social life as if it is *necessarily* a source of corruption, for human intelligence, being finite, is necessarily corrupting. In his *Défense de l'Esprit des lois*, Montesquieu answered impatiently the charge that he had failed to discuss original sin (it isn't a book on theology! he spluttered).[20] But he might well have responded that the critic was simply incorrect: *De l'esprit des lois* indicated clearly that corruption is an inevitable outcome of man's social nature and his limited intelligence.

If the tendency towards corruption is an essential element of political life, the duty of legislation is to mitigate it as much as possible. Montesquieu is so sparse in his treatment of an original condition not because he intends, obliquely, to denounce such speculation, but because he does not want to fill in human nature with false universal claims. But throughout *EL* he attacks specific institutions as unnatural, and an attentive reading of these passages gives us quite a number of rules for social life, from enjoining self-defence (and denouncing suicide) (6.13; 26.3; 6.13; 10.2; 15.16; 24.6; 26.7), to defending sexual *pudeur*, the natural regulation of sexual mores and the care for children (16.12; 26.3; 23.10; 12.14; 26.6; 23.2), to denouncing the bloodthirsty ancient republican penchant for murdering conquered peoples (10.3). Thus, for instance, Montesquieu suggested that it was a natural law for a father to feed his child, but not to give his child an inheritance – the regulation of the latter is something entirely dependent on the constitution and mores of a given state (26.6). The fundamental basis is in the four "natural laws" (which are equally natural sentiments) introduced in 1.2: the desire for peace (timidity), the need for food, the desire for sexual union, and the desire for community (born of our shared human capacity for knowledge). This is a conception of human beings as both individualistic yet born for cooperative social and sexual relations.[21] This is a very weak teleology – but a teleology nonetheless.[22]

"Dans l'état de nature, les hommes naissent bien dans l'égalité: mais ils n'y sauraient rester. La société la leur fait perdre, et ils ne redeviennent égaux que par les lois" (8.3). Laws are to give people something approaching the basic goods that they would seek in an imaginary, original condition. With regards to equality, this does not entail an "extreme equality": it entails a type of equality that threatens neither social order nor individual liberty. The laws – and the principles underpinning them – are means of mitigating the natural corruption to which human sociability tends. In different environments and different nations, different laws and psychological dispositions will be required, but there is, underlying it all, a basic conception of the good – that which does not do harm to our natural dispositions. But the "laws of nature" are too limited – they merely give us a rough outline of a natural social disposition; they say nothing about the institutions required to prevent their corruption. This is a question for the legislators of humanity: let us turn to the question of reducing corruption in the political world.

Moderate Corruption: England and the Anti-Social Passions

(A) Fear

To eliminate corruption altogether is neither possible, nor, perhaps, entirely desirable. In the *Lettres persanes*'s famous parable of the Troglodytes (Letters 10–14), Montesquieu appears to be suggesting that a fully virtuous anarchic republic cannot possibly last; certainly we have already seen that republican severity perverts our most natural affections (just as republican self-sacrifice exceeds the demands of nature). The "principles" of the different constitutions are all both natural and unnatural: they exaggerate one passion at the expense of others. Fear is one of the most fundamental passions, but when elevated to the principle of government it entirely undermines our capacity for love and solidarity. Honour makes us vain, superficial, and decadent. Excessive virtue and public-spiritedness undermine our natural familial affections. Moderate corruption of principles appears to be the basis for humane social cohesion. The ancient Germanic tribes who conquered the Roman empire and whose institutions resulted in the English constitution saw their own original republican constitution altered, and its principle diluted, by the changed conditions brought about by their success: "Il est admirable que la corruption du gouvernement d'un peuple conquérant ait formé la meilleure espèce de gouvernement que les hommes aient pu imaginer" (11.8). Montesquieu's constant call for moderation – "Le bien politique, comme le bien moral, se trouve entre deux limites" (29.1) – is an attempt to prevent psychological imbalance. The real opposite of corruption is not virtue, but rather immoderation, that which does the most violence to human nature.

The "best type of government that men have been able to imagine" is the English government championed in book 11: this is the government that has "political liberty as its object" (5). And the main force that defends this liberty is the balance of powers, the manner in which our natural tendency to attempt to usurp the social unit for personal gain is mitigated by the institutional constraint of power checking power. Now, if Montesquieu celebrates an idealized version of the English constitution, he is much more ambivalent about England generally, and this is not merely because he thinks that the English are prone to suicidal depression (14.12).[23] Despite his enthusiasm for the English, he is of the view that fear and avarice play a central role in the commercial "republic under the guise of a monarchy." Let us consider how corruption is mitigated in that constitution.

Montesquieu's treatment of liberty is quite distinct from republican celebrations of free civic life. He famously defines political liberty for a citizen as "cette tranquilité d'esprit qui provient de l'opinion que chacun a de sa sûreté; et, pour qu'on ait cette liberté, il faut que le gouvernement soit tel qu'un citoyen ne puisse pas craindre un autre citoyen" (11.6). Earlier Montesquieu defines political liberty as "pouvoir faire ce que l'on doit vouloir, et n'être point contraint de faire ce que l'on ne doit pas vouloir." Or, in a different formulation, liberty is "le droit de faire tout ce que les lois permettent" (11.3). We are very comfortable with this last formulation – it is consistent with the Hobbesian liberty of the subject, and it fully accords with the dominant liberal conception of negative liberty. But the most striking element is the psychological claim – liberty is the *feeling* derived from the *opinion* one has of one's own security. The balance of powers that Montesquieu celebrates is there to prevent people from fearing one another.

Liberty is "l'opinion que l'on a de sa sûreté" (12.2). Montesquieu offers an interesting hedge on the metaphysical problem of free will by merely defining "philosophical liberty" as being of the *opinion* that one's act is a product of one's will. That is, without actually dealing with the determinist challenge to voluntarism, Montesquieu nonetheless manages to sweep away the Hobbesian reconciliation of freedom and subjection to absolute power.[24] Whatever the objective truth is, both philosophical and political liberty are matters of subjective opinion. Most importantly, they are states free from fear: in one's "philosophical liberty" one has the opinion of having acted freely (even if a Hobbesian could point out the appetites and aversions that determined the action); in one's "political liberty," one follows the law willingly and is under the impression of not having a sword constantly hanging over one's head. Montesquieu thought that this liberty obtained in England: "Quand un homme en Angleterre auroit autant d'ennemis qu'il a de cheveux sur la tête, il ne lui en arriveroit rien: c'est beaucoup, car la santé de l'âme est aussi nécessaire que celle du corps."[25] The balance of power protects the rule of law and thus helps give liberty to a people who have neither virtue nor honour.[26]

But England's constitutional structure is no panacea: the English, having eliminated their intermediary institutions, are in grave danger of becoming slaves if they do not preserve their mores (2.4). Both mores and laws are essential for the minimization of corruption. Indeed, Montesquieu is quite clear that juridical and constitutional means alone will not suffice to cure people of corrupt mores, despite the intimate link between the two. We have seen that the two elements that most corrupt both individual souls and regimes are fear and avarice. England has both – indeed, England is replete with vicious passions, "la haine, l'envie, la jalousie, l'ardeur de s'enrichir et de se distinguer" (19.27) – but Montesquieu thinks these passions themselves are a source of energy to England. The difficulty with England is that the very things that make it successful – its fear and avarice – are equally threats to its integrity.

First of all, Montesquieu's English citizens are not in a state free from fear – on the contrary, in a free state of an English stripe, "le peuple serait inquiet sur sa situation, et croirait être en danger dans les moments même les plus sûrs" (19.27). These fears are inflamed by factionalism – party leaders in such a state "augmenterait les terreurs du peuple, qui ne saurait jamais au juste s'il serait en danger ou non" (ibid.). Indeed, people become so attached to their particular party's views of reality that they lose their capacity for judgment: writers are almost as unfree as they would be in despotic regimes: "chacun devient aussi esclave des préjujés de sa faction, qu'il le serait d'un despote" (ibid.). But unlike Machiavelli and his English heirs, Montesquieu did not condemn parties outright. Paradoxically, Montesquieu thought that the partisan tendency to lie to people about the dangers of their state, throwing around groundless accusations of conspiracies and corruption, actually served to strengthen the state, since people thereby attend more to the actions of the government (ibid.).[27] The dangers of faction were moderated by the influence of the legislative body itself, which is able to calm the populace due to the respect it, as a body, commands in popular opinion.[28] Parties cannot devolve into the type of factions that so threatened ancient republics because the constitution is mixed – but if the government were to lose its balance, liberty would be in great danger. The English attempt to become a republic failed because the English did not have sufficient civic virtue to overcome their factionalism (3.3). The danger of despotism in England is both mitigated and derived from their passionate factionalism (and we can see here why Montesquieu worried about the English tendency towards despotism). It is their constitution and their spirit of liberty that protect them from their otherwise rapacious and untrusting spirit, but it is their very distrust and rapacity that prevent the destruction of their constitution.

The security that each individual feels in England is thus not total – on the contrary, people feel constantly wary; their security is rather a security from each other, and it is due to the existence of a reliable law that is enforced with punishments. Herein lies a psychological contradiction: the main object of their fear (the government) is that which protects them from fear – with threats. Montesquieu articulated the commonplace view that punishment was corrupt and counterproductive when exercised arbitrarily. But even when it is exercised in a non-arbitrary manner it ought not to be too harsh. While the state must retain a monopoly on violence, Montesquieu argued against people being overawed by fear of the sovereign's sword. Monarchies are corrupted when a prince "change sa justice en sévérité" (8.7), and we see in Usbek the complete manifestation of this corruption in his wrathful desire to purify his harem: "Je vais punir ... nous allons exterminer le crime, et l'innocence va pâlir" (*LP*, Lettre 160). Being "tough on crime" is corrupt and corrupting. When punishments are too severe, they themselves undermine the law. "Il y a deux genres de corruption: l'un, lorque le peuple n'observe point les lois; l'autre, lorsqu'il est corrompu par les lois: mal incurable, parce qu'il est dans le remède même" (6.12) Fear is an essential human motivation, and it must be a part of any regime, but it deforms us and threatens the regime itself when it becomes overbearing.

The moderate and non-arbitrary manner in which punishment is exacted is a source of liberty. Montesquieu believes in the utility of punishment, but the fear that one feels must be directed towards *laws* and dependable institutions and not individuals. In England, "on craint la magistrature, et non pas les magistrates" (11.6). This is the basis of any moderate regime. In a monarchy it is important that punishment appear to derive from the laws, of which the king is the protector, and not from the person of the king himself (12.23). Mark Hulliung has suggested that this is a step in the direction of the Weberian bureaucracy – impersonal management.[29] But if Hulliung is correct to point to the impersonal nature of Montesquieu's ideal judiciary, it is important to note that the rule of law in Montesquieu's English constitution is defended not by a bureaucratic ethos, but rather by the political structure itself, which sets off against each other the competing interests of corrupted individuals wary that one group or another will undermine impersonal justice.

It is for this reason that Montesquieu inaugurates the modern mania for transparency. English partisanship actually serves to augment transparency. The English requirement for ministers to give an account before a public body – parliament – equally serves to keep them honest in their foreign relations (19.27). In his famous letter to Domville, expressing his optimism about English liberty surviving the well-known corruption of parliamentarians, Montesquieu wrote that while corruption would no doubt continue to affect some elections of MPs, in the English parliament "la corruption ne laisse pas que d'être embarrassée, parce qu'il est difficile de mettre un voile."[30] There is a great danger in secrecy, and a great merit to openness. Montesquieu celebrated the Roman law that stated that anyone killing a night intruder must, in the act, cry out so as to draw attention to his act (29.15) (this is the ancient equivalent of the closed-circuit video camera). At the same time, Montesquieu offers no Panopticon – the security state ought not to try to shine its light on every little act of the citizen (12.17). Indeed, Montesquieu would not have wanted transparency idolized. Liberty, we recall, is based on subjective belief, and when authority is exercised Montesquieu does not want it to be excessively transparent. Montesquieu preferred taxes on (non-essential) commodities to direct taxes on persons because when the tax on merchandise is included in the price, the payer is not made aware of the taxation (13.7, 8). Transparency must work to prevent the usurpation of power by one class or branch of government; it is not to be celebrated in itself.

The balance of power that prevents any branch of government from becoming dominant is a product of England's mixed constitution. It is for this reason that the main vice of the English – avarice – is so very dangerous. English parliamentarians are apt to be corrupt and to sell themselves to royal influence. Montesquieu lamented this in his *Notes sur l'Angleterre*, following the rhetoric of Bolingbroke's opposition to the king's "placemen" in parliament.[31] But Montesquieu ought to have seen the utility in this, given his view that excessive purity was itself a bad thing. Isaac Kramnick points out that the mixed constitution in England benefited from the king's tendency to place favourites in parliament: "Corruption preserved the mixed constitution in the eighteenth century to such an extent that one analyst claims that this period was indeed the only time when England enjoyed a truly balanced constitution."[32] Montesquieu celebrated this mixture: "L'Angleterre est à présent le plus libre pays qui soit au monde ... J'appelle libre parce que le prince n'a le pouvoir de faire aucun tort imaginable à qui se soit ... mais si la chambre basse devenait maîtresse, son pouvoir seroit illimité et dangereux ... Il faut donc qu'un bon Anglois cherche à défendre la liberté également contre les attentats de la couronne et ceux de la chambre."[33]

The famous thesis about the balance of powers between branches of government is a variation of this classical insistence on a balance between the interests of different estates (royal, aristocratic, popular). The venality of the English commons is ever a source of concern, but Montesquieu was neither apoplectic nor sanguine about placemen.[34] In a society that places such emphasis on money, parliament would always be in danger of being sold – it is therefore important that parliamentarians not be, as a body, sold to the same people. Montesquieu predicted the demise of English liberty "lorsque la puissance législative sera plus corrompue que l'executrice" (11.6). He also had a dire warning about representation:

> Lorsque divers corps législatifs se succèdent les uns aux autres, le peuple, qui a mauvais opinion du corps législatif actuel, porte, avec raison, ses espérances sur celui qui viendra après: mais, si c'était toujours le même corps, le peuple le voyant une fois corrompu, n'espérerait plus rien de ses lois; il deviendrait furieux, ou tomberait dans l'indolence. (ibid.)

Only regular elections combined with party antipathies could prevent such comfort on the part of parliamentarians. But the danger remains of an entrenched political class leading to widespread disaffection. Both the fury and the indolence that derive from this state of affairs can be harmful to liberty, the first leading to civil war and the second to servitude.

(B) Desire for Wealth and Luxury

England is a kind of commercial republic (21.7), and as such is subject to the danger facing commercial republics: that its leading members abandon those mores that keep commercial societies moderate. A brief look at what Montesquieu thinks of the English should give us pause on this score. Humanity is undermined by the spirit of commerce itself: "Dans les pays ou l'on n'est affecté que de l'esprit du commerce, on traffique de toutes les actions humaines, et de toutes les vertus morales: les plus petites choses, celles que l'humanité demande, s'y font, ou s'y donnent pour de l'argent" (20.2). This is certainly part of the English malaise – it is not just the weather that makes the English suicidal: it is their manner of interacting with each other. In contrast to the gay, sociable French subjects of a monarch, the English appear to be a dour, unfriendly, and vicious people. His early impressions of England are not laudatory: "L'argent est ici souverainement estimé; l'honneur et la vertu peu."[35] If he later altered these views somewhat (accepting that the English also value merit), he nonetheless continued to think that England's resilience and liberty largely derived from the way in which competing interests (individual interests and class interests) balance each other off in the public realm. The English regime is moderate because the English people are not; the mixed regime and the balance of powers ensure that corruption moderates corruption. As he said with regard to the passing of an anti-corruption bill in the English parliament, "le plus corrompu des parliaments est celui qui a le plus assuré la liberté publique."[36]

But England is more than a nation of devils. Commerce itself has a moderating influence – while it corrupts pure mores, it equally softens harsh mores (20.1). What takes the place of virtue in commercial republics is a moderating spirit of prudence, hard work, and economy; we have already seen how this ethic can be endangered by excessive wealth. English tastelessness and lack of polite manners is a sign that things are well – "l'époque de la politesse des Romains est la même que celle de l'établissement du pouvoir arbitraire" (19.27). How can the pursuit of wealth be prevented from entirely corrupting the city with luxury and undermining the necessary work ethic?

> Pour maintenir l'esprit de commerce, il faut que les principaux citoyens le fassent eux-mêmes; que cet esprit règne seul, et ne soit point croisé par un autre; que toutes les lois le favorisent; que ces mêmes lois, par leur dispositions, divisant les fortunes à mesure que le commerce les grossit, mettent chaque citoyen pauvre dans une assez grande aisance, pour pouvoir travailler comme les autres; et chaque citoyen riche dans une telle médiocrité, qu'il ait besoin de son travail pour conserver ou pour acquérir. (5.6)[37]

The establishment of a vast plutocracy and an industrial reserve army of unemployed is the structural basis for the corruption of mores that would sap the utility of avarice and turn England down the road to despotism. The poor must have access to the labour market, and the rich must have their wealth kept within limits so that they do not begin to indulge in the useless luxuries that define consumption in a monarchy.[38]

Montesquieu was concerned that English wealth might eventually corrupt the country, but he remained optimistic that such corruption could be contained – and would not follow the Roman pattern – due to the vast difference between English luxury (which was a product of trade and industry) and Roman luxury (which was a product of rapine and the imposition or tributes). Montesquieu thought that wealth produced from trade is not the zero-sum wealth that the corrupted Roman officers enjoyed, and he appears to have been hopeful that this would lead to fewer extremes of inequality. This is not merely a question of violent conquest versus pacific trade – it is a question of the relationship between the bellicose, militarily successful Roman republic and its lack of avarice. The difficulty with Roman virtue was that it was entirely dependent upon the equal sharing of land. In the *Considérations sur les Romains*, Montesquieu argued that the relaxation of the laws on the ownership of land had introduced avarice, sapping the virtue of the Roman citizen-soldiers; he suggested, with some nostalgia, that this corruption described modern Europe.[39] In the same text he expressed some sympathy for the Gracchi, though suggesting that their agrarian laws came too late, at a point when civic virtue had been lost.[40] But in *EL* he appears to side with Cicero in thinking the agrarian laws unjust (26.15). The key shift is that Montesquieu had come to think that inequality in the commercial world need not entail the type of universal corruption that had been the demise of the Roman republic. But this rejection of agrarian laws is not a complete rejection of the need to moderate inequality and avarice. The key to the maintenance of English liberty, he insists, is the maintenance of a large class of "gens médiocres."[41] If Montesquieu presents a somewhat idyllic portrait of eighteenth-century English inequality, we can see his clear espousal of the classical Aristotelian teaching that a large middle class is the best support for a mixed regime.

Montesquieu believed that free states always regulate their merchants, whereas despotisms create, if I may employ an anachronistic phrase, business-friendly regulatory environments (20.12).[42] He did not want merchants to be overly burdened with excessive bureaucratic formalities (20.13), but he was quite clear that the purpose of commerce is to further the good of the state, and the regulation of merchants is an essential basis for freedom. Excessive taxation would harm industry, but taxation was the reason commerce was to be celebrated by governments.[43] There is a debate about the degree to which Montesquieu championed the independent, self-regulating nature of the commercial realm; certainly he thought that commerce undermined the political sovereignty of despotic countries, running counter to their tendency to want to prevent the free movement of capital outside their borders (12.14). It is also true that Montesquieu anticipated Adam Smith's worries about government-enforced monopolies (20.10). Finally, he thought it essential for a well-ordered state that private property be respected (26.15). But property right is a product of positive law, and the state must be able to control matters such as inheritance in whatever manner necessary for their particular constitutions. Political interference in matters of property is not something that Montesquieu condemned, nor was he an outright enemy of high taxation (the most free countries are the most taxed, while the most despotic are the least 13.12, 10) – the key was merely to adjust tax policy so as not to dissuade commercial activity.

England represents a society in which the corrupt and corrupting passions of fear and greed are dominant but moderated. The English are avaricious and fearful, but their constitution is such that these passions serve to keep them united rather than to break them apart. Crucially, they so love the liberty they perceive in their state that they remain ready to sacrifice their wealth for its sake (19.27). But the danger remains that the English would sell their liberty – just as some English people are quite willing to abandon their country to go "chercher l'abondance dans les pays de la servitude même" (19.27). The balance of corruptions is precarious; an ever-present, self-interested fear is the defence against terror, and a moderately avaricious disposition, well confined by laws, is the defence against overreaching.[44]

Conclusion

Montesquieu stands somewhere between a civic-republican warning against opulence and a full Mandevillian or Smithean embrace of commercial society. The myriad advantages of commercial republics do not negate the inherent dangers of their motivating passions – fear and the desire for private gain. Self-interested bourgeois man, whose utility and independent spirit Montesquieu so admired, is equally a potential danger – if he manages to overcome the balances in his constitution, corruption will become endemic and the state will become despotic.

We have seen that, for Montesquieu, corruption entails the augmentation of the sentiments (fear and avarice) that undermine sociability. In this sense, it entails the abuse of public things for private gain, for the greater corruption there is, the less sense there is of a public. But the complete elimination of fear is impossible in human society, and the complete elimination of greed leads to an unhealthy asceticism.

His solution to the problem is one with which our liberal world is quite familiar – institutions must be designed such that public benefits derive from *moderate* private vices. The state must not be allowed to become either too heavy-handed in its wielding of the sword or too light in its control of commerce. Punishment must remain humane. Merchants and financiers must be encouraged but controlled: the liberty of commerce depends on merchants not being allowed to do what they want (20.12). Office holders may be expected to want to breach the trust given to them, and watchfulness and resentment must be encouraged in order to keep them in check. Unlike ancient founders of republics, Montesquieuan legislators no longer have purity in their sights. Above all, "il ne faut pas tout corriger" (19.6).

But make no mistake – this regime-craft entails soul-craft. A certain type of human personality is both the product and the defender of this balance (and in Montesquieu's more aristocratic moments he suggests that it is not a terribly admirable type). The passions of fear and avarice must not be allowed to become so dominant as to break apart natural human relationships and turn society into zero-sum games of exploitation. However comfortable we are with this teaching, there is something decidedly uninspiring about it. Must we truly accept that societies that produce the likes of Walpole – and the attendant outcries against them – are the greatest possible political achievements? But if Montesquieu sets his sights well below civic republican heights, he nonetheless does not offer a post-moral conception of politics in which the language of corruption loses its normative force; he retains the teaching that the extreme corruption of regimes is both a product and source of the corruption of human nature. Whether Montesquieu's account of corruption could survive the philosophical evisceration of nature as a normative source is an open question.

NOTES

1 Jarrett A. Carty's exposition of Machiavelli in this volume (chap. 6) reminds us of Machiavelli's revival of ancient republican ideals without their teleological content. This is an element of what Paul Rahe thinks made "modern" republicanism modern.

2 See, for instance, Mlada Bukovanski, "The Hollowness of Anti-Corruption Discourse," *Review of International Political Economy* 13.2 (2006), 183, who argues for a return to civic republican discourse.

3 Jacqueline Best, "Civilizing through Transparency: The International Monetary Fund," in *The Global Standards of Market Civilization*, ed. Leonard Seabrooke and Brett Bowden (London: Routledge/RIPE series, 2006), 134–45.
4 Joel Hurstfield puts this opposition well: "In the eighteenth century it was common enough to pay electors for their votes. If any parliamentary candidate today gave five shillings to a single elector he would at once be the subject of a serious criminal charge. But if he tells the same elector that, if returned to power, he will increase the elector's pension or reduce his tax by fifty pounds, he has committed no criminal offence and may indeed emerge as a self-styled benefactor of mankind." Joel Hurstfield, *Freedom, Corruption and Government in Elizabethan England* (London: J. Cape, 1973), 143.
5 The writer who has most been concerned with unveiling this tradition is, naturally, J.G.A. Pocock, whose *Machiavellian Moment* (Princeton: Princeton University Press, 1975) attempted to reveal a unified tradition from the Greek *polis* through to revolutionary America.
6 I refer in particular to self-identified "neo-republicans" such as Philip Pettit (who normally wears a sports jacket).
7 Which is to say, Dr Johnson may have been overstating the case when he declared the first Whig to be the devil.
8 One can hear echoes of Machiavelli's *Prince*, chap. 4.
9 Sharon Krause emphasizes this passage in her attempt to rehabilitate honour in liberal-democratic societies. "Politics of Distinction and Disobedience: Honor and the Defence of Liberty in Montesquieu," *Polity* 31.3 (1999), 476.
10 Voltaire, *L'ABC* (London: Robert Freeman, 1762), 21. Voltaire's charge has recently been taken up by Corey Robin, who thinks Montesquieu's account of despotism in *EL* is insufficiently analytical, lacking the thoughtful detail that is found in the *Lettres persanes*. Corey Robin, "Reflections on Fear: Montesquieu in Retrieval," *American Political Science Review* 94.2 (June 2000), 347–60.
11 This observation is at the heart of Judith Shklar's justly celebrated "liberalism of fear."
12 In this sense, Montesquieu represents an inversion of Hobbes. For Hobbes saw social unity as a product of artifice, kept together with a dominant fear; Montesquieu sees sociability as natural and undermined by the *Leviathan*'s sword. Despotism *creates* atomistic Hobbesian individuals.
13 That is, they seek wealth from state benefices; people rarely seek wealth in commercial activity under despotism, since property is so tenuous. For a detailed discussion of Montesquieu's concerns about wealth and luxury, see Roger Boesche, "Fearing Monarchs and Merchants: Montesquieu's Two Theories of Despotism," *Western Political Quarterly* 43.4 (1990), 741–61.

I will be indicating the degree to which Montesquieu was concerned about the negative psychological and political effects of avarice, but I suggest greater ambivalence in Montesquieu's thought than is evident in Boesche's presentation.

14 12.25: "Un ministre mal habile veut toujours vous avertir que vous êtes esclaves. Mais, si cela était, il devrait chercher à le faire ignorer."

15 This last point speaks somewhat to Montesquieu's experience: Rebecca Kingston points out that Montesquieu paid in taxes approximately the full amount of his income from his position in the Bordeaux parliament, and was therefore obliged to look to wine production for the bulk of his income. *Montesquieu and the Parliament of Bordeaux* (Geneva: Droz, 1996), 89 n. 71.

16 Among those arguing for the pertinence of the natural-law tradition in the interpretation of Montesquieu are C.P. Courtney (see n. 17) and Marc Waddicor, *Montesquieu and the Philosophy of Natural Law* (The Hague: Martin Nijhoff, 1970).

17 C.P. Courtney, "Natural Law," in *Montesquieu's Science of Politics*, ed. D.W. Carrithers, M.A. Mosher, and P.A. Rahe (Lanham, MD: Rowman & Littlefield, 2001), 60.

18 It is somewhat incorrect to say with Céline Spector that "while man is a double being, a sentient and an emotive creature, but also, by nature, an intelligent and free being (I, 1), fear reduces the human being to pure animality, governing his behavior as mechanically as the laws of movement that govern bodies." "Honor, Interest, Virtue," in *Montesquieu and His Legacy*, ed. Rebecca Kingston (Albany: SUNY, 2009), 52. This corresponds poorly to Montesquieu's claim that "les bêtes … n'ont point nos espérances mais elles n'ont pas nos craintes" (1.1).

19 Thomas Pangle, *Montesquieu's Philosophy of Liberalism* (Chicago: University of Chicago Press, 1973), 37.

20 Montesquieu, *Oeuvres complètes* (Paris: Gallimard, 1949), 2: 1133.

21 Montesquieu mentions a fifth law, the knowledge and love of God, but we get the sense that this law is only there to defuse pious objections; he dismisses this law quickly as excessively speculative for a pre-social being, and it plays no role in his analysis of human nature.

22 In this, I disagree with the influential view of Thomas Pangle, who would have us downplay the importance of this pre-civic human nature: "Only that part of nature which led to civil society can be of relevance to civil society." *Montesquieu's Philosophy of Liberalism*, 40.

23 Sharon Krause has correctly indicated the degree of ambivalence Montesquieu had about the English spirit, and there is a tradition of interpretation that sees him as a much more conservative defender of

the nobility in the ancien régime. It is very important to recall these less laudatory passages given our tendency to focus on Montesquieu's idealized presentation of the English constitution as the most enduring elements of his thought. Sharon Krause, "The Spirit of Separate Powers in Montesquieu," *Review of Politics* 62.2 (Spring 2000), 231–65. For one version of the nobility thesis, see Louis Althusser, *Montesquieu, la politique et l'histoire* (Paris: PUF, 1959), chap. 6. It is one of the curious things about Montesquieu that he could have been so dearly loved by the likes of Burke and yet inspire books such as that of Mark Hulliung, describing him as the radical forerunner of the revolution. *Montesquieu and the Old Regime* (Berkeley: University of California Press, 1976).

24 Montesquieu appeared to inaugurate a determinist political science; at the same time, he condemned determinism and defended himself against the charge in his *Défense de l'Esprit des lois.*

25 Montesquieu, "Notes sur l'Angleterre," in *Oeuvres complètes*, 1: 884 (hereafter *OC*).

26 Ibid.

27 Montesquieu thus offers a startling defence of Fox News.

28 I have treated faction and party as synonymous here because Montesquieu predates the philosophical distinction between these two things, a distinction developed in English theory and practice over the course of the eighteenth century and expressed most clearly in the work of Edmund Burke (a great reader of the Baron de la Brède).

29 Hulliung, *Montesquieu and the Old Regime*, 213.

30 *OC*, 1: 1449.

31 "Notes sur l'Angleterre," *OC*, 1: 880.

32 Isaac Kramnick, *Bolingbroke and His Circle: The Politics of Nostalgia in the Age of Walpole* (Ithaca: Cornell University Press, 1992), 152.

33 "Notes sur l'Angleterre," *OC*, 1: 884.

34 Celine Spector suggests that he was confident that the English love of liberty would win out, but Kramnick indicates that late in life Montesquieu appears to have been quite concerned. Kramnick, *Bolingbroke and His Circle*, 295 n. 45. (Montesquieu, *Pensées et fragments inédits* [Paris, 1909], 12.)

35 *Notes sur l'Angleterre*, 1: 878. In the *Pensées* we can read Montesquieu's later view that the English, in addition to loving money, also have esteem for merit, a point equally made in *EL*, 19.27. Nonetheless, in the *Pensées* we can also read Montesquieu expressing his preference for his own country and its mores. He also declares that in France he loves – and does not fear – the government, which is moderate. The generalizations in the *Notes sur l'Angleterre* are mostly repeated in *EL*, 19.27, particularly with regard to

the relations between the sexes in England. This barb seems to be a view he retained of the English: "Il faut à l'Anglois un bon diner, une fille, de l'aisance; comme il n'est pas répandu, et qu'il est borné a cela, dès que sa fortune se délabre, et qu'il ne peut plus avoir cela, il se tue ou se fait voleur" (877).

36 *Notes sur l'Angleterre*, 1: 881. He points out that it was passed more by accident than design.

37 Montesquieu proceeds to say that a good law would be for inheritances to be divided equally among all children in order to avoid individuals building up large fortunes. But he might have gone even further and endorsed Warren Buffet's plan not to give his immense fortune to his children. (Buffet has famously quipped, "I want to give my kids enough so that they could feel that they could do anything, but not so much that they could do nothing," thereby endorsing the work ethic that Montesquieu thinks is at the heart of commercial virtue.) This insistence on equal access to inheritance mitigates the somewhat more Lockean praise of Henry VIII for having got rid of "les hôpitaux ou le bas people trouvait sa subsistence," thereby increasing industry (23.29). Paul Rahe places emphasis on this passage, but he skips lightly over the passage calling for the suppression of extreme inequality ("Montesquieu does not dwell on this option"). Rahe is entirely silent about Montesquieu's unambiguous endorsement of a sizable welfare state in wealthy nations. This is consistent with Rahe's desire to conscript Montesquieu for the American conservative movement, whose main spring is fear of central government. See Paul A. Rahe, *Montesquieu and the Logic of Liberty* (New Haven: Yale University Press, 2009), 231 and Rahe, *Soft Despotism: Democracy's Drift* (New Haven: Yale UP, 2009). Montesquieu is the master of ambivalence, and to isolate any strand in his many-varied thought is to risk "recast[ing] the great man's thinking along the lines of [one's] own predelictions" (*Montesquieu and the Logic of Liberty*, 138), to employ the phrase with which Rahe castigates Hulliung, Keohane, Shklar, Manin, and Spector.

38 On this note, Montesquieu indicates that it is both a duty (to prevent suffering) and a sensible policy (to prevent revolts) for a wealthy state to see to the needs of the poor: "Quelques aumônes que l'on fait à un homme nu, dans les rues, ne remplissent point les obligations de l'État, qui doit à tout les citoyens une subsistence assurée, la nourriture, un vêtement convenable, et un genre de vie qui ne soit point contraire à la santé" (23.29).

39 *Considérations sur les causes de la grandeur des Romains et de leur décadence* (Paris: Gallimard, 2008), chap. 3.

40 Ibid., chap. 8, 122.

41 *OC*, 1450.

42 Equally, he suggests that taxes ought to be lowest in despotic countries (13.10).

43 Montesquieu derides tax farming as inherently corrupt, and prefers the English system, which is quicker and more predictable (20.13); he explains the success of the early Islamic conquests in terms of their less corrupt system of taxation (13.16).

44 This is not to say that England is a model that should be exported: Montesquieu's celebrated attack on uniformity (29.18) – clearly a response to the bigot's cry under Louis XIV of *un roi, une loi, une foi* – is also an attack on purity and the excessive attachment to abstract ideals. It is equally an attack on one-size-fits-all civilizing missions. Certainly Montesquieu would have been dismayed to see "freedom on the march."

9 The Fortitude of the Uncertain: Political Courage in David Hume's Political Philosophy

MARC HANVELT

Locating David Hume in relation to the tradition of civic republicanism is complicated. On the one hand, the essay "Idea of a Perfect Commonwealth" describes a Harringtonian republican model to which Hume claims he "cannot, in theory, discover any considerable objection."[1] On the other hand, Hume's support for the British constitution, including his claim that some forms of corruption are "inseparable from the very nature of the constitution,"[2] is decidedly un-republican. Many of Hume's writings pose direct challenges to the tradition of civic republicanism.[3] As Andrew Sabl has argued, Hume's political ideal is better described as "civic pluralism" than "civic republicanism" because he advocated political institutions as "the method for furthering diverse projects" and resisted the civic republican ideal, "which called for all citizens to practice an identical civic virtue for intrinsic or instrumental reasons."[4] Nevertheless, in elaborating important elements of his political thought, Hume consciously employed republican themes and republican language. As the work of a thinker who grappled with the relationship between the republican tradition and political life in a modern commercial society, Hume's writings are valuable resources for those seeking insights into questions of civic virtue and public life in contemporary democratic societies. Of particular note in this respect are the lessons to be gleaned from an aspect of Hume's thought that has received relatively little attention in the scholarly literature: his account of political courage.

Moderation is the virtue most commonly associated with Hume's political philosophy. Central to his conception of public life is an opposition of interests, which he understood to represent simultaneously the chief support of the British constitution and, because it often gives rise to factions, one of the greatest threats to the stability of the constitution.[5] In its constructive form, Hume understood the opposition of interests to be a principled form of politics undergirded by a sceptical philosophical outlook. However, the opposition of interests can easily turn to factional conflict when it involves an opposition of what Hume called abstract speculative principles. Hume's central political concern was with the effects of faction and fanaticism on British politics. He is generally understood to have endorsed a moderate form of politics, free of the bigotry and rage that he associated with the party politics of his age. However, I will argue that use of the term moderation, including Hume's own use, misrepresents the type of politics he was actually endorsing. While moderation, especially with respect to modifying existing political conventions and institutions, certainly played an important part in Hume's political thought, many of his discussions of British and English politics point towards his endorsement of a form of politics that can be more accurately described as marked by a particular type of political courage.

Hume struggled with the question of how courage, a virtue most associated with the battlefield, could play a constructive role in the political realm. His analysis serves to highlight both the positive potential and the danger inherent in any notion of political courage. When political courage is adapted from martial courage – understood as steadfastness in the face of risk on the battlefield – it can easily breed intransigence and dogmatism. What is more, by casting opposing principles as fundamentally dangerous to their own and, correspondingly, by defining the defence of their own abstract principles against challenge from others as courageous, factions can use the allure of courage to present their own members in a virtuous light or to inspire factional conflict. Such factional uses of courage require that courage be understood as martial courage transposed into the political realm. Hume recognized that this transposed martial courage – what, for the sake of conceptual clarity, I will henceforth term martial political courage – was held by common opinion as the principal definition of political courage. However, he also understood how dangerous this form of courage could be. Because individuals who are politically courageous in the martial sense exhibit a steadfast or uncritical adherence to their own beliefs or to those of their party, this form of courage actually promotes the development of factionalism and fanaticism.

In contrast to the steadfast or uncritical adherence to abstract principle that defines martial political courage, Hume invoked a second notion of political courage that is marked by a steadfast defence of the public combined with an equally steadfast resistance to the seduction of party. This form of courage is the political sibling of the philosophical courage that Hume demonstrates for his readers in the famous conclusion to book 1 of his *Treatise of Human Nature*. The philosophically courageous individual is one who eschews dogmatism and resists the siren call of demonstrative reason in favour of the humbled reason that Hume leaves us in the *Treatise*. Similarly, Hume's politically courageous individual develops stable moral and political commitments while facing the frightening reality of a world in which causal relations are not demonstrative and in which the same underlying processes of association that lead us to make sound and defensible judgments can also lead us into error.

Hume's analysis of political courage holds important insights for better understanding the form of politics that he imagined would mitigate the dangers of factionalism without requiring too many coercive measures that would limit the opposition of interests in public life. However, his analysis also offers insights for contemporary democratic citizens and democratic theorists concerned with the tenor of public discourse and the more vitriolic forms of partisanship that are, in many ways, closely analogous to the factionalism about which Hume wrote in the eighteenth century. Hume's distinctive account of political courage directly challenges the common opinion, held in his own day and arguably today also, that political courage is properly understood as martial political courage. His own conception of political courage, what he sometimes misleadingly identifies as moderation, is, in effect, a resistance to the allure of faction and to the sense of security – though his philosophy of mind shows it to be a false sense of security – that can be found in dogmatic adherence to abstract principle in the face of an uncertain world. Hume refocuses our attention on the type of political courage that is required to defend against the forces that threaten the open opposition of interests in public life, most notably the forces of faction and fanaticism. The insights he offers in this regard are as applicable to contemporary democratic politics as they were to the politics of his own time.[6]

In his discussion of the build-up to the English Civil War, Hume describes the English people as courageous. He writes,

> Never was there a people less corrupted by vice, and more actuated by principle, than the English during that period: Never were there individuals

> who possessed more capacity, more courage, more public spirit, more disinterested zeal. The infusion of one ingredient, in too large a proportion, had corrupted all these noble principles, and converted them into the most virulent poison.[7]

Immediately from this passage, we know that Hume's account of courage must be understood in opposition to religious zeal, the ingredient that, on his account had corrupted the noble principles of "courage," "capacity," "public spirit," and "disinterested zeal." Our challenge is to determine how, precisely, Hume understood the uncorrupted form of this virtue, in particular, its political form.

Courage can be broadly defined as "the quality or disposition of character that enables an individual to overcome fear in order to achieve a preconceived goal."[8] According to Ryan Balot, "the 'prototypical' meaning of *andreia* was that virtue that enabled men, and especially hoplite citizens, to overcome the fear of death on the battlefield."[9] Many of Hume's references to courage are clearly references to this type of martial courage.[10] However, he also writes of at least three other distinct forms of courage: philosophical courage,[11] courage of mind,[12] and political courage.[13] What is more, Hume's claim that, when elevated with courage, the soul "throws itself with alacrity into any scene of thought or action" makes clear that courage can be exhibited in very different fora.[14]

Hume's analysis of courage is complicated, in part, by the fact that he expresses great ambivalence about even construing it as a virtue. Hume routinely expresses a negative appraisal of martial courage and warns against its dangers.[15] For example, he writes, "men of cool reflexion are not so sanguine in their praises of [heroism or military glory]. The infinite confusions and disorder, which it has caus'd in the world, diminish much its merit in their eyes."[16] He also writes that "the unhappy prepossession, which men commonly entertain in favour of ambition, courage, enterprize, and other warlike virtues, engages generous natures, who always love fame, into such pursuits as destroy their own peace, and that of the rest of mankind."[17]

Hume's negative appraisals of martial courage strongly suggest that the different forms of courage of which he writes cannot all be understood as merely manifestations of the same virtue in different contexts. In many passages, Hume writes very admiringly of courage, suggesting that the form of courage in question is free of the problems and dangers that, to his mind, attend martial courage. Though the prototypical definition of courage might be drawn from a martial setting, Hume requires that it be fundamentally transformed, rather than simply transposed from the battlefield, in order to be considered a virtue in the political realm.[18]

The starting point for understanding Hume's account of political courage is the form of philosophical courage that he illustrates in the conclusion to book 1 of the *Treatise of Human Nature*. The *Treatise* is Hume's philosophical magnum opus. However, it is a mistake to read the *Treatise* as concerned solely with philosophical questions. Through his enquiries into questions about philosophical rationalism and the nature of belief, Hume addressed the political and moral dangers that he saw in the uncritical and dogmatic types of belief that were promulgated by faction and, in particular, by organized religion. In fact, a good argument can be made to suggest that it was these latter concerns that were foremost in Hume's mind when he wrote the *Treatise*. Jennifer Herdt has argued very persuasively that "Hume's epistemological concerns are not just secondary to practical and moral affairs ..., but they are actually driven by his concerns about the threat posed by religious belief and practice to the peace and prosperity of society."[19] As Ernest Campbell Mossner writes, "Hume's deep and abiding interests were always in philosophy and its practical applications."[20] Hume's account of philosophical courage describes a standpoint towards the generation of knowledge. This form of courage, which Hume demonstrates for us in the conclusion to book 1 of the *Treatise of Human Nature*, has a political sibling that plays an important role in his account of political discourse and public life.

After having driven his lance through the heart of demonstrative reason by showing that the necessary connection in causal reasoning is supplied by our imagination and that there is no independent, autonomous faculty of reason, but rather, that it is through the same processes of mind that we arrive at both reasonable and unreasonable conclusions, Hume steps back from his argument to address very personal words to his readers. In the conclusion to book 1 of the *Treatise*, he writes that he wishes to reflect upon the journey he has just taken, "and which undoubtedly requires the utmost art and industry to be brought to a happy conclusion."[21] Hume writes,

> Methinks I am like a man, who having struck on many shoals, and having narrowly escap'd shipwreck in passing a small firth, has yet the temerity to put out to sea in the same leaky weather-beaten vessel, and even carries his

> ambition so far as to think of compassing the globe under these disadvantageous circumstances. My memory of past errors and perplexities, makes me diffident for the future. The wretched condition, weakness, and disorder of the faculties, I must employ in my enquiries, encrease my apprehensions. And the impossibility of amending or correcting these faculties, reduces me almost to despair, and makes me resolve to perish on the barren rock, on which I am at present, rather than venture myself upon that boundless ocean, which runs out into immensity. This sudden view of my danger strikes me with melancholy; and 'tis usual for that passion, above all others, to indulge itself; I cannot forbear feeding my despair, with all those desponding reflections, which the present subject furnishes me with in such abundance.[22]

Hume recounts for his readers how his philosophical investigations into the workings of the mind have led him down a spiral of doubt. He writes that his arguments against demonstrative reason have left him with a choice "betwixt a false reason and no reason at all."[23] And this realisation has led him to despair. "The intense view of these manifold contradictions and imperfections in human reason has so wrought upon me, and heated my brain," he writes, "that I am ready to reject all belief and reasoning, and can look upon no opinion even as more probable or likely than another."[24]

Famously, Hume is delivered from his philosophical melancholy by spending an evening dining and playing backgammon with his friends. Removed from his study and surrounded by friends and merriment, he quickly recovers his spirits and even feels an ambition arise in him "of contributing to the instruction of mankind."[25] Hume's ambition is actually quite grand. "Instead of taking now and then a castle or village on the frontier," he writes, his intent is to "march up directly to the capital or center of these sciences, to human nature itself; which being once masters of, we may every where else hope for an easy victory."[26] Reinvigorated, Hume continues his enquiry into human nature and presses on to investigate the nature of the passions and of morals.

In her seminal account of Hume's *Treatise*, Annette Baier argues that in this famous passage from the conclusion to book 1, "Hume enacts for us the turn he wants us to imitate, a turn from a one-sided reliance on intellect and its methods of proceeding to an attempt to use, in our philosophy, *all* the capacities of the human mind: memory, passion and sentiment as well as a chastened intellect."[27] Baier's reading of this passage is very persuasive. And I am in agreement with much of her analysis. However, I believe that there is more going on here. Hume's description of himself as setting out to sea in a "leaky weather-beaten vessel," despite his "disadvantageous circumstances," his "memory of past errors and perplexities," and "the wretched condition, weakness, and disorder of the faculties" he must employ, suggests that the pursuit of his philosophical enquiries will involve no small measure of courage.[28]

But what type of courage will be required for this pursuit? Obviously, this cannot be the courage of the battlefield. Instead of martial courage, Hume's philosophical enquiries require a type of philosophical courage. He writes: "Courage defends us, but cowardice lays us open to every attack."[29] On Hume's account, philosophical courage differs from martial courage because the two forms defend against very different enemies. Martial courage defends against a military adversary that seeks the conquest or destruction of one's city. Courageous soldiers will defend their homeland or their city to the death. They will draw a line in the sand and resolve not to let any of their enemies cross that line while they still breathe. The strength of the soldiers' resolve, combined with the magnitude of the danger they face, determines the extent of the courage that they can be said to be exhibiting. The military dynamic, in which one is either victor or vanquished, calls for a stark form of courage. In this arena, courage consists in digging in one's heels on the battlefield, despite the very real danger that doing so will hasten one's own death, and steadfastly resisting one's enemies.

Philosophical courage involves defending against a very different type of adversary. The courageous individual who adopts Hume's philosophical method will defend against what Hume calls "our founders of systems." These are philosophical rationalists who are overly disconnected from everyday concerns and from the "gross earthy mixture" that Hume associates with the "many honest gentlemen" of England.[30] Philosophical courage requires a very different stance towards one's adversary than does martial courage. In fact, Hume often writes of martial courage in terms that could easily be applied to the "founders of systems." In describing military scenes in the *History of England*, Hume often writes of "obstinate courage"[31] or "that courage which consists in obstinacy,"[32] of "impetuous courage,"[33] or of "headlong courage."[34] Each of these characterizations (obstinate, impetuous, and headlong) can be as easily applied to martial courage as they can to the forms of philosophical dogmatism that Hume wrote his *Treatise* to dispel.

In contrast to martial courage, Hume's philosophical courage does not involve the obstinate, headlong, or impetuous defence of any particular principles or ideas. Rather, it involves a steadfast resistance to the alluring certainty and reasonableness that are promised by the "founders of systems." Philosophical courage requires that one maintain a stance of self-conscious uncertainty, that one not demand a degree of demonstrative proof that human reason cannot supply, that one develop stable commitments in a world determined by cause and effect but in which those relationships can never be demonstratively proven. Hume's "leaky weather-beaten vessel" is no luxurious craft. However, had Hume lived in 1912, the designers of the most famous of "unsinkable" luxury ocean liners would have furnished him with a perfect counter-metaphor to illustrate the dangers of following the founders of systems and of putting too much stock in the power of demonstrative reason. The founders of systems offer you luxury, security, and an unsinkable vessel. But they leave you gasping for air in the frigid waters of the North Atlantic. By contrast, the travellers on Hume's vessel live without luxury and without any strong sense of security. But they brave the open seas and live to tell the tale. They are engaged in an arduous pursuit that, in one of his letters to Gilbert Elliot of Minto, Hume described as the "perpetual Struggle of a restless Imagination against Inclination."[35]

Defending against the philosophical "founders of systems" was an enterprise that Hume connected directly to his political enterprise of challenging the forces of faction and fanaticism. Hume famously claimed that "errors in religion are dangerous; those in philosophy only ridiculous."[36] Facing off against the forces of faction and fanaticism, many of which Hume took to be rooted in errors in religion, required courage. Of his lifelong enterprise, Hume wrote, "I wantonly exposed myself to the rage of both civil and religious factions."[37] However, though his willingness to expose himself to this danger may have been wanton, Hume did not oppose the forces of faction by dogmatically championing an opposite set of abstract principles. Instead, he challenged the terms of discourse by eviscerating demonstrative reason and championing an experimental and empirical method of analysis. In this way, Hume laid the groundwork for transferring his notion of philosophical courage to the political realm.

Hume points us towards his account of political courage in a passage of the *Treatise* that contains a significant double entendre. In his discussion of the love of fame, Hume writes that "a mere soldier little values the character of eloquence: A gownman of courage: a bishop of humour: Or a merchant of learning."[38] Ostensibly, Hume's purpose in this passage is to argue that people's love of fame leads them to place little value on characteristics that they do not, themselves, possess. However, Hume is also here launching a well-aimed jab at organized religion, claiming that priests do not value political courage.

The centrepiece of this passage is the double meaning of the word "gownman," as both civilian and clergyman.[39] This double meaning would not have escaped Hume and was most likely entirely intentional on his part. The most obvious way to read the passage would be as setting up an opposition between civilians and soldiers. Soldiers place little value on eloquence, civilians on martial courage. But, of course, this claim is very easily refuted. And Hume certainly knew it to be so. The rousing speeches that great military commanders deliver to their troops are often essential for lifting their morale in difficult times or before important battles. We need only look at Hume's own account of Elizabeth I's famous 1588 speech to the troops at Tilbury who were waiting to defend against a possible invasion of the Spanish Armada.[40] The queen, Hume writes,

> exhorted the soldiers to remember their duty to their country and their religion, and professed her intention, though a woman, to lead them herself into the field against the enemy, and rather to perish in battle than survive the ruin and slavery of her people. By this spirited behaviour she revived the tenderness and admiration of the soldiery: An attachment to her person became a kind of enthusiasm among them: And they asked one another, Whether it were possible, that Englishmen could abandon this glorious cause, could display less fortitude than appeared in the female sex, or could ever, by any dangers, be induced to relinquish the defence of their heroic princess?[41]

In this passage, Hume clearly conveys both the soldiers' admiration for Elizabeth's powerful performance as well as his own. The soldiers were deeply moved by Elizabeth's speech. Therefore, while a soldier will likely be better served by a mighty courage than by a silver tongue when confronting an enemy on the battlefield, it hardly seems credible to claim that soldiers "little value eloquence."

If he was not actually making the argument that soldiers place no value on eloquence, then what was Hume actually arguing in this passage? I would suggest that his real aim was to make a claim about gownmen – understood now as dogmatic clergymen – and their lack of courage. This claim stands up much better than the claim about soldiers and highlights the distinction between martial political courage and the form of political courage that Hume endorses as a virtue.

Hume discusses martial political courage, the popular understanding of political courage, in various writings. For example, he describes Blake, a newly minted admiral during the period of the Commonwealth, as "a man of great courage and a generous disposition, the same person who had defended Lyme and Taunton with such unshaken obstinacy."[42] This notion of political courage is also apparent in Hume's discussion of Henry IV. Hume writes that Henry, "governed his people more by terror than by affection, more by his own policy than by their sense of duty or allegiance … But it must be owned, that his prudence and vigilance and foresight, in maintaining his power, were admirable. His command of temper admirable: His courage, both military and political, without blemish."[43] Of James I, Hume writes: "The same defect of courage, which held him in awe of foreign nations, made him likewise afraid of shocking the prejudices of his own subjects, and kept him from openly avowing measures, which he was determined to pursue."[44] We see martial political courage one more time in Hume's account of Arlington, a member of the Cabal that advised Charles II on foreign affairs in 1670. Hume describes Arlington as the least dangerous member of the Cabal, precisely because he lacked courage. Hume writes: "His judgment was sound, though his capacity was but moderate; and his intentions were good, though he wanted courage and integrity to persevere in them."[45]

In all four cases, those of Henry, Blake, James, and Arlington, Hume describes as political courage a type of obstinacy or steadfastness that can be considered analogous to martial courage. His assessments of the political courage of these four men are based on their respective abilities to stay the course, to steadfastly stand on principle, whatever the odds against them. However, while Hume acknowledged that this transposed martial courage constituted the popular understanding of political courage, his lifelong concerns with the deleterious effects of faction and fanaticism prevented him from approving of martial political courage as a virtue. As Jason Scorza writes, "Tragic and sometimes even deadly conflicts among political actors may occur, particularly when their admiration for courage intensifies the aggressiveness and obstinacy of their political behavior."[46]

The impossibility of coherently ascribing to Hume a view of martial political courage as a virtue becomes apparent when we consider his description of the ratification of a defensive alliance between Holland

and England that later, in 1668, became the Triple League. Hume writes:

> The articles of this confederacy were soon adjusted by such candid and able negotiators: But the greatest difficulty still remained. By the constitution of the republic, all the towns in all the provinces must give their consent to every alliance; and besides that this formality could not be dispatched in less than two months, it was justly to be dreaded, that the influence of France would obstruct the passing of the treaty in some of the smaller cities. D'Estrades, the French ambassador, a man of abilities, hearing of the league, which was on the carpet, treated it lightly; "Six weeks hence," said he, "we shall speak to it." To obviate this difficulty, de Wit had the courage, for the public good, to break through the laws in so fundamental an article; and by his authority, he prevailed with the States General at once to sign and ratify the league: Though they acknowledged, that, if that measure should displease their constituents, they risqued their heads by this irregularity. After sealing, all parties embraced with great cordiality.[47]

The courage that de Wit exhibits here is a political courage analogous to the steadfastness in the face of risk that defines martial courage. What is important to note, however, is that Hume cannot have approved of de Wit's courage as virtuous. Had one of the many factional leaders that Hume disparages in the *History* subverted the constitution in this way in order to pass a law or ratify a treaty that served the interests of their own party, we can be quite certain that Hume's tone in recounting the event would have been far more critical.

Just as Hume's discussions of martial courage show him to be very hesitant to denote it unproblematically as a virtue, his description of de Wit's actions as courageous must be taken with a grain of salt. By contrast, the tone of Hume's jab at the clergy – his claim that gownmen do not value courage – strongly suggests that, in a clear sense, he considered gownmen to lack virtue. On Hume's account, the danger posed by priests lies in their steadfast belief in religious principles and in their ability to inspire and promote uncritical belief in abstract principles in the political sphere. In other words, priests are dangerous because they are politically courageous in the martial sense of the word and because of their ability to inspire this form of courage in others. Therefore, Hume's claim that priests lack or little value courage relies upon there being an alternative form of political courage, entirely distinct from martial courage, that Hume did consider to be virtuous. This latter form of courage is the much more nuanced courage that is the political sibling of the philosophical courage described in book 1 of the *Treatise*.

Socrates is the only individual named by Hume as a model of philosophical courage.[48] Ryan Balot argues that there is a parallel Socratic notion of political courage that is evident in Plato's *Laws*. This notion of political courage is remarkably similar to that which Hume endorses. As Balot writes, Socrates's political courage was "not construed as the conventional military virtue, but rather as the capacity to act decisively and wisely while also recognizing the ambiguities of human action." On this model, "the courageous do not sit on the sidelines and bemoan the impossibility of 'having it both ways' … rather, they act so as to affirm (rather than lament) the tragedy and comedy of human existence."[49] It is not clear what direct influence this account of political courage might have had on Hume's thinking. However, the parallel is striking.[50] For Socrates, as for Hume, the politically courageous individual stands firm, not against an aggressive enemy, but in the face of the ambiguities and uncertainties of the human world which present themselves as real dangers. Facing these dangers requires no small measure of courage.[51]

It is important to recognize the centrality of danger to any notion of courage. Hume explicitly states that the extent of an individual's courage is directly related to the danger he or she faces.[52] We have already seen that the danger in question need not be physical in nature. Hume's account of James I's fear of shocking the prejudices of his people makes this clear. Ancient Athenian orators also emphasized the non-physical dangers they faced in order to highlight the political courage they exhibited in their public speaking. As Balot notes:

> Orators themselves foregrounded the dangers of free speech and argued that they deserved credit for their courage in running risks for the sake of Athens' welfare. There was a legitimate basis for their arguments in the penalties, both formal and informal, that might result from political participation. Participants' property, citizenship, and even lives were at stake in legal procedures … To these can be added the less formal risks derived from shame – unpopularity, humiliation, and loss of credibility – as well as slander … These political realities of elite competition made free speech in the deliberative context of the democracy an enormously risky venture.[53]

As Balot argues, Demosthenes "formulates civic courage as the ability to speak freely even against the *demos*' inclinations."[54]

For Hume, the key to differentiating martial political courage from the political courage he considered a virtue lies in the perception of danger that the individual faces. The individual who exhibits martial political courage faces danger from political enemies who are, in many ways, analogous to enemies on the battlefield. The individual who exhibits martial political courage defends a position of power, a specific set of abstract principles, or specific policies against political enemies who seek his or her defeat. The ancient Athenian orators faced dangers inherent to standing up to, and in some cases directly contradicting, public opinion. This notion of danger is closer to that faced by Hume's politically courageous individual. However, it is not identical with it. Hume's conception of political courage is related to the danger of uncertainty. It is an epistemological danger, rather than a physical danger or the danger of contrary political opinion. But, as we will see, standing up to the epistemological danger faced by Hume's politically courageous individual is often far more difficult.

A central element in Hume's study of human nature is his account of an innate human tendency towards fanaticism. Though he saw fanaticism manifest in both "civil and religious factions,"[55] and believed political fanaticism to be directly analogous to religious fanaticism, Hume thought the human tendency toward fanaticism was most easily explained in relation to religious belief. In his essay "Of Parties in General," Hume writes:

> Two men travelling on the highway, the one east, the other west, can easily pass each other, if the way be broad enough: But two men, reasoning upon opposite principles of religion, cannot so easily pass, without shocking; though one should think, that the way were also, in that case, sufficiently broad, and that each might proceed, without interruption, in his own course. But such is the nature of the human mind, that it always lays hold on every mind that approaches it; and as it is wonderfully fortified by an unanimity of sentiment, so is it shocked and disturbed by any contrariety. Hence the eagerness, which most people discover in a dispute; and hence their impatience of opposition, even in the most speculative and indifferent opinions. This principle, however frivolous it may appear, seems to have been the origin of all religious wars and divisions.[56]

In the *Natural History of Religion*, Hume offers his most developed account of how the tendency towards fanaticism develops. Hume argues that the original impetus that led people to contemplate the existence of divinity in the first place must have been "the ordinary affections of human life, the anxious concern for happiness, the dread of future misery, the terror of death, the thirst of revenge, the appetite for food and other necessities."[57] People sought explanations for their misery and their happiness, for death, and for the other variables in human life. Whenever people search for such explanations, Hume writes, "*unknown causes* … become the constant object of [their] hope and fear; and while the passions are kept in perpetual alarm by an anxious expectation of the events, the imagination is equally employed in forming ideas of those powers, on which [they] have so entire a dependence."[58] Hume contends that people have a natural tendency to transpose human qualities and emotions onto all beings. It is "no wonder, then," he argues, "that mankind, being placed in such an absolute ignorance of causes, and being at the same time so anxious concerning their future fortune, should immediately acknowledge a dependence on invisible powers, possessed of sentiment and intelligence."[59] According to Hume, the causal relations that produce the variability in human life are not demonstrative.[60] He writes: "We are placed in this world, as in a great theatre, where the true springs and causes of every event are entirely concealed from us."[61] But most people have difficulty accepting the limits of their cognitive powers. They are anxious to find comfort in some account of the world that offers an explanation of these springs and causes. In the end, Hume argues, people find "no better expedient than to represent them as intelligent voluntary agents, like ourselves; only somewhat superior in power and wisdom."[62]

Determining that the world must be shaped by one or more divine beings does nothing, however, to diminish the variability in peoples' lives. Therefore, Hume argues, people seek to influence their own chances for happiness by choosing a particular god as their patron, or as the general sovereign of heaven. And this, he argues, is the first step towards the development of fanaticism. Hume writes that the chosen god's "votaries will endeavour, by every art, to insinuate themselves into his favour … In proportion as men's fears or distresses become more urgent, they still invent new strains of adulation; and even he who outdoes his predecessor in swelling up the titles of his divinity, is sure to be outdone by his successor in newer and more pompous epithets of praise."[63] Once people settle upon a sole object of devotion, they come to see the worship of other deities as impious. Hume argues that the acknowledgment of a single god "seems naturally to require the unity of faith and ceremonies, and furnishes designing men with a pretence for representing their adversaries as profane, and the objects of divine as well as human vengeance."[64]

For Hume, the point of this story is to show how people seek safety from uncertainty in dogmatic faith. This type of dogmatic faith was most apparent to Hume in organized religion. But he considered his analysis to be equally applicable to dogmatic adherence to abstract political principles also. As Herdt writes, Hume's account of fanaticism teaches us "to expect zeal where belief is tottering or under fire, to expect factions to emerge to supply reinforcement, to anticipate that insignificant details will be magnified and made the heart of violent and irreconcilable disputes, and that zealous belief will be deaf to reason."[65] In his essay "Of the Independency of Parliament," Hume writes:

> Men are generally more honest in their private than in their public capacity, and will go greater lengths to serve a party, than when their own private interest is alone concerned. Honour is a great check upon mankind: But where a considerable body of men act together, this check is, in a great measure, removed; since a man is sure to be approved of by his own party, for what promotes the common interest; and he soon learns to despise the clamours of adversaries.[66]

Because party or factional membership provides respite from a world of uncertainty by supplying individuals with a set of abstract principles they can adopt as fundamental beliefs, individuals are quick to defend the interests of their party against any apparent attack or challenge. But, as Hume understood it, herein lies the paradox of faction: by seeking security in faction and dogmatic belief, individuals only open themselves, and their societies, up to greater dangers. As Herdt writes: "Members of religious factions perceive actions in defense of their party as selfless and principled, but this simply licenses them to do greater harm with a clean conscience."[67] Hume thought this problem to be particularly pertinent to the British, whom he thought, of all the nations of Europe, to be "the most under the influence of that religious spirit, which tends rather to inflame bigotry than encrease peace and mutual charity."[68]

By relating Hume's discussions of political courage to his account of the development of faction and fanaticism, we come to see that Hume's political courage is, in fact, directly opposed to martial political courage. Martial political courage contributes to the development of both fanaticism and factional conflict. And, while he acknowledged that this form of steadfastness was commonly considered to be political courage, Hume could not endorse it as a virtue for the same reasons that he could not unproblematically endorse martial courage on the battlefield as a virtue. Instead, Hume endorsed a form of political courage that involves resisting the allure of faction. Martial political courage promotes faction. Hume's political courage is a direct challenge to it. The contrast could not be more stark.

Hume concludes the sixth volume of his *History of England* with a passage that directly connects his notion of political courage to the constitution and to his account of public life. He writes:

> Thus have we seen, through the course of four reigns, a continual struggle maintained between the crown and the people: Privilege and prerogative were ever at variance: And both parties, beside the present object of dispute, had many latent claims, which, on a favourable occasion, they produced against their adversaries. Governments too steady and uniform, as they are seldom free, so are they, in the judgment of some, attended with another sensible inconvenience: They abate the active powers of men; depress courage, invention, and genius; and produce an universal lethargy in the people.[69]

Though he argues that, in the case of seventeenth-century English history, the political turmoil was extreme and some of the consequences very harmful, Hume does agree that governments that are too settled, in which there is no open opposition of interests, are both unfree and destructive of courage. This is not the only passage in which Hume connects political courage with liberty.[70] But notice the other two characteristics that Hume associates with courage in the preceding passage: industry and genius. These strongly suggest that the courage of which Hume writes in this passage is the courage to question, the courage to face uncertainty, the courage required to venture out onto the ocean in Hume's "leaky weather-beaten vessel." Dogmatism, intransigence, steadfast and unwavering defence of abstract principle, in other words, the characteristics associated with martial political courage, none of these are close bedfellows of industry and genius.

In the conclusion to his essay "That Politics May Be Reduced to a Science," Hume implores his contemporaries to "draw a lesson of moderation with regard to the parties, into which our country is at present divided; at the same time, that we allow not this moderation to abate the industry and passion, with which every individual is bound to pursue the good of his country."[71] What he is describing here is political courage. And his message is as applicable to the citizens of contemporary democratic polities as it was to his own countrymen. When taking a courageous political stand comes to be understood in the language of martial courage, in other words, when political courage comes to be understood as an unwavering defence of principle or party, blind partisanship and deafness to reason will come to dominate the political discourse of a country. These can produce factionalism that can tear at the very fabric of a political society. Hume points us towards an alternative account of political courage that safeguards rather than threatens the open opposition of interests in public life. On his account, the virtuous citizen pursues the good of his or her country in a "leaky weather-beaten vessel." In the political realm, courage is the fortitude of the uncertain.

NOTES

1 *Essays*, "Idea of a Perfect Commonwealth," 516. References to Hume's *Essays Moral, Political, and Literary* take the form *Essays* followed by the title and page number in David Hume, *Essays Moral, Political, and Literary*, ed. Eugene F. Miller (Indianapolis: Liberty Classics, 1987).

2 *Essays*, "Of the Independency of Parliament," 45.

3 See James Moore, "Hume's Political Science and the Classical Republican Tradition," *Canadian Journal of Political Science* 10:4 (December 1977), 809–39.

4 Andrew Sabl, *Hume's Politics: Coordination and Crisis in the History of England* (Princeton: Princeton University Press, 2012), 53.

5 *Essays*, "Idea of a Perfect Commonwealth," 525.

6 This is especially so if we think of democracy, as Ryan Balot encourages us to do in his chapter in this volume, as inviting a culture of critical discourse among the citizenry.

7 H 5.380. References to Hume's *History of England* take the form H followed by the volume and page number in David Hume, *The History of England from the Invasion of Julius Caesar to the Revolution in 1688*, foreword by William B. Todd, 6 vols. 1778 edition (rpt. Indianapolis: Liberty, 1983).

8 Ryan K. Balot, "Courage in the Democratic Polis," *Classical Quarterly*, new series, 54:2 (2004), 407.

9 Ibid.

10 See, for example, H 5.51, H 2.350.

11 See, for example, EPM 7.17; SBN 256. References to Hume's *Enquiry concerning the Principles of Morals* take the form EPM followed by the book and paragraph number in David Hume, *An Enquiry Concerning the Principles of Morals*, ed. Tom L. Beauchamp (New York: Oxford University Press, 1998); followed by SBN and the page number in David Hume, *Enquiries concerning Human Understanding and concerning the Principles of Morals*, ed. L.A. Selby-Bigge and P.H. Nidditch (Oxford: Clarendon Press, 1975).
12 See, for example, H 2.126.
13 See, for example, H 5.122, H 2.350, H 2.449.
14 T 2.3.8.9; SBN 435. References to Hume's *Treatise of Human Nature* take the form T followed by the book, part, section, and paragraph reference in David Hume, *A Treatise of Human Nature*, ed. David Fate Norton and Mary J. Norton (New York: Oxford University Press, 2002); followed by SBN and the page reference in David Hume, *A Treatise of Human Nature*, ed. L.A. Selby-Bigge and P.H. Nidditch (Oxford: Clarendon Press, 1978).
15 Hume's concern about the effects of martial courage is a further important basis for the critical view of the Spartan model that Varad Mehta discusses in this volume in "Sparta, Modernity, Enlightenment."
16 T 3.3.2.15; SBN 600–1.
17 H 5.51.
18 My argument here contrasts with that of Annette Baier, who writes that "courage has to be transferred from the battlefield to more peaceful fields (or to more domestic battlefields) before it gets approved as a virtue" (Annette C. Baier, *A Progress of Sentiments: Reflections on Hume's Treatise* [Cambridge, MA: Harvard University Press, 1991], 212). On my reading of Hume, political courage is a transformed, not merely transferred, form of courage.
19 Jennifer A. Herdt, *Religion and Faction in Hume's Moral Philosophy* (New York: Cambridge University Press, 1997), 9.
20 Ernest Campbell Mossner, *The Life of David Hume* (Oxford: Clarendon Press, 1980), 140.
21 T 1.4.7.1; SBN 263.
22 T 1.4.7.1; SBN 263–4.
23 T 1.4.7.7; SBN 268.
24 T 1.4.7.8; SBN 268–9.
25 T 1.4.7.12; SBN 271.
26 T Intro.6; SBN xvi.
27 Baier, *A Progress of Sentiments*, 1.
28 T 1.4.7.1; SBN 264.
29 T 2.1.7.3; SBN 295.
30 T 1.4.7.14; SBN 272.

31 H 6.203.
32 H 3.264.
33 H 6.262.
34 H 2.445.
35 *Letters*, 1.154. References to Hume's letters take the form *Letters*, followed by the volume and page number in David Hume, *The Letters of David Hume*, ed. J.Y.T. Greig, 2 vols. (Oxford: Clarendon Press, 1932).
36 T 1.4.7.13; SBN 272.
37 *Essays*, "My Own Life," xli.
38 T 2.1.11.13; SBN 322.
39 *Compact Oxford English Dictionary*.
40 "… therefore I am come amongst you, as you see, at this time, not for my recreation and disport, but being resolved, in the midst and heat of the battle, to live and die amongst you all; to lay down for my God, and for my kingdom, and my people, my honour and my blood, even in the dust. I know I have the body but of a weak and feeble woman; but I have the heart and stomach of a king, and of a king of England too, and think foul scorn that Parma or Spain, or any prince of Europe, should dare to invade the borders of my realm" (http://www.britannia.com/history/monarchs/mon45.html).
41 H 4.266.
42 H 6.41.
43 H 2.350.
44 H 5.84.
45 H 6.241.
46 Jason A. Scorza, "The Ambivalence of Political Courage," *Review of Politics* 63:4 (2001), 639.
47 H 6.221.
48 EPM 7.17; SBN 256.
49 Ryan K. Balot, "Politics, Philosophy, and Likelihood" (unpublished).
50 Of course, Socrates operates with conceptions of demonstrative truth and of philosophy that are very different from Hume's.
51 Though describing risks more specifically physical in nature, the discussion that Timothy Burns offers in his chapter in this volume of Thucydides's account of the courage of the Plataeans similarly points to a willingness to accept the world as it is as comprising an important dimension of courage.
52 H 4.xlii.
53 Ryan K. Balot, "Free Speech, Courage, and Democratic Deliberation," in *Free Speech in Classical Antiquity*, ed. Ineke Sluiter and Ralph M. Rosen (Leiden, Netherlands: Koninklijke Brill, 2004), 243.
54 Ibid., 247.

55 *Essays*, "My Own Life," xli.
56 *Essays*, "Of Parties in General," 60.
57 David Hume, *The Natural History of Religion*, ed. H.E. Root (Stanford: Stanford University Press, 1957), 28.
58 Ibid., 29.
59 Ibid., 30.
60 These causes are unknowable, according to Hume, because of his contention that "we cannot go beyond experience" (T Intro.8; SBN xvii).
61 *Natural History of Religion*, 28.
62 Ibid., 40.
63 Ibid., 43.
64 Ibid., 49.
65 Herdt, *Religion and Faction*, 216.
66 *Essays*, "Of the Independency of Parliament," 43.
67 Herdt, *Religion and Faction*, 205.
68 H 5.164.
69 H 6.530.
70 See also H 5.15.
71 *Essays*, "That Politics May Be Reduced to a Science," 27.

10 Sparta, Modernity, Enlightenment

VARAD MEHTA

"Republicanism was the ideology of the Enlightenment."[1] This bold proclamation by the historian Gordon Wood is certainly exaggerated. Nonetheless, it derives from sound premises, for he rightly identifies as one of the chief catalysts of eighteenth-century interest in civic republicanism[2] an intensification during the Enlightenment of the habitual early modern fascination with ancient history and politics.[3]

Antiquity's increased allure in the eighteenth century was a consequence of the advent of modernity. An idea whose essence has proved as elusive as it has protean, modernity is best thought of as a way of understanding man's relationship to his past, as well as the relationship itself, a relationship transformed during and by the Enlightenment.[4] Modernity so conceived owes primarily to the conviction that the present is entirely new and therefore wholly distinct from the past.[5] A conscious distancing of present from past is indispensable to the reconfiguration of the past and of man's relationship to it that modernity entails. But sealing the past off from the present is not in itself enough to achieve modernity. The critical step is opening the future. The perception that one lives in a new time generates an awareness that the future is now "open and indefinite, and society must go on advancing into it."[6] The crux of modernity, therefore, is that it is whatever the future makes of it.[7]

The future cannot be understood without the past. The emergence of modernity spurred the eighteenth century's turn to antiquity. Indeed, the one could not have been envisioned without the other. As Jürgen Habermas recognized, the perception of modernity was sharpest just when it was needed to repel appeals to antiquity. "The term 'modern' appeared and reappeared exactly during those periods in Europe when the consciousness of a new epoch formed itself through a renewed relationship to the ancients – whenever, moreover, antiquity was considered a model to be recovered through some kind of imitation."[8] The future would be – had to be – different. Ever since the Enlightenment, therefore, "modernity has explicitly been defined as a categorical *rejection* of the example of antiquity."[9]

The example of antiquity, on the other hand, was for its adherents no less a rejection of modernity, especially of the changes which were remaking European society during this period and thereby threatened to cut it adrift from its historical moorings: the expansion of commerce and consumption; the reorientation, grounded in a conception of liberty based on the new ideology of natural rights, of the individual's relationship to society to favour the former over the latter; and, above all, the denial of the validity of measuring the achievements of the present by those of the past. Antiquity's ideals offered a compelling vision to those sceptical of or even hostile to these transformations because the nostalgic, utopian image of the ancient republic was the primary alternative available to those wishing to cast a critical eye upon the contemporary state of Europe. Throughout the Enlightenment, both those who embraced modernity and those who did not conceived of it "in relation to an archaic world that helped define it, rather like a reverse image."[10]

This inversion generated much of the symbolic energy of classical republicanism, which thrived in the eighteenth century as an ideological vehicle for antagonism to modernity, antagonism which manifested itself most powerfully in the nebulous congeries of ideas and impressions known variously as the Spartan mirage, legend, or tradition.[11] Sparta represented a bastion against the encroachments and enticements of an age inimical to the ideals that critics of modernity believed integral to the preservation of society: the concord of private and public interest; the civic virtue and engagement of the citizen; a widely diffused martial spirit; the denial of luxury and a concomitant vigilance against corruption; and, especially, a civic solidarity anchored in a unitary conception of the common good binding on all. The Sparta of myth seemed most fully to embody these values, which were also the aspirations of classical republicanism. So it became, at least for the eighteenth century, the pre-eminent exemplar of the modes and values of classical politics.

The Spartan legend was remembered again during the Enlightenment because of all historical alternatives, it appeared most unlike the present. The purpose of the Spartan way of life was to prevent the future.

Sparta's mirage of immutability galvanized those who wished to keep things as they were. Those who liked what had become of their world and hoped it would keep changing, by contrast, anathematized Sparta as an obsolete barbarism because they feared its resurrection would imperil the century's considerable material and moral progress, especially its catalyst, the new understanding of the future that saw it not as closed and unalterable, but as open and indeterminate.

A census of such a large and diverse group of thinkers would not be feasible in a short essay such as this. Instead, I shall focus on a select few in whose writings Sparta was especially prominent, and who may therefore be taken as representative of the broader trends in eighteenth-century commentary on Sparta. Andrew Fletcher, Adam Ferguson, John Brown, Gabriel Bonnot de Mably, and Jean-Jacques Rousseau were among Sparta's most ardent, eloquent apologists; David Hume, Charles-Louis de Montesquieu, and Joseph Priestley three of its sternest, most incisive foes. For those on either side, the Enlightenment conflict about Sparta was a conflict about the nature and direction of modernity. As such, it was also a conflict about history. "Whatever else then seemed to be in question, it was history – how to understand, reconstruct, and use the past – that was undoubtedly at the heart of the matter."[12] The future, no less than the past, was at stake.

"The truculent Scots patriot"[13] Andrew Fletcher of Saltoun (1653–1716) is little remembered now, but in his day he was as renowned for his fierce temper and peccadilloes as for his fierce loyalty to Scotland. A significant precursor of the Scottish Enlightenment, he was one of the leading voices in the decade-long debate over Scotland's future which culminated in the Union of 1707, which he opposed from his seat in the Scottish parliament.[14]

Sparta provided Fletcher with a mechanism to reconcile the imperatives of modernizing statehood with the ideals of classical republicanism at a moment when Scotland's justification for joining England's empire, namely, to partake of its burgeoning commercial prospects, was rendering "the classical *polis*-confined republican model all but obsolete."[15] His advocacy for the rejuvenation of Britain's moribund militias and his proposal of a reform program to rescue Scotland from the economic dislocations of the 1690s both had Spartan antecedents. The former, propounded in the tract *A Discourse of Government with Relation to Militias* (1698), is predicated on the notion that public liberty will be preserved where there is a public militia. Fletcher accepts that Britain's defunct militias will never be viable military forces again. The militia's purpose is to realize his conviction that "the whole free people of any nation ought to be exercised to arms." To that end, he wants several camps set up in England and Scotland in which all young men will enrol upon turning twenty-two in order to spend the next two years training in military arts. Mostly what they will learn, however, is how to be better men.[16]

Fletcher's regime of martial discipline resembles a truncated, modernized version of the *agoge*, the Spartan system of military training-cum-education. What matters to him is the formative influence on young men his scheme could have. He wants to mould Scotland's youth. "Such a camp would be as great a school of virtue as of military discipline ... Virtue imbibed in younger years would cast a flavour to the utmost periods of life. In a word, they would learn greater and better things than the military art, and more necessary too, if anything can be more necessary than the defence of our country."[17]

Fletcher follows the traditional civic republican equation of virtue with militarism, but subtly alters the balance to favour virtue in light of the militia's irrelevance to modern European warfare. James Buchan exaggerates only slightly when he claims Fletcher aspired to create in Scotland a society based on the aristocratic and martial virtues of ancient Sparta.[18]

Sparta's shadow looms as well over the remedies for Scotland's economic underdevelopment he advances in the second of his *Two Discourses concerning the Affairs of Scotland* (1698). Inspired by how he imagined the ancients would have resolved it, Fletcher's answer to the problem of the apparent rise of vagabondage in Scotland is the creation of a massive new servile class. "Every man of a certain estate in this nation should be obliged to take a proportionable number of those vagabonds" and put them to labour.[19] Fletcher denies this constitutes slavery, for they will be subject to the laws, not the arbitrary will of their masters. They may be bought and sold, but in exchange for the expropriation of their labour shall be clothed and fed, an improvement over their present penury.

Having expropriated the elite's wealth to pay for the privilege of becoming masters, Fletcher sets about curing the woeful state of Scottish agriculture by expropriating their land. His program has several steps, including the abolition of interest, the substitution of payments for rent in kind, and a mandated reallocation of land to put it in the hands of those with the greatest ability to improve it. Those with plots too small to be economically viable and those with too much land to improve it themselves would be forced to sell to those who could use it most efficiently and productively. "All sorts of men would in a little time fall into that easy method for their affairs, which is proposed by the project."[20]

A bizarre jumble of the ancient and modern, Fletcher's schemes represent a massive attempt at social engineering. If "the impracticality of his own proposals reflects a forced, even archaic analysis of the problems,"[21] the paradox is the result of his own conceptual limitations. Fletcher attempted to institute ancient solutions even though he knew he was applying them in a context in which they were no longer valid. The problems he tried to solve were the result of a "total alteration in the way of living, upon which all government depends." This alteration had begun around 1500 and had not stopped. Fletcher does not "pretend that the present governments can be restored" to their former situations. In his own words, his historical investigations "show[ed] the impossibility of it."[22]

Fletcher's thought was proleptic, foretelling Sparta's (and republicanism's) career over the course of the century. Already with him we see the idea that the movement of history opens a divide between past and present which can no longer be crossed. He perceived that something was wrong and what; but not why or how to rectify it. Hence, the clash between the atavistic and the futuristic in his prescriptions. Trying to accommodate these new realities he stretched republican politics to its limits. Yet if it could not explain Scotland's new economic and political realities, then perhaps it was not the new society which came up short but rather the civic ideal.[23] Republicanism could apprehend the approach of modernity, but not grasp it. Accepting the imperatives of modern statecraft but unable to jettison his antiquated moral assumptions, Fletcher tumbled into the chasm between them.

Moral qualms made Adam Ferguson's (1723–1816) embrace of civic republicanism more ambivalent than it may otherwise have been. A son of the Highlands who became professor of moral philosophy at Edinburgh, Ferguson was one of the most influential figures of the Scottish Enlightenment and a forerunner of modern sociology. He was also one of the most sensitive critics of the new and improved Scotland.[24] Ferguson, too, explored the limits of classical politics in the modern age, but what Fletcher had only glimpsed had become for his countryman the way things were. The thesis of his masterpiece, *An Essay on the History of Civil Society* (1767), is simple: "The boasted refinements, then, of the polished age, are not divested of danger."[25] Yet he was no reactionary republican misoneist. He was cognizant that civic republicanism offered "no answers for the new respectability of wealth and social refinement, which eighteenth-century Scots came to associate with the modern age."[26] Nor did he try to prove otherwise.

Rather, he defended the continuing relevance of civic values. This justification, however, departed considerably from the traditional civic view because though he accepted its political premises he eschewed its economic bases.[27] Ferguson applied republican ideals to commercial society in order to unite them. His unique contribution to the Enlightenment was a theory of commercial modernity upheld by a revised, updated version of the civic creed.[28] By reworking republican precepts he hoped to revitalize them and make them accessible to modern society.

Ferguson feared that the blandishments and achievements of the modern age, vaunted as a higher stage of civilization, would actually subvert it. He worried that at the present stage of historical and social development, that of modern commercial society, men, who naturally "prefer the occupation, improvement, and felicity of our nature, to its mere existence," would become so engrossed in their private pursuits that they would lose sight of everything else, including the civic bonds which made their activities possible by fostering the society in which they take place. Not only would the community collapse if those ties were severed, but so would the reason for those pursuits, as both are contingent upon interaction with one's fellows.[29]

Ferguson's mandate was to rekindle "that habit of the soul by which we consider ourselves as but a part of some beloved community, and as but individual members of some society, whose general welfare is to us the supreme object of zeal, and the great rule of our conduct." Yet if this higher calling is to be answered, then more mundane desires must be sacrificed. He indicates this when he states that "if we are asked, Where the pursuit of trifling accommodations should stop, in order that a man may devote himself entirely to the higher engagements of life? we may answer, That it should stop where it is. This was the rule followed at Sparta." Moreover, in ancient times the public counted for everything and the individual for nothing, a sharp contrast to the modern arrangement, which is the reverse.[30] But Ferguson does not contend things can be turned back. His commitment to his historical scheme foreclosed that possibility. Hence, he harbours no desire to stop the progress of the arts. Nor could there be a return even if he desired it. Sparta occupied an earlier moment not only in time, but in the development of civilization. It is as impossible to return to the one as it is the other.

Ferguson's appreciation that Sparta is irretrievable affords him a detached perspective from which he can view Sparta's positive and negative aspects. This imparts to his treatment a certain historicist quality. Anachronistic the term may be, but it points to the subtext of Ferguson's observations on ancient Lacedaemon, namely, that if one does not wish to judge contemporary society by Sparta, then Sparta should no more be judged by contemporary society.

Unlike many of his counterparts, who wonder how others could "subsist under customs and manners" they would find intolerable and therefore dismiss as barbaric, Ferguson recognizes that "every age hath its consolations as well as its sufferings." Sparta's "consolations" nearly transport him. The Spartan constitution alone pulled off the nearly impossible feat of stifling the ruinous "passion for riches." It did this by making the citizen regard himself "as the property of his country not as the owner of a private estate." This living public property was "active, penetrating, brave, disinterested, and generous." All told, there was a dignity and grandeur to the Spartan which made him something to behold.[31]

But this dignity and grandeur were bought at the terrible price of the suffering of the thousands who were devoured to make it possible, suffering which may be overlooked for a moment but cannot be forgotten. "When we think only of the superior order of men in this state ... we are apt to forget, like themselves, that slaves have a title to be treated like men." We are apt to forget; but we can *forget* it only because we once *knew* it. The ancients never knew it at all. Waking from his reverie, Ferguson recognizes the slave, and remembers that Sparta too had suffering.

> Women, or slaves, in the earliest ages, had been set apart for the purposes of domestic care, or bodily labour ... Freemen would be understood to have no object beside those of politics and war. In this manner, the honours of one half of the species were sacrificed to those of the other; as stones from the same quarry are buried in the foundation, to sustain the blocks which happen to be hewn for the superior parts of the pile. In the midst of our encomiums bestowed on the Greeks and the Romans, we are, by this circumstance, made to remember, that no institution is perfect.

From the modern point of view, that pile appears very much a ruin. It leaves the ancients "a sorry plea for esteem with the inhabitants of modern Europe."[32]

But perhaps this is only because the plea falls on deaf ears. Moderns, Ferguson suggests, simply may not be "sufficiently instructed" in the nature and purpose of the Spartan state to attain a true understanding of it. If that is so, it is a futile gesture to condemn or condone Sparta. Futile too because the progress of history obviates the prospect of establishing a standard applicable to both societies. Each is legitimate according to its own lights. If the modern age is measured by levels of politeness and civilization or the progress of commerce, "we shall be found to have greatly excelled any of the celebrated nations of antiquity."[33] By their own standards, moderns surpass antiquity. That is all that matters. Sparta occupied an earlier stage of historical development. Modern society occupies another, later stage. Time's advance confers no moral legitimacy on the one nor delegitimizes the other. But the earlier stage has been superseded, and there can be no return. Sparta is history.

That same history consoled others less sanguine than Ferguson about the morality of progress. Self-appointed social guardians who harboured few doubts that progress threatened human happiness were drawn to Sparta because its educational apparatus offered a bulwark against what they feared was progress's primary hazard, a freedom of thought liable to sunder communal bonds. The solution was to mould individuals in such a way that the harmful effects of their mental independence were neutralized. The Spartans had pulled off the feat of allowing individuals to think for themselves, but only what they had been taught to think. If the British hoped to preserve their society from ruin they would have to do the same.[34]

This was the demand made bluntly, and from his opponents' perspective obnoxiously, by John Brown (1715–66). A playwright and poet with a reputation for being "a rather peculiar character," Brown was best known for several social and political tracts espousing the views of the English opposition, of which he was one of the loudest voices of the 1750s and 1760s. He spelled out his views on the necessity of adopting Spartan education in his *Thoughts on Civil Liberty, on Licentiousness, and Faction* (1765), published shortly before his despair about the state of contemporary England drove him to slit his own throat.[35]

Brown was motivated by abhorrence of the "fatal Principle" of change, which undermines "that Identity and Integrity of Manners and Principles, which is the Soul and Security of every free state." No free community built on the maxims of unrestrained thought and action, he avows, is long for the world. Some mechanism is necessary which will check man's innate selfishness and prevent liberty from sinking into licentiousness. Modern law lacks an "inward Controul" powerful enough to "penetrate the secret Recesses of the Soul" and "reach the dark Intentions of the Heart of Man." The history of free states confirms the necessity of such a "controul," inculcated via a system of instruction and moral suasion that begins with birth. "Thus was the famed Republic of Sparta strongly fortify'd, by the united and concurrent Power of Manners and Principles, all pointed to the same End, the Strength and Duration of the State."[36]

Moderns may revile the ends to which Sparta's manners and principles were put, but what attracts Brown is their success. Britain's potentially fatal flaw is its lack of a uniform, national mode of education. It needs a power like Sparta had to uphold the manners and principles necessary to preserve its way of life.[37] For Brown, the spartanization of education is the only way to extirpate the woes of licentiousness and faction, thereby preserving liberty.

Fascination with Sparta was not British property. Admiration for Lycurgus's legendary prowess in remaking human nature was an elemental aspect of the thought of the French theorist Gabriel Bonnot, abbé de Mably (1709–85), a one-time royalist who switched allegiances and produced what was arguably the most important body of republican thought in eighteenth-century France, if not all Europe.[38] Mably's sketch of Lycurgus and Sparta forms the centrepiece of his *Observations sur l'histoire de la Grèce* (1764). Divided and violent until his intervention, Lycurgus remade his people by imposing his will on them. He "opposed his genius to that of the Spartans, and dared to take up the hard task of making them into a new people ... Without any right other than that conferred by a love of the good and the safety of the people, he forced the Lacedaemonians to become wise and happy."[39] Mably's Lycurgus is a man of implacable volition, a revolutionary willing to defy the proclivities of his countrymen in order to realize their better natures.

Lycurgus's superior knowledge of "the reciprocal action of the laws on *moeurs*, and of *moeurs* on the laws" facilitated his economic program, the linchpin of his system. Aware of the problems that industry and avarice could entail, Lycurgus "descended, so to speak, right to the hearts of his citizens, and stamped out the germ of the desire for wealth." As any republican would have desired, he limited the Spartans' needs to those sanctioned by nature. Thereafter, luxury and its supports fled

Sparta, wealth became useless and contemptible, "and Sparta became a fortress inaccessible to corruption."[40]

Adherence to the principles of republicanism, and its capacity to sustain a certain dialectic tendency in his thinking,[41] only partially explain Mably's unstinting admiration for Sparta and his ceaseless allusions to it. He turned to it above all because it was an outlet for a profound yearning for a way of life whose attraction was all the more powerful because it existed only in his imagination. Several passages in his *Entretiens de Phocion* (1763) evince a deep nostalgia for the days of antique (let us describe it, *faute de mieux*, as) authenticity. None is more evocatively plangent than this one, uttered by Mably's eponymous spokesman:

> I delight in the simplicity of *moeurs* portrayed in Homer: kings who know the number of cattle, goats, and sheep in their flocks and can prepare their own food; queens who weave the very garments their husbands wear; princesses who descend to the river in humble carts in order to wash their families' clothes. Each person finding glory in being his own artisan. The gods willing, perhaps the wisdom of our *moeurs*, the simplicity of our needs, and the equality of our fortunes can still make this possible![42]

Phocion's plaint crosses the divide of centuries not once, but twice. The chasm between Mably and Homer is vast, almost two and a half millennia. But that between Phocion and Homer is not inconsiderable, either. The *Entretiens* is set in the fourth century BC, meaning that Homer's age had already fallen into the dark dim depths of time immemorial not by Phocion's day, but by that of his forgotten ancestors. Phocion's nostalgia redounds to Mably's; they reinforce and amplify each other. Mably looks back to Phocion, who looks back to Homer – and in this double vision they both look to the past and away from the present and the future.

Mably has a strong title to being the greatest "laconomaniac" of the era.[43] Jean-Jacques Rousseau's (1712–78) is stronger. Sparta was his talisman, keeping at bay the forces of a modernity he could neither fully reject nor accept. Rousseau's attachment to antiquity – which pervades his entire philosophical outlook – was the pendant of his alienation from contemporary Europe. If the Genevan philosopher became the "arch-priest of laconism," he did so through his scourging of the Enlightenment and the modern world it championed.[44]

Rousseau exalted "that Republic of demi-Gods rather than of men," as he described it in his very first tract, the *Discourse on the Arts and*

Sciences (1750),[45] from the beginning of his career to its end, but never more fatefully than in *The Social Contract* (1762). The outstanding expression of his Spartan passion, in this as in so many other respects, it must be regarded as the outstanding expression of his mind. Rousseau's paramount task in that book is to explain how man, despite being born free, wound up in chains, and to offer a model of political organization which would prevent this enslavement from recurring. The freedom he strives to recreate therein is that freedom whose most perfect earthly incarnation, he believed, had been ancient Sparta. Seen from this perspective Rousseau's proposals have a markedly laconic cast. His portrait of the lawgiver, who as Brent Cusher notes in his essay "play[s] such a central role for Rousseau's civic republicanism,"[46] is deeply coloured by the legend of Lycurgus, who took a community which was fractious in precisely the way one riven by the unfettered play of particular wills would be, and moulded it into a new people which placed the general above every particular will. The general will itself is more readily imagined in a small place like ancient Sparta where political decision making occurred on a face-to-face basis.[47] The civil religion mimics those Spartan festivals whose performance he believed was necessary to republics. It nurtures that "sweet uniformity" in which the Spartans had lived, and republican citizens should live.[48] Rousseau's antipathy to representation also finds justification in Sparta and the other Greek republics, where citizens managed public affairs not only in their own names but on their own behalf. In a "well-conducted city everyone flies to the assemblies" because public affairs take priority over private. As "the sum of the common happiness contributes a greater share to each individual's happiness," there is no need to seek private fulfilment.[49]

Sparta was a society in which men were free of the chains they wore in the present. If they were once free they could be again. The ancients showed the way. Rousseau's dilemma was that few would be willing to follow it even if they could. By framing Sparta and modernity as antithetical he negated any grounds by which the claims of the one could be validated against the other. Rousseau knew this. The whole point of referring to antiquity was to turn one's gaze to the future.[50] Gaze he may have upon the past, but what he saw was the future. In this way, if no other, Rousseau was a modern.

Yet if the point of turning to the past was to seek the future, perhaps it was best to find it on its own terrain lest the seeker or, worse, the future itself be lost. This was the argument made by the enemies of the Spartan legend, who feared that its resurrection threatened the very ideals of modernity and enlightenment that at long last were allowing the future to escape the past. The Scottish philosopher and historian David Hume (1711–76) was a committed foe of the continued dalliance with political models inspired by nostalgia for the ancient republics, which he considered hopelessly irrelevant to the modern age. Hume's *Essays Moral, Political, and Literary* (1758), which like his histories were as highly regarded in his day as his seminal philosophical works are today, is a vindication of modernity.[51] For Hume, republican citizenship belonged to an earlier, irretrievable stage of history. It had been superseded by the economic and political system which had prevailed in Britain over the preceding half-century. Hume believed that "private life and private virtues are not an unsatisfactory alternative to life on the public stage"; not only could one be fully human despite not living in a *polis*, life in a commercial republic is indeed preferable.[52]

Such ideas were antithetical to the classical tradition. The *Essays* announces Hume's rejection of this tradition; it is a sustained criticism of ancient politics. Hume assails Sparta with especial gusto, not only in its own right, but also for the infatuation its memory seems to inspire in his more susceptible fellows. Hume's argument is one that would become common to eighteenth-century critics of Sparta and republicanism: even if those ideals had once flourished, there is no way of accommodating them in the modern world without shattering it.

History teaches that there is no escape from the historical process which has made modernity inhospitable to those ideals. This is the basis of Hume's case against classical politics in the essay "Of Civil Liberty." The ancients' theories fit their world and experience because they were based on what the ancients knew. What they did not know is everything that came after. Only by ignoring the subsequent two millennia of history could anyone pretend those theories remained viable – an absurd proposition. "Such mighty revolutions have happened in human affairs, and so many events have arisen contrary to the expectations of the ancients, that they are sufficient to beget the suspicion of still further changes." History, Hume implies, in some sense *is* change. To deny either would be a useless gesture. And a misguided one, for change and history have benefited mankind, at least when it comes to politics. All governments have "undergone, in modern times, a great change for the better."[53]

That change owes much to the expansion of trade and commerce. Classical political theory scorned these, yet they form the basis of modern statecraft. On this score Hume is convinced that modern politics is more realistic, as it makes better accommodation for human nature than ancient, whose paragon was Lycurgus's labour to stifle and reshape human nature. Modern political doctrine is superior because it acknowledges that a state's greatness is inseparable from the people's happiness. What often makes them happy, Hume proposes in his essay "Of Commerce," is commerce. Such happiness and its cause were impossible in ancient times, when "a kind of opposition between the greatness of the state and the happiness of the subject" existed, as the state seized the private endeavours of its citizens in its quest for greatness. This expropriation, this "want" of commerce was the reason the ancient states seemed more powerful than their modern counterparts. Contemporary statesmen might be tempted to revive this policy, but any such prospect is

> almost impossible; and that because ancient policy was violent, and contrary to the more natural and usual course of things. It is well known with what peculiar laws Sparta was governed, and what a prodigy that republic is justly esteemed by every one, who has considered human nature as it has displayed itself in other nations, and other ages. Were the testimony of history less positive and circumstantial, such a government would appear a mere philosophical whim or fiction, and impossible ever to be reduced to practice.

Were it not for history's abundant testimony, Sparta would be dismissed as a fantasy conjured from the depths of imagination. As far as Hume is concerned, it may as well be just that. Whatever circumstances had once permitted Sparta to thrive no longer obtain. Modern politicians, properly informed by history, must realize that "the best policy [is] to comply with the common bent of mankind, and give it all the improvements of which it is susceptible."[54]

Charles-Louis de Montesquieu (1689–1755) agreed. At one time a judge in the *parlement* of Bordeaux, Montesquieu authored two of the most important works of the first half of the eighteenth century, the *Persian Letters* (1721) and *The Spirit of the Laws* (1748). Unlike Hume, he was not hostile to the antique mode of politics, but he nevertheless took for granted its incompatibility with modernity. Considered as a whole, his thought offered a new vision of liberty, one founded in the conviction that the republican form no longer had a place in the modern age. As such he is rightly considered one of the progenitors of modernity.[55]

Montesquieu treats antiquity as having customs, institutions, and mentalities quite distinct from those of the modern world.[56] Taken on its own terms, the antique model would seem to have been quite successful, and this is the tack he takes early in his sprawling masterwork, *The Spirit of the Laws*. Sparta provides him with the finest example of what he calls a democratic republic, that is, a republic founded on virtue. "Virtue, in a republic, is a very simple thing: it is love of the republic." Love of the republic is but the love of one's homeland and its laws, a love citizens express by preferring the common interest to their own. Montesquieu attributes Sparta's great virtue to its "singular institutions," its system of education and Lycurgus's success in guiding his people away from any other sources of fulfilment than their pursuit of "greatness and glory."[57]

Montesquieu lets Sparta's strangeness flow from his portrait of its way of life; his description neither criticizes nor emphasizes. Yet in later sections of his great book he underscores the pillars of republicanism which have crumbled since antiquity. For one thing, institutions such as Sparta's are possible only in a small state because only there is the population tiny enough to be guided down a singular path. "It is in the nature of a republic to have only a small territory; otherwise, it can scarcely continue to exist." The republic stayed small; it was the world that got bigger. "The compass opened the universe, so to speak."[58] With it came commerce not just of goods but of peoples and ideas, and a vast expansion of humanity's horizons.

With all these changes the scope and nature of government changed. Perhaps the most dramatic change, certainly the most important, came in its relationship to the individual. The statutes of the ancient legislators were more concerned with the community than the citizen, "and the citizen more than the man. The law sacrificed both the citizen and the man and thought only of the republic." This attitude, that the individual's good must yield to the public good, Montesquieu dismisses as a "fallacy." Government must follow the bent of its citizens. Only such a government may be reckoned just, or natural. "It is better to say that the government most in conformity with nature is the one whose particular arrangement best relates to the disposition of the people for whom it is established."[59]

No Enlightenment figure was more adamant that meeting this obligation required hurling Sparta into the abyss of history than the radical political theorist, Dissenter, and discoverer of oxygen, Joseph Priestley (1733–1804). Priestley's case against Sparta, articulated in the *Essay on the First Principles of Government, and on the Nature of Political, Civil, and Religious Liberty* (1768, 1771), is simple. Humanity has made great strides in morality and knowledge over the course of history, especially recently. The engine of this progress is the freedom of the human mind. Resurrecting Sparta would destroy this freedom, and with it progress and all hope of a better future.

It is a faculty of the mind that it can contemplate the past, present, and future, thereby accumulating knowledge and experience. As it does, the intellect improves. What is true of the part is true of the whole. "The human species itself is capable of a similar and unbounded improvement; whereby mankind in a later age are greatly superior to mankind in a former age." Those living today, therefore, enjoy "much greater power, to be, and to make happy" than those who lived centuries ago. For the same reason, those who will live centuries from now shall be superior to us.[60]

Those adhering to the maxim that the collective wisdom of all the members of society taken together "must be preferable to that of individuals" would bring that improvement to a calamitous halt if they were able to reimpose on men's minds the shackles which have only recently fallen away. Priestley therefore opposes vehemently the clamour for a system of uniform education. "The great object of civil society is the happiness of the members of it." But this happiness each member must find for himself. As much as education conduces to this pursuit, then, "the right of conducting it should be inviolably preserved to individuals." It must be, for history and experience reveal that those arts "stand the fairest chance of being brought to perfection" which have the greatest scope for experimentation, for trial and error.[61]

Only the unfettered play of the mind leads to the continuous perfection of all its arts. Fixing those arts as they are would fix them in their "infancy," unformed and only partly understood. Education is particularly susceptible to this danger. Putting education "in its present imperfect state into the hands of the civil magistrate, in order to fix the mode of it, would be like" giving clothes to a child and refusing to let it replace them as it grows.[62]

The civil art too is immature, and just as imperilled by the prospect of being bound to its present limits. Society and the state, like the men and women who constitute them, must grow, change, adapt, and learn. Even the best government in the world, Priestley warns, would, if "fixed in its present condition," one day become the worst. Some states, though, did not have to become the worst; they always had been.

> What advantage did Sparta (the constitution of whose government was so much admired by the ancients, and many moderns) reap from those institutions which contributed to its longevity, but the longer continuance of, what I should not scruple to call, the worst government we read of in the world … The convulsions of Athens, where life was in some measure enjoyed, and the faculties of body and mind had their proper exercise and gratification, were, in my opinion, far preferable to the savage uniformity of Sparta.[63]

Priestley loathes uniformity because it destroys progress by subverting the freedom of thought which facilitates the improvement and change upon which progress depends. Only when minds in all their glorious variety are allowed to roam freely and wantonly can men create the progress that leads them to the future. Should the desire to immobilize the mind just when it has taken its first steps into a wider world be realized, "it would, I apprehend, put an effectual stop to all the noble improvements of which society is capable."[64] To try to keep things as they are and impose uniformity, in other words to resurrect Sparta, is to surrender the possibility of man ever emerging from his self-imposed immaturity.

By placing the individual as the bearer of progress at the centre of his political vision, Priestley subverted both the Spartan mirage and the classical republicanism it inspired. Belief in progress demands a concomitant belief that the future can – and should – be different from the present and past. Both these beliefs were inimical to the Spartan and republican ideals. Sparta's *telos* was to withstand the future. Thwarting the individual's ability to have any aspirations other than those of the community was a primary means towards this end. From these principles, Priestley articulated a moral case that Sparta is incompatible with Enlightenment, and thus human progress – a case which, by Priestley's lights, could have but one verdict: if mankind is to have any hope of enlightenment, of progress, of a future, the only place Sparta can have in the modern world is none.

We may marvel at the eighteenth century's fascination with Sparta, so pervasive it astonishes us now.[65] Yet this enthusiasm was a product of the very forces which cause our astonishment today. It was both a cause and consequence of "man's quarrel with his own history, that most characteristic feature of the modern mind."[66]

Sparta was an ideal arsenal for this conflict because it could furnish weapons to both sides. E.N. Tigerstedt noted fifty years ago that the Spartan mirage has been resolved into so many contrasting visions that one cannot help wondering if "'Sparta' is nothing more than a projection of the present into the past, a wishfulfilment that has been given a historical label."[67] Sparta in the Enlightenment was just that, a projection of the present into the past, but it was no less a projection of the past into the present. Convinced of it themselves, the champions of the Enlightenment sought to convince their brethren that granting that wish would bring only disaster. Sparta had to be projected out of the present and made fast against the desires of time. The longing of the present would henceforth be for the future.

Admiration for ancient Sparta had been a pillar of Western thought for two millennia. Hume, Montesquieu, Priestley, and others chipped away at it. Their successors were even more trenchant and devastating in their assaults. None more so than Emmanuel Joseph Sieyès (1748–1836) and Benjamin Constant (1767–1830), two of the most prominent political writers of the French Revolution and each a founding father of liberalism. Both blamed the Reign of Terror on the Jacobin infatuation with classical antiquity, especially Sparta. That calamity proved that applying the wisdom of the past to the problems of the present could have lethal effects.

The existence of this volume (and series)[68] shows that the desire to learn from antiquity has not been extinguished. Ancient politics can – and does – instruct modern. But it must be our teacher, not our master. As with any other authority, we may not follow where it will not lead. Thanks in no small part to Sparta's eighteenth-century enemies, scepticism, even suspicion and distrust, of modern attempts to reclaim antiquity have themselves become part of those attempts.

Perhaps this, then, was the moral of the Enlightenment's confrontation with antiquity: that henceforth its lessons would have to be learned with great, and applied with even greater, caution. The past might serve as guide, but the modern world had to chart its own course into the future. Once this conviction took hold, Sparta's sway over the European imagination diminished greatly, and both it and civic republicanism departed the eighteenth century far weaker than they had entered it.

NOTES

1 Gordon Wood, *The Creation of the American Republic, 1776–1787,* 2nd ed. (Chapel Hill: University of North Carolina Press, 1998), viii.
2 Throughout this essay I use "civic republicanism" and "classical republicanism" interchangeably.
3 Jennifer Tolbert Roberts, *Athens on Trial: The Antidemocratic Tradition in Western Thought* (Princeton: Princeton University Press, 1994), 156.
4 "The beginning of modernity (*Neuzeit*), with all the difficulties that arise out of this concept, was manifested for the first time in the Enlightenment, which had identified itself as the standard-bearer of a new time (*neue Zeit*)." Reinhart Koselleck, *The Practice of Conceptual History: Timing History, Spacing Concepts,* trans. T.S. Presner et al. (Stanford: Stanford University Press, 2002), 160.
5 Michael Kwass, "Big Hair: A Wig History of Consumption in Eighteenth-Century France," *American Historical Review* 111 (2006), 632.
6 J.G.A. Pocock, *Virtue, Commerce, and History: Essays on Political Thought and History, Chiefly on the Eighteenth Century* (Cambridge: Cambridge University Press, 1985), 100.
7 "As a 'project' modernity is less a realised set of relationships, institutions and experiences than a series of claims and attempts to make and remake the future." Miles Ogborn, *Spaces of Modernity: London's Geographies 1680–1780* (New York: Guilford Press, 1998), 28.
8 Jürgen Habermas, "Modernity versus Postmodernity," *New German Critique* 22 (1981), 3.
9 Tilo Schabert, "A Note on Modernity," *Political Theory* 7 (1979), 125.
10 Elena Russo, "The Youth of Moral Life: The Virtue of the Ancients from Montesquieu to Nietzsche," in *Montesquieu and the Spirit of Modernity,* ed. David W. Carrithers and Patrick Coleman (Oxford: Voltaire Foundation, 2002), 105.
11 François Ollier, *Le mirage spartiate: Étude sur l'idéalisation de Sparte dans l'antiquité grecque de l'origine jusqu' aux Cyniques,* 2 vols. (Paris: É. de Boccard, 1933–43); E.N. Tigerstedt, *The Legend of Sparta in Classical Antiquity,* 3 vols. (Stockholm: Almqvist and Wiksell, 1965–78); Elizabeth Rawson, *The Spartan Tradition in European Thought,* 2nd ed. (Oxford: Oxford University Press, 1991).
12 Joseph M. Levine, *The Battle of the Books: History and Literature in the Augustan Age* (Ithaca: Cornell University Press, 1991), 7.
13 James Buchan, *Crowded with Genius: The Scottish Enlightenment: Edinburgh's Moment of the Mind* (New York: HarperCollins, 2003), 20.

14 For additional background on Fletcher, see John Robertson, *The Case for the Enlightenment: Scotland and Naples, 1680–1760* (Cambridge: Cambridge University Press, 2005), 161–84.

15 Fania Oz-Salzberger, "The Political Theory of the Scottish Enlightenment," in *The Cambridge Companion to the Scottish Enlightenment*, ed. Alexander Broadie (Cambridge: Cambridge University Press, 2003), 166.

16 Andrew Fletcher, *Political Writings*, ed. John Robertson (Cambridge: Cambridge University Press, 1997), 21–8.

17 Ibid., 29.

18 Buchan, *Crowded with Genius*, 13–14.

19 Fletcher, *Political Writings*, 68.

20 Ibid., 78.

21 Robertson, *Case for the Enlightenment*, 171.

22 Fletcher, *Political Writings*, 6, 4.

23 Oz-Salzberger, "Political Theory," 158; Robertson, *Case for the Enlightenment*, 181–2.

24 Marco Geuna, "Republicanism and Commercial Society in the Scottish Enlightenment: The Case of Adam Ferguson," in *Republicanism: A Shared European Heritage*, ed. Martin van Gelderen and Quentin Skinner, 2 vols. (Cambridge: Cambridge University Press, 2002), 2: 177–95; Lisa Hill, *The Passionate Society: The Social, Political and Moral Thought of Adam Ferguson* (Dordrecht: Springer, 2006).

25 Adam Ferguson, *An Essay on the History of Civil Society*, ed. Fania Oz-Salzberger (Cambridge: Cambridge University Press, 1995), 219.

26 Oz-Salzberger, "Political Theory," 169.

27 Geuna, "Republicanism and Commercial Society," 183.

28 Oz-Salzberger, "Political Theory," 168.

29 Ferguson, *Essay*, 225, 197, 173, 170.

30 Ibid., 53, 234, 57.

31 Ibid., 103–4, 152–3, 176.

32 Ibid., 177, 176, 189.

33 Ibid., 153, 193.

34 Peter Miller, *Defining the Common Good: Empire, Religion and Philosophy in Eighteenth-Century Britain* (Cambridge: Cambridge University Press, 2004), 113, 336.

35 For further information on Brown, see ibid., 105–17, 333–5. As Miller notes (335), Brown's views in the *Thoughts* stand in stark contrast to his early receptiveness to free inquiry.

36 John Brown, *Thoughts on Civil Liberty, on Licentiousness, and Faction*, 2nd ed. (London: Davis and Reymers, 1765), 75, 25, 50.

37 Ibid., 83, 157.
38 Johnson Kent Wright, *A Classical Republican in Eighteenth-Century France: The Political Thought of Mably* (Stanford: Stanford University Press, 1997).
39 Gabriel Bonnot de Mably, *Collection complète des oeuvres de l'Abbé de Mably*, 15 vols. (Paris: Ch. Desbriere, 1794–5), 4: 14.
40 Ibid., 4: 22.
41 Chantal Grell, *Le dix-huitième siècle et l'antiquité en France, 1680–1789* (Oxford: Voltaire Foundation, 1995), 473–4.
42 Mably, *Collection complète des oeuvres*, 10: 120.
43 Rawson, *Spartan Tradition*, 245; Wright, *Classical Republican*, 16.
44 Rawson, *Spartan Tradition*, 243. See also Roberts, *Athens on Trial*, 166; Paul Cartledge, "The Socratics' Sparta and Rousseau's," in *Sparta: New Perspectives*, ed. Stephen Hodkinson and Anton Powell (Swansea: Classical Press of Wales, 1999), 311–37.
45 Jean-Jacques Rousseau, *The Discourses and Other Early Political Writings*, trans. Victor Gourevitch (Cambridge: Cambridge University Press, 1997), 11.
46 See next chapter.
47 Colin Jones, *The Great Nation: France from Louis XV to Napoleon* (London: Penguin Books, 2002), 221.
48 For a fuller discussion of the civil religion as an aspect of republican culture see Lee Ward's chapter (12).
49 Jean-Jacques Rousseau, *The Social Contract and Other Later Political Writings*, trans. Victor Gourevitch (Cambridge: Cambridge University Press, 1997), 113.
50 Yves Touchefeu, "Le sauvage et le citoyen: Le mythe des origines dans le système de Rousseau," in *Primitivisme et mythes des origines dans la France des Lumières, 1680–1820*, ed. Chantal Grell and Christian Michel (Paris: Presses de l'Université de Paris-Sorbonne, 1989), 188 n. 50.
51 The *Essays* has a complex publication history. It consolidates several separate volumes that were published in the 1740s and 1750s, not reaching this form until 1758. For additional information see David Hume, *Essays Moral, Political, and Literary*, ed. Eugene F. Miller (Indianapolis: Liberty Fund, 1987), xii–xiv.
52 John Danford, "'Riches Valuable at All Times and to All Men': Hume and the Eighteenth-Century Debate on Commerce and Liberty," in *Liberty and American Experience in the Eighteenth Century*, ed. David Womersley (Indianapolis: Liberty Fund, 2006), 334.
53 Hume, *Essays*, 89, 93.
54 Ibid., 257, 259, 260.
55 Judith N. Shklar, "Montesquieu and the New Republicanism," in *Machiavelli and Republicanism*, ed. Quentin Skinner et al. (Cambridge: Cambridge

University Press, 1990), 270, 266; David W. Carrithers, "Introduction: Montesquieu and the Spirit of Modernity," in *Montesquieu and the Spirit of Modernity*, ed. David W. Carrithers and Patrick Coleman (Oxford: Voltaire Foundation, 2002), 26.

56 Carrithers, "Introduction," 17.

57 Charles-Louis de Montesquieu, *The Spirit of the Laws*, trans. Anne Cohler et al. (Cambridge: Cambridge University Press, 1989), 42, 36, 37. Robert Sparling addresses Montesquieu's conception of republican virtue at greater length in his chapter (8) above.

58 Ibid., 38, 124, 390. That the compass had transformed European civilization was a widely shared sentiment. "The invention of the needle" was one of the causes of the "total alteration in the way of living, upon which all government depends" that Andrew Fletcher lamented. See Fletcher, *Political Writings*, 5–6.

59 Montesquieu, *Spirit of the Laws*, 528, 510, 8.

60 Joseph Priestley, *Political Writings*, ed. Peter N. Miller (Cambridge: Cambridge University Press, 1993), 8–9.

61 Ibid., 29, 46, 52, 42.

62 Ibid., 43.

63 Ibid., 109.

64 Ibid., 117.

65 David W. Carrithers, "Democratic and Aristocratic Republics: Ancient and Modern," in *Montesquieu's Science of Politics: Essays on* The Spirit of Laws, ed. David W. Carrithers et al. (Lanham, MD: Rowman and Littlefield, 2001), 130.

66 Pocock, *Virtue, Commerce, and History*, 98.

67 Tigerstedt, *Legend of Sparta*, 1: 17.

68 See Preface, n. 6.

11 A Master of the Art of Persuasion: Rousseau's Platonic Teaching on the Virtuous Legislator

BRENT EDWIN CUSHER

Jean-Jacques Rousseau's doctrine of the legislator, that highly virtuous human type who designs foundational laws for the polity, is in many ways the core element of his civic republicanism. That this should be so, however, is perhaps not readily evident. After all, Rousseau is clear that republican legitimacy is conferred by a social contract, to which all the people equally consent. And surely this need for popular consent stands in some tension with the presence of a vastly superior individual – one of the "images of authority," as Judith Shklar has memorably put it,[1] in Rousseau's political thought. Still, Rousseau is just as clear that healthy civic life depends decisively on the legislator's authoritative guidance, for his activity is necessary for resolving a formidable dilemma on the part of the people. Referring in the *Social Contract* to the people as a "blind multitude," Rousseau says that collectively it "often does not know what it wants because it rarely knows what is good for it."[2] The problem for republican politics, then, is a deficiency of vision. The people vaguely sense that there is a good for itself as a group, namely, the general will, but remain unable to make an accurate judgment about its content. Rousseau explains furthermore that certain private individuals can see what is good for the group, but that these men reject it in favour of more parochial interests. Hence, for Rousseau's republican model to enjoy success, the people need "guides" to show them what they cannot see. Individual men need a wise and persuasive legislator to demonstrate that it would be advantageous for them to unite and live together under the general will, and the group needs to be shown what the general will is in the first place.

What is the nature of this figure playing such a central role for Rousseau's civic republicanism? While this question is impossibly broad for a chapter-length study, I shall attempt to take a modest step towards answering it by exploring Rousseau's conception of the legislator's most important task. Taking into account the dilemma of popular vision, as sketched above, it should be apparent that this figure's key function is to provide political instruction for the people, which task requires a form of communication with them. In other words, while Rousseau's vision of civic republicanism is in essential agreement with those others treated in the present volume, in the sense of being animated by the insight that the public must be deeply concerned with its government, Rousseau highlights the task of the individual who moulds and inspires such concern. He explains that the legislator must be a master of the art of persuasion: his speech must be supremely effective at moving the people to accept laws in accordance with the general will. And Rousseau refers to this special kind of communication by the formula "to persuade without convincing (*persuader sans convaincre*)."

Yet what is most striking about Rousseau's conception of legislative persuasion, I shall argue, is that it shares essential elements with models of persuasion found in ancient political thought. To raise the question of Rousseau's conception of persuasion, then, is to raise the larger question of his sources for developing the legislator. Worthwhile not merely from the perspective of the history of ideas, this subject can yield political knowledge too, for it promises to clarify the deep influences on Rousseau's civic republicanism. As Geoffrey Kellow indicates in the introduction to this volume, early modern thinkers frequently drew lessons from ancient examples in formulating their own models of republican politics, and Rousseau's teaching on the legislator is one area where this pattern clearly comes to light. Now, scholarly treatments of Rousseau's legislator have most frequently identified Niccolò Machiavelli's armed prophet as its chief forebear.[3] And there are sound reasons to believe that Rousseau had Machiavelli in mind when constructing the legislator, one of which being his citation of Machiavelli's *Discourses on Livy* in his chapter "On the Legislator" from the *Social Contract*.[4] But however useful it may be to draw this connection, I shall provide evidence in this chapter for seeing Rousseau's legislator rather as an incarnation of the ancient Platonic model, which he learned through careful meditation on Plato's *Laws*.[5] And it is precisely the remarkable relationship between Rousseau and Plato on the matter of legislative persuasion that both underlies and animates this argument. In the following sections, then, I shall discuss Rousseau and Plato individually on the nature of legislative persuasion and conclude with reflections on the parallels between the two, stressing what these parallels reveal about Rousseau's civic republicanism.

Passion and the Art of Persuasion in Rousseau's Political Thought

That the legislator's instruction must be a form of communication between himself and the people is a simple enough truth to perceive; the difficulty, according to Rousseau, rests in the nature of this communication. As he explains in the *Social Contract*, the legislator cannot simply communicate with the people what is truly in its interest because the two parties speak in different languages.

> Wise men who want to use their own language rather than that of the common people cannot be understood by the people. Now there are a thousand kinds of ideas *that are impossible to translate into the language of the people.* Overly general views and overly remote objects are equally beyond its grasp. Each individual, appreciating no other aspect of government than the one that relates to his private interest, has difficulty perceiving the advantages he should obtain from the continual deprivations imposed by good laws.[6]

Because the principles of political right are either too abstract or too remote from the immediate concerns of common individuals, such principles fail to be grasped by them. True political wisdom is, for Rousseau, the province of a few. His formulation implies a grave truth about the relationship between wisdom and society.[7] If, for example, one is translating from one spoken language to another – French to English, say – then one must find the word signifying approximately the same idea in the new language as it had in the old. The assumption is that the various languages are merely different ways of expressing ideas common to humanity. By contrast, Rousseau implies that knowledge of the true principles of political right does not lend itself to translation into the people's language at all. There is no vocabulary in the common language capable of capturing the content of the lawgiver's wisdom. Regardless of how virtuous the legislator finds a particular people, he will not be able to reason with them, as Rousseau holds that one cannot reason with the commonality of men.[8]

This insight is the basis for Rousseau's formula "to persuade without convincing": the legislator must get the people to accept legislation not because they are convinced that they should, but for different reasons.

What, then, does Rousseau mean by this peculiar kind of persuasion? The answer to this question is not entirely clear from the *Social Contract* itself. Instead of explaining what it means to persuade in this manner, Rousseau moves immediately to give an example of such speech, by expounding on the legislator's use of the gods as a mouthpiece during the act of legislation. Still, he does not neglect to define this term in other sections of his corpus. Christopher Kelly, who has written the richest treatment of this type of persuasion, indicates that the most comprehensive discussion of it is found in Rousseau's *Essay on the Origin of Languages*.[9] The *Essay* is the chief text of Rousseau's that investigates the nature of communication as such, speculating on the origins of non-verbal communication, speech and language, writing, and music. But, remarkably, when discussing the character of the earliest language, Rousseau uses the same terminology as he does when describing legislative persuasion.

> Instead of arguments [the first language] would have aphorisms; it would persuade without convincing, and depict without reasoning (*elle persuaderoit sans convaincre et peindroit sans raisonner*). It would resemble Chinese in certain respects, Greek in others, and Arabic in others. Develop these ideas in all their ramifications, and you will find Plato's *Cratylus* is not as ridiculous as it seems to be.[10]

In order to understand Rousseau's model of legislative persuasion, then, it is necessary to investigate his conceptualization of the first language.

The central thesis of the *Essay on the Origins of Languages* is that spoken languages originated in the moral passions, not in a faculty of speech with which all humans are endowed and not because speech was instrumental in satisfying physical needs. For human beings living in the state of nature and experiencing nothing other than purely physical needs, all communication would have been conducted non-verbally, such as by physical gestures and signs. The test of visible signs is accuracy, and because expediency is most important when one is looking to satisfy practical needs, the use of signs would have been the most efficient way of accomplishing this goal. But as soon as human beings developed factitious needs or desires and the habit of living together – a process that Rousseau sketches in detail in his *Discourse on the Origins of Inequality among Men* – they began to communicate in spoken languages. "From where," Rousseau asks, "could [the origin of languages] derive? From the moral needs, the passions. The passions all bring men together, but the necessity of seeking their livelihood makes them flee one another. Neither hunger nor thirst, but love, hatred, pity, anger wrested the first voices from them."[11] Rousseau explains here that the simple passions of hunger and thirst, namely, those related to *amour de soi*, are themselves alone incapable of bringing human beings to develop languages, but that the passions related to *amour-propre* are.[12] Satisfaction of the sophisticated moral passions demands a more sophisticated manner of expression than mere gestures. And it is not simply that spoken languages originate in the *amour-propre* in the speaker: according to Rousseau, speech is meant to appeal to the passions of *amour-propre* in the auditor as well. Discourse is necessary "when it is a question of moving the heart and enflaming the passions."[13]

Rousseau explains that the first language would have expressed figurative rather than literal meaning. Metaphor would have been, in all likelihood, the way by which early men described the objects of nature, because their first sensory experience in encountering other objects would have been the "illusory image offered by the passions" of *amour-propre*.[14] Furthermore, Rousseau calls the first language that developed "tuneful and passionate." That it was melodious depends on its being passionate. Early men confronted with the need to communicate passions to the hearts of others would do so in the appropriate medium: they would sing rather than speak. For Rousseau, the medium of feeling is song.[15] The first language would "neglect grammatical analogy to stick to the euphony, number, harmony, and beauty of sounds."[16] It is for this reason that Kelly, as well as John T. Scott, have maintained that the language of Rousseau's legislator would itself be musical.[17] "The first stories, the first harangues, and *the first laws* were in verse," Rousseau explains; "poetry was discovered before prose; this had to be so, since the passions spoke before reason."[18]

Rousseau gives a vivid example of the moving power of this first language when discussing the character of oriental languages, such as Arabic or Persian. In contrast with the Northern European languages, those "of men who help one another, who coolly reason with one another, or of quick-tempered people who get angry," the oriental languages express their meaning through musical accent and aim at moving the heart. Rousseau indicates, moreover, that they represent the type of communication with which "the wise giv[e] laws to peoples." They represent the sort of language that must be used by the legislator in communicating with the people. But merely to understand a language like Arabic, for example, would not be enough to qualify one for the legislative task. Rousseau's legislator must be a master of the art of so speaking.

> Someone who can read a little Arabic smiles when leafing through the Koran; had he heard Mohammed in person proclaim it in that eloquent and rhythmic language, with that sonorous and persuasive voice which seduced the ear before the heart, and constantly animating his aphorisms with the accent of enthusiasm, he would have prostrated himself on the earth while crying out: great Prophet, Messenger of God, lead us to glory, to martyrdom; we want to conquer or to die for you.[19]

According to Rousseau, then, Mohammed's persuasiveness was achieved by the rhythmic and accented character of his speech and the resonant nature of his voice. Mohammed was capable of moving his followers by means of these instruments because they took direct aim at the principal motivating forces in human beings, that is, the moral passions.

The example of Mohammed here is significant. While it is often noted that Lycurgus of Sparta was the example foremost on Rousseau's mind when thinking about the legislator, as Varad Mehta has persuasively demonstrated in this volume, so too were the examples of other historical figures involved in the project of shaping peoples. Indeed, the founder of the Islamic religion is one of the few legislators to whom Rousseau expressly refers in the *Social Contract*. The "law of the son of Ishmael," he remarks, as well as the Jewish law, "still bear witness today to the great men who formulated them."[20] In short, the description of Mohammed's method of communication is also a description of Rousseau's legislator's, and as such it is a clear indication of what it means to persuade without convincing. So, what does this term mean? This brief analysis has shown that to persuade without convincing involves a sharp distinction between communication with the passions and communication with reason, and that it prefers to employ the former. To communicate with reason would be to attempt to convince: in the *Essay on Languages*, Rousseau compares persuasion without convincing to using aphorisms instead of arguments, on the one hand, and depicting without reasoning, on the other. Now it would be misleading to claim that reason is categorically excluded from the legislator's art, for the use of verbal communication implies that reason is functioning to some extent. Still, the people are not moved to accept the legislator's work by rational argument. As has been demonstrated, they cannot be so moved because true political wisdom cannot be translated into the language of the people.[21] The legislator's language and method of persuasion is therefore decisively sub-rational in character, in two ways. It speaks directly to the heart or the passions of its audience, avoiding direct appeal to the reasoning faculty, and it speaks with the language of the heart, especially with music in its melodious accents and rhythms.

Legislative Persuasion in Plato's *Laws*: The Athenian Stranger on Preludes to Laws

In his *Discourse on Political Economy*, Rousseau calls attention to an aspect of Platonic jurisprudence that reflects his ancient predecessor's extraordinary understanding of the legislative art. Because he knows that "the power of the laws depends even more on their own wisdom than on the severity of their ministers ... Plato considers it a very important precaution always to place at the head of edicts a sensible preamble (*un préambule raisonné*) which shows (*montre*) their justice and utility."[22] In the midst of his discussion of civil law and the legislator's task to establish it, Rousseau bestows high praise on Plato for his teaching on these same themes.

The particular institution to which Rousseau refers in this passage is the prelude (*prooimion*), which the Athenian Stranger, the chief interlocutor of Plato's *Laws*, calls a wholly innovative aspect of his jurisprudence.[23] What is a legal prelude? The Athenian introduces the subject in *Laws* 4 by indicating that there are things the lawgiver ought to say that cannot be presented "in the shape of law" yet must be given as "an example ... for himself and for those he will give laws to."[24] Such an "example" is intended to explain the law in more detail than can be found in the legal prescription alone. The legislator must, therefore, either give a speech or compose a text containing these things and attach it to the beginning of the law so as to herald the expression of the law proper.[25]

Yet what makes this institution so important in the context of our present inquiry – and certainly *one* reason why Rousseau directs our attention to it – is that the prelude is intended to be the principal embodiment of legislative persuasion. The Athenian remarks that it is crucial from the perspective of the lawgiver that the people "be as persuadable as possible (*eupeithestatous*) with regard to virtue,"[26] the loftiest goal of legislation in the *Laws*. But making the people persuadable, or indeed, simply persuading them, cannot be the task of the law itself. "Is [the legislator]," the Athenian asks, "just going to explain straightaway what must and must not be done, add the threat of a penalty, and turn to another law, without adding a single encouragement or bit of persuasion to his legislative edicts (*paramuthias de kai peithous tois nomotheoumenois mēde en prosdidō*)?"[27] As the framing of this question implies, the answer is no. The wise lawgiver must instead establish laws in a double form: what the legislator gives will express the law proper and the penalty, which is likened to a "tyrannical command," in addition to the prelude, which itself represents "persuasion."[28] Indeed, the distinction here seems to harmonize with Jeffrey Dirk Wilson's compelling argument in this volume that the good lawgiver, for the Athenian in Plato's *Laws*, will strive to mix the principles of despotism/order and liberty into the regime. These two principles appear very clearly as "tyrannical command" and "persuasion" in the establishment of laws in a double form.

Rousseau's assessment of the preludes in his *Political Economy* raises a key question as regards the nature of Platonic persuasion. Rousseau has described the preambles of the *Laws* as being *raisonné*, which has been rendered as "sensible" but which is the adjective related to the past participle of *raisonner*, to reason. What is the relationship of the Platonic preludes to reason? Recently, the scholarly literature on Plato's political thought has been augmented by several studies devoted to interpreting the preludes, many of which take the strong position that they function as agents of rational persuasion. Chief among these is Christopher Bobonich's *Plato's Utopia Recast*, in which Plato is interpreted as having become rather sanguine about the prospects for general enlightenment in his late dialogues, the latest being the *Laws*. Bobonich contends that the task of the preludes is to educate citizens by means of "good epistemic reasons for thinking that the principles lying behind the legislation are true." If this is the case, then it should be clear that Bobonich interprets the preludes to be rational in character. "The preludes are thus designed to be instances of rational persuasion," he argues, "that is, attempts to influence the citizens' beliefs through appealing to rational considerations. They are not intended to inculcate false but useful beliefs or to effect persuasion through non-rational means."[29]

This interpretation of the *Laws*, and others similar to it,[30] draw heavily on the Athenian's discussion of the art of medicine in book 4, in which he distinguishes between two types of doctor. On the one hand, there are doctors who understand the nature of the human body and treat patients in light of this knowledge. The Athenian refers to these as "free doctors," for they tend to treat free citizens. On the other hand, there are doctor's servants who have nothing more than the experience of observing their masters' methods. These servants are called "slave doctors," for they go around treating sick slaves. The slave doctor cannot give or receive "an account of each malady"; nonetheless, "claiming to know with precision, he gives his commands just like a headstrong tyrant and hurries off to some other sick domestic slave." The method of the free doctor, however, is radically different.

> The free doctor mostly cares for and looks after the maladies of free men. He investigates these from their beginning and according to nature, communing with the patient himself and his friends, and he both learns (*manthanei*) something himself from the invalids and, as much as he can, teaches (*didaskei*) the one who is sick. He doesn't give orders until he has in some sense persuaded (*ou proteron epetaxen prin an tē sumpeisē*); when he has on each occasion tamed the sick person with persuasion (*meta peithous hēmeroumenon*), he attempts to succeed in leading him back to health.[31]

The Athenian's intention in describing these two kinds of doctor is to clarify the general purpose of the preludes. Whereas a simple law and its penalty for disobedience would correspond to the activity of the slave doctor, a law with its penalty and prelude would be similar to the activity of the free doctor. And it is this latter method that the Athenian prefers.

This passage sheds bright light on the reason why interpreters have contended that the preludes undertake the rational persuasion of citizens. The free doctor, after all, appears to engage primarily in the education of his patients. But there are several reasons why we should be cautious about interpreting the preludes as appealing primarily to reason. First, it is possible to teach by means that fall short of rational argument – the sense of *didaskō* in the passage on the free doctor encompasses this broader kind of teaching[32] – and it is possible for education to aim at instructing the affections rather than reason. There is, in other words, a distinction between civic and philosophic education.[33] In the text cited above, the Athenian also qualifies the notion that the free doctor teaches his patient, claiming that he tries to do so as "as much as he can." Furthermore, the goal of "communing" with the patient is to tame (*hēmeroumenon*) him by means of persuasion so that the doctor can attempt to lead him to health. Such language implies that the objective of the free doctor is to govern and shape the disposition of the patient: that an individual has been "tamed" implies that his passions have been calmed, which calming represents a new disposition of soul. Having been made gentle, the sick individual is in a better position to be brought to health. Earlier in the *Laws*, the Athenian had described the conversation between doctor and patient by saying that it "would contribute something to making the hearer listen in a more tame and agreeable mood (*hēmerōteron … kai eumenesteron*) to the advice,"[34] the change in mood being the essential purpose of the conversation.

Finally, when concluding his theoretical elaboration of the preludes, the Athenian summarizes what has been said, stating their primary purpose:

> For it became clear to me that this whole speech, which the speaker gives in order to persuade, is delivered with just this end in view: so that he who receives the law uttered by the legislator might receive the command – that is, the law – in a frame of mind more favorably disposed and therefore more apt to learn something (*eumenōs, kai dia tēn eumeneian eumathesteron*). That's why, according to my argument at least, this would correctly be called a "prelude" (*prooimion*) rather than an "argument" (*logos*) of the law.[35]

To be sure, the text indicates that the goodwill (*eumeneia*) brought about by the prelude might help the hearer to learn something: the prelude contains an explanatory justification of the law.[36] Still, its immediate aim is to alter the "frame of mind" of the citizen, or, in other words, his disposition. For this reason, the prelude should not be viewed as an instance of rational argument (*logos*).

The persuasion embodied in the preludes, then, appears to be directed at the sub-rational elements of the citizen's soul.[37] With respect to its ability to convey the reasons behind the law, at best we might say that the prelude strives to inculcate good civic opinion and not knowledge.[38] Analysis of two models of preludes from the *Laws* may serve to illustrate this point further. The first explicit example of a legal prelude, presented in *Laws* 4, concerns the law making marriage mandatory for everyone between the ages of thirty and thirty-five. Now, it is clear that the city would have an interest in seeing its citizens marry and produce children in stable family life: childbirth is a condition of the city's continuation. The prelude, however, focuses on the selfish desire that all human beings have for immortality and fame after death, explaining that we best satisfy this desire by having children. But the relation between marriage and children, on the one hand, and the natural desire for immortality, on the other, is susceptible to serious questions. Though the prelude indicates that everyone desires immortality, it is not clear whether everyone should seek satisfaction of this desire in the family. As Thomas Pangle indicates referring to Plato's own decision not to marry: "Surely in the case of the author ... the family was not the way he chose to express his desire for immortality."[39] This observation suggests, of course, that it might not be simply true that the family is a necessary condition for human flourishing. Surely it gainsays the notion that the imperative to marry is categorical, as the prelude implies.

An additional example is the prelude to the law against impiety, from *Laws* 10.[40] The Athenian's proof of the existence of the gods and their providence begins in his claim that human beings need "persuasion" about these matters "so as to make them as tame"[41] as the legislator can, and the Cretan Clinias, with whom the Athenian is speaking, quickly agrees. After having begun to discuss the nature of soul with his interlocutor, though, the Athenian suddenly breaks off their conversation in order to continue it alone.

> Now the argument coming up is rather swift and perhaps almost unfordable for your strength. Lest it create in you a dizziness and whirling, sweep you away by asking unfamiliar questions, and engender an unpleasant unsightliness and unseemliness, it seems to me that I ought now to proceed thus: first I should question myself, while you listen in safety, and then after this I again should answer myself, and go through the entire argument this way until what pertains to soul is completed and it has been demonstrated that soul is prior to body.[42]

Plato indicates several times in the *Laws* that Clinias is not a mean sort of human being, having distinguished himself as an intelligent man among the Cretans. Yet despite his virtue, he is incapable of following the Athenian's argument in the prelude to the law on impiety.[43] Clinias himself indicates that he is unable to follow the reasoning. This could only imply, however, that ordinary citizens would be unable to follow the argument, and that the prelude could not educate by means of sound rational argument. Indeed, the Athenian's image of the unpleasant "dizziness and whirling" that would accompany his argument in *Laws* 10 calls to mind the painful bedazzlement experienced by the individual going through philosophic education in the *Republic*'s allegory of the cave.[44] The drama of Clinias, who is spared the shock attending an education in philosophy, shows that the legislator cannot persuade by rational means.

For these reasons, Glenn Morrow has referred to Platonic preludes as "a species of enchantment" (*epōdē*) and has argued that it represents "a training of the sentiments."[45] But though the prelude is the chief form of persuasion at the legislator's disposal, it is not the only form of enchantment in the *Laws*, and the Athenian explains that the legislator will use other forms in his persuasive art.[46] The Athenian contends, for example, that the lawgiver must establish public festivals that feature choruses in singing and dancing. The songs and dances are not simply entertainment: they are established so that those participating in the choruses, as well as those watching the performances, will undergo an education of the affections, which training helps individuals to acquire the proper qualities of citizenship. The Athenian maintains that young children watching the choruses will have their souls accustomed in the ways of the regime, while older citizens will keep their habituation in the same ways preserved. In short, the songs and dances represent another form of persuasive enchantment by which the lawgiver conducts the work of legislation.[47] And as enchantments, they aim at the affections of the citizenry. This is precisely the sense of Platonic persuasion as contained in the preludes.

Rousseau's Platonic Teaching on Legislative Persuasion

Having separately considered Rousseau's and Plato's positions on legislative persuasion, it is fitting to approach our conclusion by asking a question about Rousseau's reading of Plato. As discussed above, Rousseau describes the preludes as being *raisonné*, yet analysis of crucial passages from the *Laws* has shown that the primary aim of the preludes is to influence not reason, but rather the sentiments. Is Rousseau's description of the preludes, and hence his understanding of Platonic persuasion, unreliable? Or, is it possible to offer a different explanation of what he intends in this statement from the *Political Economy*? The answer to this question is crucially important, for on it turns the matter of Rousseau's engagement with the political thought of his ancient predecessor.

The context of Rousseau's characterization of Platonic preludes is his elaboration on what he calls the first maxim of legitimate government, that is, "to follow the general will in all matters." He concludes that the legislator, to meet this maxim's demands, must make the laws conform to the general will and ensure that the citizens respect them. So, Rousseau asks, how does one promote such respect? One certainly cannot do so by means of force or severity of punishments: overwhelming force provokes the citizen body to feel only terror, which is a vain source of attachment to the law. Indeed, this insight points to the paramount reason for being sceptical that Rousseau's legislator and Machiavelli's armed prophet are intimately similar. Machiavelli famously indicates that the founder conducts his legislation in part by means of force, maintaining that the impressive example of violence well used can effectively compel men to accept "new modes and orders."[48] Yet Rousseau denies this last teaching. In the *Social Contract*, he clarifies that "the legislator is … unable to use either force or reasoning."[49] There must be other methods, and these turn out to be the province of the supremely virtuous legislator. As we have seen, the art of persuasion is the legislator's most important tool.

When Rousseau cites Plato, then, he does so in support of his argument that healthy republican politics can be established only by non-coercive, persuasive means. In context, the chief purpose of calling the legal prelude *raisonné* in the *Political Economy* is to indicate that it achieves its goal by means other than force. Rousseau means to say that the intention of each preamble is to convey (i.e., to "show [*montre*]") the wisdom embodied in the law to the people living under it – as it is for Plato.[50] But this is not to make a strong claim on how the wisdom is to be conveyed. In other words, it is not to make a strong claim that the persuasion of Plato's preludes is fundamentally rational in character. Taking into account this chapter's examination of Rousseau on communication, it is clear that he is well acquainted with methods of conveying wisdom that do not appeal to rational argumentation.

Ultimately, Rousseau and Plato are remarkably similar as regards their understanding of legislative persuasion.[51] To be sure, it would be possible to point to slight differences. Plato, for instance, wishes for persuasion to become institutionalized in the form of preludes, whereas Rousseau, with his teaching on persuading without convincing, does not. Yet even this is less of a disagreement than it might seem at first: Rousseau argues in the penultimate chapter of the *Social Contract* that the persuasive powers of the legislator are, in fact, to become institutionalized in the form of civil religion. There is a perhaps unexpected but strong resonance between this insight, on the one hand, and Lee Ward's careful analysis of Rousseau on civil religion in this volume, on the other. Ward shows that Rousseau's view on the public entertainments most suitable for republican citizens is tied closely together with his views on the purposes of civil religion. Clarity on Rousseau's doctrine of the legislator, however, suggests just how much the objectives of legislative persuasion are intended to be built into these institutions of public entertainment and civil religion, for the greater purpose of educating and sustaining republican citizenship.

The point that bears more directly on the immediate discussion, however, is that both Rousseau and Plato take persuasion to be an indispensable ingredient of healthy republican politics. And they are in agreement on the nature of legislative persuasion as well. Both argue that its primary objective is to shape and govern the citizens' affections; both show that it will not take the form of rational argument. Indeed, for both philosophers, the character of republican communication is musical. Whether it is the melody and rhythm of a sonorous voice, or singing and dancing occurring in a chorus, the good lawgiver must employ these forms of music in establishing a political community.

NOTES

1 Judith N. Shklar, *Men and Citizens: A Study of Rousseau's Social Theory* (Cambridge: Cambridge University Press, 1969), 127–64.

2 Jean-Jacques Rousseau, *On the Social Contract, with Geneva Manuscript, and Political Economy*, ed. Roger D. Masters, trans. Judith R. Masters (New York: St Martin's Press, 1978), 67. All citations of Rousseau in this chapter will be to various editions in English translation. For the French original, I have used Jean-Jacques Rousseau, *Oeuvres complètes*, general ed. Bernard Gagnebin and Marcel Raymond, 5 vols. (Paris: Éditions Gallimard / Bibliothèque de la Pléiade, 1959–95).

3 For examples, see Joseph Masciulli, "The Armed Founder versus the Catonic Hero: Machiavelli and Rousseau on Popular Leadership," *Interpretation* 14.2–3 (May–Sept. 1986), 265–80; Roger D. Masters, *The Political Philosophy of Rousseau* (Princeton: Princeton University Press, 1968), 364–8; and Maurizio Viroli, *La théorie de la société bien ordonnée chez Jean-Jacques Rousseau* (Berlin: Walter de Gruyter, 1988), 156–60. Cf. Barbara Silberdick Feinberg, "Creativity and the Political Community: The Role of the Law-Giver in the Thought of Plato, Machiavelli and Rousseau," *Western Political Quarterly* 23:3 (Sept. 1970), 471–84; Harvey F. Fireside, "The Concept of the Legislator in Rousseau's *Social Contract*," *Review of Politics* 32:2 (Apr. 1970), 191–6; and Paul A. Rahe, *Soft Despotism*,

Democracy's Drift: Montesquieu, Rousseau, Tocqueville and the Modern Project (New Haven: Yale University Press, 2009), 119.

4 Rousseau, *Social Contract*, 70, footnote.

5 Rousseau was intimately familiar with Plato *Laws*: see M.J. Silverthorne, "Rousseau's Plato," *Studies on Voltaire and the Eighteenth Century* 116 (1973), 235–49. There is, at present, a rapidly growing body of scholarship on Rousseau's Platonism more generally, the contributions to which seek generally to demonstrate the profound influence that Platonic political philosophy had on Rousseau. See, e.g., Melissa Butler, "Rousseau and Plato on Women: An Analysis of Book V of *Émile* and Book V of the *Republic*," in *Rousseau and the Ancients / Rousseau et les Anciens*, Proceedings of the Durham, NC, Colloquium (May 1999), ed. Ruth W. Grant and Phillip Stewart (Montreal: Pensée Libre [no. 8], 2001), 140–50; Laurence D. Cooper, *Eros in Plato, Rousseau, and Nietzsche: The Politics of Infinity* (University Park: Pennsylvania State University Press, 2008); Eve Grace, "Justice in the Soul: The *Rêveries* as Rousseau's Answer to Plato's Glaucon," in *Rousseau and the Ancients*, 114–26; Eric Nelson, *The Greek Tradition in Republican Thought* (Cambridge: Cambridge University Press, 2004), 186; Clifford Orwin, "Rousseau's Socratism," *Journal of Politics* 60.1 (Feb. 1998), 174–87; Leonard R. Sorenson, "Rousseau's Socratism: The Political Bearing of 'On Theatrical Imitation,'" *Interpretation* 20.2 (Winter, 1992–3), 135–55; Zev M. Trachtenberg, "Rousseau's Platonic Rejection of Politics," in *Rousseau and the Ancients*, 182–97; and David Lay Williams, *Rousseau's Platonic Enlightenment* (University Park: Pennsylvania State University Press, 2007).

6 Rousseau, *Social Contract*, 69, emphasis supplied.

7 See, more generally, Rousseau's *Discourse on the Sciences and Arts* for his views on the contradiction between wisdom and society: Jean-Jacques Rousseau, *The First and Second Discourses*, ed. Roger D. Masters, trans. Roger D. and Judith R. Masters (New York: St Martin's Press, 1964), 33. Cf., in this connection, Orwin, "Rousseau's Socratism," 174–85; and Leo Strauss, "On the Intention of Rousseau," *Social Research* 14 (Dec. 1947), 461–8.

8 For a reading of Rousseau on language seeing him as more optimistic about the possibility of "popular enlightenment," see J. Patrick Dobel, "The Role of Language in Rousseau's Political Thought," *Polity* 18.4 (Summer 1986), 650ff.

9 Christopher Kelly, "'To persuade without convincing': The Language of Rousseau's Legislator," *American Journal of Political Science* 31.2 (May 1987), 327. For a very different approach to interpreting Rousseau's persuasion "without convincing," see Saguiv A. Hadari, "'*Persuader sans convaincre*':

A Rousseauan Approach to the Insoluble Problem of the *Social Contract*," *Western Political Quarterly* 39.3 (Sept. 1986), 504–19.

10 Jean-Jacques Rousseau, *Essay on the Origin of Languages and Writings Related to Music*, trans. and ed. John T. Scott, in *The Collected Writings of Rousseau*, vol. 7 (Hanover, NH: University Press of New England, 1998), 296. That Rousseau refers to Plato's *Cratylus* in the context of the persuasion used by the legislator is significant for the present study. This dialogue, in which Socrates and his interlocutors investigate the relation between language and nature, features a god whose task is to assign names to the various objects. The word Plato uses to name this god is *nomothetēs*. The most commonly available translation of the *Cratylus*, that by C.D.C. Reeve, renders this word "rule-setter" to specify the intellectual distance between this word's meaning in the *Cratylus* and the usual notion of political lawgiving. But the most immediate meaning of *nomothetēs* is "lawgiver." Though it is not possible to develop this theme here, one might suggest that Plato, through the *Cratylus*, teaches that legislation at its highest level involves dividing nature and giving definition to the things of nature by means of names. See, e.g., Plato, *Cratylus*, 389a2–3; cf. Genesis 1.

11 Rousseau, *Languages*, 294.

12 On the distinction between *amour de soi* and *amour-propre*, two different kinds of self-love, see Jean-Jacques Rousseau, *Emile, or On Education*, ed. and trans. Allan Bloom (New York: Basic Books, 1979), 211–16; and Rousseau, *First and Second Discourses*, 221–2. See also Laurence D. Cooper, *Rousseau, Nature, and the Problem of the Good Life* (University Park: Pennsylvania State University Press, 1999), 115–81; and Clifford Orwin, "Rousseau on the Sources of Ethics," in *Instilling Ethics*, ed. Norma Thompson (Lanham, MD: Rowman and Littlefield Publishers, 2000), 74–9.

13 Rousseau, *Languages*, 291.

14 Ibid., 295. So, for instance, the fear of seeing another man in nature would lead one to call him a "giant." Only when the fear eventually subsides can one see another man as he is and therefore refer to him as he is.

15 See Victor Gourevitch, "The Political Argument of Rousseau's *Essay on the Origin of Languages*," in *Pursuits of Reason: Essays in Honor of Stanley Cavell*, ed. Ted Cohen, Paul Guyer, and Hilary Putnam (Lubbock: Texas Tech University Press, 1993), 24–9.

16 Rousseau, *Languages*, 296.

17 Kelly, "'To persuade without convincing,'" 328–30; and John T. Scott, "Rousseau and the Melodious Language of Freedom," *Journal of Politics* 59.3 (Aug. 1997), 824–5.

18 Rousseau, *Languages*, 318, emphasis supplied.

19 Ibid., 317. On the subject of fanaticism – and Rousseau's qualified endorsement of it – see Rousseau, *Emile*, 312–14 (footnote).

20 Rousseau, *Social Contract*, 70.

21 Consider Kelly, "'To persuade without convincing,'" 326: "The discussion [of civil religion in the *Social Contract*] indicates Rousseau's judgment about the mistake of relying on rational argument alone." See also Shklar, *Men and Citizens*, 156–8.

22 Rousseau, *Social Contract*, 215; my modification of Masters's translation. Masters renders the phrase "*un préambule raisonné*" as "a well-reasoned preamble." But Rousseau's text does not warrant such a strong translation. After all, Rousseau has not said "*un préambule bien raisonné.*" (For *bien raisonné* as an idiom meaning "well-reasoned," cf. *Le Grand Robert de la langue française*, s.v., *raisonner*.) Victor Gourevitch, in his translation, renders the phrase "a reasoned preamble." See Jean-Jacques Rousseau, *The Social Contract and Other Later Political Writings*, ed. and trans. Victor Gourevitch (Cambridge: Cambridge University Press, 1997).

23 Plato, *Laws*, 722b4–c4. All citations to Plato's *Laws* will be made according to the Stephanus numbers, available in all editions of Plato. I have used the Oxford edition of Plato's works: Plato, *Platonis opera*, ed. John Burnet, 5 vols. (Oxford: Clarendon Press, 1902). Direct quotations from the *Laws* have been taken from Thomas L. Pangle's translation: Thomas L. Pangle, *The* Laws *of Plato*, trans., with notes and an interpretative essay (Chicago: University of Chicago Press, 1988).

24 Plato, *Laws*, 718b5–c1.

25 Cf. the interesting uses of "prelude" in the *Republic*: e.g., 357a1–2, 432e8, and 531d7–8.

26 Plato, *Laws*, 718c8–9.

27 Ibid., 719e8–20a2.

28 Ibid., 722e7–3a4.

29 Christopher Bobonich, *Plato's Utopia Recast: His Later Ethics and Politics* (Oxford: Clarendon Press, 2002), 104. See also Christopher Bobonich, "Persuasion, Compulsion, and Freedom in Plato's Laws," *Classical Quarterly*, new series, 41.2 (1991), 373. Cf. Andrea Wilson Nightingale, "Writing/Reading a Sacred Text: A Literary Interpretation of Plato's *Laws*," *Classical Philology* 88 (1993), 291–3; and Harvey Yunis, "Rhetoric as Instruction: A Response to Vickers on Rhetoric in the *Laws*," *Philosophy and Rhetoric* 23.2 (1990), 125–32.

30 Consider, e.g., Josiah Ober, "Law and Political Theory," in *The Cambridge Companion to Ancient Greek Law*, ed. Michael Gagarin and David Cohen (Cambridge: Cambridge University Press, 2005), 407; Thanassis Samaras,

Plato on Democracy (New York: Peter Lang, 2002), pp. 310–18; and John R. Wallach, *The Platonic Political Art: A Study of Critical Reason and Democracy* (University Park: The Pennsylvania State University Press, 2001), 371–77.

31 Plato, *Laws*, 720c6–e2. The most thorough discussion of the Athenian's treatment of the medical art in the *Laws* is Randall Baldwin Clark, *The Law Most Beautiful and Best: Medical Argument and Magical Rhetoric in Plato's* Laws (Lanham, MD: Lexington Books, 2003). For a discussion of how Plato's teaching on the medical art in the *Laws* relates to his teaching on the same in other dialogues, particularly the *Gorgias*, see Jacques Jouanna, "Le médecin modèle du législateur dans les *Lois* de Platon," *Ktema* 3 (1978), 82–91.

32 See *Liddell and Scott's Greek Lexicon*, s.v., *didaskō*. While the primary sense of this verb is "to instruct (a person) or teach (a thing)," its second sense is "to show by argument" or "to prove."

33 This important distinction is central to Crystal Cordell Paris's reading of Aristotle, in the first part of this volume. Paris demonstrates that the art of rhetoric, which is for Aristotle "the necessary corollary of the ruling activity of the citizen," is a form of communication that will seek to move citizens on an emotional level rather than speaking to them on an analytic level. In other words, the "methods and conditions of its [i.e. rhetoric's] exercise are to be distinguished from those of science" (117). Aristotle's views on rhetoric seem here to be similar to Plato's views on legislative persuasion.

34 Plato, *Laws*, 718d.

35 Ibid., 723a2–7.

36 For interpretations viewing the preludes as admixtures of rational and non-rational persuasion, see Glenn R. Morrow, "Plato's Conception of Persuasion," *Philosophical Review* 62.2 (Apr. 1953), 242; and Paul Shorey, "Plato's *Laws* and the Unity of Plato's Thought. I," *Classical Philology* 9.4 (Oct. 1914), 366–9.

37 For similar readings, see George Klosko, *The Development of Plato's Political Theory*, 2nd ed. (Oxford: Oxford University Press, 2006), 244–5; André Laks, "The *Laws*," in *The Cambridge History of Greek and Roman Political Thought*, ed. Christopher Rowe and Malcolm Schofield (Cambridge: Cambridge University Press, 2000), 289; R.F. Stalley, "Persuasion in Plato's *Laws*," *History of Political Thought* 15.2 (Summer 1994), 157–77; Leo Strauss, *The Argument and the Action of Plato's* Laws (Chicago: University of Chicago Press, 1975), 61–5; and Brian Vickers, *In Defence of Rhetoric* (Oxford: Clarendon Press, 1988), 143–7. Because it discusses Plato's generally pessimistic views on rational persuasion in dialogues other than the *Laws*, the following article serves to illuminate Klosko's position, cited in this note: George Klosko, "Rational Persuasion in Plato's Political Theory," *History of Political Thought* 7.1 (Spring 1986), 15–31.

38 This position has been defended by scholars such as M.J. Silverthorne and Eduard Zeller: M.J. Silverthorne, "Laws, Preambles and the Legislator in Plato," *Humanities Association Review* 26.1 (Winter 1975), 15; and Eduard Zeller, *Plato and the Older Academy*, trans. Sarah Frances Alleyne and Alfred Goodwin (New York: Russell and Russell, 1962 [1876]), 522–33. See also Luc Brisson, *Lectures de Platon* (Paris: Librairie Philosophique J. Vrin, 2000), 235–62; and compare the following statement by Jeffrey Dirk Wilson in this volume (chap. 14): "The preamble works primarily through praise and blame; it may sometimes attain to the level of the rational. Its method of operation, however, is not its goal, which is ontological: in an indiscernible way and at an indiscernible moment the puppet becomes *human* being."

39 Pangle, "Interpretative Essay," in *The* Laws *of Plato*, 448. Consider Pangle's illuminating discussion of the theory of the preludes at 445–9.

40 The Athenian calls the argument of book 10 a prelude at 907d4–5.

41 Plato, *Laws*, 890c6–8.

42 Ibid., 892e5–3a7; cf. 896e4–5, 897d5–6. For further evidence that the Athenian must condescend to the capabilities of Clinias and Megillus, consider 804b7–c1 and context.

43 See also Glenn R. Morrow, *Plato's Cretan City: A Historical Interpretation of the* Laws (Princeton: Princeton University Press, 1993 [1960]), 483: "These mathematical curves involved are difficult to grasp and they would be beyond the powers of the Athenian's two companions."

44 Cf. Plato, *Republic*, 515c4–d7.

45 Glenn R. Morrow, "Plato's Conception of Persuasion," *Philosophical Review* 62.2 (Apr. 1953), 240 and 238. Cf. David Cohen, "Law, Autonomy, and Political Community in Plato's *Laws*," *Classical Philology* 88.4 (Oct. 1993), 310; E.R. Dodds, *The Ancient Concept of Progress and Other Essays on Greek Literature and Belief* (Oxford: Clarendon Press, 1973), 110–11; and Pangle, "Interpretive Essay," 449: "The enchanting power, for ordinary citizens, of the Athenian's brief example [of the prelude on marriage] is proven by its effect on Megillus."

46 See, e.g., 659c9–e2, 664b3–c2, 665c2–7, 666c6, 671a1, 812b9–c7.

47 For more on the connection between enchantment and persuasion, see Plato, *Laws*, 773d5–e2 and 837e5–6. On this subject in the context of the prelude of *Laws* 10, see 887d2–5 and 903b1–2. See, finally, Morrow, "Plato's Conception of Persuasion," 238–42.

48 See, e.g., Niccolò Machiavelli, *The Prince*, 2nd ed., trans. and ed. Harvey C. Mansfield (Chicago: University of Chicago Press, 1998), 21–5, 37–8; and Niccolò Machiavelli, *Discourses on Livy*, trans. and ed. Harvey C. Mansfield and Nathan Tarcov (Chicago: University of Chicago Press, 1996), 28–30.

49 Rousseau, *Social Contract*, 69. See, in this connection, Tim Collins, "Romanticism and Rousseau's Legislator," in *Rousseau and Criticism / Rousseau et la Critique*, ed. Lorrarine Clark and Guy Lafrance (Ottawa: Pensée Libre [no. 5], 1995), 212–13.

50 Support for this reading is found in *The Oxford-Hachette French Dictionary*, s.v., *raissoné*. "*Rationnel*" is the fourth meaning of the adjective, and the first three, namely, "*prudent*," "*contrôlé*," and "*sensé*," all fall short of indicating "well-reasoned" or "rational."

51 Hence, R.W. Hall remarks, in a discussion of Rousseauan persuasion, that "Rousseau surely has in mind the innovation Plato introduced in the *Laws* of prefacing his important laws by preambles which were to add to the rational content of the laws persuasion to obedience based on their appeal to sentiment or feeling." R.W. Hall, "Rousseau and Plato," *Apeiron* 16.1 (1982), 15–16. (This appears to be a departure from Hall's earlier position on the Platonic preludes, in which he had emphasized their rational content. See R.W. Hall, *Plato and the Individual* [The Hague, The Netherlands: Martinus Nijhoff, 1963], 203–8.) Cf. Bryan Garsten, *Saving Persuasion: A Defense of Rhetoric and Judgment* (Cambridge, MA: Harvard University Press, 2006), 59–62. For Garsten, Rousseauan persuasion is very different from the classical conception of persuasion. But by the classical conception, Garsten means Ciceronian eloquence. His treatment of Rousseau does not, at any rate, compare persuasion "without convincing" to Platonic persuasion.

12 Civil Religion, Civic Republicanism, and Enlightenment in Rousseau

LEE WARD

As the introduction to this volume reminds us, the term republic is fraught with ambiguity in the modern world. It is used to describe regimes as diverse as the theocratic Islamic Republic of Iran and the militantly atheistic People's Democratic Republic of North Korea. Both of these contemporary manifestations of republics are a far cry from the classical ideal of citizenship long associated with republicanism. I will argue that Jean-Jacques Rousseau is a modern who provides a unique glimpse into the morality and psychology of the classical republics.

Rousseau is typically seen as one of the most prominent early modern critics of the Enlightenment. His frequent appeals to the classical republic as the peak of political possibilities for human flourishing are central to his apparent rejection of modern times.[1] I propose, however, to reconsider Rousseau's stance towards modernity by re-examining his account of the complex relation between civil religion and civic republicanism. As Jonathan Israel demonstrates in his recent works on Enlightenment philosophy, the critique of Christianity was integral to the radical Enlightenment project.[2] I will argue that Rousseau's endorsement of civil religion as an alternative to, and correction of, traditional Christianity thus, in a crucial respect, aligns his version of republicanism with the secularizing tendencies of the Enlightenment.

This study builds upon the insights of others who identify Rousseau's understanding of the dilemma confronting religion in modernity.[3] On the one hand, Rousseau excoriates the pernicious universalism of Christianity, but acknowledges its edifying moderation and humanness. On the other hand, Rousseau extols the civic virtues produced by the ancient pagan cults, while deploring their tendency towards superstition and xenophobia. In this light, the logical solution to the problem of modern religion appears to require combining classical republican particularism with significant elements of humane Christian moralism.

It seems natural then to turn to Rousseau's discussion in the *Social Contract* of the simplified theology he endorsed and found embodied in an idealized version of Geneva, one of the few glimmers of ancient virtue left in modern Europe. However, I will argue that Rousseau's commitment to principles of civic republicanism does not support accommodation with reformed Christianity in Geneva. Rather, what we see in Rousseau's treatment of classically inspired public entertainments, social customs, and practices he insists were "born" in the republics of antiquity is a sustained critique of Christianity that seeks to replace theology and traditional piety with a new cultural orientation towards a secular and ahistorical conception of communal life.[4] Indeed, Rousseau's celebrated criticism of the proposal to establish a professional theatre in Geneva may have less to do with the corrupting effects of Enlightenment high culture than it does with his awareness of the serious challenges involved in transforming even Geneva into a true civic republic. With his analysis of the complex relation between public entertainments and civil religion, Rousseau thus employs classical concepts not only to critique liberal modernity, but also, perhaps paradoxically, to advance the Enlightenment project of establishing post-Christian and post-feudal republican polities.

1. Civil Religion

In order to understand how Rousseau viewed the relation between republicanism, on the one hand, and religion, on the other, it is important to consider the main elements of his key treatment of civil religion in book 4 of the *Social Contract*. Here Rousseau asserts that polytheism is the primal religious fact: "At first men had no other kings but the gods, and no other government than a theocratic one," and thus in the early stages of society "there were as many gods as there were peoples."[5] In this context, the rise of Christianity can be explained as a consequence of Roman imperialism insofar as the "theological and civil intolerance" inherent in polytheism meant that "there was no other way of converting a people except by enslaving, nor any missionaries than conquerors."[6] Historically speaking, Christian universalism was thus in some sense a predictable outcome of paganism.

However, Rousseau's account of civil religion also identifies a taxonomy of religion based on three categories: the "religion of man," the "religion of the citizen," and a third arrangement dividing political and religious authorities into two distinct sovereign jurisdictions. Rousseau dismisses the latter form, which he identifies with Roman Catholicism, as "bizarre" and productive of a "perpetual jurisdictional conflict that has made good polity practically impossible in Christian states," for "whatever breaks up social unity is worthless." The religion of man, or "natural divine law," is a humane rationalist teaching about the true duties of morality based on the "pure and simple religion of the Gospel," while civic religion, or "positive divine law," Rousseau identifies with the "early peoples" who viewed every other nation as "infidel, alien, and barbarous." According to Rousseau, civil religion of the pagan cults has the salutary effect of melding service to the state with worship of the gods, and thus "unites the divine cult with love of the laws."[7] However, it also was based on outrageous lies that made the people superstitious, bloodthirsty, and intolerant, a condition which is "harmful" to the long-term security of the state. Natural theology, by contrast, is a truer account of "eternal moral duties." However, insofar as natural divine law establishes no particular relation to the body politic, "one of the great bonds of a particular society remains ineffectual." The homeland of the true Christian, Rousseau insists, is "not of this world."[8]

The problem of civil religion is then the conflicting tendencies of natural and civil theology. Rousseau does not see an inverse relation between the metaphysical truth of a religion and its political utility, for he acknowledges that the ultimate political usefulness of pagan civil religion was fatally undermined by the parochial and superstitious character of these civic cults. Rousseau's ideal civil religion would be one that combines the rationalist and moderate tendencies of natural theology with the strong nativist impulse and emotional connection of classical civil religion. He indicates that some form of civil religion is indispensable for a healthy regime: "For it is of great importance to the state that each citizen has a religion that causes him to love his duties."[9] However, the dogmatic core of such a civil religion should, according to Rousseau, be reducible to a few simple beliefs such as the existence of God, divine judgment, and the sanctity of the social contract and a single negative prohibition on intolerance. While Rousseau insists that the sovereign power has the right to regulate all religious beliefs, he maintains that its primary responsibility is to encourage "sentiments of sociability," and not to advance a specific set of theological propositions.[10] Civil religion is then a fundamentally political response to a religious problem.

The intersection of Rousseau's account of civil religion and his commitment to civic republicanism lies in the cobbled streets of his native Geneva, a regime characterized by both egalitarian republican politics and an influential version of reformed Christianity. Geneva represents the possibility for establishing a civil religion that is at once patriotic and non-sectarian, socially edifying and intellectually respectable. That is to say, Geneva's combination of classical virtue and reformed theology will demonstrate the limits and possibilities for addressing the problem of civil religion in modernity.

2. The Problem of the Theatre

Rousseau's most important discussion of Geneva's republicanism emerges in the context of the controversy surrounding the suggestion by the doyen of French intellectuals, Jean le Rond d'Alembert, that the freedom-loving, but parochial and unsophisticated, Genevans would benefit from the establishment of a Parisian-style professional theatre in the city. Notably, Rousseau practically begins his response by expressing outrage about d'Alembert's characterization of the clergy in Geneva as covert socianian rationalists who only maintain a public appearance of orthodox Calvinism in order to avoid scandalizing their more traditional flock. At least initially, then, Rousseau presents austere Calvinism, effectively the civil religion of Geneva, as the antithesis of the enervating cosmopolitanism of the theatre. Indeed, far from being a marginal event with interest only for aficionados of the stage, Rousseau contends that the introduction of Enlightenment high culture would produce "a revolution in our practices" that has the potential to completely undermine Geneva's republican institutions.[11]

In part, Rousseau's opposition to the theatre is a function of the natural conservatism he associates with small polities concerned to preserve their distinct, but delicate, social structures, for "in a state as small as the republic of Geneva, all innovations are dangerous and ... ought never to be made without urgent and grave motives."[12] However, the more specific problems he identifies are threefold. First, Rousseau warns about the socio-economic inequality and desire for luxury associated with high culture. Inequality is both a spur to the arts and a product of the desires enflamed by the theatre, especially the vain desire to be recognized as sophisticated and glamorous by one's fellows. Second, Rousseau inveighs against the corrupting effects the theatre has on public morality both with respect to the dissipated example of actors, and especially actresses, but also regarding the content of the plays, especially comedies, which Rousseau claims either present virtue as an object of derision by making the good man "a ridiculous figure" (*un personnage ridicule*), or at the very least makes "fun of the vices without ever making virtue loved."[13] Unable to make virtue a beautiful spectacle, the theatre can only corrode the virtue it has no part in cultivating.

The third and most important problem of the theatre has to do with the potential transformation of the subjective life of the citizens with the introduction of a seductive new realm of emotional interiority that has a disturbing solipsistic effect among the citizens: "People think they come together in the theater, and it is there that each is isolated. It is there that they go to forget their friends, neighbours and relations in order to take interest in fables, in order to cry for the misfortunes of the dead, or to laugh at the expense of the living."[14] Whereas the citizen should experience the immediacy of civic life in the propinquity of flesh and blood relations, Rousseau claims that the theatre operates on its own principles of representation which eviscerates what he takes to be the authentic moral life of the citizens.

The theatre is a threat to Geneva's republican government. However, this threat manifests primarily in public opinion. All governments, Rousseau claims, are creatures of public sentiment: "Opinion, queen of the world, is not subject to the power of kings; they are themselves her first slaves."[15] For Rousseau, the conceptual link between the operation of opinion, on the one hand, and the political principles of the regime, on the other, is his notion of taste (*le goût*). Taste, he insists, "stems from several things" such as mores, religion, and socio-economic class, but its principal effect is to act as an unofficial, extra-legal determinant of right.[16] While the theatre would be a cause of corruption in republican Geneva, Rousseau suggests that it is relatively benign in Paris, where *mores* are already so corrupt that the performances are a mild distraction from the sophisticated capital's many criminal attractions. The real danger for Geneva, however, lies in the possibility that once tastes change as a result of exposure to high culture, "our innocent pleasures will have lost their charm[;] the theatre will have taken away our taste for them forever."[17] By this measure, institutional change is at best a lagging indicator of fundamental shifts in the public's perception of what is and is not laudable, and even acceptable, conduct.

Rousseau's conjecture about the corrupting effects of the theatre on the egalitarian mores and coarse, simple tastes of Genevans is intended to be a lesson about the limits of government control over society. That is to say, government controls morality not primarily through laws and coercive instruments, but rather indirectly by shaping public opinion: "There is no well constituted state in which one does not find practices which stem from the form of government and help to maintain it."[18] The two examples Rousseau adduces to illustrate the awesome, but indirect, power of opinion and taste are the inability of the French government to stop duelling, and the ascendancy of women as the arbiters of taste in the modern world.

Rousseau's discussion of duelling is a reminder that the unofficial laws of taste operate in all manner of regimes, even if they operate somewhat differently in monarchies than republics. He attributes the failure of the French monarchy's attempts to change public opinion about duels to its insensitivity towards the power of opinion. For Rousseau, the key to understanding the French public's attitudes towards duelling is to recognize the pivotal role of honour in establishing French tastes. Laws bearing the severest penalties for duelling were ineffective because they left men's assumptions about courage and honour largely unchallenged: "Thus it was wrong to begin by condemning all duellists indiscriminately to death; this created straight off a shocking opposition between honour and law; for even the law cannot oblige anyone to dishonour himself."[19]

The subtle, but awesome, power of opinion makers is perhaps most clearly demonstrated for Rousseau by the ascendancy of women as the arbiters of taste in modern society. In contrast to the martial spirit of the ancient republics such as Sparta and Rome, Rousseau sees in modernity the gradual feminization of taste. This is the central truth of the time that the French tribunals trying to eradicate duelling failed to appreciate. Indeed, Rousseau declares that any attempt at large-scale social change can only succeed by enlisting the active support of women "on whom depends in large measure men's way of thinking."[20] Duelling will sooner cease when it displeases women in France than it ever will out of fear of severe punishment.

The specific issues raised by the theatre in Geneva casts in sharp relief the role of women in shaping public opinion. According to Rousseau, the modern theatre is designed to reflect the tastes of women, as especially witnessed in the literary fixation with romances. Love, he insists, "is the realm of women. It is they who necessarily give the law in it."[21] The effect on society is a vicious circle in which women (and men trying to please them) fill the theatres to see romances, while simultaneously the cultural celebration of romantic themes further extends "the empire of sex, to make women and girls the preceptors of the public."[22] Rousseau sees the political implications of this feminization of taste heavily favouring monarchy with its encouragement of delicacy and luxury over the austere, manly virtues of the classical republic. To this end Rousseau strikingly contrasts the paragon of Parisian high society – the aristocratic lady in her salon – surrounded by a "harem of men more women than she" with the rugged entertainments of the hardy warriors of antiquity who established the standards of taste for their entire society.[23]

3. Republican Political Culture

Rousseau insists that contrary to the assertions of Parisian snobs like d'Alembert, the professional theatre would not in fact fill a cultural vacuum in Geneva. Indeed, one vital source of the cultural life of the republic is the male and female circles, which Rousseau claims still preserve "some image of ancient morals among us."[24] The classical bona fides of these "decent and innocent institutions" suit austere republican morals and simple tastes, however the theatre makes the circles appear antiquated and boring: "The moment there is drama, goodbye to the circles."[25] What is at stake with respect to the status of the circles is, according to Rousseau, nothing less than the moral foundation of republican freedom as he warns: "Let us not flatter ourselves that we shall preserve our liberty while renouncing the morals by which we acquired it."[26] But why do the circles have such importance?

In Geneva, the classical republican goal of weaving the rulers and ruled into a seamless whole rests upon the institutionalization of gender difference. The male circles are private associations of twelve to fifteen men who rent "comfortable quarters" at "common expense" at which they all meet every afternoon for companionship and conviviality.[27] That these glorified frat houses are often dens of gambling and inebriation, Rousseau does not deny. He is quite candid that the male circles often encourage personal vices and hurt domestic family life.[28] However, the great virtue of the circles, which outweighs all other disadvantages, is that by excluding women the circles allow men to be men. The great service of the circles to republicanism lies in their capacity to promote a classical ideal of male friendship: "These decent and innocent institutions combine everything which can contribute to making friends, citizens, and soldiers out of the same men, and, in consequence, everything which is most appropriate to a free people."[29]

In their circles men develop their civic personality in a milieu where they can "speak of country and virtue without passing for bores."[30] Rousseau identifies speaking and acting coarsely, or at least with little concern for the opinion of women, as a hallmark of the republican simplicity "which preserves a good constitution as well as good morals."[31]

The female circles are less formal gatherings in which women and girls "meet in societies at one another's homes."[32] Men are not "severely excluded," but few ever attend. Rousseau concedes that these female gatherings are hotbeds of gossip, but he defends them primarily as a device to encourage a climate of surveillance among women.[33] Both versions of the circles address the particular needs and inclinations of the gender to which they apply. Nature, by giving "different tastes to the two sexes," dictates that they "ought to come together sometimes and live separately ordinarily."[34] Rousseau provides the example of England as a society "in which the morals of the two sexes appear at first glance to be most contrary," and yet it manages to combine a social practice of sexual differentiation with a considerable degree of political liberty.[35] For Rousseau, the role the circles play in encouraging modesty in women is at least as important as providing a female-free zone for men to develop civic and fraternal bonds. Surveillance in the circles, and society more generally, reinforces notions of female modesty, and provides its own formidable sanction in the form of reputation and opinion. It is with respect to female modesty that Rousseau intones: "Never has a people perished from an excess of wine; all perish from the disorder of women."[36]

Rousseau identifies female modesty as the virtue laying the foundation of the private family. Modesty is central to his notion of gender roles: "Man can be audacious, such is his vocation; someone has to declare. But every women without modesty (*sans pudeur*) is guilty, is depraved because she tramples on a sentiment natural to her sex."[37] However, it is the needs of society rather than nature strictly speaking which establishes the moral urgency of female modesty: "If the timidity, chasteness, and modesty which are proper to them are social inventions (*des inventions sociales*), it is necessary for society that women acquire these qualities; they must be cultivated in women, and any woman who disdains them offends good morals."[38] Thus, the circles clearly are not a celebration of the naturalness of the private family.[39] Rather Rousseau saw them as elements in the classical project of denaturing, by which the family is subordinated to the republic. Indeed, it is the inherently public character of the circles which draws Rousseau's approbation: "Of all the kinds of relations which can bring individuals together in a city like ours, the circles form incontestably the most reasonable, the most decent, and the least dangerous ones, because they neither wish nor can be hidden, because they are public and permitted."[40] The circles thus are simply irreplaceable in Geneva because they institutionalize on the level of opinion – more formidable than laws – the subjection of the private sphere to the public interest.

4. Republican Entertainments

The circles represent the conservative aspect of Rousseau's response to the introduction of the theatre in Geneva. They are what Genevans already have and need to protect. However, his discussion of republican "entertainments" (*les spectacles*) such as open-air festivals and publicly sanctioned balls signifies the innovative dimension of Rousseau's reflections on republican culture. In contrast to the segregationist logic of the circles, republican entertainments operate as unifying forces in society. The central premise of Rousseau's treatment of republican alternatives to the theatre is the notion that civic virtue is not antithetical to pleasure. Pleasure was not the object of the circles. Rousseau admits that the replacement of the older and more boisterous "dining societies" held in taverns by the smaller and more sedate circles came about as a response to the "civil discords" of the past (*nos discords civiles*); that is to say, the circles represent an effort to dampen passions in the city.[41] However, Rousseau insists that entertainments are not only permissible in republics, but that "they were born" in, and are the product of, popular genius.[42] He thus explicitly associates the republican alternatives to the theatre in Geneva with the classical tradition. In ancient Sparta and Rome, the forms of entertainment that "flourish with a truly festive air" were not works of literature, but rather open-air festivals and contests of skill and strength.[43] The activities Rousseau associates with the origin of entertainments are not dependent on literary expression. Rather, Rousseau suggests that the ancient theatre originated as a reflection of real life; that is to say, the truest art is the life of a people.

Rousseau's inclination towards the simple entertainments of the classical republics gives his reading of the relative virtues and vices of ancient theatre a particular focus. While his aim in the *Letter to d'Alembert* is clearly not to present ancient theatre as an alternative to the modern form, Rousseau does contrast contemporary French theatre unfavourably with that of classical Greece.[44] His central claim in this respect is that ancient theatre reflected a kind of sociological realism rooted in the vital national traditions of a people. This realism served the distinct moral or political purpose of encouraging civic virtue: "The ancients had heroes and put men on their stages; we, on the contrary, put only heroes on the stage and hardly have any men. The ancients spoke of humanity in less affected phrases, but they knew how to exercise it better."[45] Rousseau emphasizes the ancient insistence on the connection between art and practice when he compares modern theatre to the sophisticated youths in Plutarch's famous story who taunt the old man in the crowded amphitheatre rather than offer him a seat. Ancient drama, Rousseau analogizes to the plain-spoken Spartan who actually practises virtue – surrendering his seat – rather than simply speaking about it.

The important civic dimension of ancient theatre gave it, according to Rousseau, a relevance that transcended even conventional morality. For instance, insofar as ancient tragedy constituted, on one level, a celebration of the national traditions and political life of a people, then Rousseau feels it is possible to explain why the public display of terrible deeds such as parricide, infanticide, and incest performed by Orestes, Agamemnon, Medea, and others did not have the deleterious impact on public morality that one would expect, particularly among modern audiences. As Rousseau relates: "If the Greeks put up with such theatre it was as representative of their national traditions, which were always running among the peoples, which they had reasons to recall constantly; and even its odious aspects entered their view."[46] In contrast to the cultural uniformity he identifies in modern Europe, the ancient Greeks were able to integrate universal questions of justice – even in shocking examples – into distinct founding narratives of self-governing peoples.

For Rousseau the peculiar genius of ancient theatre was that it did not facilitate the withdrawal of the individual from his or her community. Rather art at its best helped to anchor the individual in civic life. It is precisely the experiential and participatory aspect of ancient entertainments that Rousseau contrasts sharply with the pernicious effects of the modern theatre. Republican entertainments are bounded neither by literary form nor by physical space: "It is in the open air, under the sky, that you ought to gather and give yourself to the sweet sentiment of your happiness."[47] The essence of these republican festivals is simplicity: "Plant in the middle of the square a stake crowned with flowers, gather the people together there, and you will have a festival."[48] Rousseau contrasts the simplicity and informality of republican spectacles with the "exclusive entertainments" in the theatre "which close up a small number of people in a melancholy fashion in a gloomy cavern."[49] The implicit identification of the modern theatregoer with the unfortunate denizens of Plato's cave in book 7 of the *Republic* is more than just a shot against the Enlightenment pretensions of d'Alembert. Rousseau's more fundamental point is that open-air festivals filled with a variety of activities are a more authentic form of human leisure than the arts as they have developed into high culture.[50] Republican entertainments thus embody the experience of communal living out of which the literary arts are never more than a deeply distorted reflection.

A number of key principles emerge in Rousseau's treatment of republican entertainments. First, we see Rousseau's willingness to embrace theatrical devices even as he rejects the theatre.[51] Whereas the circles signify a Rousseauian equivalent to reality television, the republican festivals are the essence of performance art. He practically effaces the distinction between performer and audience: "Make the spectators an entertainment to themselves; make them actors themselves; do it so that each sees and loves himself in the others so that all will be better united."[52] It is community building through participation. Second, there is also Rousseau's lack of concern for the content of these festivals. It is the mere act of gathering the people that constitutes a festival. These events should avoid celebrating the symbols of authority, the "prisons, lances, soldiers, and afflicting images of servitude and inequality" that inhabit modern drama.[53] Rather than prescribed content, Rousseau advocates a depoliticized event filled with competitions. The effect of such contests is not only to provide a pleasant distraction for the audience, but also to animate the contestants in all manner of skills, trades, and sports. But is there not considerable tension between Rousseau's praise for competitions and his republican commitment to the principle of equality? Indeed, we know that this was a very real concern of Rousseau's from his claim in the *Second Discourse* that competition among singers and dancers ended the golden age of humanity by producing the first sparks of vanity (*amour-propre*), which "eventually produced compounds fatal to happiness and innocence."[54] From the *Letter* it seems that Rousseau's amendment to his treatment of vanity in the earlier work rests on the realization that the age of natural innocence is unrecoverable. In modernity vanity can only be managed not eradicated, and thus at best may be channelled into publicly sanctioned events. Only in this way can the community capitalize on this potentially dangerous subjectivity and place it in the service of deeper social bonds.

The third element of Rousseau's account of republican entertainments is the central role of pleasure. The contours of Rousseau's argument about pleasure are complex. On the one hand, he identifies a hedonic root to social order. Not only must people in a republic "live in their stations," they "must live in them pleasantly (*agréablement*)."[55] Equality and civil peace, then, presuppose a sense of contentment among the public: "Deceit and the spirit of intrigue come from uneasiness and discontentment, everything goes badly when one aspires to the job (*l'emploi*) of another."[56] This idea of contentment represents the transformation of Genevans at play: "They are no longer that steady people which never deviates from its economic rules."[57] Festivals thus supply part of the hedonic correction to Geneva's natural austerity insofar as they provide respite from the drudgery of commercial life. It is in this sense that we can interpret Rousseau's famous claim that "there is no pure joy other than public joy."[58] Pure joy is not dependent on contingent extrinsic goods such as family, wealth, or status; that is to say, it is necessarily public because true pleasure presupposes that private interest is indistinguishable from the public good. It is only in their festivals that Genevans truly embrace the public: "All the societies constitute but one, all become common to all."[59] Pleasure then is the unifying principle that holds the differentiated elements of republican society together.

The connection between pleasure and republican spectacles is nowhere more apparent that in Rousseau's proposal for the institution of balls and dances in the winter season. This is the major innovation that Rousseau puts forth in the context of his attack on the theatre. In fact, the balls constitute a criticism of what Rousseau takes to be the excessively dour moralism of Geneva. As Starobinski astutely observes, this section of the *Letter* is saturated with the phrase "*je voudrais*" ("I would like"), Rousseau's most personal expressions of wish, preference, and imagination in the entire *Letter*.[60] Rousseau suggests that Geneva needs to do more to strengthen the hedonic foundation of the republic. His proposal is to introduce balls open to all marriageable young people. There should be a public figure who attends these balls in the person of a lord commissioner representing the governing council. There should also be a box of honour set aside for seniors. Married women can attend, although for modesty's sake they would be forbidden from dancing themselves. Finally, Rousseau encourages competition for a queen of the ball title going every year to the young woman "who during the preceding one has comported herself most decently, most modestly, and has most pleased everyone."[61]

Perhaps the most striking feature of the balls is Rousseau's attempt to replicate the participatory form of the open-air festivals in the highly charged erotic environment of the dances. The balls occupy a middle ground between a family wedding and a coronation as they blur the distinction between the private and the public realms. The predisposition towards surveillance that characterized the female circles dominates the balls as well. Transparency produced by public scrutiny is the key for innocent courtship, much as "vice is a friend of the shadows."[62] The public character of the balls also ensures that an egalitarian spirit prevails in them. Open to all marriageable youth, the balls are not solely for privileged debutants. Indeed, the free operation of personal preference and erotic attraction will, Rousseau suspects, break down the twin pillars of aristocracy, namely, traditional patriarchy and dynastic marriages. The democratizing effect of romantic love would be profound: "The relations becoming easier, marriages would be more frequent, these marriages, being less circumscribed to the same rank, would prevent the emergence of parties, temper excessive inequality, and maintain the body of the people better in the spirit of its constitution."[63] Even the queen of the ball honour, which appears to encourage elitism, is presented by Rousseau as perfectly consistent with republican virtue. As one commentator observes, the award is given to the unmarried woman who has made "the best display of a reluctance to display oneself."[64] Even if the prize degenerates into a beauty context, Rousseau prefers that the community defer to nature by celebrating the most beautiful women, rather than the richest.

The balls represent the theoretical peak of Rousseau's treatment of republican entertainments. Whereas the circles divide on the basis of gender, the open-air festivals and especially the balls would periodically reconstruct the social whole by bringing together the two sexes and the multiple generations of the polity. The fact that Geneva does not already have some version of the balls is a problem. Rousseau implies that a misguided cultural and religious predisposition towards excessive distrust of pleasure, combined with the public authority's neglect to attend properly to the erotic and familial attachments of their people, has left Geneva dangerously exposed to the harmful effects of the theatre. In other words, Rousseau feared that Geneva's civil religion and its republican culture were in deep tension.

5. How to Solve a Problem like Geneva?

Rousseau presents Geneva in the *Letter* as both an inspiration and a problem. It is an inspiration for republicans because of its political institutions and egalitarian mores. But it is a problem inasmuch as its religious beliefs and social customs only imperfectly support republican culture. The *Letter* thus in a generic sense demonstrates the interdependence between political culture and political institutions, or perhaps even the priority of culture over institutions in Rousseau's thought.[65] Geneva also, however, plays a more specific role in assessing Rousseau's stance towards the Enlightenment. Geneva embodies the problem of civil religion in modernity. It is a regime that tries to combine classical republican practices such as gender differentiation and promotion of civic virtue with a theological core derived from Calvinist Christianity. The uneasy relationship between these two constituent parts of Geneva's civic identity dominates Rousseau's account of his native city. We will conclude by suggesting that Rousseau's advocacy of classically inspired entertainments in Geneva signifies his commitment to the creation of a broadly secularized republican political culture to replace traditional Christianity. For Rousseau, modern republican civil religion is a product of a process that is practically indistinguishable from Enlightenment secularization.

From Rousseau's account of the circles, open-air festivals, and balls a few key features of republican political culture emerge. First, there is the pivotal role of gender differentiation, which involves the normal separation of the sexes in the circles and their periodic reintegration on a general scale in the festivals and balls. Contrary to the suspicions of the dour Calvinist moralists in Geneva who see only vice and anarchy in pleasure and thus oppose dancing in any form, Rousseau contends that the desire for pleasure properly channelled into publicly sanctioned activities can be an important source of social stability. Connected with this idea of pleasure is Rousseau's emphasis on the participatory character of healthy republican entertainments. A republican people should become an object to themselves, an object of enchantment to the individuals who identify themselves with the civic whole. With this blurring of the distinction between audience and performer, republican entertainments contribute to the construction of the general will of society by politicizing leisure, while simultaneously injecting patterns of theatricality into practically all aspects of public life.

The common idea running through the various aspects of republican entertainments is the notion of spontaneity. By spontaneity Rousseau does not primarily mean a temporal phenomenon as in something unplanned or ad hoc. Rather the political significance of spontaneity operates on the level of sentiment. Spontaneity in the Rousseauian sense reflects an existential condition approximating naturalness, and is thus inseparable from equality. Expressions of spontaneity are reminders of a vestigial sense of natural equality that survives dimly even in grossly unequal civil societies. Rousseau's assumption is that social inequality is conventional and the spontaneous sentiments of the heart always lead to some form of solidarity with others. The opposite of spontaneity is not calculation, but rather "dignity" that "daughter of pride (*l'orgueil*) and mother of boredom (*l'ennui*)."[66] For Rousseau, dignity is not a personal virtue, but rather a pernicious artifice created by political inequality and socio-economic class differences. Thus, an important aim of Rousseau's defence of spontaneous republican entertainments against the dignified arts is to encourage the taste for equality among republican peoples.

One story near the conclusion of the *Letter* perfectly encapsulates this Rousseauian ideal of spontaneity. It recounts the young Jean-Jacques's impressions of the impromptu dance of the men of the St Gervais militia regiment at the end of their manoeuvres. This "rather simple entertainment (*spectacle assez simple*)" is a combination of the circles and the balls, in which the women and children at home at the start of the dance eventually join their husbands and fathers on the square.[67] The patriotic and martial spirit of the dance displays a remarkable melding of national-security needs and personal pleasure. However, the most important feature of the dance as Rousseau presents it is its spontaneity. In principle this event is inimitable insofar as a contrived simulation would never be a genuine reflection of the spontaneous sentiments that produced the dance. This is not to deny the highly conventional character of the distinction between Genevans and non-Genevans, which ostensibly grounds the patriotism that occasioned the militia manoeuvres in the first place.[68] Spontaneity, Rousseau suggests, flourishes perhaps only in a limited social and political horizon.

The episode with the St Gervais regiment serves a double duty in the *Letter* both as an illustration of what Rousseau's republican political culture includes, as well as an implicit indicator of what is alien to it. In particular, it is striking that Rousseau's spontaneous republican entertainments are neither religious nor antiquarian. The republican festivals and events in Rousseau's idealized Geneva are not organized around the Christian calendar. There is never the slightest suggestion that republican entertainments are anything but secular. Why would this be the case, given the venerable tradition of festivities such as Easter and Christmas? On the one hand, there is Rousseau's denunciation of what he takes to be the enfeebling universalism of Christianity. Republican entertainments therefore must be secular in order to connect individuals on an emotional level to each other and to their society. The otherworldliness and transnational character of Christianity estranges the individual from authentic civic life and communal identity. As a general philosophical proposition the particular attachments and civic bonds that republican customs are meant to solidify are inevitably undermined by the permanent presence of Christian holidays and sacred days in a people's calendar.

The other problem with religion is more specific to Geneva's origins in the Reformation. The city of Calvin was undoubtedly founded as a theocracy and Rousseau admits that Genevans historically have in fact tended to define themselves on religious rather than republican terms. He observes that in the past Genevan cultural life was so immersed in the imagery of Reformation era theology that it would have been impossible to craft an indigenous form of tragedy on a Genevan stage without crudely demonizing the House of Savoy (with whom Geneva in the 1750s was then at peace) or even peopling the stage with stock pantomime versions of the "Devil and the Antichrist [i.e., the pope]."[69] While Rousseau indicates a certain embarrassment about Geneva's religious heritage, the reason why republican entertainments should avoid this heritage seems to have to do principally with political considerations in the present. Secular entertainments are unlikely to become a source of theological dispute and may even provide a locus of authority to rival that of the clergy in Geneva. For example, it is worth noting that the lord commissioners of the balls represent the council, not the churches. More importantly, the implicit criticism of Geneva in Rousseau's proposal for the balls is that the legacy of austere Calvinism is an unhealthy hostility to pleasure. In this respect at least, Rousseau shares the Enlightener d'Alembert's concern to alter Genevan *mores* by rehabilitating pleasure, albeit through simple entertainments rather than the theatre.

Rousseau's republican entertainments are also manifestly not antiquarian. While these festivals are undoubtedly classically inspired, they do not celebrate national history or commemorate past events.[70]

Spontaneity it seems requires liberation not only from social class, but also from the burden of tradition. This is shown indirectly by Rousseau's efforts to avoid discussing the celebrations associated with the Escalade, a holiday commemorating the 1602 victory of the Genevans over the Savoyards. As d'Alembert observed in his original article for the *Encyclopédie*, this Genevan victory "marked the beginning of this republic's tranquility" and the de facto security of its political independence.[71] Why does Rousseau discuss republican entertainments in Geneva at considerable length but mention this seminal event and annual celebration only in passing? Coleman suggests that Rousseau wished to de-emphasize this holiday because it stirred up primitive, nativist passions among Genevans.[72] While there is perhaps much truth in this suggestion, it is also likely that Rousseau's concerns about antiquarianism are in service of his larger point about the nature of political founding. Republics, unlike monarchies, do not require deeply rooted traditions. While republics need founders, these founders need to disappear from the cultural life of a people. The problem with the Escalade is the inherent sadness involved in commemoration; that is to say, the inevitable estrangement experienced by the present generation which cannot participate in, and thus feels no real ownership of, these past events. Herein Rousseau points to a tension between the progressive dynamic of a democratic society, on the one hand, and the perceived need for reverence of republican political institutions, on the other. Will a free people revere institutions of their own creation if they experience them as their own products rather than as an inheritance from a hallowed past?

In this respect, Rousseau's analysis of the problem that history and tradition poses for democracy recalls Pericles's statement of the problem in his celebrated "Funeral Oration" to the Athenian people in the opening phase of the Peloponnesian War. According to Thucydides, Pericles expressed ambivalence about his role as keynote speaker at the traditional mass burial of the Athenian war dead. The premier Greek statesman's praise of Athenian democracy and the valour of the war dead stands in considerable disjunction with his reservations about the customs handed down by the ancestors, which require a public eulogy. Pericles expresses his concern that the custom cannot properly fulfil the goal for which it was intended, namely, to honour the dead, because the weakness of mere words can never do justice to the sacrifices of the fallen. His indirect criticism of the "ancestors" is unmistakable: "For myself, I should have thought that the worth which had displayed itself in deeds would be sufficiently rewarded by honors also shown by deeds ... And I could have wished that the reputations of so many brave men were not to be imperiled in the mouth of a single individual, to stand or fall according as he spoke well or ill."[73] Indeed, one of the underlying themes of Pericles's oration is a certain democratic irreverence towards the past.[74] While praising "our remote ancestors" who first founded Athens, as well as "our own fathers," who added to this inheritance the "empire we now possess," Pericles seems to give pride of place to the present generation – "those of us here" – who have augmented the empire and made Athens capable "to depend on her own resources whether for war or for peace."[75] For Pericles, insofar as freedom is an inheritance, it is not properly a subject of ritualistic devotion, but rather a celebration of a spirit of tolerance and self-expression. In Athens, he boasts, "we live exactly as we please."[76]

Rousseau's treatment of Geneva imbibes this wisdom of the ancients, albeit in a form distinct from its original. The civic traditions of Christian Geneva will never be more than a very rough approximation of the classics. For instance, a Genevan Pericles is almost inconceivable in a society dominated by the churches. However, Rousseau's dismissal of public entertainment as political or historical commemoration still reveals a dimension of his political thought that is at once both classical and profoundly progressive. A republican society is by definition not captive to its own past. This presumably is the great danger the Escalade poses in Geneva, not to mention reverence for the original theocratic order established in the city by Calvin. Rousseau's concern is that natural sentiments and the desire for pleasure must be directed away from investing an excessive emotional attachment to institutions. The reification of consent in political institutions is perhaps the most pernicious disease afflicting republics as the public forgets that institutions only acquire legitimacy from active support of the people. In this sense, the self-generating and spontaneous entertainments of the people parallel the radically democratic foundations of the social contract by replicating on the social level the formal structure of the general will.[77] That is to say, a people trained in its habits and taste to revere the past are unlikely to follow Rousseau's recommendation that every assembly open each new session by voting on the question: "Does it please the sovereign to preserve the present form of government"?[78]

Rousseau fears that Geneva is in some respects captive to its past, especially to its religious heritage. The Escalade restricts Genevan political imagination to the parameters of a Reformation era context that casts an austere and gloomy aspect over modern republicanism. Spontaneous, secular republican entertainments offer emancipatory possibilities for Genevan society. Even just the introduction of the balls would, Rousseau suspects, produce a great transformation in the quality of life for Genevans. Towards the conclusion of the *Letter* Rousseau admits that the Genevan "inclination to travel" means that "half of our citizens, scattered throughout the rest of Europe and the world, live and die far from their country."[79] While Rousseau claims that the poorness of the soil requires this heavy emigration, his account of republican entertainments suggests that Geneva has also been deficient in providing the entertainments that make an individual "like one's station and prevent him craving a sweeter one."[80] The prospects for Geneva are thus problematic because republican institutions in the city cannot rely upon the enduring taste for equality among the citizens. The dour moralism of Geneva's heritage makes it vulnerable to the allure of the theatre precisely because the theatre appeals to a deep and long suppressed yearning in the Genevan soul for pleasure and beauty. It is to remedy this condition that Rousseau's classically inspired entertainments are directed.

Conclusion

Rousseau's account of Geneva represents the stark challenges confronting any effort to establish authentic republican polities in modernity. The tension between the particularistic needs of the civic republic and the universalistic pretensions of monotheistic religion is, according to Rousseau, perhaps ultimately irremediable. Insofar as Rousseau's treatment of civil religion rests on the assumption that modern republicanism is inseparable from the political management of religion, then it is reasonable to conclude that at least in this crucial area of politico-religious affairs Rousseau's beliefs align him with some of the most radical elements of the Enlightenment he publicly claimed to despise. Central to this reconsideration of Rousseau's relation to modernity is his use of classical concepts to challenge some of the prevailing prejudices of modern political theology. This is not to suggest that Rousseau's orientation was either wholly classical or wholly modern. Rather I mean to assist in the process of rediscovering Rousseau's relationship to the Enlightenment by observing the possible underlying intellectual thread uniting his classically inspired public entertainments for Geneva and the revolutionary Festivals of Reason in Year II.

NOTES

1 See, for example, Judith Shklar, *Men and Citizens: A Study of Rousseau's Social Theory* (Cambridge: Cambridge University Press 1969), 1–32 and Mark Hulliung, *The Autocritique of Enlightenment: Rousseau and the Philosophes* (Cambridge, MA: Harvard University Press, 1994), 125–37.
2 Jonathan Israel, *Enlightenment Contested: Philosophy, Modernity and the Emancipation of Man, 1670–1752* (Oxford: Oxford University Press, 2006), 63–71 and Jonathan Israel, *A Revolution of the Mind: Radical Enlightenment and the Intellectual Origins of Modern Democracy* (Princeton: Princeton University Press, 2010), 22–8.
3 Ronald Beiner, "Machiavelli, Hobbes and Rousseau on Civil Religion," *Review of Politics* 55.4 (Autumn 1993), 631–8 and Arthur M. Melzer, "The Origin of the Counter-Enlightenment: Rousseau and the New Religion of Sincerity," *American Political Science Review* 90.2 (June 1996), 344–51.
4 Jean-Jacques Rousseau, *Lettre à M. D'Alembert sur son article Genève* (Paris: Garnier-Flammarion, 1967 [1758]), 233. All translations are my own.
5 Rousseau, Jean-Jacques, *On the Social Contract*, trans. Donald A. Cress (Indianapolis: Hackett Publishing, 1987 [1762]), 96.
6 Rousseau, *Social Contract*, 97.
7 This and all prior quotations in this paragraph are from Rousseau, *Social Contract*, 98–9.
8 Ibid., 100.
9 Ibid., 102.
10 Ibid.
11 Rousseau, *Lettre*, 192. An earlier version of portions of the following discussion appeared in chapter 2 of Lee Ward, *Modern Democracy and the Theological-Political Problem in Spinoza, Rousseau, and Jefferson* (New York: Palgrave Macmillan, 2014), reproduced with permission of Palgrave Macmillan.
12 Ibid., 230.
13 Ibid., 163, 96, 94.
14 Ibid., 66.
15 Ibid., 154.
16 Ibid., 119.
17 Ibid., 232.
18 Ibid., 192.
19 Ibid., 146.
20 Ibid., 151.
21 Ibid., 113.

22 Ibid., 113.
23 Ibid., 197.
24 Ibid., 202.
25 Ibid., 202, 194.
26 Ibid., 214.
27 Ibid., 193.
28 Ibid., 206.
29 Ibid., 203.
30 Ibid., 202.
31 Ibid., 214.
32 Ibid., 194.
33 As Rousseau wryly remarks: "Combien scandals publics ne retient pas la crainte de ces sévères observatrices?" (ibid., 204).
34 Ibid., 205, 195.
35 Ibid., 166–7.
36 Ibid., 209.
37 Ibid., 171–2.
38 Ibid., 175.
39 Nicole Fermon, *Domesticating Passions: Rousseau, Woman and Nation* (Hanover, NH: Wesleyan University Press, 1997), 120.
40 Rousseau, *Lettre*, 207.
41 Ibid., 193.
42 Ibid., 233.
43 Ibid., 233. As Brent Edwin Cusher describes in the previous chapter in this volume, the Athenian Stranger in Plato's *Laws* also contends that the philosophic lawgiver must establish public festivals in order to train the sentiments and inculcate the proper qualities of citizenship.
44 Famously, in the *Discourse on the Arts and Sciences* Rousseau identified the emergence of the theatre as one of the major stages of corruption in Athens, and an important reason for its inferiority to Sparta, which thrived in its "happy ignorance" (Jean-Jacques Rousseau, *The First and Second Discourses*, trans. Roger Masters [New York: St Martin's Press, 1964 (1754)], 43–4). Thus, we must recall that from Rousseau's perspective any form of drama is a product of, or contributory to, alienation of individuals from an authentic human life. However, the narrower claim that Rousseau believed modern theatre much inferior to ancient drama still holds.
45 Rousseau, *Lettre*, 89–90.
46 Ibid., 91.
47 Ibid., 233.
48 Ibid., 234.

49 Ibid., 233.
50 Ibid., 235.
51 Elizabeth Wingrove, "Sexual Performance as Political Performance in the *Lettre à M. d'Alembert sur les Spectacles*," *Political Theory* 23:4 (Nov. 1995), 587 and Patrick Coleman, *Rousseau's Political Imagination: Rule and Representation in the Letter à d'Alembert* (Geneva: Librairie Droz, 1984), 153.
52 Rousseau, *Lettre*, 234.
53 Ibid., 233.
54 Rousseau, *Second Discourse*, 149.
55 Rousseau, *Lettre*, 234.
56 Ibid., 234.
57 Ibid., 235.
58 Ibid., 249.
59 Ibid., 236.
60 Jean Starobinski, *Jean-Jacques Rousseau: Transparency and Obstruction*, trans. Arthur Goldhammer (Chicago: University of Chicago Press, 1988), 102.
61 Rousseau, *Lettre*, 239–40.
62 Ibid., 238.
63 Ibid., 241–2.
64 Wingrove, *Sexual Performance*, 605.
65 Daniel Cullen, *Freedom in Rousseau's Political Philosophy* (DeKalb: Northern Illinois University Press, 1993), 128.
66 Rousseau, *Lettre*, 249.
67 Ibid., 248.
68 Coleman, *Political Imagination*, 138.
69 Rousseau, *Lettre*, 226.
70 Cullen, *Freedom in Rousseau*, 135.
71 Jean le Rond d'Alembert, "Article on Geneva," in *Politics and the Arts: Letter to d'Alembert on the Theatre*, trans. Allan Bloom (Ithaca: Cornell University Press, 1960), 141. For more on the cultural importance of the Escalade as a symbol of national independence in eighteenth-century Geneva, see "Introduction," in *The Identity of Geneva: The Christian Commonwealth, 1564–1864*, ed. John B. Roney and Martin I. Klauber (Westport, CT: Greenwood Press, 1998), 7.
72 Coleman, *Political Imagination*, 131.
73 Thucydides, *The Peloponnesian War* in *The Landmark Thucydides*, ed. Robert Strassler (New York: Free Press, 1996), 111. As Timothy Burns astutely observes in chapter 1 of part 1 of this volume, Pericles's political purpose is not only to criticize custom, but rather it is also fundamentally a secularizing project that celebrates Athenian intelligence and

resourcefulness over and against the traditional idea of divine care for the *polis*.

74 Pericles does not hereby contradict Rousseau's point about the traditional or customary appeal of Greek drama. The ownership Greek audiences felt about their own national arts signified a kind of horizontal ownership distinct from that of other peoples. What Pericles is describing is the problem of generational or vertical ownership, which can stand in real tension with inherited national traditions. Rousseau, I would argue like Pericles, sees a conception of generational fidelity to certain principles – fluid with regard to structures but strong in its commitment to the general idea of republicanism – as the most promising way to reduce this tension.

75 Thucydides, *Peloponnesian War*, 111–12.

76 Ibid., 113.

77 See for example, Rousseau, *Social Contract*, book 1, chapter 7. See also Victor Gourevitch, "Rousseau on the Arts and Sciences," *Journal of Philosophy* 69.20 (Nov. 1972), 743.

78 Rousseau, *Social Contract*, 79.

79 Rousseau, *Lettre*, 243.

80 Ibid., 234.

13 Mary Wollstonecraft and Adam Smith on Gender, History, and the Civic Republican Tradition

NEVEN LEDDY

This chapter focuses on the transmission of civic republicanism in the eighteenth century through the moral philosophy and political history of the ancients. In the process of elucidating Mary Wollstonecraft's engagement with civic republicanism, we will also touch on her response to Adam Smith, and his effort to buttress traditional ethics and politics with a sentimental education. Mary Wollstonecraft's *Vindication of the Rights of Woman* (1792) can be understood as an exposition of her anxiety that eighteenth-century women were denied access to ancient history and moral philosophy. She argued that instruction in citizenship was restricted to those men schooled in the liberal arts, since they alone were exposed to the civic republican tradition through the study of history; since women were cut off from the moral and political teachings of civic republicanism, their capacity for conventional political virtue was badly undermined. She suggested that the moral philosophy of Cicero could be replaced by conscience, but for the lack of exemplary political and moral actions contained in ancient history Wollstonecraft saw no remedy but the education of women in classics and the liberal arts.

Only two years earlier, in the revisions to the final edition of his *Theory of Moral Sentiments* (1790), Adam Smith expressed his own anxiety that the canon of ancient history and moral philosophy was too narrow to provide an effective Enlightenment education for young men. Smith's proposal was to enlarge the textual basis of Enlightenment education to include the distinctly feminine voice of sentimental novelists. For her part, Wollstonecraft despaired that women's reading – and consequently their entire education – was limited to just such novels. In their respective suggestions that boys be educated more like girls and that girls be educated more like boys, Smith and Wollstonecraft shared a concern that traditional Enlightenment education was not adequately serving either gender. The crux of the matter for both figures lay in the Enlightenment practice of the history of ideas.

While Wollstonecraft made specific reference to the moral philosophy of Cicero in the *Vindication*, her far more frequent references to history as the vehicle for civic republicanism were never linked to a particular historian, either ancient or modern. It would seem that Wollstonecraft was more concerned with the content of ancient history than with specific historians. Moreover, the legacy of antiquity was so much a part of the intellectual world of the eighteenth century that what we might call "common knowledge" references to antiquity were not always flagged as such. Regularly name-checked by Enlightenment writers, certain Roman figures appeared under familiar Enlightenment aliases (Tully for Cicero) or at least in formulations unfamiliar to twenty-first-century readers (Antoninus for Marcus Aurelius). In his lectures on rhetoric and belles-lettres, in contrast, Adam Smith referred explicitly to Tacitus as the most accessible of ancient historians, and it is commonly assumed that Tacitus can be taken as representative of ancient historians to the eighteenth-century mind.

Current scholarship on the gendered production and reception of historical writing does not address Wollstonecraft's engagement with Smith, but nevertheless illuminates their respective approaches to the discipline. Mark Salber Phillips explains Wollstonecraft's complaint about the gendering of historical education by suggesting that history was moving beyond narratives of political deeds towards social and sentimental concerns in the latter half of the eighteenth century, but that it retained a specifically masculine audience.[1] Phillips acknowledges that this is a stereotype, and that the "reading habits of actual readers were far more varied,"[2] but for our purposes here it is important to emphasize that it is a stereotype that Wollstonecraft accepted. J.G.A Pocock has also weighed in on this question to point out that even if the reading of history was not a gendered process, the writing of history was an overwhelmingly male occupation.[3]

As usual Pocock has been the fountainhead of commentary on his chosen topic, since followed by Sylvana Tomaselli and Mary Catherine Moran. Moran's historiographical argument is that the Scottish literati, in particular, were actively undermining the classical practice of history as past (and exemplary) politics.[4] Tomaselli explains that women were disinclined to engage with eighteenth-century conjectural histories because they presented women as passive agents of men's passion.[5] This historiographical case does not necessarily undermine the view that Wollstonecraft was clamouring for access to just that tradition. In this case, the secondary literature on Smith and Wollstonecraft conflicts, productively.

In order to make his point about gendered access to the study of history, Pocock elaborates on the Tacitean historical method. Pocock suggests that the Enlightenment take-up of Tacitus is best understood if we look at Tacitus as the most modern of the ancients. Pocock shrinks the distance between ancient and early-modern practices of history by emphasizing the sophistication of the ancient Tacitean tradition:

> The classical narrative had in fact never been confined to the simple narrative of exemplary actions. It had been also a macronarrative of the foundation and decay of political forms, and part of the "philosophical" component inherited from Tacitean historiography had been the question how, and whether, the actions of individuals could be made the occasions of moments of systemic change.[6]

On this reading, Enlightenment conjectural history was a firmly Tacitean enterprise. In short, Pocock intimates that Tacitus was the Enlightenment's favourite historian because he was the least ancient of ancient historians. For Wollstonecraft, though, ancient history was political history; Pocock's comment is more appropriate to Smith's presentation of Tacitus.

It is entirely possible to reconcile these conflicting interpretations of the civic republican tradition in the eighteenth century if we accept that Smith and Wollstonecraft might have been tunnelling from opposite ends, but working towards the same goal. Smith and Wollstonecraft were in agreement that the ancient accounts of Roman history and philosophy, as vehicles for civic republicanism, were not adequate for their respective social aims. For Smith the content of ancient history and especially philosophy was too narrow for a complete Enlightenment education: his solution was to broaden that corpus to include modern sentimental novels.[7] For Wollstonecraft the civic message of those same texts was not sufficiently disseminated, particularly to women: her solution was to broaden the readership of the canonic texts. In simple terms, Smith argued for the inclusion of a feminine (or feminizing) voice within the canon, while Wollstonecraft wanted to hear the existing canon read in a female voice.

Wollstonecraft's central concern in the *Vindication* was the inability of women to effectively perform their duties as citizens. The education reforms that she outlined were meant to enable women to earn political and social equality with men. Her model of the new woman was of one who read history rather than novels, and was rational rather than sentimental. In her attempts to live up to her ideal, Wollstonecraft was consistent in denouncing feminine traits which she believed fell short of that ideal. She announced, for example, that she would "try to avoid that flowery diction which has slided from essays into novels, and from novels into familiar letters and conversations."[8] Wollstonecraft alternated between exposing the civic failings of her gender and identifying the causes of those failings. This approach revealed a vicious circle in which domestic education undermined by sentimental novels limited the intellectual horizons of women and prevented them from taking a broader national perspective on their own lives and actions.

In the introduction to the *Vindication* Wollstonecraft outlined her methodology as a kind of teleological social criticism. She emphasized that she aimed at a result in a future stage of social development, characterized by gender and political equality, as she vehemently criticized her contemporary world. This chapter takes up two examples of this method, while tracing Wollstonecraft's sustained engagement with Adam Smith. Throughout the *Vindication*, Wollstonecraft demonstrated the eclipse of the virtue of the citizen in a domestic prison. Following her avowed method, this social criticism was equally a program for improvement: by educating girls like boys and providing them with similar experience in the world, those girls would mature into citizen-wives capable of virtue. The second example of this methodology concerned the matter of that education, which was to expose girls to the civic republican tradition through the study of history.[9]

Domestic Citizenship / Domesticating Smith

In her efforts to expose the limitations of domestic education, and illuminate an exit from that predicament, Wollstonecraft rather surprisingly redeployed Adam Smith's moral psychology in her improved model of domestic life. She used Smith's concept of sympathy to criticize the limits of matrimonial harmony in a couple with typically divergent educations. She then held up Rousseau's choice of partner as an example of the pernicious consequences of masculine lust. Ultimately, Wollstonecraft presented the study of history by girls as the solution to gender inequality within marriage, and the social inequality it represented.

Wollstonecraft envisaged properly educated citizen-wives who would be respected and respectable, rather than flattered and stunted.[10] In this discussion she followed Smith's distinction between praise for, and the praiseworthiness of, a wife. Smith had explained the distinction between the two concepts with reference to conscience and the Impartial Spectator: "The jurisdiction of the man without, is founded altogether in the desire of actual praise, and in aversion to actual blame. The jurisdiction of the man within, is founded altogether in the desire of praise-worthiness, and in the aversion to blame-worthiness."[11] Wollstonecraft suggested that the citizen-wife should follow the second course, that "whether she be loved or neglected, her first wish should be to make herself respectable."[12] She explained that to be pursued by gallants is no success at all when compared to establishing respectability vis-à-vis a husband.

Wollstonecraft further employed Smith's moral psychology to demonstrate the importance of an educated wife in a manner that I am certain would never have occurred to Smith:

> The man who can be contented to live with a pretty, useful companion, without a mind, has lost in voluptuous gratifications a taste for more refined enjoyments; he has never felt the calm satisfaction, that refreshes the parched heart, like the silent dew of heaven, – of being beloved by one who could understand him. – In the society of his wife he is still alone, unless when the man is sunk in the brute. "The charm of life," says a grave philosophical reasoner [Smith], is "sympathy; nothing pleases us more than to observe in other men a fellow-feeling with all the emotions of our own breast."[13]

Her model of marriage is very much like Smith's model of friendship among equals. Smith, however, would likely have considered marriage "constrained," and claimed that "those who would confine friendship to two persons, seem to confound the wise security of friendship with the jealousy and folly of love."[14] Wollstonecraft was more optimistic, suggesting that love – though (and perhaps because) it is temporary – educates the affections in a useful manner.

> In order to fulfil the duties of life, and to be able to pursue with vigour the various employments which form the moral character, a master and

> mistress of a family ought not to continue to love each other with passion. I mean to say, that they ought not to indulge those emotions which disturb the order of society, and engross the thoughts that should be otherwise employed. The mind that has never been engrossed by one object wants vigour – if it can long be so, it is weak.[15]

This is a remarkably unsentimental stance, and represents the idealized role of Wollstonecraft's citizen-wife. Her criticism of contemporary gender relations focused on Rousseau's sentimental novel as emblematic of the failings of girls' education.

The particular target here is Rousseau, whom Wollstonecraft excoriates for broadcasting the idea that love is eternal.[16] The results of this delusion are intensive, crowding out even the pursuit of other virtues: "Love, in their bosoms, taking place of every nobler passion, their sole ambition is to be fair, to raise emotion instead of inspiring respect; and this ignoble desire, like the servility in absolute monarchies, destroys all strength of character."[17] Having established that Smith's model of friendship is a better model for marriage than Rousseau's anguished portrayal of Julie and St-Preux in the *Nouvelle Héloïse*, Wollstonecraft turned to the role of education in creating an equal partnership.

As an example of the gulf that girls' and boys' education can create, Wollstonecraft pointed to its effect in subsequent marriage: "But it is no less true, that an improved understanding only can render society agreeable; and it is a melancholy thing for a father of a family, who is fond of home, to be obliged to be always wrapped up in himself, and to have nobody about him to whom he can impart his sentiments." In the previous sentence she had allowed that virtue may be accessed through conscience, rather than learning: "Our own conscience is the most enlightened philosopher. There is no need to be acquainted with Tully's offices, to make a man of probity: and perhaps the most virtuous woman in the world, is the least acquainted with the definition of virtue."[18] While women might not need a theory of virtue, Wollstonecraft insisted that they need the example – and the same example as men, the shorthand for which in the secondary literature is usually Tacitean history.

Smith had similarly invoked Cicero and explicitly deployed Tacitus; his use of the latter is of particular interest on this topic. In his lectures on belles-lettres, Smith compared Tacitus to contemporary French novelists in their emphasis on motivation and psychological insight. "Marivaux and Crebillon resemble Tacitus as much as we can well imagine in works of so conterary a nature. They are Allways at great pains to account for every event by the temper and internall disposition of the several actors in disquisitions that approach near to metaphysicall ones."[19] Smith here emphasized the similarity of Tacitean psychological insight for history to that supplied by sentimental fiction. In the sentimental fiction that informed Smith's early moral theory the reader is privy to all of the necessary data for assessment, much like the ideal Impartial Spectator. It is on this point that Smith linked Tacitus to Crébillon and Marivaux,[20] and by the same token suggested that those sentimental novelists were a necessary addendum to the ancient sources of moral philosophy.

It would seem safe to dismiss the idea that Smith's variety of analytical literature might replace – for Wollstonecraft – the canon of civic republicanism. Nor, it must be added, was this Smith's intention; he proposed the sentimental novel, and those of Madame Riccoboni in particular, as a useful complement to the rigours of Stoic-Enlightenment education. It would seem, however, that there might be an unexpected middle ground in this engagement: While Wollstonecraft clamoured for access to the masculine bastions of moral philosophy and the classics, Smith suggested that this canon need to be expanded to include a feminine – though not necessarily female – voice.[21]

Public Citizenship and Benevolence

Wollstonecraft conceived of civic virtue as an expression of benevolence on a national scale. Her principal complaint concerning the education of girls was that domestic education restricted the scope of their benevolence. Her alternative vision of public education would teach virtue through exemplary political history for girls as well as boys. Following on from this co-educational grounding in public virtue, Wollstonecraft advocated political representation for citizen-wives on the assumption that women would earn that right by embracing civic education. While earlier she initially claimed that Cicero's *Offices* was not a prerequisite for virtue, she concluded that a grounding in political history was essential to fulfil the obligations of citizenship.

> They might also study politics, and settle their benevolence on the broadest basis; for the reading of history will scarcely be more useful than the perusal of romances, if read as mere biography; if the character of the times, the political improvements, arts, &c. be not observed. In short, if it be not considered as the history of man; and not of particular men, who filled a niche in the temple of fame.[22]

This contextual approach to history approaches what we now call the Cambridge school of the history of ideas in context. In Wollstonecraft's terms, she urged women to discard their novels and read history like men. On this point Wollstonecraft would certainly agree with Ryan Balot's point that manliness had colonized too much of the territory of virtue, which might more productively be shared by both genders. Unlike in Ryan Balot's reading of contemporary and ancient modes of manliness centred on military courage as a means to exclude women's virtue, Wollstonecraft suggests that this exclusion is achieved through the monopolization of the study of history.[23]

Wollstonecraft outlined the root and branch reform of education that she saw as the way to effect a revolution in female manners. She argued that public instructors were more effective than private tutors – whom she dismissed as patronage appointments – or private school masters – who she said are subservient to the demands of overprotective parents.[24] Her overarching structure aimed to educate the affections of children, so that they might learn the duties of citizenship.[25] Wollstonecraft's point about educating the affections spoke to the tendency to send children away to school, disrupting the bonds of family. She claimed that this disruption undermined children's capacity for national benevolence:

> Few, I believe, have had much affection for mankind, who did not first love their parents, their brothers, sisters, and even the domestic brutes, whom they first played with. The exercise of youthful sympathies forms the moral temperature; and it is the recollection of these first affections and pursuits that gives life to those that are afterwards more under the direction of reason.[26]

Extrapolating from the family to the nation, Wollstonecraft made the bold claim that boys and girls should be educated together.[27]

Wollstonecraft's civic pedagogy might be summarized as "citizenship begins at home." On this point she was in agreement with Smith's conclusion that intimacy does and should incur loyalty. Wollstonecraft argued that domestic intimacy should be the springboard for a broader benevolence which she refers to as national in scope.[28] In the absence of such a broad engagement, Wollstonecraft again pointed to a vicious circle. While she privileged political engagement over other aspects of moral life, her broader point is not about the type of engagement, but about "events" of any type: "The mighty business of female life is to please, and restrained from entering into more important concerns by political and civil oppression, sentiments become events, and reflection deepens what it should, and would have effaced, if the understanding had been allowed to take a wider range."[29] A limited horizon leaves women stunted and solipsistic. Sentimental solipsism, in turn, stunts women's capacity to educate themselves out of their predicament:

> But, confined to trifling employments, they naturally imbibe opinions which the only kind of reading calculated to interest an innocent frivolous mind, inspires. Unable to grasp any thing great, is it surprising that they find the reading of history a very dry task, and disquisitions addressed to the understanding intolerably tedious, and almost unintelligible.[30]

Particularly interesting on this point is her explanation of women's inability to engage with history.

To demonstrate her solution to this lacuna, Wollstonecraft offered her own historical anthropology of gender:

> It is plain from the history of all nations, that women cannot be confined to merely domestic pursuits, for they will not fulfil family duties, unless their minds take a wider range, and whilst they are kept in ignorance they become in the same proportion the slaves of pleasure as they are the slaves of man. Nor can they be shut out of great enterprises, though the narrowness of their minds often make them mar, what they are unable to comprehend.[31]

She referred to historical evidence of the corrupting role of women in politics, as court favourites and mistresses. Her conclusion on this point is that women lack the rationality to engage positively in civic life, which fed into the vicious circle by encouraging solipsism.

Wollstonecraft here claimed that exclusion from political life encourages female sentimentality:

> Females, in fact, denied all political privileges, and not allowed, as married women, excepting in criminal cases, a civil existence, have their attention naturally drawn from the interest of the whole community to that of the minute parts, though the private duty of any member of society must be very imperfectly performed when not connected with the general good.[32]

Wollstonecraft then turned to women's stereotypical substitute for what we might call "character-building" experience: the novel. She followed up on her claim that exclusion from political life encouraged female sentimentality, which results in a vicious circle. Wollstonecraft explained that the very limited scope of women's activities narrow their horizon until every interaction becomes a rivalry, which women fail to rise above. It is important to note the alternatives she offered to this narrow-mindedness: "… for they have not any business to interest them, have not a taste for literature, and they find politics dry, because they have not acquired a love for mankind by turning their thoughts to the grand pursuits that exalt the human race, and promote general happiness."[33] While men interact with one another through the study of the past and in the contemporary world – though they may not be friends, they are not all direct rivals – women interact with one another only in the domestic sphere, where every other woman is a rival for the attention of men. On this reading the narrow education of women impedes broader national or universal benevolence, which excludes women from a social or political perspective on their own lives. On this point, Wollstonecraft reproduced the Enlightenment trope whereby the isolation of women retards cultural development, with repeated references to Islam.[34]

In section 6 Wollstonecraft offered the political conclusions – in some very loaded language – that might result from her proposed reformation of female manners:

> To render women truly useful members of society, I argue that they should be led, by having their undertakings cultivated on a large scale, to acquire a rational affection for their country, founded on knowledge, because it is obvious that we are little interested about what we do not understand. And to render this general knowledge of due importance, I have endeavoured to shew that private duties are never properly fulfilled unless the understanding enlarges the heart; and that public virtue is only an aggregate of private.[35]

She here linked with Smith on another of his anxieties, giving the corrupting potential of wealth a gendered reading: "For as marriage has been termed the parent of those endearing charities which draw man from the brutal herd, the corrupting intercourse that wealth, idleness, and folly, produce between the sexes, is more universally injurious to morality than all the other vices of mankind collectively considered."[36] Where Smith wrote of the destructive power of baubles,[37] on Wollstonecraft's reading those baubles would have been acquired in the immodest attempts by men to seduce women.

This is an unexpected emphasis by way of conclusion. Wollstonecraft seemed here to suggest that men's sexual pursuit of ignorant women is the most nefarious of social ills. On this point she seemed to have abandoned her hope that male chastity might be encouraged, to instead suggest that educated women were better placed to resist their bauble-laden attempts at seduction. Implied in this is the idea that an educated citizen-wife would be more effective in restraining the unenlightened lust of men. Men of the world, Wollstonecraft seems to say, should marry historians. Rather that teaching girls abstinence, Wollstonecraft seemed to suggest, we should teach them history.[38]

NOTES

1 Mark Salber Phillips, *Society and Sentiment: Genres of Historical Writing in Britain, 1740–1820* (Princeton: Princeton University Press, 2000), 163.

2 Ibid., 114.

3 J.G.A. Pocock, *Barbarism and Religion*, vol. 2: *Narratives of Civil Government* (Cambridge: Cambridge University Press, 1999), 181.

4 Mary Catherine Moran, "'The Commerce of the Sexes': Gender and the Social Sphere in Scottish Enlightenment Accounts of Civil Society," in *Paradoxes of Civil Society: New Perspectives on German and British History*, ed. Frank Trentmann (Oxford and New York: Berghahn Books, 2000), 61–84.

5 Sylvana Tomaselli, "Civilization, Patriotism and Enlightened Histories of Woman," in *Women, Gender, Enlightenment*, ed. Sarah Knott and Barbara Taylor (Basingstoke: Palgrave, 2005), 117–35.

6 Pocock, *Barbarism and Religion*, 2: 10.

7 Adam Smith, *Theory of Moral Sentiments*, ed. D.D. Raphael and A.L. Macfie (Indianapolis: Liberty Fund, 1982 [6th ed.1790]) 3.3.15 / 143. See also Neven Leddy, "Adam Smith's Moral Philosophy in the Context of Eighteenth-Century French Fiction," *Adam Smith Review* 4 (2008), 158–80.

8 Mary Wollstonecraft, *A Vindication of the Rights of Woman*, ed. Sylvana Tomaselli (Cambridge: Cambridge University Press, 1995 [1792]), 77.

9 Brent Cusher explains, in his contribution to this volume, that "the character of republican communication is musical" (p. 239, above). My claim here is that the method of republican education is historical. In the same vein, Lee Ward, in this volume, suggests that the theatrical method of civic education, as suggested by d'Alembert, was seen by Rousseau as a challenge to a uniquely Genevan mode of civic republicanism.

10 Wollstonecraft was brutally disparaging of men who take up with women of limited intellectual resources, with Rousseau as her favourite target. She demonstrates this point with reference to Rousseau's relationship with Thérèse Lavasseur, who is said to have possessed only sexual sensibility – a flaw which is extended to included most "powerful" women in history. Her point is that girls (and boys, but that is tangential to the main claim here) who have not had their affections educated cannot engage in benevolent interpersonal relations beyond the sexual. Wollstonecraft, *Vindication*, 271.

11 Smith, *Theory of Moral Sentiments*, 3.2.32 / 131.

12 Wollstonecraft, *Vindication*, 97.

13 Ibid., 171.

14 Smith, *Theory of Moral Sentiments*, 6.2.1.18 / 225.

15 Wollstonecraft, *Vindication*, 100.

16 Ibid., 102.

17 Ibid., 107.

18 Ibid., 169.

19 Adam Smith, *Lectures on Rhetoric and Belles Lettres*, ed. J.C. Bryce (Indianapolis: Liberty Fund, 1985 [delivered 1748–63]), Lecture 20, p. 112.

20 Phillips has addressed the novelty of Smith's linkage of Tacitus to eighteenth-century sentimental fiction:

> "As Smith well knew, this is an extraordinary comparison to make; after all, Tacitus's name had long been a byword for a ruthless, unsentimental acceptance of political reality, while in Britain more recently Tacitus had figured as the scourge of tyrants and the champion of last republican virtue." Phillips, *Society and Sentiment*, 87.

21 For a further development of this tendency in Smith see Neven Leddy, "Adam Smith's Moral Philosophy in the Context of Eighteenth-century French Fiction," *Adam Smith Review* 4 (2008): 158–80; and "Grave, Philosophical and Cool Reasoner: Mary Wollstonecraft on the Use of Gender in Adam Smith," *Adam Smith Review* 7 (2014).

22 Wollstonecraft, *Vindication*, 238

23 Wollstonecraft would also scoff at the idea that military life is either very courageous, or even particularly masculine; for which see Wollstonecraft, ibid., 235–6.

24 On this last point she dissents from Smith's position that education should not be wholly funded by the state. See Adam Smith, *An Inquiry into the Nature and Causes of the Wealth of Nations*, ed. R.H. Campbell and A.S. Skinner (Indianapolis: Liberty Fund, 1981), 5.1.f / 758–88.

25 Wollstonecraft, *Vindication*, 252.

26 Ibid., 256.

27 Along the way she happily outlined the nefarious effects of the English model of "public" schooling for both boys and girls. She implied that co-educational establishments would act as a brake on sodomy and masturbation amongst boys, but more important, that it would prepare both genders for eventual marriage. Ibid., 259–60.

28 For her references to national benevolence see *Vindication*, 74, 87, 291.

29 Ibid., 282.

30 Ibid., 282.

31 Ibid., 270.

32 Ibid., 281–2.

33 Ibid., 286.

34 Ibid., 74, 87.

35 Ibid., 291.

36 Ibid., 292.

37 Smith, *Wealth of Nations*, 3.4.10–17 / 418–22.

38 Without any electives in literature, obviously.

14 Pinocchio and the Puppet of Plato's *Laws*

JEFFREY DIRK WILSON

To compare Carlo Collodi's *The Adventures of Pinocchio* with Plato's *Laws* is to invite a smile, whether of bemused curiosity or wry disdain. The *Laws* is the carefully worked, sometimes even laboured, last word of a great genius. *Pinocchio* is an accidental novel written by an Italian republican who served as a soldier and public official and worked as a journalist,[1] albeit in each capacity a man of the second or even third tier. Plato (427–347 BC) without the *Laws* remains what he is. Collodi (AD 1826–90) without *Pinocchio* fades into obscurity. That having been said, it is possible for the genius and the journalist to observe the same kind of political crisis which they rightly perceive to be a moral crisis first and a political crisis second, neither of which can be resolved without resolving the other. Both knew what Plato's pupil put most succinctly, that to get politics right, it is necessary to get education right. Aristotle opines in the opening lines of the final book of his *Politics*:

> No one will doubt that the legislator should direct his attention above all to the education of youth; for the neglect of education does harm to the constitution. The citizen should be moulded to suit the form of government under which he lives. For each government has a peculiar character which originally formed and which continues to preserve it. The character of democracy creates democracy, and the character of oligarchy creates oligarchy; and always the better the character, the better the government.[2]

What Plato – at least in the *Laws* – and Collodi shared was their commitment to the best possible (rather than the best conceivable) government and, therefore also, to the best possible education. The present chapter compares a single motif from Plato, his puppet in the *Laws*, and the entirety of Collodi's most memorable and important work, his children's novel *The Adventures of Pinocchio*. That comparison is made in relation to a political state of affairs in their respective countries about which each man felt both satisfaction and frustration. Some part of their ideals had become actual, and yet each saw how precariously situated were the best parts of the regime under which he lived. Nine years after Plato's death (347 BC), Philip of Macedon brought Athens decisively within the sphere of his power. By 322, Macedonian hegemony was complete, and the glory days of Athens were in the past. For the forty years after the publication of *Pinocchio*, Italy wavered between uncertainty and chaos until 1922 when Mussolini marched on Rome, and Italy's republican vision yielded to fascism. In parallel contexts, each man offered his contemporaries the notion of a puppet as metaphor for human formation and fulfilment as citizen. In both cases, the prophetic character of that metaphor went unheeded. From the comparison, finally, a few observations shall be derived which might help clarify a republican vision for the future.

If one simply adds together the pages of the *Republic*, *Statesman*, and *Laws*, one sees that Plato committed more than a third of his writing to explicitly political themes. Moreover, those themes can be traced throughout the body of his work. One such theme is his concern for the rational pursuit of virtue as a necessary precondition for the realization of the right political constitution. Whether Plato's political dialogues be read as a call for revolution or merely reform, it is clear that he was profoundly dissatisfied with the status quo in Athens. Otherwise, why would he have written so much in urging the establishment of a different state of affairs? Glenn R. Morrow writes:

> The *Laws* shows that Plato thought the Athenians of his own day had departed from the moderation that characterized their ancestors. In the *Gorgias* Socrates refuses to accord the name of statesman to the great leaders of the age following the Persian Wars (515c–519a). It is true that they provided the city with walls, docks, shipyards, and all the attributes of wealth and power, but they failed to make the citizens better; in fact they made them worse, and this shows that they lacked the fundamental requirement of the political art. In the *Republic*, Plato pictures democracy as close to the lower limit in the scale of political value … The faults he finds with it … are those he saw in the democracy he knew best, that of fourth century Athens. But there is another view of Athens sometimes presented in the dialogues … In the *Meno* (93e, 94b,d) and *Protagoras* (319e)

> the great statesmen described in the *Gorgias* – Themistocles, Pericles, Thucydides, Aristides – are cited as examples of wisdom and civic virtue. How they acquired their excellences seems to be a mystery, and it is clear they did not know how to teach them to their sons.[3]

The "sons" of "the great statesmen" sentenced Socrates to death. The grandsons were those who managed Athenian affairs in the first half of the fourth century. Though they did make Athens safe for philosophy – clearly a Platonic prerequisite for the right kind of politics – nevertheless they were not able to thwart Philip of Macedon.[4] Over the course of Plato's lifetime, Athens was in decline. When he was born, Athens had already been at war with Sparta for four years, and he was twenty-three when Athens was finally defeated. Athens's citizenry then engaged in mutual recrimination, of which Socrates was a casualty. There ensued a quarter-century when Athens regained a position of regional strength, but under the democratic constitution which had made possible the capital sentence against Socrates. Then, during the final dozen years of Plato's life, Athens as political entity lived increasingly in the shadow of Macedon while Philip successfully advanced his imperial agenda.[5] It was against such a political backdrop that Plato inscribed his final work, the *Laws*, onto wax tablets.

Plato's principal character in the *Laws* is the Athenian Stranger, who discusses the best possible constitution with Clinias of Crete and Megillus of Sparta. The convergence of representatives from three different cities bespeaks the proposal of the *Laws*, that the best polity will blend elements from constitutions of different countries. The Athenian Stranger observes that to rule men and women requires first the mean of measure:

> If one neglects the rule of due measure (*to metrion*), and gives things too great in power to things too small – sails to ships, food to bodies, offices of rule to souls – then everything is upset, and they run, through the excess of insolence, some to bodily disorders, others to that offspring of insolence, injustice ... To guard against this, by perceiving the due measure (*to metrion*), is the task of the great lawgiver.[6]

This constitutional "due measure" or mean is no mere average, nor like Aristotle's Golden Mean that stands between two opposite extremes; rather, it is a mean of mixture. He praises this quality in the Spartan constitution in which monarchy, exemplifying the despotic principle, and democracy, exemplifying the principle of freedom, are blended.[7] The Athenian Stranger identifies the fault in the constitutions of Athens and Persia, respectively, which ultimately necessitated catastrophe. Each is based on a single principle, liberty in the case of Athens and despotism in the case of Persia.[8] The Spartans, by contrast, founded their constitution on the mean which admixes despotism, perhaps better understood as order, and liberty. André Laks explains this model of mixed polity:

> In other words, a mixture is required not simply between the ingredients (external mixture) but also within them (internal mixture). There is a democratic aspect to the "monarchical" (= competent) magistrate, who looks after the interests of the community, as the tyrant fails to do; and there is the monarchical aspect to the "democratic assembly," which selects most of the magistrates. In the city of the *Laws* the competence of the assembly is extensive, and liberty itself belongs to all.[9]

Internal mixture gives content to the external mixture, and the external mixture gives structure to the internal mixture. It is the dynamic tension in the mixture of the two mixtures which makes the constitutional mean in which order and liberty are in perfect balance such that the maintenance of one ensures the preservation of the other. The Athenian Stranger explains his goal: "our idea being that a State ought to be free and wise and in friendship with itself."[10] Thus, through a blending of principles a political mean is achieved which is not possible in a constitution founded upon a single principle.

In the following analysis of Plato's text, care shall be paid to the order and relative placement of motifs and discussions. This care arises from a commitment to Plato's authorial method which communicates philosophical insight not only through the content of the speeches, rather also through the structure and dynamic interplay of the dialogue itself. Leo Strauss, taking a phrase from the *Phaedrus* (264b7), calls this quality of Plato's writing "logographic necessity." He then characterizes it: "Every part of the written speech must be necessary for the whole; the place where each part occurs is the place where it is necessary that it should occur; in a word, the good writing must resemble the healthy animal which can do its proper work well."[11] Jacob Klein may have put this interpretive principle most succinctly, "Every word in a Platonic dialogue counts."[12] Though the principle of logographic necessity arises from the texts of Plato, once identified it can be used in analysis of other texts. It is also thus employed here in the analysis of *Pinocchio*.

The discussion of the puppet in the *Laws* provides a basis for reflecting upon this mean of mixture. The introduction of the puppet image comes early in the work, about three-quarters through book 1, which is to say, well before the lengthy discussion of monarchy and democracy in book 3. The image of the puppet, however, prepares the reader for the later thematic introduction of the mean of mixture. The treatment here returns to the metaphor of the puppet after the mean of mixture has been discovered. The Athenian Stranger introduces the puppet by inviting his fellows to play pretend with him. "Let us suppose ...," he says, not entirely unlike the trope "Once upon a time." He imagines aloud a game within the game of pretend, the play of puppeteering:

> Let us suppose that each of us living creatures is an ingenious puppet of the gods, whether contrived by way of a toy of theirs or for some serious purpose – for as to that we know nothing; but this we do know, that these inward affections of ours, like sinews or cords, drag us along and, being opposed to each other, pull one against the other to opposite actions; and herein lies the dividing line between goodness and badness.[13]

The Stranger continues to analyse the puppet – the description is very like what in modernity is known as a marionette – especially the cords which suspend and control it, the golden cord of *logos* embodied in the law and the other non-golden cords which are also necessary to make the marionette work properly. Without multiple cords made from a variety of materials, the marionette will "fall flat."[14] A marionette works precisely through the mean accomplished by a mixture of cords. Without the mixture, the marionette falls flat, which is what happens to a city with an unmixed polity, as exemplified by the extreme of democracy (as in Athens) or of monarchy (as in Persia). In the passage just cited about the marionette, after the words, "these inward affections of ours, like sinews or cords, drag us along and, being opposed to each other, pull one against the other to opposite actions," I suggest one could insert the phrase, "like democracy and monarchy." One could argue, against this view, that the Stranger here is contrasting the golden with the non-golden cords, *logos* in contrast to the passions. Upon closer examination, however, one sees that it is the non-golden cords, "the inward passions," pulling in opposite directions and thus suspending the marionette, which allows the golden cord to do its work. In the *polis* it is monarchy and democracy, representing the passionate forces of politics, which must be opposed to each other. The marionette must be kept in an easy suspension so that *logos* can be operative. Held too tight, and movement is not possible; too loose, and the puppet goes slack or even falls flat. Seth Benardete comes close to this point without quite reaching it when he writes, "The puppet is suddenly a composite, with an inside that can be made to respond to the golden thread outside."[15] It is curious that having made such an observation Benardete does not advance to describe how the puppet stands as the metaphor of the mean of mixture, the puppet specifically as the citizen seeking to live the good life in the puppet theatre of the city.

An aim of framing laws is to free humans to live according to *logos*, even while being constrained by passions and even external force. The puppeteer cannot coerce such freedom, but can, through the right laws, so habituate the citizen to external acts that conform with *logos* but for reasons other than *logos*. The person's external actions are brought into alignment with *logos* before a person's internal logic comes into alignment with *logos*. Citizenship is a category of becoming in accord with *logos*; it is an ontological category of seeming as being. The citizen is both a human being who, under rare and excellent circumstances, can live according to *logos*; he is also a puppet who can seem to live according to *logos* but who is actually being manipulated by the puppeteer. In a way that cannot ever quite be explained, when the citizen as puppet forgets that he is a puppet he actually becomes a human being, by acting like a human being, namely, by living in *logos*. The laws of the *polis* hold him in easy suspension, creating the possibility for *logos* to do its work. The more extensive orchestration of all the puppets approximates the life of the *polis* itself: the game within a game, the puppet citizen in the political life of play pretend *is* the political life.

That conclusion need not be reached by inference alone. The Athenian Stranger introduces the theme of the puppet in book 1 and recurs to it in book 7, which is to say as near the beginning of the *Laws'* second half as the introduction was near the beginning of the first half. The Stranger commends giving one's self to the condition of a marionette in the hands of God when he considers "by what means and by what modes of living we shall best navigate our barque of life through this voyage of existence." He continues:

> What I assert is this … that the object really worthy of all serious and blessed effort is God, while man is contrived, as we said above, to be a plaything of God, and the best part of him is really just that; and thus I say that every man and woman ought to pass through life in accordance with

> this character, playing at the noblest of pastimes, being otherwise minded than they now are.[16]

This claim by the Stranger is extraordinary and – to the modern or postmodern mind, at least – counter-intuitive: the Stranger affirms that human beings are the puppets of God as a statement of hope and of freedom rather than of despair and of resigned determinism. Human beings, as citizens, should earnestly play at being marionettes in the puppet theatre of the *polis*.

The dialogue is entitled *Laws*, and thus it must be asked what role laws play in this marionette theatre. The laws are the cords which keep the marionette from falling flat. In times past, the Stranger says, laws were "unblended" (*akratos*).[17] This in itself shows how far Plato has integrated into his methodology the mean of mixture as the ideal of possibility. Like the slave doctor who prescribes without any explanation or comfort, unblended laws order people to comply with the dictates of the law and threaten them with punishment if they do not comply. Brent Edwin Cusher, in chapter 11, discusses the work of the free doctor in contrast to the slave doctor. The slave doctor does not, perhaps cannot, explain to his patient – a fellow slave – why the cure must be followed. The free doctor, however, persuades his free patient. It is easy to imagine that moment. The free doctor holds up to his free patient the juxtaposition of conflicting passions: fear of the disease versus fear of the cure (e.g., the danger of gangrene and the shattering pain of amputation and cauterization). At the moment that the one fear is held in check by the other, the free patient is psychologically disposed to listen to reason. For the free patient as for the marionette, it is the equipoise of conflicting inward passions which allows the golden cord of *logos* to do its work. In this context, it is fitting to consider one of Plato's great innovations in this dialogue, the preamble[18] (*proemium*), which explains the purpose of the law and why compliance with the law is best for the person and the *polis*, promising honour for the law-abiding and shame for the law-breaker to which is attached the prescription itself; thus, the preamble transforms being subject to legislation from a condition of slavery to one of freedom.[19]

If the metaphors of the double form of the law and of the marionette cords are themselves blended (the internal mixture and the external mixture), one can imagine the cords as laws. The puppet can be kept from falling flat by the single, steely cord of coercion, the monarchical principle, but he is both rigid and lifeless, without any resemblance to life lived in *logos*. The role of the preambles is to be the "easy" part of the "easy suspension," the democratic principle. Without the cord of coercion, however, this easy suspension permits flaccidity, and therefore the puppet is again without resemblance to life lived in *logos*. It is the blending of the two, persuasion and coercion, that can yield actions in the puppet which resemble life lived in *logos* and which, in an indiscernible way and moment, become truly human being.

André Laks observes that the legislator waits as long as possible to see if the persuasive part of the law (*proemium*) can do its work before the coercive part of the law is brought into play.[20] There is this second sense of suspension, not merely of the puppet but of legislation. For as long as possible, the puppet is held in suspense by the deferral of coercive legislation, to see if the cords of persuasion do their work before the puppeteer finally engages that steely cord of coercion, forcing the puppet to go through the motions of *logos*, and making it seem that the golden cord is operative when it is not. Coercive legislation becomes the last rather than the first recourse of the legislator. In his discussion of "the status of persuasion in the *Laws*," Laks summarizes the two prevailing views of the preamble's function. He writes: "Against the tendentious but widespread interpretation which reduces the preamble to an exercise in manipulative rhetoric, some commentators have recently insisted that the persuasion at issue in the work is in principle rational."[21] Cusher reviews those two views at some length. The view argued here constitutes a third understanding to the two outlined by Laks and analysed by Cusher.[22] The preamble works primarily through praise and blame; it may sometimes attain to the level of the rational. Its method of operation, however, is not its goal, which is ontological: in an indiscernible way and at an indiscernible moment the puppet becomes *human* being. Putting the puppet through the motions of *logos* is transcendently transformative. The denizen of the city was previously less than fully human, but his being has now become fully human through the work of the persuasive and coercive cords. The denizen who seemed to live according to *logos* has become a citizen who does truly live according to *logos*. Laks comes very close to this understanding, though without quite embracing it, when he writes in conclusion about the preamble: "It also confirms Plato's attention, in his late political work, to what one might call the spontaneous manifestations of rationality of the 'human prodigy.'"[23] The Stranger seeks to create every possibility of setting the puppet free to be human with all the necessary safeguards in place to prevent him from falling flat.

The human marionette is perhaps only a plaything of the gods, perhaps something else, but both despite the cords and because of the cords, it *seems* not to be merely a puppet, but actually *to be* a human being. This is an important point which Seth Benardete seems to miss. He announces that the purpose of his book on the *Laws* is "to try to uncover its concealed ontological dimension and explain why it is concealed and how it comes to light."[24] He comes closest to recognizing the puppet as a principal metaphor by which the ontology of the *Laws* "comes to light" when he writes: "The puppet represents us as being put under a microscope, in whose field the stop-and-go character of our actions would become evident."[25] He misses the more obvious point of the puppet as a Pinocchio-like story, the puppet who by acting like a boy becomes a boy and, as the case in the *Laws*, the puppet who becomes human by acting like a citizen.[26] Pinocchio runs through all the extremes in the human appetites and passions but as a puppet. When he is guided by reason and virtue he becomes truly human and the wooden puppet is no longer necessary as a means to becoming and being. Thus, the story ends with the limp puppet "propped against a chair," and Pinocchio the boy is full of joy.[27]

The puppet appears only at two critical moments in Plato's *Laws*, but the puppet makes up the whole of Collodi's book. When he set pen to paper "rather grudgingly" in 1881 for the first chapter in the magazine serial which would become the children's classic, Italy had been united for twenty years.[28] After the initial excitement of having achieved most of the Risorgimento's major aims, the new Italy was mired in internecine strife among the various parties which had sought unity but on different premises of political philosophy. Royalists (followers of the triumphant Victor Emmanuel) and hard-line republicans (among whom Giuseppe Mazzini was the foremost) fought each other even as both sought to create a new national unity. It was not, however, merely factional strife which threatened the new nation. There was also a lack of coherent vision to inspire virtuous self-denial among those who welcomed the success of Italy over old local distinctions as well as against the two political entities with larger claims, the Papal States and Austria as hegemon of north-eastern Italy. Benedetto Croce (1866–1952) writes of the period 1871–90: "Where decadence, in comparison with the preceding period, can really be observed in Italy is with regard to vigour and breadth of thought."[29] Croce grew up and came of age during this period, and writes of it as an eyewitness observer. He acknowledges that "orthodox Catholicism, which was not wholly exhausted by clericalism ... continued to guide souls along the paths of virtue."[30] There were others, however, who had sought guidance from secular lights. Mazzini (1805–72), for example, was influenced by the French philosopher Saint-Simon (1760–1825), and thus was committed to a new civil religion of humanity which required an educational program to make possible and then to support the new political regime.[31] By the time of Mazzini's death, the energy of that secularist vision was spent. Croce writes: "After the middle of the century, however, the current was arrested and grew stagnant, owing to an obstacle that was not so much materialism ... as naturalism, with its corollary, agnosticism."[32] He offers an incisive comment about education, reflecting presumably upon his own experience: "Theories of education were full of hygiene and medicine, and empty of spiritual values."[33] The revolutionaries who had contributed so much to Italy's nationhood seemed merely old-fashioned to the generation emerging in the 1870s and 1880s. Again, Benedetto Croce comments: "The men of the old Left ... inherited something of the heroic age, and always responded to great ideas, thus showing that they had not followed Mazzini in vain, and had not for nothing dreamed of a moral and religious revival in Italian social life. But the new generation, which was growing up about 1880, was prosaic and narrow-minded."[34] Reading Croce's assessment of nineteenth-century Italy, one recalls how Morrow assessed Plato's view of Athens. In each case, a heroic generation had done its work, but had not been able to form a successor generation to consolidate and build upon its monumental achievement.

It was precisely at this moment that a man "of the old Left" evidenced his commitment to the "moral and religious revival in Italian social life" – albeit the civil religion of Saint-Simon – as well as his disillusionment with the way Italians made use of their newly won status as citizens of a nation: in 1881, Carlo Collodi commenced writing *The Adventures of Pinocchio*.[35] The end sought not only by Mazzini and his followers but by all the factional leaders of the Risorgimento was best expressed by Massimo Taparelli, Marchese d'Azeglio (1798–1866), that "now Italy was made, what remained to be done was to make Italians."[36] The Risorgimento had been successful in creating the structure of political unity; the leaders of the new Italy then discovered the work of creating cultural and social cohesion to be far more challenging. As David Tabachnick and Toivo Koivukoski note in this work's preface, political structure alone is inadequate to make a true republic; a correspondent political culture is needed as well. It was to that need which Collodi wrote.

While much has been written about *The Adventures of Pinocchio*, there is little information available in the English literature about the book's author, Carlo Lorenzini, who wrote under the name Carlo Collodi after the Tuscan village where his mother had been born.[37] His parents arranged for him to receive priestly formation, which left him "steeped … in classical literature and thought."[38] In 1848 – the momentous year of revolutions – Lorenzini had just come of age. Like Mazzini, he embraced armed revolt as an appropriate and necessary means to achieve a unitary Italian state.[39] Lorenzini participated in the campaigns of 1848 and 1859 against Austria.[40] He also engaged the work of unification through his journalism and through his entry into the new genre of children's literature.[41] In 1875, he began his apprenticeship as a children's author with the translation into Italian of the French fairy tales by Charles Perrault. It was as the translator of those stories that Lorenzini first adopted his pen name.[42] Lorenzini wrote for adults; Collodi for children. As Collodi, he went on to write a series of "successful pedagogical" novels about boy heroes.[43] In 1881, he began his serialized novel about Pinocchio, which he intended to end with chapter 15 when Pinocchio is hanged. Italian children insisted that Pinocchio must live, and Collodi responded by completing and thereby also transforming *The Adventures of Pinocchio*. He seems not to have suspected the power of his own story, as indicated both by his plan to end the book prematurely and by his characterization of it as puerile in a letter to his publishers: "I'm sending you this baby-talk … Do what you like with it."[44] It is lovely to think that precisely the children whom he was determined to improve recognized the genius of the work not recognized by Collodi himself. That historical occurrence has a fascinating literary parallel in Plato's *Laws*, when the Athenian Stranger imagines a pleasure contest among various entertainments in which, as Seth Benardete observes, "the very small children" give the prize to the puppeteer.[45]

Ann Lawson Lucas calls into question the ideological appropriations of Collodi's book, whether Marxist, Freudian, or Christian allegorical, summing up her critique in a sentence: "Many of these elaborate theories now seem dated, but *parti pris* interpretations will continue to emerge following each new intellectual vogue."[46] If we freely accept Lucas's implicit warning, nevertheless, underlying every work of art is some kind of philosophical framework. The attempt here is to discover some part of that framework as disclosed in the text of *Pinocchio*. Although Lucas writes as a literary critic, her own estimation of the currents running throughout the book are consonant with the philosophical themes which shall be adumbrated here. She writes: "*Pinocchio* has hidden depths; it is, indeed, imbued with Lorenzini's most fundamental perceptions, not only of human nature, but of life in society; his sympathy for the poor, his criticism of social and political institutions, and his detestation of hierarchies are all here."[47] Collodi's life and commitments in relation to the Risorgimento serve as blinders in the best sense to keep the reader attentive to his text, discovering what is salient in it without importing the critic's views into the text.

Pinocchio has become an icon of popular culture, a circumstance carefully documented by Richard Wunderlich and Thomas J. Morrissey in their *Pinocchio Goes Postmodern: Perils of a Puppet in the United States*. This is a case, however, of a book more famous than read.[48] For that reason, it may be useful to rehearse the outline of the story, especially with respect to those members of the *dramatis personae* to be discussed here. The book opens with a piece of wood about to be turned into a table leg by Master Cherry, who is startled when the piece of wood talks to him. Geppetto knocks at Master Cherry's door, and asks for a piece of wood to transform into a puppet. After an argument and scuffle, Geppetto leaves with the piece of wood. He begins carving the figure of a puppet, and as he does so, the puppet becomes increasingly lively. Pinocchio begins his wayward adventures through disobedience and then by running away. The rest of the story is a kind of odyssey in which Pinocchio tries to find his way back home. He soon arrives in the company of the Fox and Cat, who defraud and seek to murder him. The Blue Fairy intervenes as she does for the balance of the story, though in various guises. It is part of Pinocchio's special insight that he is able to recognize the Blue Fairy even when she in no way resembles herself in previous rescues. There is an ape judge who jails Pinocchio because he has been robbed, a farmer who literally puts him in the doghouse, a policeman who wrongly arrests him, a fisherman who endeavours to fry him as side-meat for breakfast, Lampwick who seduces him to travel to Toyland where he becomes an ass, Mini-Man who sells Pinocchio the ass to a circus, the Ringmaster who abuses him, the subsequent purchaser who throws him into the sea, and, finally, the Shark, which eats him. In the Shark's belly, Pinocchio is reunited with his dear daddy, Geppetto, and then devises a means of escape, carrying Geppetto on his back out of the Shark, which is reminiscent of Aeneas carrying Anchises from burning Troy. Pinocchio and Geppetto return home, where they live happily ever after, Pinocchio having become "a proper little boy,"[49] and, it must also be said, Geppetto having become a proper father. That is the story, but there is much more to the book than just the story.

One finds on the very first page important claims both metaphysical and political. Here are the oft-quoted first lines:

> Once upon a time there was …
>
> "A king!" my little readers will say at once.
>
> No, children, you're wrong. Once upon a time there was a piece of wood.[50]

Collodi begins with the fairy-tale formula. This is not merely a work of fiction, but also a make-believe story in which anything might happen. At the same time, this fairy tale begins by addressing a political premise and expectation, namely, that there should be a king. The Mazzinian republican, Carlo Lorenzini a.k.a. Collodi, is telling the children of Italy's citizens, that is, the future citizens of Italy, that they have made a mistake by beginning their new nation with a king. The story begins with a very different metaphysical and political premise, "a piece of wood." Though Collodi was classically educated, one does not have to suppose he was thinking of Plato and Aristotle as he wrote *Pinocchio* in order to see principles of Platonic and Aristotelian philosophy in his pages. One may note, for example, that wood is material and, further, that the Greek word for "wood," *hulē*, was Aristotle's choice to designate matter.[51] This piece of wood surprises Master Cherry by speaking, much as the people of Italy surprised dukes, kings, and even an emperor by speaking up. The piece of wood was not matter only; it was also ensouled. This piece of animated matter is the first premise of the new nation, because the challenge before Italy after 1861 was not whether they could make kings – there were more than enough of them about – but whether they could make citizens – of which there were all too few. Could the human-like denizens of the new Italy become fully human as citizens? That was the question on the mind of Collodi.

The second chapter of *Pinocchio* can be read as displaying the problem of establishing public discourse. The nascent citizen, still only a talking piece of wood, overhears his betters, Master Cherry and Geppetto, arguing in a fashion not unlike that of parliamentary debates in the new Italy. Geppetto wore a wig which reminded children of a bowl of "cornmeal mush." The piece of wood calls Geppetto by his street nickname, "Corn Head." Geppetto supposes that the epithet must have come from

Master Cherry. They engage in an exchange of which the Monty Python "Argument Clinic"[52] is reminiscent:

> "Why are you insulting me?"
> "Who's insulting you?"
> "You called me Corn Head."
> "It wasn't me."
> "Oh, I suppose you're saying it was *me*? I say it was you."
> "Was not."
> "Was too."
> "Was not!"
> "Was too!"
> As tempers flared, words gave way to deeds, and they scratched, bit, and battered each other as they fought.[53]

That pointless exchange parodies the scenes in the Italian parliament which Christopher Duggan describes with scholarly nuance:

> In the early 1880s the situation appeared to be getting worse ... But the problem in Italy was that it coincided with a general revulsion towards parliament and growing anxieties about the country's "decadence" ... The blurring of party lines and the sense that the Chamber was dissolving into a quagmire of unprincipled factions held together by the bargaining skills of the pliable but personally honest Depretis (one leading contemporary compared him to an English water closet that stayed clean despite the filth passing through it).[54]

Passion, sentiment, and parochialism abounded. The means of civil debate eluded the people and politicians of the new Italy. One reasonably then asks what the root causes were of such public irascibility.

Like the dual nature of the puppet, the problem of Italians' readiness to squabble also has both material and spiritual causes. In chapter 3, Collodi points to the philosophical counterpoint of seeming and being which underlies the material challenge to creation of a true republic. He describes Geppetto's room in terms of broken furniture and general disarray. The impression of dire poverty is complete when he tells the reader, "On the rear wall you could see a fireplace with a glowing fire, but it was a painted fire, and above it was a painted pot, which boiled merrily and gave off steam that really looked like steam."[55] He signals that Pinocchio is "Everyman," when Geppetto explains his rationale for the choice of the puppet's name, "I once knew an entire family by that name ... The richest one was a beggar."[56] There are other signs of extreme poverty throughout the novel.[57] Corresponding to material want is spiritual appetite. It is tempting to think of appetite as material, but the strange fact about appetite is that material goods are necessary but not sufficient conditions for the satisfaction of appetite. Pinocchio attempts to eat from the painted pot on the wall. Unsatisfied, his hunger leads to reflection about his disrespectful treatment of Geppetto, his "daddy"; thus, material want leads him to awareness of a purely spiritual want.[58] Night falls, but Pinocchio searches for food. There was a thunderstorm which terrified him, "but his hunger was greater than his fear" and despair was added to the opposing forces within him.[59] Pinocchio repeatedly bumps into the world in his various states, and Collodi presents those encounters as occasions for the experience of injustice, usually in hues of the darkest comic relief. On "the dark and stormy night" – the storm, by the way, is a dry one without rain – Pinocchio begs for food from a householder who appears at an upstairs window. He promises food to the supplicant, but instead dumps water on his head. The householder, in a sense, provides the rain which the storm had not. Nature inspires fear, but no sustenance. What nature withheld is provided by man, but only as retribution. Umberto Eco begins a brief reflection on the opening lines of *Pinocchio* by observing, "Certainly the author has, at his disposal, particular genre signals that he can use to give instructions to his model reader; but frequently these signals can be highly ambiguous."[60] His assessment is apposite to the entire novel and not merely its opening lines. After Pinocchio's drenching, the reader may well ask, "Is there no justice in the world?" The immediate and superficial response is that there is not. Pinocchio was promised bread, but was given an unwanted bath. Instead of being nourished, he was humiliated. Here one notes the ambiguity. At a deeper and more enduring level, there is justice in the story. He was hungry, afraid, despairing, and – in the end – wet because he had been disobedient. His lack of virtue, his wilful pursuit to satisfy appetites and passions is justly rewarded. The dynamic of the unjust entity unknowingly distributing justice as an instrument in the hand of providence – if only a secularized notion of providence – persists throughout the story. That is true of Pinocchio's encounter with the Fox and the Cat, the ape judge, the farmer, the policemen, the fisherman, Lampwick and Mini-Man, the Ringmaster, the buyer of the ass, and the Shark. At the same time, there are limits set for those who would do him ill. An unequal dualism is at work throughout the novel. Good and evil engage each other in the person of Pinocchio, but every malevolent being is mysteriously subordinate to the benevolent providence of the Blue Fairy. At least for those who have discernment enough to recognize the hand of that benevolent providence – and Pinocchio, for all his failings, is blessed with such a gift – there is actually something better than justice in the world, namely, redemption.

The *volta* of the story comes in chapter 25, just past the book's halfway point and, significantly, well after that point where Collodi continued because the children of Italy had insisted. Pinocchio has attained a certain virtue because of his strenuous efforts to find his "daddy," Geppetto. He has landed on "an island in the middle of the sea,"[61] where he meets "a good little woman," whom Pinocchio recognizes as the Blue Fairy.[62] Pinocchio expresses his amazement that the Blue Fairy has "grown up" from the girl he had known before to the woman she is now. As the being who intervenes on behalf of Pinocchio, she is a providential power. In the counsel she gives him, she is the golden cord of *logos* who seeks to guide him even as his passions pull him in opposite directions. He has come to himself and declares his heartfelt wish to grow up too:

> "But you can't grow," replied the Fairy.
>
> "Why not?"
>
> "Because puppets never grow. They're born as puppets, they live as puppets, and they die as puppets."
>
> "Oh, I'm sick of always being just a puppet!" shouted Pinocchio, smacking himself on the forehead. "It's about time I grew up too and became a man."
>
> "And you will, if you can earn it."
>
> "Really? How do I earn it?"
>
> "It's the easiest thing in the world: just practice being a proper boy."[63]

There follows a checklist of qualities which "a proper boy" must possess. In short, he must evidence virtue and reason. Here is a marvellous point about the relationship of human-like Italian to truly human citizen and, equally, of seeming, becoming, and being. One can become a truly human citizen by seeming like such a citizen. Performing citizen-like activities (e.g., telling the truth, pursuing knowledge, having a good heart, working hard, and contributing to the common good through a worthy art or trade)[64] transforms a person from a bundle of appetites and passions into an integral human citizen. That is to say, if a person acts like a citizen continuously, then that person will *be* a citizen and thereby also achieve the end of *being* fully *human*. In a sense, Collodi had given up on the governing generation of 1881. He had sensed that, as in the kingdom of God, it would also be true in the modern secular nation state that "a little child shall lead them."[65] Collodi gives to Geppetto a key statement in the final dozen lines of the book: "When children who were once naughty become nice, their whole families change and become happier."[66] It is not the adults who will convert the children, rather the children who will transform Italy. Clearly, that transformation will take place through education afforded children by adults, but it is even clearer throughout the novel that many adults are irredeemable. Their instrumentality in the hand of a benign providence will remain unwitting. The family of the Italian nation shall rise or fall by the puppet children who either will or will not become fully human citizens. Pinocchio, for his part, discovers his highest good by escaping puppethood. In the final two sentences, he exclaims, "How funny I was when I was a puppet! And how happy I am now that I have become a proper little boy."[67] Until the final pages, the reader does not know which of Pinocchio's sentiments will prevail, his baser passions or his real love and appreciation for both Geppetto and the Blue Fairy. It is with Pinocchio as the Athenian Stranger observed: "These inward affections of ours, like sinews or cords, drag us along and, being opposed to each other, pull one against the other to opposite actions; and herein lies the dividing line between goodness and badness."[68] Pinocchio's passions keep him (and Collodi's audience) in suspense, so that the golden cord of reason can do its work in both the puppet and the audience. In attending to Collodi's lifelong commitments, the reader learns from Pinocchio and his adventures that the human being attains happiness as a citizen living in accord with virtue and reason, fully engaged in the political community.

Brand and Pertile, writing in *The Cambridge History of Italian Literature*, assess the place of *Pinocchio* in Italian culture: "Critics agree that *Pinocchio* may be read as a kind of *Bildungsroman*, aimed at showing that for a child to grow into a good citizen he must abandon the puppet within him and become trustworthy, dependable and respectful of society's rules."[69] They are certainly right to speak of what is necessary in order "for a child to grow into a good citizen," and it may be added that in order for the puppet-like child to become a fully mature adult, it is necessary at the same time to become a well-formed citizen. That is to suggest a premise underlying Collodi's novel, namely, to be truly human one must be rightly engaged in the political community. Not only, pace Aristotle, is the human being the political animal, but in order to be more than animal, the human must be political.

The civil body politick, rightly constituted, comprises the system of cords which does not ensure that humans attain to being, but only creates the *opportunity* for humans to attain to being, that is, to live the good life in the well-ordered *polis*. At the end of book 3 of the *Laws*, it is this that the Athenian Stranger says is "the object of all these discourses": "to discover how best a State might be managed, and how best the individual citizen might pass his life."[70] This is the happy symbiosis of which Geoffrey Kellow writes here in the "Introduction": the being of the *polis* nurturing the being of citizens and in turn the *polis* nurtured by her citizens. The former necessarily fails without the latter. Although Collodi does not provide us with a corresponding declaration in *The Adventures of Pinocchio*, the same aim is implicit throughout: human life is as citizen in the city. Plato and Collodi both chide and encourage their countrymen to recalibrate their standards of citizenship. Read retrospectively, one sees the prophetic character of their puppets; there is an admonitory forth-telling and a foretelling of inevitable consequences if the prophetic word is not heeded. Athens – given to the democratic principle alone – became subject to Macedon and, thereafter, never again attained real political importance. The new Italy in all its cascading constitutions has vacillated between the lawlessness of chaos and the lawlessness of tyranny. The fatal flaw has been the unblended or – at very best – the improperly blended presence of the despotic and democratic principles. In this regard, Plato saw much more clearly than Collodi. The puppet conjured by the Athenian Stranger worked. He was a marionette which functioned properly. A point often missed about Pinocchio is that he was a failure as a puppet. In chapter 10, Pinocchio's entrance into the puppet theatre "triggered a small revolution." There was a family reunion of sorts among the puppets, but it brought the performance to a halt.[71] Collodi celebrates this failure; the scene depicts the escape from tyranny to freedom. For the Athenian Stranger, by contrast, the marionette had to operate effectively in the puppet theatre. In this life, there is no escaping the performance in the theatre: that is the life of the citizen in the city. On the stage of the city, the puppeteer legislates the steely cords of the marionette and coaxes the marionette with preambles, thereby putting the puppet through the motions of the rational life of virtue in the hope that the golden cord may descend and take hold. This is the part of the story that Collodi and Italy miss. Freedom must be a means to order, and coercion a means to freedom. The despotic and democratic principles must be admixed both externally and internally, keeping citizens and city alike in suspense. Pinocchio is, indeed, held in suspense by his passions, but Collodi has omitted the passionate rule of despots. His is, after all, a book which begins by *not* being about a king; it ends with praise for Pinocchio's devotion to his daddy, but a father who has long since ceased to be a despot. The beauty of the Athenian Stranger's proposal is that he does not ask humans to be better than they are. He proposes to juxtapose two of the worst human tendencies – the passion to dominate another and the passion to be completely free from such domination. They counteract each other, thus giving virtue and reason a momentary chance *to be.*[72] Plato understood well how precarious is every human effort towards nobility in life. His Athenian Stranger sets forth the mean of mixed polity as a path of ascent, all the while understanding that in any attempted ascent to rational and virtuous being the human often hangs not by a cord, golden or steel, but by the merest thread.

NOTES

1 Collodi "broadly sympathized with the ideas of Mazzini, Risorgimento theorist, idealist, and insurrectionist whose aim was an egalitarian Republic of Italy." Ann Lawson Lucas, "Introduction," *The Adventures of Pinocchio,* by Carlo Collodi (Oxford: Oxford University Press, 1996), xii. Quoted in Richard Wunderlich and Thomas Morrissey, *Pinocchio Goes Postmodern: Perils of a Puppet in the United States* (New York: Routledge, 2002), 3–4.

2 Aristotle, *Politics* 8.1337a11–19. Aristotle, *The Complete Works of Aristotle: The Revised Oxford Translation,* 2 vols., ed. Jonathan Barnes (Princeton: Princeton University Press, 1984), 2: 2121.

3 Glenn R. Morrow, *Plato's Cretan City: A Historical Interpretation of the "Laws"* (Princeton: Princeton University Press, 1993), 86–7.

4 For a different view, T.H. Irwin writes: "However much [Plato] objects to democracy, he assumes that, practically speaking, the Athenian democracy is stable, and that no feasible alternative is likely to be superior." T.H. Irwin, "The Intellectual Background," in *The Cambridge Companion to Plato,* ed. Richard Kraut (Cambridge: Cambridge University Press, 1999), 62. Irwin makes clear that this is, in fact, his own view and that he thinks he is merely agreeing with Plato. His view, further, is that Plato – satisfied that politically things cannot be much better than they are – is led "back to ethical

problems." Ibid., 63. Though Irwin makes reference to both *Republic* and *Laws*, he does not seem to have taken them seriously into account. Neither the constitution proposed in the former, led by guardians, nor the mean of mixed polity advocated in the latter – a theme to be examined below – accord with Irwin's conclusions. Why would Plato write his final dialogue, concerned with every aspect of the civil body politick and synthesizing multiple political traditions, if he was satisfied with the current state of affairs in Athens? Even Irwin acknowledges that Plato "objects to democracy."

5 Arnold Wycombe Gomme and Nicholas Geoffrey Lemprière Hammond, "Athens (Historical Outline)," in *The Oxford Classical Dictionary*, ed. N.G.L. Hammond and Howard Hayes Scullard (Oxford: Oxford University Press, 1978), 140–1.

6 Plato, *Laws*, trans. R.G. Bury Loeb Classical Library, vols. 10 and 11, nos. 187 and 192 (Cambridge, MA: Harvard University Press, 2001), 216–17 (3.691c1–d5). Hereafter, *L.* 3.691c1–d5; Bury 1.216–17.

7 *L.* 3.691d8–92b1 and 3.701e1–8.

8 *L.* 3.699e1–6.

9 André Laks, "The *Laws*," in *The Cambridge History of Greek and Roman Political Thought*, ed. Christopher Rowe et al. (Cambridge: Cambridge University Press, 2000), 279.

10 *L.* 3.693b1–5; Bury 1.216–17.

11 Leo Strauss, *The City and Man* (Chicago: Rand McNally and Co., 1964), 53. Stanley Rosen follows his mentor on this point: "It is now very widely accepted that one cannot understand Plato's philosophical teaching apart from the most careful consideration of its literary presentation." Stanley Rosen, *Plato's "Republic": A Study* (New Haven: Yale University Press, 2005), 353. Jacob Howland makes a similar point, "One cannot understand Plato without paying due attention to his style." Jacob Howland, *The "Republic": The Odyssey of Philosophy* (New York: Twayne Publishers, 1993), 25.

12 Jacob Klein, *Lectures and Essays*, ed. Robert B. Williamson and Elliot Zuckerman (Annapolis, MD: St John's College Press, 1985), 310.

13 *L.* 1.644d7–e4; Bury 68–9.

14 *L.* 1.644e4–45c6.

15 Seth Benardete, *Plato's "Laws": The Discovery of Being* (Chicago: University of Chicago Press, 2000), 48.

16 *L.* 7.803b2–c8; Bury 2.52–5.

17 *L.* 4.723a1–2.

18 Cusher translates this Greek term as "prelude" (p. 232).

19 *L.* 4.719c1–b5. The key passage is 4.722e.1–23b6.

20 Laks, "The *Laws*," 265.

21 Ibid., 289.
22 Thus, while appreciating Cusher's rich treatment of the preamble of the *Laws*, my own conclusion differs from his. In the end, his position is that the preamble is not rational, citing the "dizziness and whirling" caused by argument (*Laws* 10.892e5–93a7) and the necessary taming of the citizen (10.890c6–8). In fact, in the former cited passage, the Stranger proposes proceeding carefully through this argument until demonstration is complete.
23 Laks, "The *Laws*," 290.
24 Benardette, *Plato's "Laws,"* xii.
25 Ibid., 48.
26 Laks also stumbles on this point. Laks, "The *Laws*," 277.
27 Carlo Collodi, *The Adventures of Pinocchio*, trans. Geoffrey Brock, intro. by Umberto Eco and afterword by Rebecca West (New York: New York Review Books, 2009), 160.
28 Christopher Duggan, *The Force of Destiny: A History of Italy since 1796* (Boston: Houghton Mifflin, 2008), 281.
29 Benedetto Croce, *A History of Italy: 1871–1915*, trans. Cecilia M. Ady (New York: Russell and Russell, 1963), 126.
30 Ibid., 127.
31 Duggan, *Force of Destiny*, 128–9.
32 Croce, *History*, 127.
33 Ibid., 132.
34 Ibid., 139.
35 Lucas, "Introduction," xxi.
36 Ibid., xx.
37 Rebecca West, afterword to *The Adventures of Pinocchio* (2009), 165. "Biographical information in English is not abundant." Wunderlich and Morrissey, *Postmodern*, 3.
38 Wunderlich and Morrissey, *Postmodern*, 3.
39 Duggan, *Force of Destiny*, 119, 130. Mazzini was "above all a terrorist." Rosario Romeo, in *La Repubblica* (Rome), 20 April 1977, quoted by Denis Mack Smith in *Mazzini* (New Haven: Yale University Press, 1994), 230.
40 Wunderlich and Morrissey, *Postmodern*, 4.
41 Lucas characterizes Lorenzini's journalism both before and after his second service as a soldier in 1859. Before that date, he was a cultural, and in particular a literary, commentator. After 1859, he "plunged again into his career in journalism." Lucas, "Introduction," xvii. His work was sufficiently noteworthy that "he was commissioned by the new government to write a polemical pamphlet against a reactionary apologist for the *ancien régime* of the Grand Dukes." Ibid., xvii.

42 Ibid., xix.
43 West, "Afterword," 166. Wunderlich and Morrissey, *Postmodern*, 4.
44 Lucas, "Introduction," xxii.
45 Benardete, *Plato's* "Laws," 68; *L.* 2.658c10–11.
46 Lucas, "Introduction," xliv–v. One may add to her list the feminist interpretation as exemplified by West's afterword to Brock's 2009 translation.
47 Ibid., xii.
48 When I use Pinocchio in my course on philosophy of human nature, I ask my students how many know the character (everyone), how many have seen the Disney movie (nearly everyone), and how many have read the book (hardly anyone).
49 Collodi, *Pinocchio*, 160.
50 Ibid., 3.
51 Henry George Liddell, Robert Scott, and Henry Stuart Jones, *A Greek-English Lexicon*, 9th ed. with a revised supplement (Oxford: Oxford University Press, 1996), s.v. *hulē*.
52 See http://www.montypython.net/scripts/argument.php and https://www.youtube.com/watch?v=kQFKtI6gn9Y.
53 Collodi, *Pinocchio*, 6–7.
54 Duggan, *Force of Destiny*, 318–19.
55 Collodi, *Pinocchio*, 9.
56 Ibid., 9.
57 E.g., "And Pinocchio, though he was a very cheerful boy, grew sad, too, because poverty, if it's true poverty, is understood by everyone, even children." Ibid., 25.
58 Ibid., 16–17.
59 Ibid., 19.
60 Umberto Eco, *Six Walks in the Fictional Woods* (Cambridge: Harvard University Press, 1994), 10.
61 Collodi, *Pinocchio*, 84.
62 Ibid., 87–9.
63 Ibid., 90–1.
64 Ibid., 91–2.
65 Isaiah 11:6 (Authorized Version).
66 Collodi, *Pinocchio*, 160.
67 Ibid.
68 *L.* 1.644d7–e4; Bury 68–9.
69 Peter Brand and Lino Pertile, eds, *The Cambridge History of Italian Literature* (Cambridge: Cambridge University Press, 1996), 471. On *Pinocchio* as

Bildungsroman, see also Wunderlich and Morrissey, *Postmodern*, 9, and Umberto Eco, "Introduction," *The Adventures of Pinocchio* (2009), x.

70 *L.* 3.702a7–b1; Bury 250–1.

71 Collodi, *Pinocchio*, 30–1.

72 Tabachnick and Koivukoski discuss Machiavelli's two types of human nature, that is, "those who want to oppress others" and those whose "desire [is] simply not to be oppressed." Speaking anachronistically, Plato transcends Machiavelli by recognizing that everyone has these two tendencies and that it is the equipoise achieved by juxtaposition of the two in any given person which creates the possibility of truly human being.

15 Unity in Multiplicity: Agency and Aesthetics in German Republicanism

DOUGLAS MOGGACH

Between the French Revolution and the revolutions of 1848, German republicanism derives its specific features from an extension and elaboration of Kant's juridical and ethical thought. It applies to political relations and interactions the concept of autonomy, the rational self-legislation of modern subjects. It takes account of decisive characteristics of modern political experience which differentiate it from antiquity: namely, the diversity, and not the homogeneity of interests (hence ruling out the Spartan model as inapplicable); the conflict among such interests, and the central political problem of effecting their harmonization; and the self-given rather than naturally determined character of the ends of action, opening up the prospect of active self-change rather than the mere assertion of particular interests. In this way two sets of contrasts appear: between the ancient and the modern forms of state, and between liberal and republican versions of the latter. The ancient is taken to represent the immersion of the citizen in the body politic, with inadequate attention to subjective effort and initiative in shaping, criticizing, and validating public norms; and the liberal is taken to consecrate existing private interests, and thus to constrain and distort the potentially transformative effects of public life. German republicanism defends autonomy against both heteronomous submersion in communal values and the blandishments of possessive individualism. This is its achievement and its legacy.

Kant describes the Enlightenment as an epochal turning point for humanity: the shaking off of self-imposed tutelage, marking the historical maturation of the species.[1] Traditional and transcendent sources of authority are deprived of their unreflective influence, and yield to critical adjudication and self-legislation by rational subjects. Kant had formulated a similar idea earlier, in the first edition of the *Critique of Pure Reason*:

> Our age is the genuine age of *criticism*, to which everything must submit. *Religion* through its holiness and *legislation* through its majesty commonly seek to exempt themselves from it. But in this way they excite a just suspicion against themselves, and cannot lay claim to that unfeigned respect that reason grants only to that which has been able to withstand its free and public examination.[2]

Enlightenment subjects no longer derive their ethical and political standards from the supposition of a fixed natural order, but from an idea of the self and its purposes. The primacy of freedom does not entail antinomianism or denial of all law, but places law on a new basis, requiring an interrogation into what the self may rightfully claim and do. The task is to reconcile the freedom of each individual with the freedom of all, within a political order which is not merely given, but constructed; harmony is not pre-established, but achieved. This problem of the compossibility of freedoms is at the heart of German political thought from Kant onwards, and it finds expression in the specific forms of German republicanism, attested in Schiller and in members of the Hegelian School, foremost among whom is Bruno Bauer. While giving political substance to Kant's moral idea of autonomy, these ideas are also shaped by aesthetic considerations, by ideas of beauty and sublimity. The result is an aesthetic republicanism which is particularly responsive to the problems of cohesiveness and division in modern society: the unity of unity and multiplicity.

While building on Enlightenment conceptions, the Kantian tradition also undertakes a critique and reformulation of these ideas. Empiricist and materialist theorists in the Enlightenment (Helvetius, Holbach, and later Bentham, with Hobbes as an early progenitor) understood the centrality of the modern subject through categories like utility and its cognates; the world existed as material for the satisfaction of need, and the maximization of happiness. On the Kantian account, however, these currents had failed to grasp the nature of subjectivity. While focusing on human needs and the conditions of their fulfilment, the materialists had promoted too naturalized a view of the subject, subsuming its activities under natural necessity; and they had produced a simplistic, reductionist account of agency. According to this model, subjects were largely determined in their desires by the effects of sensibility or of nature upon them;[3] second, these desires (in conjunction with beliefs formed on the basis of previous experience) immediately determined action, or were a sufficient incentive to it; third, reason was reduced to an ancillary restraining role in the guise of prudence, also under the influence of empirical beliefs. Such subjects (as Marx, too, later observed)[4] are essentially passive, merely responding to natural imperatives, and completely integrated within the causal nexus of the natural order.[5] While nature is divested of its earlier meaning as a normative order, natural necessity continues to control subjects through the mechanisms of their needs and desires: their emancipation from nature remains incomplete. For Kant and the German idealists who further developed his thought, the error of the materialists is to minimize the capacity of subjects to abstract from motives of sensibility and immediate interest and to submit these to rational examination and critique. The error is to deny to subjects their intrinsic spontaneity.

Kant and his successors thus redefine the model of rational agency which underlies the Enlightenment project. The key to this redefinition is the notion of spontaneity. This is one of the central and distinctive concepts of German philosophy since Leibniz,[6] and while the Leibnizian and Kantian versions differ significantly, the core idea is the ability not to be ruled from without, but to be self-determining. This idea underlies the imperative to bring the external and internal worlds under rational direction, which is the hallmark of German idealism in its development of the Enlightenment project. Theoretically, Kant characterizes spontaneity as the mind's power of producing representations out of itself.[7] Practically, it refers to the will's capacity to exempt itself from external causal determination, and to direct its course according to self-imposed rules or maxims which are themselves not causally derived. On Kant's account, subjects are sensibly affected, but not, as Enlightenment materialists maintain, sensibly determined.[8] Practical reason endows subjects with the ability to abstract from the workings of natural causes or desires, as these arise in the medium of sensibility; and to initiate in the phenomenal world new causal series, whose origin lies in an act of will, and not in an antecedent determining cause.[9] For Kant (as too for the Stoics,[10] the enlightened idealists of the ancient world), desires do not directly necessitate action, but operate through the medium of practical judgments, after being sifted and assessed in light of their fitness for subjects' teleological projects. This consideration does not apply exclusively to moral activity, but to rational agency in general: it yields a broader perspective on the freedom which subjects enjoy in the satisfaction of desires, because they remain at liberty to choose among them, or to reject them. As one noted commentator puts it, a desire constitutes a cause for acting not automatically, but only insofar as subjects incorporate this desire within their maxims, that is, posit or adopt it as a rule for action.[11] Just as in the Stoic refutation of Epicureanism, pleasure and pain are not immediate, primary data which determine the totality of our responses, but are materials for the will; insofar as they figure as an incentive to conscious action (and not merely as a cause of instinctive reaction), they must be taken up or recognized as pleasurable or painful within the individual's prior self-conception. Negative freedom in Kant's sense is precisely this independence of the will from desires, and the capacity to adjudicate among them; the will is not directly determined by objects of desire, but only by causes which it itself admits, or allows to operate.[12] From spontaneity flow the other concepts which Kant adduces in his account of agency: autonomy, heteronomy, and determinability. These notions will also be central to post-Kantian political thinking.

Autonomy is self-legislation in accord with the moral law, and out of the motive of duty: it implies inner as well as outer compliance. It is spontaneity under the command of practical reason, the governing of one's actions in accord with maxims which can be willed universally without contradiction. These maxims are derived neither from motives of sensibility or interest, nor from the supposition of a teleological order of nature, but from reason in its practical capacity.[13] For humans as imperfectly rational beings, a composite of intellect and sensibility, morality assumes the form of imperatives issued by reason to assess desires and bring them under its command. This conception of adjudicative and legislative reason involves a broadening of rationality beyond its typical Enlightenment role, as a servant of the passions and interests.[14] In response to materialist notions of instrumental rationality, Kant proposes a distinction between empirical and pure practical reason. The former is the domain of need satisfaction, happiness, and utility, which, while a vital component of rationality, is not exhaustive, because its concern is with the efficiency of means, but not the assessment of appropriate ends. This latter is the function of *pure* practical reason, the domain of self-legislation and morality, upon which, for Kant, the spheres of juridical right and moral virtue, in their specific differences, are founded. Through pure practical reason, subjects exercise autonomy by testing their maxims for validity and universalizability, and acting on the basis of duty rather than inclination, wherever these conflict.[15]

The imperatives of pure practical reason are categorical, not hypothetical. They are moral rules that are valid for their own sake, not for any ulterior ends. Freedom here appears in its most exalted form as self-legislation, in which subjects prescribe the moral law to themselves, and do not rely on external authority to dictate their conclusions. The source of value and normativity lies within, in the rational faculties, and not in any external standards. This recognition marks the end of self-imposed tutelage, and the dawning of genuine enlightenment.

If it is the contrary of autonomy, heteronomy, or taking the law from elsewhere, is nonetheless a manifestation of spontaneity. In acting heteronomously, subjects are determining *themselves* in conformity with a desire,[16] and in opposition to duty; it is not the case that the desire simply determines the subjective will, as on the materialist model, but rather that the will actively colludes in this determination. This self-determination of the will satisfies the basic condition of spontaneity, even in pursuit of illegitimate ends. Nor does the reproach of heteronomy apply to all need satisfaction; it does so only when a conflict arises with duty or moral imperatives. "To be happy is necessarily the desire of every rational but finite being."[17] But happiness is an indeterminate goal, open to an infinite variety of satisfactions; and it becomes problematic only when it risks leading us astray, into heteronomous opposition to what we ought to do.

Kant's account of rational agency is rounded out by the concept of determinability, which will play a central role in post-Kantian thought. This refers not so much to the *malleability* of the self, which would imply moulding by external forces: literally a hammering into shape. It refers rather to the capacity of the self to determine its own empirical properties, or to contribute to the realization of one possible experiential world rather than another, by selecting from a range of options, in accord with some (moral or non-moral) evaluative standard;[18] this process is operative in both empirical and pure practical reason. Such a creative power is not absolute and unbounded, because not all empirical properties of the self are open to variation through the will; but for Kant it covers a wide range of activities, whereby the self gradually becomes consonant with freedom and reason. Determinability is simply spontaneity by another name, as a process of self-shaping, and so it will be understood by Schiller and other post-Kantians. The concept is not, however, redundant or eliminable. It is through determinability that the aesthetic dimensions of freedom will come to the fore.

The Kantian account of rational agency has direct implications for political thought, Kant's own and that of his followers, where these implications lead in different directions, but always from the same conceptual base. The preceding considerations set up the debate between typically liberal ideas of freedom and those of German republicans,[19] though the lines of demarcation between these approaches were fluid in Kant's day, and important commonalities exist. According to the standard account, liberalism, whose theoretical origins lie in Enlightenment materialism, maintains that one is free if unimpeded in his or her empirical desires. This constitutes negative liberty, not in Kant's sense as the absence of external causes, but in the sense of non-interference with the objects of desire;[20] or as Hobbes puts it (taking him as offering a liberal view of the self, if not of the state): the absence of obstacles between persons and the objects of their will.[21] We can now see that the liberal definition of negative freedom as non-interference depends on an implicit equation of freedom with happiness, utility, or the satisfaction of desires: we are free to the extent that nothing hampers us in fulfilling our wants, whatever these may be. Kant's achievement here is to differentiate these terms, freedom and happiness, and to assign them to distinct, yet connected, spheres within the system of practical reason.

Unlike the liberal version, Kantian negative freedom is the absence of external determination, based on the recognition of spontaneity as the capacity to abstract from empirical desires, and to incorporate them selectively into maxims. This reference to external determination has important consequences, as it relates, first, to other wills; and second, to the objects of desire. First, as such external determination would include the hegemony of an alien will over the subject, Kant's conception of negative liberty accords with that of recent proponents of republicanism, who define freedom not as the absence of interference, but as the absence of domination or of the possibility of *arbitrary* interference.[22] For republicans, one can be unfree not simply because the will and power of another pose empirical impediments to one's purposes, as Hobbes would have it; but by virtue of the *possibility* of any such intervention, whether it be exercised or not, insofar as the decision to suspend or exert such power remains at the discretion of this alien will. To be subject to the possibility of such interference is to be *sub potestate*, under the constraint of another, and thus to lack the status of the free person.[23] It is to be deprived of freedom, even if the pursuit of happiness be (empirically) unconstrained. Though Kant's own idea of non-determination is more far-reaching in its repudiation of any unexamined cause of desire, it is compatible with the republican approach in regard to other wills. Second, the Kantian concept of freedom depends further on the primacy of self-relation and self-consciousness over desire, pleasure, and pain, following the line described by the Stoics. Freedom is not the fulfilment of indiscriminate desires, but precisely entails the ability to discriminate and to judge. It is this primacy of self-consciousness which is captured in the Kantian notion of right, the recognition of the self as the independent source of practical, technical, and pragmatic judgments,[24] while the empirical quest for satisfaction occupies the sphere of welfare. Kant's distinction between happiness, right, and virtue is rooted here.

In his *Metaphysics of Morals* of 1797, Kant sets out his system of practical reason, and in particular the political doctrine of right, the juridical relations among free and independent subjects.[25] Although for Kant happiness cannot be the foundation of ethical and political theory, it still enjoys an ample and legitimate sphere. Happiness is too subjective and variable to provide a firm basis for ethical thinking, but it is to be accommodated within universal rational principles, which determine the proper scope of subjects' satisfaction-seeking activities. As distinguished from morality, which involves full autonomy in Kant's sense of moral self-legislation, the juridical sphere, or sphere of right, regulates *external* actions so as to ensure that subjects can pursue their own ends without violating the conditions of free activity for others. Right concerns only the external or observable aspects of action, not its maxim or principle. In considering them as legal subjects, Kant explicitly leaves the motivations of individuals out of account. In the sphere of right, individuals determine their choices of particular goods or objects of happiness, and seek these insofar as they are mutually compatible with others' choices. It is here that their spontaneity has free play, limited only by the necessity that others must be able to practise their own freedom simultaneously. Political prescription of these specific choices would be an infringement of spontaneity and right, and would constitute despotism;[26] the state may not legitimately determine for its subjects the manner of seeking happiness, though it must prevent them from encroaching on the capacity of others to exert free agency themselves.

In his account of right, Kant reflects on the achievements of modern political thought, presenting his own version of a social contract doctrine. But he continues to differ in important respects from Hobbes and Locke. Prudential calculation may be a sufficient ground for action *within* the sphere of right (we are not required to have moral motives when we act rightfully, but may, for example, refrain from harming others for fear of consequences); but prudence does not establish this sphere in the first place.[27] The imperative to leave the putative state of nature and establish rightful relations in civil society is a moral one, a command of pure practical reason: "Let there be rights" is a moral decree, and not one based upon utility. It enables freedom (in the form of spontaneity) as well as satisfaction, and thus is rooted in pure practical reason, while releasing empirical practical reason to pursue its own workings and securing its specific terrain. Moreover, the sphere of right is always situated in the larger context of morality; right does not designate the ultimate form of rational freedom, but is an important subordinate, and relatively independent, expression. The pure autonomy of moral self-determination is exercised beyond the sphere of right; morality transcends right without suppressing it, and without making it dispensable.

Welfare is the sphere where desires are fulfilled, or at least satisfaction sought, according to the teleological projects of their initiators; right is the sphere where subjects secure a place for these welfare-seeking activities, and where they evaluate them. Right for Kant is a formal property, which abstracts from material ends, from what is actually chosen. But it makes the exercise of such choices possible for each subject within a defined area of juridical space; and it seeks to enable the compossibility of choices among all subjects by establishing a system of limits where each may pursue his or her own material ends without interference or domination, while leaving space for others to act likewise.[28] Kant's juridical republicanism addresses the compossibility problem through reciprocal limitation, and coercion defined as mutual exclusion from individuals' respective fields of activity, guaranteed by the state. As related to the subjective capacity for spontaneous choice, right is a manifestation of pure and not empirical practical reason. Because its justification is transcendental, as guaranteeing freedom, and not teleological, as promoting happiness, the principle of right cannot be overridden by appeals to welfare, though these may have their place in morality. Right issues from a categorical imperative.

The categorical foundation of right, however, is not incompatible with a certain flexibility in its application. The fact that juridical subjects need not be morally motivated in their strictly legal interactions has already been noted. Moreover, while rights impose specifiable obligations on subjects to forbear from impeding one another in their projects,

Kant maintains that each subject is not duty-bound to insist on the full panoply of rights at all times and to the last detail, as long as the general conditions of agency are respected.[29] He thus allows room for mutual adjustment and the exercise of prudence in rightful interaction, an idea that is at the heart of Schiller's political project. Nor should the Kantian position on the categorical character of right be interpreted, as it is by the young Wilhelm von Humboldt, to foreclose any significant possibilities of state intervention in the economy or in social concerns such as education, health, and so on.[30] As Fichte correctly saw,[31] such interventions may be justified on Kantian terms insofar as they promote and extend the conditions of free agency: insofar as they are designed to enhance freedom, and not primarily happiness (though Kant even allows a modest prudential role to the latter in the context of international rivalries).[32]

The concepts of spontaneity, autonomy, and determinability, and the distinctions among happiness, right, and virtue, are the pillars upon which post-Kantian political thought is erected. Among the principal elaborations are the increasing politicization of the concept of autonomy, involving a reconfiguration of the virtue/right distinction; and an aestheticization of determinability, in response to perceived problems in the articulation of welfare and right. These problems, it is thought, are amenable to solution by aesthetic renderings of the modern self: for Schiller in the register of beauty, for Bruno Bauer through the sublime. Beauty mandates harmonious mutual adjustment rather than litigious confrontation among rights-bearing subjects; and this possibility reposes in turn on aesthetic education, which promotes suppleness rather than inflexibility of interests. From the perspective of the sublime, however, the compossibility problem arises not only because private interests in modern civil society are fragmentary and rigidly asserted, but because they are incompatible in their substance. The ways of pursuing happiness have impinged on the structures of right, and threaten to overwhelm them. The requisite response is thus not adjustment but transformation, a radicalization of determinability as sublime transcendence of particular interests. On this terrain two distinct structures of aesthetic republicanism emerge.

Schiller wrote his major work in aesthetics, *The Aesthetic Education of Man in a Series of Letters*,[33] in 1793–4, during the Jacobin ascendancy in the French Revolution. Its publication thus precedes Kant's *Metaphysics of Morals*, with its canonical distinctions of welfare, right, and morality. Nonetheless, Schiller had available to him not only the *Critique of Judgement*,

Kant's principal contribution to aesthetics, but also Kant's major writings in practical philosophy from the previous ten years, which lay out the nature of Enlightenment and modern subjectivity,[34] the various kinds of imperatives, the concepts of autonomy and heteronomy,[35] determinability and negative liberty,[36] and the distinction between freedom and happiness.[37] Schiller thus had ample materials at his disposal to produce a model of political interaction consistent with the main lines of Kantianism, and he deploys the appropriate Kantian concepts regularly in his writing. Moreover, at Jena Schiller was at the centre of a circle of colleagues and correspondents involved in his journalistic projects, and here the political and aesthetic dimensions of Kant's thought were widely and profoundly debated.[38] Schiller was fully immersed in Kant when he wrote the *Aesthetic Letters*, and his argument can be understood against the backdrop of Kant's own ongoing development of republican themes.

The aesthetic character of Schiller's republicanism comes to the fore in his distinction between the perfect and the beautiful, which he renders as the difference between autonomy and heautonomy.[39] The latter is a term derived from the *Critique of Judgement*, and Schiller uses it to underline processes of self-generated change. He takes autonomy to mean that the rational idea is manifest in objectivity; thought has determined its object in accord with its own mandate. Heautonomy, however, stresses that the adequacy of object to idea is a result brought about by free and conscious activity, by spontaneity, and not by accident or by imposition from without.

> The perfect can have autonomy insofar as its form is determined by its concept; but only the beautiful has *heautonomy*, because in it, form is determined by inner essence. The perfect, exhibited [*dargestellt*] with freedom, is transformed directly [*sogleich*] into the beautiful …
>
> Beauty, or rather taste, treats all things as ends-in-themselves, and simply does not tolerate that one [thing] serve the other as means, or bear the yoke [of subjection]. In the aesthetic world, every natural being is a free citizen, having equal rights with the noblest, and must never suffer constraint for the sake of the whole, but must simply in all cases give consent.

The central political question for Schiller is the attainment of a unity that is compatible with difference, and that is brought about by spontaneous self-determination rather than by forcible imposition.[40] The distinction of autonomy and heautonomy is reflected in Schiller's two definitions of form in *Aesthetic Education*: one is externally imposed form as brittle and lifeless, because not animated by an internal energy, but merely juxtaposed from outside. The other, aesthetic form, is flexible and spontaneous, describing the movements of the particulars who generate it.[41] It is the latter which is beautiful, because in it multiplicity is held in unity, and not suppressed in monotone uniformity; but this integration is not extraneous to its elements. It is their very product, the reflection of multiplicity back into unity. In contrast, a system based on perfection, as in the tradition of Leibniz and Wolff, may exhibit its complete concept, or achieve a kind of amalgamation of its content, but this is effected as an external synthesis, not as a genuine harmony among the particulars, achieved by their own spontaneous self-shaping. Adapting the argument from Kant's newly published text "Theory and Practice," Schiller contends that even if such a perfectionist system could secure the happiness of its subjects, it would do so at the cost of their liberty. It would sacrifice pure to empirical practical reason. It would be a system of domination or tutelage which, even if benevolent, would fail the test of republican freedom.

As a symbol of this republican freedom, beauty, by contrast, is a self-directing movement, wherein the mutual compatibility of the elements is sustained by their own cooperation. The unity of unity and diversity here results from harmonious accord, reciprocal recognition, and consent.[42] By respecting the freedom of others, we elicit from them, under the influence of aesthetic education, a commitment to limit their own freedom in turn: this voluntary mutual recognition and adjustment will be the essence of the republican state. Through his development of the autonomy-heautonomy distinction, and its political application, Schiller broadens Kant's account, and illustrates spontaneity at work in aesthetic determinability and self-formation. In aesthetic education, spontaneity trains and elevates itself to a moral standpoint, where the demands of duty and of sensibility are no longer in contention.[43] The boundaries between welfare, right, and virtue are more permeable than in Kant, and the conflicts between them less acute. Autonomy is not confined to moral life or to the determination of maxims, but refers the subject to an institutional matrix, in which freedom permeates social and political relations. Self-legislation is taken to be a characteristic of the practice of right, as well as of morality.

If the tutelary state fails to meet the test of beautiful freedom, Schiller implies a similar criticism of the imposed unity of the revolutionary Jacobin state. As Schiller affirms, "A political constitution will be very imperfect if it can bring about unity only by the suppression [*Aufhebung*] of multiplicity."[44] It is incumbent upon the state to respect "not only the objective and generic, but also the subjective and specific character"[45] of its citizens. Schiller believes that the French Revolution had failed to accommodate diversity, seeking to impose coercively a uniform political identity. He proposes a new ideal, implying neither uniformity nor confusion,[46] but centring on aesthetic processes of spontaneous change, the realization of beautiful unity, in conditions of modernity. Starting from the recognition of diverse interests, it seeks a possible compatibility among these. It treats interests in relations of right as determinable, and as capable of resolution or synthesis, and thus it aims to produce a universal interest, a commonality of purpose, formulated and sustained by individual effort, insight, and virtue. If this process is opposed, in its historical context, to the disciplinary grinding down of particularity under Jacobin rule, it would equally oppose, by anticipation, the celebration of mere multiplicity or diversity, or the affirmation of a particularistic politics of identity which comes to prominence in subsequent political discourse. Instead, Schiller is attentive to the possibility that new, polyphonic harmonies can be created.

Schiller is particularly alert to the conditions of modern subjectivity and freedom in which the problem of difference is posed. The concord of particular and universal interests can no longer simply be presupposed, but must be created. Modern aesthetically engendered unity cannot be modelled upon that achieved by the Greeks, because the ancient sense of wholeness and harmony requires a citizenry which, in comparison with the modern division of labour, is largely undifferentiated in interest and function, and thus is no longer an attainable, or indeed desirable, ideal.[47]

The Greek conception of beautiful individuality, depicting the citizen as a microcosm of his *polis*, lacks the modern principle of reflection, according to which the self is not only as part of an encompassing whole, but is recognized as an independent centre of judgment and valuation, relating to and separating itself critically from its world. While shattering the apparently immediate harmonies of Greek antiquity, modernity opens new prospects for the mediation of unity and diversity through self-determining and spontaneous action.

Schiller offers a more differentiated analysis of the Greek world, and its *apparent* immediate unities, an analysis consistent with a Kantian theoretical framework. First, the *polis* secures the unity of self and community through the political coercion of morality, a consequence of the denial of the autonomy and spontaneity of the self. The Kantian distinction of right and morality[48] represents significant progress in this respect, admitting coercion only in the sphere of legality or outward action, but prohibiting the forcible imposition of virtue. Second, Schiller acknowledges that within the ancient Greek world, important distinctions exist in the relation between happiness and virtue. Against more austere forms of Greek unity like the Spartan model, Schiller inclines towards the vigour and expansiveness of Athens, which, within the confines of the ancient conception, renders possible a continuous striving for perfection of the mind and culture, as well as a wider range of material satisfactions. This assessment, too, is in accord with the emerging lines of Kant's political thought.[49]

Modernity poses anew the question of the unity of unity and multiplicity. New kinds of diversity, rooted in the modern division of labour, open up an unprecedented range of tensions among private interests, and make it necessary to rethink the political bonds among citizens. In Schiller's account, the modern fragmentation of labour is detrimental to the individual producer, whose activity and perspectives on self, society, and the world are truncated and deformed. "Everlastingly chained to a single little fragment of the Whole, man himself develops into nothing but a fragment."[50] While specialization and division of labour promote progress in knowledge for the species, they mutilate the individuals who are the agents of the process. Hence arises an imperative to redress this state of diremption, to discover prospects for wholeness and integrity compatible with the differentiations of modern life, and to place political unity on a new foundation.

Unity is not to be equated with ancient homogeneity or Jacobin suppression of particularity, but depends upon determinability and self-fashioning. Schiller takes the interests of modern civil society to be diversified but potentially reconcilable. He proposes a politicized account of autonomy according to which desires or private interests are not immediately causal for political action, but must rather be consciously examined, and treated as determinable by the self. Only in the mutual adjustment by the particulars of their limited private ends can diremption and fragmentation be overcome, and a genuine universal interest be formulated. This spontaneous activity is the essence of aesthetic education. The mutual delimitation which Kant will take to characterize the juridical space is here presented as a work of freedom. Schiller employs the concept of determinability[51] to emphasize the potential of the self to modify its properties and the objective forms of its appearance. The rational subject is not the bearer of fixed ends set by a natural order, as in classical Greek philosophy, nor a creature of fixed natural attributes, as in Enlightenment materialism, but is free and spontaneous. The determinability of individuals according to the insights of reason allows them to acquire new abilities and forms of interaction through aesthetic education. Schiller's critical ideal is an aesthetic state of beautiful and harmonized life conditions and relations, a juridical sphere characterized by mutual adaptation rather than coercion and conflict.

Besides the tutelary and Jacobin states, Schiller distinguishes two possible routes along which the modern state may evolve. The state may simply reflect and intensify the culture of diremption and its intractable conflicts, or it may promote the acquisition of new capacities for freedom through aesthetic determinability of the self. One possible outcome is the "dynamic state" based upon collisions among self-assertive individuals, who rigidly insist upon their own private rights, and who relate to others through competition for material advantage. This result represents a disjunctive idea of reciprocity, or mutual exclusion. Here, anticipating the modern liberal state, Schiller describes unity as effected at best instrumentally through self-interest. These interests are taken to be valid as given, and are expressed through the clash of conflicting forces (captured in the idea of "dynamism"). On the other hand, Schiller describes the aesthetic state as a modern form of republicanism, based on collaborative action and mutual recognition.[52] This ideal designates not a final, utopian condition, but a process of constant renewal. It is order as produced, not given; but produced by free play, not under duress. It seeks a higher unity that preserves diversity while enhancing cooperation. The active reciprocity of the aesthetic condition involves the determination of the self and its properties in the light of the universal. From a Kantian perspective, this is virtue penetrating into the relations of right, and modifying their workings. It accords with republican ideas which conceive of the centrality of virtue for political life.[53]

Aesthetic education teaches us to exclude certain ways of advancing one's own teleological projects, the rigid insistence on particular interests typical of the modern culture of diremption, and to cultivate others, including the ability to contribute to a common good, to promote perfection through one's own acts. It liberates subjects from the reign of unbridled sensuousness, for Schiller an affliction of the ancient Greeks; but also from the grip of a too austere morality, which holds the sense world to be alien and hostile to itself (as Schiller sometimes reads Kant).[54] It requires subjects to train their spontaneity up to the level of autonomy (though the relations between these concepts, and likewise between beauty and sublimity, are not unambiguous in Schiller, and remain vexed issues for him).[55] But the self-discipline and self-direction of spontaneity does not imply the eradication of the particular, as in Jacobinism or rigorist moral systems. "Man," affirms Schiller, "must learn to desire more nobly, so that he may not need to will sublimely."[56] Schiller's aesthetic ideal is the elevation of the self to a higher ethical plane, and the tempering but not the sacrifice of the self's own particular perspectives.[57] The political synthesis which he envisages avoids the absorptive universality of the ancient Greek *polis*, the imposed unity of the French Revolutionary state, and the unrestricted particularism of the "dynamic state." The historical outcome is uncertain on Schiller's reading. There is no triumphalism or bland optimism here, but doubt and hesitation about the adequacy of the proposed solution and the means to effect it. Modernity, liberating individuals from traditional relationships, makes possible the creation of new forms of interaction and individuality, while threatening to engulf them in struggles over the satisfaction of desires. For Schiller, aesthetic education at least offers prospects that rational emancipation can be realized, through a program of self-formation intended to wed spontaneity and autonomy, and to do so in ways compatible with modern diversity.

A later form of post-Kantian aesthetic republicanism enjoins precisely a rigorist ideal of the subordination of particularity to the demands of universality; it identifies freedom not primarily with beautiful harmony, but with the sublime struggle against inner and outer domination, against the power of unexamined desires and of irrational political hegemony. That such sublime willing is imperative for social unity and progress is a conclusion of Bruno Bauer's analysis of the world of the French Revolution and its aftermath. The interests that constitute modern civil society are not only diverse, but also locked in mutual opposition. With Kant, Schiller had understood interactions in the juridical sphere as mutually limiting, but potentially reconcilable; civil society did not appear to generate necessarily *opposing* interests; interests were indeed fragmentary, and too unilaterally and unbendingly asserted, but potentially compatible in their substance once appropriately understood and exhibited. The emergence of the social question in the early nineteenth century elicits a contrary conclusion, and leads to a further reappraisal of the relations among the spheres of Kantian practical reason. The impinging of property and economic interests on political freedom becomes one of the central theoretical issues for the Hegelian Left, whose interpretations of Kant and Hegel are intended to promote social transformation and justice.

Unlike the compossibility of external spheres of activity posited in Kant's own view of juridical space, Bauer, a leading figure in the Left Hegelian movement of the 1840s, sees civil society as marked by incompatible and deeply conflicting private interests.[58] The political problem for him is not merely to accommodate these interests through compromise and pragmatic adjustment, or even through the delicate balancing of aesthetic education. They must instead be changed before they can be harmonized, or rather, the individual bearers of these interests must change themselves. The determinability of such selves is grasped through aesthetic categories, as in Schiller, but now it is the sublime rather than the beautiful which provides the appropriate reference. Sublimity appears in two dimensions: subjectively, in quelling particular interests in the self, a more stringent process of self-transformation than that envisaged by Schiller, since the issue is no longer the rigidity of interests, but their *incommensurability*; and objectively, in contributing to the ongoing historical struggle to realize reason and freedom in social and political life.[59] Such a position places Bauer much closer to the Jacobin solution which Schiller had repudiated, insofar as particularity itself can appear as the adversary of rational freedom; but Bauer continues to insist that individuals must emancipate themselves from the grip of irrational interests, desires, and affiliations, and cannot be emancipated by another. It is not the state which frees its subjects, but they who free themselves through the struggle to construct the republican order.

As in Schiller, modernity for Bauer presents a stark alternative, as a culture of diremption or of freedom. Breaking the traditional hierarchical order of estate society, modernity releases individuals to reconstruct social relations, either by simply following the bent of private interest, or by submitting these interests to critique. This critical freedom, designated "universal self-consciousness," stipulates that individuals not be determined by their desires, but that they must be able to emancipate themselves from their particular interests and identities wherever these conflict with the general interest in progress. Critique involves theoretical assessment of one's own values as well as social practices and institutions, and an examination of their validity claims; and it also mandates practical intervention, challenging and expunging all irrational relations.[60] Through his concept of universal self-consciousness, Bauer adapts Kantian practical reason. In taking up the standpoint of the general interest, and rationally deliberating on the maxims of their action, ethical subjects exhibit spontaneity, liberating themselves from determination by external causes or unexamined inner drives. Political virtue is the subjection of the particular to the discipline of the universal. Desires and drives do not constitute one's deepest, authentic self,[61] but may be hindrances to freedom, insofar as they are determined heteronomously.

Bauer extends the idea of autonomy by taking Kantian moral premises as a basis for political and juridical actions and relations. He thus replaces virtue into the sphere of right, from which Kant had extracted it. Political virtue means that the ends of political (as well as moral) action require universalistic sanction and rational justification, based on promoting the conditions for freedom. Personal utility or welfare may not override considerations of the general good. Recognizing the ability of all subjects to claim moral and juridical equality, this universality repudiates inherited distinctions of rank, status, rights, and privileges associated with the old pre-Revolutionary order.[62] In Bauer's view, these must be expunged as merely "positive," merely historical vestiges without claim of rational justification.

The economic interests of modern emancipated individuals must also be submitted to critique; the shift of virtue into right is occasioned by a new conception of civil society and its limits, and is not a theoretical regression behind Kant. The Left Hegelian conception of the opposition between citizenship and acquisitive individualism is informed by insights into the characteristics and problems of modern civil society.

One of the characteristics of ancient Roman republicanism was that, instead of the direct and transparent relations which, ideally, prevailed in the Greek political community, it had conceived of citizens as linked in relations mediated by property.[63] Roman thought thus introduced a tension into the idea of citizenship between juridical and political status, between the abstract legal person and the active co-legislator. The apparent immediate unity of the Greek *polis* is lost, and in place of Greek "beautiful individuals," persons emerge as private proprietors endowed with rights, demarcating a private sphere and an absolute dominion over property unprecedented in Greek practice. On this basis a distinction arises in Cicero, for whom two levels of duty exist, *kathekon* and *katorthoma*, one which governs the transactions among politically passive legal persons, the other which applies to holders of political office, who must maintain higher ethical standards in the interest of preserving the state from internal and external threat.[64] Cicero's perfectionist ethic enjoins magistrates to act in the general interest and to uphold the republic unconstrained, where necessary, by the conventions and norms that govern the transactions of private life. Bruno Bauer will adapt this republican rigorism to the exigencies of civil society marked by the conflict of interest rooted in the modern division of labour.[65]

The danger to freedom now arises from the tendency of property to disfigure the political domain. Individuals become frozen in their private spheres of interest, intractably opposed to each other and to historical progress, while the universal is arrogated by the state as a transcendent power, acting in the interests of the ruling groups. In this account, virtue and commerce are in conflict because the market promotes heteronomy and the opposition of interests. It inclines subjects to maximize property to the detriment of their political commitments. This is a repetition of the older republican criticism of chrematistic,[66] which Bauer attempts to vindicate through his reflections on the emergence of the modern state and economy. Originating as an emancipatory struggle against irrational privilege and hierarchy, the French Revolution became, after the overthrow of the Jacobins, a vehicle for rapacity and imperial conquest in the interests of the French bourgeoisie.[67] The post-revolutionary world, according to Bauer, is on the verge of dissolution into an indeterminate mass society. Individuals in such a world are particularistic in pursuit of their immediate interest, but indeterminate: they surrender the powers of spontaneity and autonomy which modernity uniquely makes possible. Republican virtue must vanquish these new forms of heteronomy, realizing autonomy within the practices of right and in the pursuit of happiness. Bauer contrasts a virtuous citizenry, or the people as a self-determining political entity, to mass society[68] on the grounds that the former has immunized itself from the dissolving and exclusionary effects of property and private interest, in order to act decisively and determinately in the general interest. The future republican state must assure the extension of relations of right, reciprocity, and justice throughout all spheres of activity. The practices of right are to reform the institutions of welfare.

Bauer's republican program in the revolutionary ferment of the 1840s was a rousing defence of popular sovereignty, a refusal to compromise with the monarchical state in its deceptive veneer of reform, a critique of liberalism as the political transposition of private interest and as profoundly compromised with the old order by reason of its proprietary concerns, and a polemical engagement with emergent socialism as incompatible with free individual self-determination.[69] All these claims share a common basis in the rejection of particularism, the defence of universal interests contained in the doctrine of infinite self-consciousness. For Bauer the force of particularism can only be vanquished by the sublime determinability of the self, a process of stringent self-change. Willingly beautiful can no longer suffice in conditions where private interests are diametrically opposed.

Bauer's writings after the failure of the Revolutions of 1848 are highly problematic.[70] His 1840s critique, however, is of abiding interest. It identifies forms of domination and heteronomy concealed in contemporary economic relations, and defends modern republican options, the extension and promotion of the sphere of right, and the virtues of active citizenship. Bauer's republican rigorism is not blithely optimistic; it invites subjects to adopt a sublime, and highly demanding, ideal of self-change, without offering metaphysical guarantees of success. It is rather an elicitation of new practices and understandings of freedom, under the guiding idea that "nothing is impossible for spirit."[71] This affirmation of the power of spontaneity is the essence of German idealism, and of its republican politics.

NOTES

The author acknowledges the support of the Social Sciences and Humanities Research Council of Canada and of the University of Ottawa Research Chair in Political Thought.

1 I. Kant, "An Answer to the Question: 'What is Enlightenment?'" (1784) in *Kant's Political Writings*, ed. Hans Reiss (Cambridge: Cambridge University Press, 1970), 54–60.

2 I. Kant, *Critique of Pure Reason*, ed. P. Guyer and A. Wood (Cambridge: Cambridge University Press, 1998).

3 Even among less deterministic accounts, many do not escape this problem insofar as they take subjective preferences as essentially arbitrary, with reason relegated to an instrumental function. Such apparent arbitrariness conceals the "hidden mechanism of nature," the effects of unexamined and unresisted natural causality upon the will. For a discussion of one such voluntarist theory, see Douglas Moggach, "The Subject as Substance: Bruno Bauer's Critique of Max Stirner," *Owl of Minerva* 41.1–2 (2009–10), 63–86.

4 Karl Marx, "Theses on Feuerbach," in *Collected Works*, vol. 5 (New York: International Publishers, 1976), 3–5.

5 Thin, non-Kantian versions of autonomy define the term to mean consistent rank ordering of preferences, and efficiency of means. For recent reflections on this subject, see John Cristman and Joel Anderson, eds, *Autonomy and the Challenges to Liberalism: New Essays* (Cambridge: Cambridge University Press, 2005).

6 Spontaneity has a technical sense here of self-causing action. This meaning is to be distinguished from popular usage, which implies that an action is undertaken without reflection. G.W. Leibniz, *Monadology*, ed. Nicholas Rescher (Pittsburgh: University of Pittsburgh Press, 1991), esp. sections 11–13; Donald Rutherford, "Leibniz on Spontaneity," in *Leibniz: Nature and Freedom*, D. Rutherford and J.A. Cover (Oxford: Oxford University Press, 2005), 156–80. For a stimulating and lucid discussion of Leibniz and German idealism, see Ernst Cassirer, *Freiheit und Form: Studien zur deutschen Geistesgeschichte*, ed. R. Schmücker (Hamburg: Meiner, 2001).

7 Kant, *Critique of Pure Reason*, B75/A51.

8 The standard reference is Hobbes's *Leviathan*, part 1, which polemically redefines Stoic *horme/aphorme* (involving practical decisions by subjects to adopt or reject a maxim of action in relation to objects) as a mechanical pull or push exerted by the object on a subject. For a discussion of related models of agency, see Henry E. Allison, *Kant's Theory of Freedom* (Cambridge: Cambridge University Press, 1990), 5–6, 39–40, 60–1, 191–8. The sensibly affected/determined distinction appears on p. 60.

9 Allison, *Kant's Theory of Freedom*, 85. The Third Antinomy of the *Critique of Pure Reason* establishes the possibility of freedom in respect to natural causality (A 452–5, B 480–3; A 534–8, B 562–6); the *Critique of Practical Reason* is intended by Kant to demonstrate the reality of freedom. I. Kant, *Critique of Practical Reason*, trans. L.W. Beck (London: Macmillan, 1956). See Dieter Henrich, *Between Kant and Hegel: Lectures on German Idealism*, ed. D.S. Pacini (Cambridge, MA: Harvard University Press, 2003), 46–61.

10 See A.A. Long, ed., *Problems in Stoicism* (London: Athlone, 1971).

11 Allison, *Kant's Theory of Freedom*, 40.

12 Kant, *Critique of Practical Reason*, § 8 (5: 33).

13 See I. Kant, *Groundwork for the Metaphysics of Morals*, ed. L. Denis (Peterborough, ON: Broadview, 2005), 98–100 (4: 441–3) on empirical and rational heteronomy, respectively.

14 Albert O. Hirschman, *The Passions and the Interests: Political Arguments for Capitalism before Its Triumph* (Princeton: Princeton University Press, 1977).

15 Kant, *Groundwork*, 98 (4: 440–1).

16 See above, note 13.
17 Kant, *Critique of Practical Reason*, 24 (5: 25).
18 Ibid., 43 (5: 42–3).
19 The full case for Kant's place as a republican as opposed to a liberal theorist cannot be mounted here. The intent is rather to indicate important affinities of Kant with republican ideas of freedom, without claiming that these affinities are exclusive. Cf., for a liberal interpretation, John Rawls's quasi-Kantian *A Theory of Justice* (Cambridge, MA: Harvard University Press, 1971); and note the comments on this construal of Kant by Robert Pippin in *Idealism as Modernism: Hegelian Variations* (Cambridge: Cambridge University Press, 1997), 86–7 n. 56. With these reservations noted, Kant serves as a basis for the republican conceptions described below. See further Daniel Weinstock and Christian Nadeau, eds, *Republicanism: History, Theory and Practice* (London: Cass, 2004); and Martin van Gelderen and Quentin Skinner, eds, *Republicanism: A Shared European Heritage*, 2 vols. (Cambridge: Cambridge University Press, 2002).
20 I. Berlin, *Four Essays on Liberty* (Oxford: Oxford University Press, 1969).
21 For Hobbes, the will is understood only as desire, not as an adjudicative and legislative capacity. On freedom, see Thomas Hobbes, *Leviathan*, ed. R. Tuck (Cambridge: Cambridge University Press, 1996), esp. chaps. 14 and 21; and Quentin Skinner, *Visions of Politics*, vol. 3: *Hobbes and Civil Science* (Cambridge: Cambridge University Press, 2002), 209–37.
22 Philip Pettit, *Republicanism: A Theory of Freedom and Government* (Oxford: Oxford University Press, 1997); Quentin Skinner, *The Foundations of Modern Political Thought*, 2 vols. (Cambridge: Cambridge University Press, 1978); Q. Skinner, *Visions of Politics*, vol. 2: *Renaissance Virtues* (Cambridge: Cambridge University Press, 2002); Annabel Brett and James Tully, with Holly Hamilton-Bleakley, eds, *Rethinking the Foundations of Modern Political Thought* (Cambridge: Cambridge University Press, 2006).
23 Quentin Skinner, *Liberty before Liberalism* (Cambridge: Cambridge University Press, 1998).
24 Kant, *Groundwork*, 76–7 (4: 416–17).
25 I. Kant, *The Metaphysics of Morals* (1797), trans. Mary Gregor (Cambridge: Cambridge University Press, 1991).
26 I. Kant, "On the Common Saying: 'This may be true in theory, but it does not apply in practice'" (1793), in *Kant's Political Writings*, ed. Hans Reiss (Cambridge: Cambridge University Press, 1970), 74.
27 Otfried Höffe, "Recht und Moral: Ein kantischer Problemaufriss," *Neue Hefte für Philosophie* 17 (1979), 1–34.

28 Douglas Moggach, "The Construction of Juridical Space: Kant's Analogy of Relation in *The Metaphysics of Morals*," in *Proceedings of the Twentieth World Congress of Philosophy 7, Modern Philosophy*, ed. Mark Gedney (Bowling Green, OH: Philosophy Documentation Centre, 2000), 201–9.

29 On Kant's review of Hufeland, where this argument is advanced in 1785–6, see Michael Rohls, *Kantisches Naturrecht und historisches Zivilrecht: Wissenschaft und bürgerliche Freiheit bei Gottlieb Hufeland* (1760–1817) (Baden-Baden: Nomos Verlag, 2004), 41 n. 121, 49.

30 Wilhelm von Humboldt, *Ideen zu einem Versuch die Grenzen der Wirksamkeit des Staates zu bestimmen* (1792), in *Gesammelte Schriften*, vol. 1 (Berlin: Reimer, 1903).

31 J.G. Fichte, *Der geschloßne Handelsstaat* (1800), in *Werke*, vol. 3 (Berlin: de Gruyter, 1971).

32 Douglas Moggach, "Freedom and Perfection: German Debates on the State in the Eighteenth Century," *Canadian Journal of Political Science* 42.4 (2009), 1003–23.

33 F. Schiller, *On the Aesthetic Education of Man in a Series of Letters* (1795), bilingual edition, ed. and trans. E. Wilkinson and L.A. Willoughby (Oxford: Clarendon Press, 1967).

34 Kant, "What Is Enlightenment?" 54–60.

35 Kant, *Groundwork*, passim.

36 Kant, *Critique of Practical Reason*, 43–4 (5: 42–3).

37 Kant, "Theory and Practice," 61–92.

38 Moggach, "Freedom and Perfection," 1010, 1014–15.

39 F. Schiller, "Brief an Gottfried Körner" (1793) at http://www.wissen-im-netz.info/literatur/schiller/briefe/vSchiller/1793/179302231.htm (my translation). I present a similar but more detailed analysis of Schiller in my article "Schiller's Aesthetic Republicanism," *History of Political Thought* 28.3 (2007), 520–41.

40 Wilkinson and Willoughby, "Introduction," in Schiller, *Aesthetic Education*, lxxxviii.

41 This distinction emerges in the discussion of the aesthetic state. Schiller, *Aesthetic Education*, Letter 16.

42 See M. Kern, "Zur Geschichtsphilosophie Friedrich Schillers," in *Aufklärung-Geschichte-Revolution: Studien zur Philosophie der Aufklärung*, ed. M. Buhr and W. Förster, vol. 2 (Berlin: Akademie Verlag, 1986), esp. 271–98.

43 This is an aspect of Schiller's *criticism* (and not mere development or application) of Kant whose import must be noted but cannot be fully assessed here. See Schiller's remark recorded in Denis's edition of Kant's

Groundwork, 177; and John McCumber, "Schiller, Hegel, and the Aesthetics of German Idealism," in *The Emergence of German Idealism*, ed. Michael Baur and Daniel O. Dahlstrom (Washington, DC: Catholic University of America Press, 1999), 135–6.

44 Schiller, *Aesthetic Education*, Letter 4.3 (my translation).

45 Ibid., Letter 4.3 (my translation).

46 Ibid., Letter 4.7.

47 Friedrich Schiller, "Über naive und sentimentalische Dichtung," in *Sämtliche Werke*, vol. 5 (Munich: Hanser, 1962), 694–780, esp. 716. For a discussion, see Joseph Chytry, *The Aesthetic State: A Quest in Modern German Thought* (Berkeley: University of California Press, 1989), 92, 96, 103.

48 Adumbrated by Kant in "Theory and Practice" of 1793, subsequent to Schiller's text on Lycurgus and Solon of 1789 (below, n. 49), the relevant distinction had emerged in the debates ignited by Kant's writings of the late 1780s. See Moggach, "Freedom and Perfection," 1014–15.

49 Friedrich Schiller, "Die Gesetzgebung des Lykurgus und Solon" (1789), in *Sämtliche Werke*, vol. 4 (Munich: Hanser, 1962), 805–36. Cf. the contribution of Mehta in this volume (chap. 10). For Schiller, Sparta does not offer a valid alternative, as that model reposes on the homogeneity and forced conformity of its members.

50 Schiller, *Aesthetic Education*, Letter 6.7.

51 Ibid., Letter 20.

52 E.g., *Aesthetic Education*, Letters 14.1 and 16.1. See Chytry, *The Aesthetic State*, 81–5, 101–2.

53 Frederick Beiser, *Schiller as Philosopher: A Re-Examination* (Oxford: Oxford University Press, 2005). Cf. the contributions of Sparling and Balot in this volume (chaps. 8, 7).

54 McCumber, "Schiller, Hegel," 136–7.

55 Friedrich Schiller, *Sämtliche Werke*, vol. 5: "Über Anmut und Würde" (1793), 433–88; "Vom Erhabenen" (1793), 489–512; and "Über das Erhabene" (1801), 792–808.

56 Schiller, *Aesthetic Education*, Letter 23.8 (Wilkinson/Willoughby translation).

57 Ibid., Letter 4.2.

58 Bruno Bauer, *Die gute Sache der Freiheit und meine eigene Angelegenheit* (Zurich and Winterthur: Verlag des literarischen Comptoirs, 1842), 199 ff.; (anon.), "Das Wohl der arbeitenden Klassen," *Norddeutsche Blätter* 9 (March 1845), 52–66.

59 Douglas Moggach, *The Philosophy and Politics of Bruno Bauer* (Cambridge: Cambridge University Press, 2003).

60 Bruno Bauer, *Die Posaune des jüngsten Gerichts über Hegel den Atheisten und Antichristen: Ein Ultimatum* (Leipzig: Otto Wigand, 1841). For an analysis, see Moggach, *Bruno Bauer*, 99–118.

61 Cf. the critical discussion of a recent version of claims about the primacy of desires in self-definition, in Allison, *Kant's Theory of Freedom*, 191–8.

62 Bruno Bauer, *Geschichte der Politik, Kultur und Aufklärung des achtzehnten Jahrhunderts, Erster Band: Deutschland während der ersten vierzig Jahre des achtzehnten Jahrhunderts* (Charlottenburg: Verlag von Egbert Bauer, 1843).

63 G.A. Pocock, "The Ideal of Citizenship since Classical Times," in *Theorizing Citizenship*, ed. Ronald Beiner (Albany: State University of New York Press, 1995), 29–52; Eric Nelson, *The Greek Tradition in Republican Thought* (Cambridge: Cambridge University Press, 2004).

64 Marcus Tullius Cicero, *De Officiis* (Cambridge, MA: Harvard University Press, 1913). Cicero has been criticized for incoherence in holding simultaneously an intersubjective and a monological, or political and judicial, account of citizenship: Cary Nederman, "Rhetoric, Reason, and Republic: Republicanisms Ancient, Medieval, and Modern," in *Renaissance Civic Humanism: Reappraisals and Reflections*, ed. James Hankins (Cambridge: Cambridge University Press, 2000), 249–59; but these are better seen as applying to two distinct audiences.

65 Douglas Moggach, "Republican Rigorism and Emancipation in *Vormärz* Germany," in D. Moggach, *The New Hegelians: Politics and Philosophy in the Hegelian School* (Cambridge: Cambridge University Press, 2006), 114–35.

66 Istvan Hont and Michael Ignatieff, eds, *Wealth and Virtue: The Shaping of Political Economy in the Scottish Enlightenment* (Cambridge: Cambridge University Press, 1983); Raimund Ottow, *Markt, Tugend, Republik* (Berlin: Akademie Verlag, 1996). There are clear echoes here of Rousseau, whose Discourse of the Origins of Inequality links the loss of freedom to the effects of the division of labour and the skewed distribution of private property. For Bauer, Rousseau's solution, as mediated by Kant, is not to absorb the individual in the community, as on the ancient model, or to restore a civic religion, but to stress the element of self-legislation and self-modification by the emancipated individual will. Cf. the contributions of Cusher and Ward in this volume (chaps. 11, 12).

67 B. Bauer et al., *Denkwürdigkeiten zur Geschichte der neueren Zeit seit der Französischen Revolution. Nach den Quellen und Original Memoiren bearbeitet und herausgegeben von Bruno Bauer und Edgar Bauer* (Charlottenburg: Verlag von Egbert Bauer, 1843–1844). For Bauer on the French Revolution, see Moggach, *Bruno Bauer*, 126–7, 149–54.

68 On *die Masse* and its problems, see Moggach, *Bruno Bauer*, 150–62.

69 Bruno Bauer, "Erste Wahlrede von 1848," in Ernst Barnikol, *Bruno Bauer: Studien und Materialien*, ed. P. Riemer and H.-M. Sass (Assen: Van Gorcum, 1972), 526–9.

70 For a brief discussion of these later views, see Moggach, *Bruno Bauer*, 180–7.

71 Bruno Bauer, "Die Fähigkeit der heutigen Juden und Christen, frei zu werden," in *Feldzüge der reinen Kritik*, ed. H.-M. Sass (Frankfurt am Main: Suhrkamp, 1968), 195.

Contributors

Ryan K. Balot is professor of political science and classics at the University of Toronto. The author of *Greed and Injustice in Classical Athens* (Princeton University Press, 2001), of *Greek Political Thought* (Blackwell, 2006), and of *Courage in the Democratic Polis: Ideology and Critique in Classical Athens* (Oxford University Press, 2014), and editor of *A Companion to Greek and Roman Political Thought* (Blackwell, 2009), Balot specializes in early modern and classical political thought.

Timothy W. Burns is professor of political science at Baylor University. He is the author of *Shakespeare's Political Wisdom*, co-author (with Thomas L. Pangle) of *Introduction to Political Philosophy*, editor of *After History? Francis Fukuyama and His Critics*, editor of *Recovering Reason: Essays in Honor of Thomas L. Pangle*, editor of *Brill's Companion to Leo Strauss' Writings on Classical Political Thought*, and co-editor (with Bryan-Paul Frost) of *Philosophy, History, and Tyranny: Re-examining the Debate between Leo Strauss and Alexandre Kojève*. He is translator of Marcellinus's "Life of Thucydides," and author of articles on Homer, Thucydides, Aristophanes, Dionysius of Halicarnassus, Shakespeare, Hobbes, Chesterton, Strauss, Fukuyama, Putnam, and modern liberal republican theory. He is also co-editor (with Thomas L. Pangle) of Palgrave Macmillan's "Recovering Political Philosophy" series, and editor-in-chief of *Interpretation: A Journal of Political Philosophy*.

Jarrett A. Carty is an associate professor at the Liberal Arts College at Concordia University, Montreal, where he teaches the history of philosophy, political theory, the history of Western civilization, and the history of science. His specialty is the early modern period in political thought, concentrating on the Reformation, the Renaissance, and the late Middle Ages. His publications include *Divine Kingdom, Holy Order: The Political Writings of Martin Luther* (2012).

Wendell John Coats, Jr is professor of government at Connecticut College, New London, CT, where he teaches courses in the history of Western political theory, ancient, medieval, and modern. He has published extensively on various themes in political theory, including civic republicanism, armed force and the political, and the thought of Michael Oakeshott.

Crystal Cordell Paris is an affiliated researcher at the Centre d'études sociologiques et politiques Raymond Aron of the École des hautes études en sciences sociales in Paris, France, and teaches at the Institut d'études politiques, Middle Eastern–Mediterranean campus. A specialist of political thought and the history of ideas, she is the author of *La philosophie politique* (Ellipses, 2013).

Brent Edwin Cusher is assistant professor in the Department of Leadership and American Studies at Christopher Newport University, in Newport News, Virginia. He has a BA from Carleton College and a PhD from the University of Toronto, both in political science, and has held appointments at Carleton College, Rhodes College, the University of Alaska–Anchorage, and Christopher Newport University.

Marc Hanvelt is assistant professor of political science at Carleton University. His primary research interests are in the history of modern political thought, the Enlightenment in the Atlantic world, the political thought of David Hume, liberalism, and democratic theory. His published work includes *The Politics of Eloquence: David Hume's Polite Rhetoric* (University of Toronto Press, 2012).

Geoffrey C. Kellow is an assistant professor at the College of the Humanities, Carleton University. He studies the Enlightenment in the Atlantic world and has published on Adam Smith, seventeenth-century economic thought, and the enduring influence of Cicero.

Toivo Koivukoski is associate professor of political science at Nipissing University and director of the Nipissing University Peace Research Initiative. He is author of *The New Barbarism and the Modern West:*

Recognizing an Ethic of Difference (2014), *After the Last Man: Excurses to the Limits of the Technological System* (2008), and co-editor with David Tabachnick of a series of books on classical regimes theory, including *On Oligarchy* (2011), *Enduring Empire* (2009), and *Confronting Tyranny: Ancient Lessons for Global Politics* (2005), along with *Globalization, Technology and Philosophy* (2004). His current research and teaching are focused on the topics of love and justice through a comparative study of Plato's *Symposium* and *Republic.*

Neven Leddy studies the migration of people and ideas in the Atlantic world with a focus on Scotland, Geneva, and the early American Republic. He teaches history and the humanities at Concordia University in Montreal.

Varad Mehta is an independent scholar. His main research interests are eighteenth-century intellectual history and political thought, the philosophy of history, and popular culture.

Douglas Moggach is distinguished university professor in the School of Political Studies and Department of Philosophy at the University of Ottawa. He is honorary professor of philosophy at the University of Sydney, and has held visiting positions in Beijing, Cambridge, Münster, Queen Mary University of London, and Pisa. He has published widely in German philosophy and the history of political thought.

David Roochnik is the Maria Stata Professor of Classical Greek Studies at Boston University. He is the author of five books and some thirty articles on ancient Greek philosophy. His most recent work is *Retrieving Aristotle in an Age of Crisis* (State University of New York Press, 2013).

Robert Sparling is an assistant professor of political studies at the University of Ottawa. He is author of *Johann Georg Hamann and the Enlightenment Project* (University of Toronto Press, 2011) and co-editor of *A Companion to Enlightenment Historiography* (Brill, 2013). He has published work in the *Review of Politics,* the *European Journal of Political Theory,* and *Political Theory.* He is currently working on the concept of corruption in modern European political thought.

David Edward Tabachnick is professor of political science at Nipissing University. His research focuses on linking ancient political thought to contemporary ethics and politics. He is the author of *The Great*

Reversal: How We Let Technology Take Control of the Planet (University of Toronto Press, 2013) and is a founding editor of the *Ancient Lessons for Global Politics* book series.

Lee Ward is Alpha Sigma Nu Distinguished Associate Professor of Political Science in Campion College at the University of Regina. He previously taught in the Department of Political Science at Kenyon College in Gambier, Ohio, and was the Bradley Post-doctoral Fellow in the Program in Constitutional Government at Harvard University. He is the author of *The Politics of Liberty in England and Revolutionary America* (Cambridge University Press, 2004), *John Locke and Modern Life* (Cambridge, 2010), *Modern Democracy and the Theological-Political Problem in Spinoza, Rousseau and Jefferson* (Palgrave Macmillan, 2014) and co-edited with Dr Ann Ward *The Ashgate Research Companion to Federalism* (Ashgate Publishing, 2009) and *Natural Right and Political Philosophy: Essays in Honor of Catherine Zuckert and Michael Zuckert* (University of Notre Dame Press, 2013). He has also written articles on John Locke, Aristotle, Montesquieu, Algernon Sidney, Plato, Spinoza, Rousseau, and Irish republicanism that have appeared in several academic journals.

Michael Weinman is professor of philosophy at Bard College Berlin. He is the author of two books, on pleasure in Aristotle's ethical thought and on the connection between Continental philosophy and modernist literature, as well as several articles and book chapters on issues in Greek and political philosophy.

Jeffrey Dirk Wilson is clinical assistant professor of philosophy at the Catholic University of America in Washington, DC, where he specializes in metaphysics and ancient Greek philosophy. He lives and works on a farm in Street, Maryland.

www.ingramcontent.com/pod-product-compliance
Lightning Source LLC
LaVergne TN
LVHW090149080826
844660LV00013B/734/J